teaching
and learning
in
secondary
schools

# teaching and learning in

WADSWORTH

ROLAND C. FAUNCE
CARROLL L. MUNSHAW
*Wayne State University*

# secondary
# schools

PUBLISHING COMPANY, INC., BELMONT, CALIFORNIA

*To our sons, Tom and Randy,*
*whose high school experiences*
*impelled us to write this book.*

ROLAND C. FAUNCE
CARROLL L. MUNSHAW

*Second printing: July 1965*

TEACHING AND LEARNING IN SECONDARY SCHOOLS
*by Roland C. Faunce and Carroll L. Munshaw*

*L. C. Cat. Card No.: 64-18139*

*Printed in the United States of America*

# preface

During the past forty years, the authors of this book have been looking at teaching methods, first as teachers and administrators, and more recently as professors of secondary education. In our study of the ways in which teachers work with their students, we have gradually reached certain conclusions. It seems clear to us, for one thing, that methods not only implement purposes; they are, in fact, a rather faithful reflection of the real purposes held by any teacher, whether consciously or otherwise. When methods appear to violate the stated purposes of the teacher, it may be because these statements of goals do not reach very far below the verbal level. In many instances, too, there are mutually contradictory methods in use by a teacher, a fact that may reflect confusion or contradiction in his beliefs about teaching and learning.

The decision to adopt a particular teaching method instead of some other seems often to be opportunistic or based on unexamined assumptions. In some cases it is born of desperation. The authors believe rather firmly that improvement in our methods of teaching is generally needed, and that such improvement will come about only as the link between purposes and methods is carefully examined and thoroughly understood.

One example of this needed connection between goals and

methods is a central theme of this book. We believe that the twin goals of understanding individual differences and adapting instruction to those differences are the most important frontiers for the vital task of developing more effective secondary schools. Our national efforts to bring about universal secondary education are still hampered by conditions that cause almost one-third of our youth to reject the schools before graduation. As never before, secondary school teachers must make intelligent efforts to understand and accept their students as individuals, and to adapt instruction boldly to individual differences. Such efforts call for clear thinking about goals. We are presently hearing a good deal about new discoveries in teaching methods and school organization. Our decisions to try this or that departure from traditional practice can only be made with clear-cut and defensible purposes, if schools are to be improved. It is our hope that this book will offer present and future teachers some help in their efforts to find better ways.

Many persons and groups have helped us to write this book. Our past and present students, the teachers with whom we have worked for many years, our colleagues and our families who have shared their ideas with us—all of these deserve our profound thanks. Special appreciation is due six of our colleagues who have read the manuscript and helped us revise it: Dr. Delmo Della-Dora, Associate Superintendent of Schools, Dearborn, Michigan; Dr. Earl C. Kelley, Distinguished Professor of Secondary Education, Wayne State University; Dr. Theodore D. Rice, Professor of Secondary Education, Wayne State University; Dr. Harold Alberty, Professor Emeritus, The Ohio State University; Dr. Paul Klohr, Professor of Education, The Ohio State University; and Dr. Victor B. Lawhead, Associate Dean and Director of Undergraduate Programs, Ball State Teachers College. Three other colleagues who worked with us on the concepts and basic issues of the book were Mr. Roy Robinson, Director of Placement and Off-Campus Services, Wayne State University; Dr. Wendell Hough, Assistant Superintendent of Schools, Garden City, Michigan; and Dr. Morrel J. Clute, Associate Professor of Secondary Education, Wayne State University.

Roland C. Faunce
Carroll L. Munshaw

# contents

# I

# Introducing the American secondary school

The American secondary school is a unique achievement. No other nation has attempted to provide free, universal education for all children and youth to age eighteen. As one result of our wealth in natural and human resources, and of our continued pursuit of our national dream of equal opportunity for each individual, we have now reached the point where we enroll in schools about 87 per cent of our young people through age seventeen. Whether you are already a teacher in a secondary school, or are now planning to become such a teacher, you have a right to feel a glow of pride in the privilege of being an important part of this enterprise, which is so basic to the success of our dream of democracy.

We realize, of course, that our dream has not been completely achieved. Nearly one-third of our youth reject the secondary schools before graduation. The causes of this alarming drop-out rate should be examined with care by every responsible educator. Why do young people leave the schools when there is no prospect of employment to entice them? What exactly is wrong with a business that loses almost a third of its customers, in the face of no competition?

Our secondary schools are often unsuccessful in meeting the needs of youth. Over twelve million students enroll in our secondary schools; every one of these young people is different. Our central

1

failure in the schools has been due to our apparent inability to gear our curricula, and to adapt our methods of teaching, to the varying needs, interests, abilities, and plans of the individual learners. In the chapters that follow, we shall speak of working with groups and individuals, of studying the individual and guiding his adjustment, of helping him participate in student activities, of knowing his home background and parents, and of using them as resources in learning. We shall be directing our main attention to the problem of meeting individual differences, the central problem involved in improving teaching methods.

*Secondary schools under attack.* During the decade of the 1950's, secondary education in the United States came under severe attack especially in the public press. Typical of these attacks is the following:

> Many a brilliant youngster nowadays finds his high school has assumed the aspects of a carnival. In one room pretty girls practice twirling batons. The sound of cheers is heard from the football field. The safe-driving class circles the block in new automobiles. Upstairs in the chemistry lab Mr. Smith is wearily trying to explain to a few boys that studying science can be fun—but who pays any attention to him?
>
> It is hard to deny that America's schools have degenerated into a system for coddling and entertaining the mediocre. The facts of the school crisis are all out in plain sight and pretty dreadful to look at. Most students avoid the tough basic courses. Only $12\frac{1}{2}$ per cent are taking any advanced mathematics, only 25 per cent are studying physics. A modern foreign language is studied by fewer than 15 per cent. Ten million Russians are studying English, but only 8,000 Americans are studying Russian.
>
> The diploma has been devaluated to the point of meaninglessness. Bernard Leibson, principal of a New York City junior high, recently admitted that while signing diplomas, he suffers "great pangs of pedagogical conscience." Although Johnny cannot read above fifth grade level and Mary has barely mastered fourth grade arithmetic, we perpetuate the fiction that they have completed the course of study with a satisfactory record.[1]

[1] Sloan Wilson, "It's Time to Close Our Carnival," *Reader's Digest* (June 1958), pp. 31–32. Reprinted by permission of Willis Kingsley Wing. Copyright © 1958 by Sloan Wilson.

By no means all of the articles about education which appeared during this period were derogatory, but unfavorable criticism predominated. The American people were getting an image of their schools which inevitably must cause them grave concern. Criticisms centered on the abundance of "fads and frills," such as music, art, homemaking, safety education, athletics; the low percentage of students who enroll in the "tough," "solid" subjects, e.g., algebra, chemistry, physics, trigonometry, and foreign languages; and the fact that the star athlete often enjoys greater status among the students than the valedictorian. It was charged that in the effort to be all things to all people standards have been lowered so much as to be all but nonexistent. Courses, the critics said, had been "watered down" in order that even the dull and the lazy students could be given passing grades. The high school diploma had come to be considered a right instead of a privilege, a token of time spent rather than a reward for achievement based on sustained effort. According to the critics, young people were pampered by parents and teachers. Because the students were thought to need time for the development of social and recreational skills, teachers were reluctant to assign homework, at least in any sizable quantity. So went the charges!

The schools have not been unresponsive to these accusations. Homework assignments have become commonplace at least as far down as the later elementary grades, and the assignments have become longer. In many schools it is not unusual for junior high youngsters to spend several hours each evening doing homework. Since there are definite limitations on the kinds of study activities for which most homes are equipped, and since most young people encounter obstacles which they need help to overcome before being able to continue, much of the homework is bound to be little more than busy work. One wonders how many young people have been prevented from participating in desirable learning experiences because all of their available time had to be spent completing homework assigned by a harried teacher who couldn't take a chance on being accused of having "low standards."

In many schools students of average ability and above are "guided" out of the vocational, industrial, and business courses as well as homemaking, art, and music and into a program of the so-called college preparatory subjects, especially mathematics and science. The college preparatory course of study enjoys a higher status than the other curricula and in some schools is the only really respectable program in the eyes of the students, teachers, or parents.

Ability grouping is back in vogue, and advanced placement, accelerated courses, and programs of enrichment are commonplace. Standards are supposedly being "raised" by the device of giving fewer A's and B's and more C's, D's, and E's. The graduates of some high schools are actually finding college less demanding than high school. Apparently, the lower the grades given, the harder the students are expected to study.

The schools, like our other social institutions, are by no means perfect. Whether they are better or worse, relatively, than the family, the church, or the courts, for example, is a matter of opinion. Unfortunately, most of the critics of recent years who, in effect, advocated a return to the "good old days" did a disservice to education through failure to deal with the real issues. In other words, most of the things which have recently come under fire were the wrong ones; seldom was any mention made of the most serious weaknesses of the schools. Such adjustments as have been made to satisfy the critics have tended to weaken the total educational pattern rather than to strengthen it.

*Development of secondary education in the United States.* In order to appreciate the significance of recent criticisms, we must consider the manner in which education developed in this country.

The earliest schools in the colonies were what we would now refer to as primary schools, teaching the rudiments of reading, writing, and arithmetic. In the southern colonies education was considered to be a responsibility of the home and the church, so no tax money was used for school operation. In the New England colonies the local governments were required to maintain schools. In the middle colonies both private and church schools existed, some receiving partial support from public funds. Compared with today, life was simple, and so were the expectations people held for their schools. Education, to the extent that it was believed desirable for all, had as its purpose the teaching of reading so that men could read the Scriptures for themselves and understand the political issues of the times. Many of the Founding Fathers were convinced that popular government was impossible without an informed electorate. This was probably the compelling reason why the support and control of education became predominantly public early in our history.

The secondary school made its appearance almost as early as the primary school, but its purposes were different and it was many decades before it was clearly established as a public institution. The first secondary school, the Boston Latin School, was founded in 1635. Similar institutions, which came to be known as Latin grammar schools, began to be established soon thereafter and continued as the agency of secondary education in the colonies until the last half of the eighteenth century. The purpose of the Latin grammar school was primarily to prepare boys for entrance to a collegiate institution in which they would study for the ministry. The curriculum was extremely narrow by today's standards, being devoted almost exclusively to the classical languages, which were thought to be useful in developing the intellect in addition to equipping seminary students for the task of reading the Bible in its early forms.

Dissatisfaction with the narrow purposes and curriculum of the Latin grammar schools gradually developed, so that in 1751 a new secondary institution, the academy, came into being. The academy differed from the Latin grammar school in that it was privately supported and controlled, whereas the earlier institution had been established by law and supported by public taxation. The curriculum of the academy was somewhat broader, and some opportunity for election of subjects was provided. Furthermore, girls were admitted to the academy. Its philosophy, however, was still strongly oriented toward the theory of mental discipline, i.e., the mind is like a muscle and is therefore strengthened by exercise. As in the case of the Latin grammar schools, the major purpose of the academy was preparation for college.[2]

By the beginning of the nineteenth century the nation had developed to the extent that some thought was being given to the need for more education for students who did not intend to go to college. The first secondary institution supposedly designed for both college and non-college bound students was established in Boston in 1821. Our present comprehensive high school may be said to have sprung from this Boston High School. Although the early high schools were intended to serve students whose vocational aspirations did not include education beyond grade twelve, the curriculum and methods

[2] A brief description of the various theories of learning that have influenced school organization and teaching methods through the years will appear in Chapter 4.

were not substantially different from those of the academy. On several occasions committees at the national level reviewed the purposes and curriculum of the high schools and issued reports. In each case the domination of the colleges was evident; in fact, most of the committee members were college personnel. In general, the effect of the committee reports was to emphasize the high schools' responsibility to prepare students for college and to reaffirm the belief that the curriculum which best served this purpose was also the proper curriculum for students who would not attend college. Although high schools were in operation in most of the larger cities by the middle of the nineteenth century, much litigation was required before the right of a district to use tax money for the support of the institution was established. The most influential of these cases and the one which is often credited as the turning point was decided by the Michigan Supreme Court in 1874 as a result of a friendly suit in which the Board of Education of the School District of the City of Kalamazoo was the defendant. Finally, in 1918 the United States Bureau of Education, in a report that took cognizance of the varied needs of the youth of high school age, set forth the first comprehensive statement of purposes for secondary education in the United States.[3]

The fact that secondary education was available did not guarantee that all youth in the appropriate age range would take advantage of it. Those who enrolled often did so at considerable personal inconvenience, having to walk many miles each day to and from the school and having to forego the opportunity to contribute financially to their own support and that of their families. It is little wonder that secondary students continued to be a rather select group for nearly a century after the establishment in 1821 of the Boston High School. Many of the "folkways" of our secondary schools developed during this period. Among these were college preparation as the primary purpose of secondary education with great dependence on reading as a means of learning and on printed materials as almost the only resource of instruction. In addition, we should note the practice of gearing instructional materials and methods to the mythical average student (thus disregarding the facts of individual differ-

---

[3] Commission on the Reorganization of Secondary Education, *Cardinal Principles of Secondary Education*, Bulletin No. 35 (Washington, D.C.: U.S. Bureau of Education, 1918).

ences), as well as the assigning of marks on the basis of a single standard of achievement without regard to ability. Is it surprising that these traditions were not destined to serve us well when the secondary schools finally began to receive "all the children of all the people"?

## A closer look at recent criticisms

An examination of the more common criticisms should help us to understand better some of the problems and issues facing those who want to help American schools serve our society to the greatest extent possible. As members of the profession primarily charged with providing both the leadership and operating manpower for one of our major institutions, we must understand the alleged weaknesses of the institution, determine the accuracy of the charges, and consider means of alleviating the problem.

A substantial portion of the criticism has been directed at an ill-defined, much maligned, and broadly misunderstood phenomenon known as progressive education. Although the life span of progressive education cannot be precisely identified, its influence was probably strongest, at least in terms of results, between 1930 and 1950. The "life adjustment" [4] emphasis during the late 1940's was a phase of this influence. What many of the critics seemingly have failed to realize is that the progressive influence in education, as Cremin [5] has so ably pointed out, was simply one aspect of the evolution of a culture, a part of the inevitable adjustment of our social institutions to meet the challenges presented by scientific and technological change.

Although the schools have been criticized frequently for their failure to respond to cultural changes, they are probably more responsive to social pressures than are any of our other institutions. The extent to which the scientific management movement and the goal of efficiency in business and industrial enterprise have influenced educational practice through several decades is illustrative of

---

[4] J. Dan Hull, *A Primer of Life Adjustment Education for Youth* (Chicago: American Technical Society, 1949).

[5] Lawrence A. Cremin, *The Transformation of the School* (New York: Alfred A. Knopf, Inc., 1961).

the sensitivity and vulnerability of our educational institutions to the values of the larger society.[6]

We have noted that the American secondary school has changed from a highly selective institution to one which, in theory at least, is available to serve all young people between the ages of twelve and eighteen. In 1900 only about 11 per cent of the youth aged fourteen to seventeen years actually were attending high school. By 1960 attendance had increased to more than 85 per cent! Progress in the percentage of youth attending high schools from 1890 to 1960 is shown in Table I.

TABLE I

COMPARISON OF ENROLLMENT IN GRADES 9–12 IN PUBLIC AND NONPUBLIC SECONDARY SCHOOLS IN THE UNITED STATES WITH THOSE AGED 14–17 YEARS IN THE GENERAL POPULATION [7]

| SCHOOL YEAR | ENROLLMENT, GRADES 9–12 AND POSTGRADUATE | NUMBER OF YOUTH AGED 14–17 IN GENERAL POPULATION | NUMBER ENROLLED PER 100 PERSONS AGED 14–17 IN GENERAL POPULATION |
|---|---|---|---|
| 1889–90 | 359,949 | 5,354,653 | 6.7 |
| 1899–1900 | 699,403 | 6,152,231 | 11.4 |
| 1909–10 | 1,115,398 | 7,220,298 | 15.4 |
| 1919–20 | 2,500,176 | 7,735,841 | 32.3 |
| 1929–30 | 4,804,255 | 9,341,221 | 51.4 |
| 1939–40 | 7,123,009 | 9,720,419 | 73.3 |
| 1949–50 | 6,453,009 | 8,404,768 | 76.8 |
| 1959–60 | 9,590,000* | 10,985,000* | 87.3* |

* Estimate by Bureau of Census.

*Enrollments in science and mathematics—past and present.* The charge has often been made that present-day secondary schools enroll a decreasing percentage of students in science and mathematics.

[6] Raymond E. Callahan, *Education and the Cult of Efficiency* (Chicago: University of Chicago Press, 1962).

[7] Adapted from *Progress of Public Education in the United States of America 1960–61* (Washington, D.C.: U.S. Department of Health, Education and Welfare, Office of Education, 1961), p. 17.

According to one outspoken critic of American secondary schools:

> The high school no longer aims chiefly to prepare students for college; it now provides educational, occupational, civic, and cultural training for every child. Under pressure from various groups, courses are being given whose educational value is questionable. Nearly half of our high schools offer little or no instruction in physics, chemistry, or in mathematics beyond introductory algebra. The percentage of high school pupils today who study scientific subjects is indicative of this: physics—23% (1900), 4% (1950); chemistry—10% (1900), 7% (1950); algebra—52% (1900), 27% (1950); and geometry—27% (1900) and 13% (1950).[8]

These and similar figures have been widely publicized in several magazines having nationwide circulation. Such comparisons are grossly misleading because they represent only a small portion of the relevant data. These figures do not reveal the fact that in 1900 only 11.4 per cent of the nation's high-school-age youth were actually enrolled in high school, whereas in 1950 the percentage was nearly 77. Since the secondary school population in 1900 was an intellectually and academically elite group as compared with the 1950 high school population, who came much closer to a true cross section of the total age group, we would expect to find a higher percentage of the 1900 students enrolled in advanced science and mathematics courses. Although this expectation holds true for physics, the difference in chemistry enrollment is slight.[9] Differences in enrollments in advanced mathematics courses are also slight.[10]

*The "fads and frills."* Much criticism has been made of the "fads and frills" alleged to have been added to the high school curriculum in response to pressures from one interest group or another. This is a charge which has been especially popular with local citizens seeking to obtain the defeat of a millage or bonding proposal. What constitutes a fad or a frill is subject, of course, to a great variety of

[8] H. G. Rickover, "The Situation in American Engineering and Scientific Education," *School and Society*, 83:2086 (May 26, 1956), 177. Reprinted by permission.

[9] "High School Science Teaching and Today's Science—Related Manpower Shortage," *The Science Teacher*, 24:3 (April 1957).

[10] See especially Harold C. Hand, "Black Horses Eat More than White Horses," *Bulletin of the American Association of University Professors*, 43:2 (Summer 1957), 266–279.

definitions depending upon the particular interests and motives of the person or group making the charge. In some instances all vocational subjects, athletics, and the fine and practical arts, in short, everything except the traditional subjects, are labeled fads and frills. Such subjects as English, history, geography, economics, biology, and geometry are seldom considered fads and frills.

Some of the activities found in the comprehensive secondary school are, perhaps, more important than others. But to establish a rank order of these activities, with a range from most important to least important, would be difficult indeed. Few communities could agree on such a ranked listing. That which is of great significance to one person is relatively low on the list of values of another. Some parents would consider the band the most important activity, others mathematics, and still others swimming. If these parents were reacting on the basis of benefits to be derived from these activities by their respective children, they could well be right! Young people's needs and abilities vary; some profit most from one kind of activity, some from another. Additionally, most youth develop more readily when they can participate in a variety of activities than when restricted to a few.

Although the expansion of the high school curriculum has been affected by pressure groups, it does not rest on so flimsy a base. The motivation for the expansion of the curriculum was twofold: (1) a belief that certain important elements in our culture were not represented by the academic subjects and (2) a desire to include experiences that would be interesting, meaningful, and useful to students whose motives, previous experience, and abilities were not conducive to satisfying participation in the traditional subjects. In other words, the subjects and activities often labeled fads and frills were added to the secondary school curriculum in order to provide a more complete education for all students, and a more meaningful education for those who could not, or would not, tolerate the academic subjects, at least as an exclusive diet.

The deletion of music, art, homemaking, business, vocational and industrial subjects, and athletics from the secondary school program would strip the school of whatever capability it now has to minister to the needs of perhaps as much as 60 to 75 per cent of its present population, to say nothing of the youth of high school age who do not now attend school. Such action would also reduce the appeal of the school for many of the youngsters in the remaining 25 to 40 per

cent. The school already suffers in competition with such commercial media as motion pictures, television, and radio; it would
become completely impotent in the eyes of many youngsters if its
curriculum were reduced to the traditional academic subjects.

*The "tough," "solid" subjects.* "Tough" and "solid" as used by
the critics seem to be synonymous with "academic" and "traditional." The referents are sometimes limited to physics, chemistry,
algebra, geometry, trigonometry, and foreign languages. Even English and history sometimes fail to be brought into the fold! The assumption seems to be that the "tough" subjects deal with concepts
that are hard to understand, require much memorization, are dull
and uninteresting, or require more time to master. One wonders
about the hours required to master a musical instrument, to learn to
type sixty words per minute, or to maintain a position on the basketball team. Some young people breeze through chemistry but find
achievement at the same level in shorthand extremely demanding. It
would seem that "tough" and "solid" are not properties inherent in
subjects; difficulty varies according to a multitude of factors, including the aptitude and interest of the learner and the methods and
materials used by the teacher.

## The unfinished business of secondary education

In a free society constructive criticism of social institutions is an
obligation of each citizen. Many of the present-day critics of the
schools, though they are sincere, have based their position regarding
the role of the school on assumptions that are not in harmony with
American social goals. In addition, some of the critics appear to
have disregarded the inevitable results of the actions which they
advocate.

The criticisms of recent years are primarily *destructive* rather than
*constructive,* since they have the effect of subverting the role of the
school in our kind of society. Had the criticisms been directed to
the major weaknesses of American secondary education, we could
have been well on our way toward alleviating some of our serious
educational problems instead of returning in many instances to educational practices that were anachronistic even during the latter part
of the nineteenth century when they were in vogue. As Melby has
stated:

There *are* educational wastelands. Not because we educate too many too highly, but because we educate too few and each not enough; not so much because schools are doing the wrong things, but more because they have not yet learned to do the right things well; not because schools are under the control of anti-intellectualists, but because schools and colleges have a tough time resisting anti-intellectual forces in our society; not because we are controlled by "an interlocking directorate of educationists," but because we are engaged in a hard and often losing struggle to get teachers, buildings, and facilities of the quality we need.[11]

What are some of the major weaknesses of secondary education in the United States? Perhaps "unfinished business" is a more accurate term than "weakness," especially in view of the many successes that secondary schools have to their credit. The school is an evolving institution subject to continuous re-evaluation and improvement.

*The drop-out.* Symptomatic of some of our most urgent unfinished business is the large number of youth who leave school without being graduated. A number of studies dealing with the problem of drop-outs have been made, most of them at the local district level. Whereas most of the earlier studies were focused on the reasons given by young people for their failure to continue in school, more recent studies have tended in the direction of attempting to find out what the drop-out is like. Because the reasons given by the drop-out or his parents or teachers are likely to be the "respectable reasons" rather than the true reasons, the latter technique is useful. Although there are differences from community to community and from school to school, generalizations are possible.

The average [typical] drop-out is 16 years old; often he has been marking time, waiting to reach the age when he may legally quit school. He is most likely to quit between the ninth and tenth, or between the tenth and eleventh grades. It is especially likely that he will not return after a summer vacation.

As a rule, the drop-out has shunned participation in extra-curricular activities, and he may have failed to become part of a social group within the school.

Usually his relationships with his teachers and with many of his fellow students indicate tension, suspicion, and strain. His

11 Ernest O. Melby, "Where and What Are the Educational Wastelands?" *School and Society*, 83:2080 (March 3, 1956), 74. Reprinted by permission.

poor attendance record, lack of interest, and failure to cooperate have contributed to his being retarded by about two years. Before leaving school, he may have spent as many years there as one who graduates, but because he has probably been held back rather than promoted regularly, he will not have completed the full program by the end of his attendance period.

The typical drop-out's parents are unimpressed with the value of education; often they openly scorn "book learning." In addition, the family is likely to regard school as a financial burden; not only does it cost something to keep a child in school, but the family is deprived of the money which the boy or girl could be contributing to the budget.[12]

The drop-out problem is not of recent origin. As shown in Table II the percentage of youth who leave school without being graduated has actually been decreasing, rapidly from 1900 to 1940 and more slowly since that time. There are compelling reasons, however, why the drop-out rate should be considered still much too high.

The entire free world is threatened with domination by an ideology that is the antithesis of our own democratic traditions and ideals. We have built our defense on the proposition that our national interest will be served best if we remain strong. It seems most unlikely that the United States can match population with the Soviet Union, to say nothing of China. It would seem, therefore, that our strength will have to be measured in terms of our technology and the *quality* of our human resources rather than the size of our manpower pool. Civilization has advanced to the extent that more and more education is required to produce the effective adult citizen. The time is probably near at hand when at least two years beyond high school will be a minimum for as much as two thirds of our population. It seems obvious that our nation can ill afford to continue to tolerate a condition in which 30 per cent of our citizens do not even complete high school.

It was easier to discount the seriousness of the drop-out problem some years ago on the basis of our need for an unskilled labor force of substantial size. It was sometimes argued that too much education tended to make people dissatisfied with work requiring little or no training. Our requirements for unskilled labor, however, have been

12 "High School Drop-Outs," *NEA Research Bulletin*, 38:1 (February 1960), 11–12. Reprinted by permission.

TABLE II

HIGH SCHOOL GRADUATES * COMPARED WITH YOUTH
17 YEARS OF AGE IN GENERAL POPULATION [13]

| SCHOOL YEAR | POPULATION 17 YEARS OF AGE | HIGH SCHOOL GRADUATES | NUMBER GRADUATED PER 100 PERSONS 17 YEARS OF AGE IN GENERAL POPULATION |
|---|---|---|---|
| 1869–70 | 815,000 | 16,000 | 2.0 |
| 1899–1900 | 1,489,146 | 94,883 | 6.4 |
| 1909–10 | 1,786,240 | 156,429 | 8.8 |
| 1919–20 | 1,855,173 | 311,266 | 16.8 |
| 1929–30 | 2,295,822 | 666,904 | 29.0 |
| 1939–40 | 2,403,074 | 1,221,475 | 50.8 |
| 1949–50 | 2,034,450 | 1,199,700 | 59.0 |
| 1951–52 | 2,040,800 | 1,196,500 | 58.6 |
| 1953–54 | 2,128,600 | 1,276,100 | 60.0 |
| 1955–56 | 2,270,000 | 1,414,800 | 62.3 |
| 1957–58 | 2,324,000 | 1,505,900 | 64.8 |

* Includes graduates from public and nonpublic schools.

decreasing rapidly, i.e., from 38.5 per cent in 1940 to 28.9 per cent in 1950, to an estimated 24.4 per cent in 1965.[14] The youth who fails to complete high school is bound to find it more and more difficult to secure a job of any kind. Those who do obtain work will find promotion almost impossible. We have noted that only about sixty-five of every hundred youth remain in high school long enough to graduate. Since this is a national average, the figure does not reveal the fact that the incidence of early school leaving varies greatly from one sector of our society to another. Generally speaking, school retention is highest in the suburbs and the well-to-do residential parts of the cities and lowest in the city slum areas. According to James B. Conant, in one slum area in one of our large cities 63 per cent of the male population between the ages of sixteen and twenty-one who had left school prior to graduation were unemployed. In

13 Adapted from *Progress of Public Education in the United States of America 1960–61,* p. 18.
14 "High School Drop-Outs," *op. cit.,* p. 12.

another city slum area "roughly 70 per cent of the boys and girls ages sixteen to twenty-one were out of school and unemployed." [15] "Social dynamite is building up in our large cities in the form of unemployed out-of-school youth, especially in the Negro slums." [16]

If the drop-out is as described in the quotation on page 12, the charge to the American secondary school seems clear. Schools will have to provide a curriculum that includes experiences appropriate to the recognized needs and interests of *all* youth. Teachers will have to use methods and materials appropriate to the abilities of *all* youth, not just those who are academically able. Teachers will have to abandon such practices as expecting every student to achieve at the same level, read the same amount in the same book, and cover the same ground. Grades will have to be assigned in relation to ability as well as achievement. Teachers will have to make certain that each youth spends some part of the school day with others of his own age and level of social maturity. Administrators will have to give more attention to extracurricular programs so that a wider variety of interests and needs are met. Greater encouragement must be given to all students to become involved in extracurricular programs. Teachers will have to show a real interest in each student. Perhaps parents will have to become more involved in school-related activities. Since parents, especially those in the lower socio-economic classes, get most of their ideas about school from their children, it may be that their attitude toward the value of an education will become quite positive when the school experience becomes meaningful for *all* American youth. The community will have to help much more than it has helped thus far in providing opportunities for young people to earn while they learn. While lack of money is rarely the major reason for dropping out of school, it is a significant factor when coupled with some other dissatisfactions. Young people should be able to find constructive work for which they are paid.

Those young people who fail to complete high school are not the only ones who are being served inadequately by typical secondary schools. A curriculum geared in most respects to the student of "middle ability" is just as inadequate for the gifted youth as it is for the potential drop-out. As a matter of fact, some of the drop-outs

[15] James B. Conant, *Slums and Suburbs* (New York: McGraw-Hill Book Co., Inc., 1961), p. 34.
[16] *Ibid.*, p. 146.

are actually highly able students who find the school program boring and meaningless. If teachers made a concerted effort to discover the needs, interests, and abilities of each secondary school student and then conducted their classes in such a way that each could progress toward his educational goals as rapidly as his ability and effort would permit, it would not be necessary to think about special schools and segregated classes for those of exceptional ability.

*Goals and purposes.* Secondary schools deserve to be criticized for their inability to define the goals of individual courses in particular and the total school program in general. Few members of the profession of education have taken the time or the trouble to analyze and think through what they really ought to attempt to accomplish with the students who come to their classes. If teachers did consider this matter carefully, they would become less willing to allow a textbook to dominate their total endeavor, and they would stop giving grades primarily on the basis of the students' ability to remember facts. American high schools will not be as strong as they should be until both faculties as groups and teachers as individuals become clear concerning the general goals of secondary education and the specific contributions to those purposes which they as individual teachers are suited to make. Closely related to a better understanding of and more concern with goals is the gearing of the processes of evaluation to all of the goals in place of only those purposes that can be readily measured by conventional examinations.

*Citizenship education.* The critics might also properly accuse the schools of failure to provide a realistic and effective citizenship program. The citizenship goal has appeared in every significant discussion of the purposes of American education during the past half century, but the schools have failed to provide ample opportunities for youth to practice democracy. Nor have they opened the doors to involvement and participation in community affairs. Citizenship training has been confined to learning about citizenship, rather than to practicing it. Student councils are usually restricted to dealing with trivia, and student government is too often dominated by the faculty sponsors.

*Work experience programs.* Secondary schools have done too little in developing work experience programs for youth. Those programs which are in operation are available to only a small minority of students, usually those in commercial or trade and industry courses. Seldom are school-sponsored work experience programs available to students on the college preparatory program. Yet many essential skills and attitudes are developed best in a work situation. A program of education that does not make this experience available to all students is incomplete.

*Individual differences.* Central to all the unfinished business is the schools' failure to structure a total program of secondary education on the basis of individual differences. Provision for optimum educational development for every youth according to his individual needs, aptitudes, and interests is not only essential but possible within the framework of our present comprehensive secondary school. The people of the United States have built a society that is unique in the experience of man; they have created an educational system which is also unique, one which in its broad framework is the envy of the entire world. We agree with James Conant that the historians in the year 2059 "will regard the American high school, as it was perfected by the end of the twentieth century, not only as one of the finest products of democracy, but as a continuing insurance for the preservation of the vitality of a society of free men."[17] We believe the key to such an achievement is an honest acceptance on the part of both the educators and the lay citizens of the fact of individual differences and a conviction that educational goals, methods, and materials must be designed to take account of this fact.

It seems clear that a society which accepts the existence of individual differences as a fact and respects the dignity of the individual will reveal the influence of this commitment in the goals and purposes established for its schools. In like manner, the teacher who understands the ways in which young people differ from each other, who is determined to take advantage of these differences rather than ignore them or attempt to reduce them, will conceive his role differently from the teacher who is not so inclined. The fact and the consequence of individual difference must affect the manner in which the teacher plans and selects resources with his students, the

[17] James B. Conant, *The Child, the Parent, and the State* (Cambridge, Mass.: Harvard University Press, 1959), p. 103.

means he employs to guide learning, and the way he and his colleagues organize the curriculum in their school.

Although educators must continue to refine and clarify their understanding of individual differences and the implications thereof, they need no further data to establish the fact of their existence. What they do need is to learn better how to deal with these differences in the school setting. In one sense this is the theme of this book; how can teachers discover the unique needs, interests, and aptitudes of each secondary school student? And, having discovered and identified these, how can they design an educational program that will provide for his optimum development?

*In conclusion.* Other aspects of the unfinished business are the dependence on "book learning" as the basic business of the schools, the premium placed on conformity with the consequent absence of encouragement to creativity, and the failure to make use of research findings. The schools will continue to be vulnerable to attack until they have made substantial improvements in these matters.

We have examined some of the major criticisms of American secondary schools. We have seen that the school is responsive to public criticism and that modifications result, even though the changes may not be as comprehensive as the critics would wish. We have analyzed certain of these criticisms and noted that the real weaknesses of our secondary schools have seldom been mentioned in the national circulation media. It seems that some of the changes now being advocated by critics are in opposition to American social ideals and goals. What are those ideals and goals, and how have they been translated into purposes for our secondary schools? We turn to these questions in Chapter 2.

## FOR FURTHER READING

Brown, Kenneth E., and Ellsworth S. Obourn, *Offerings and Enrollments in Science and Mathematics in Public High Schools.* Pamphlet No. 120. Washington, D.C.: U.S. Department of Health, Education and Welfare, Office of Education, 1956. An authoritative report that presents the facts on the extent of enrollment by high school students in mathematics and science courses.

Callahan, Raymond E., *Education and the Cult of Efficiency.* Chicago: University of Chicago Press, 1962. The influence on the schools of the goal of efficiency in business and industry, particularly as exemplified by the scientific management movement, is presented with careful documentation.

Cremin, Lawrence A., *The Transformation of the School*. New York: Alfred A. Knopf, Inc., 1961. The author presents the progressive education movement as a product of changing social forces and traces the history of the movement from 1876–1957.

Douglass, Harl R., *Trends and Issues in Secondary Education*. Washington, D.C.: Center for Applied Research in Education, Inc., 1962. Chapters 1 and 2 present a succinct summary of trends and issues in basic theory and philosophy in relation to the current socio-economic setting.

Educational Policies Commission, *Education for All American Youth, A Further Look*. Washington, D.C.: The National Education Association, 1952. Revision of the first volume published in 1944. Descriptions of simulated rural and urban school communities and school programs, identifying problems and needs and revealing "best" practice. A good resource for the reader who desires an introduction to the comprehensive high school and the community school concept.

————, *The Central Purpose of Education*. Washington, D.C.: The National Education Association, 1961. A concise analysis of *one* of the major purposes of education in the United States (thinking) by a source widely recognized as authoritative.

Hand, Harold C., "A Scholar's Devil Theory," *The High School Journal*, 41:7 (April 1958), 270–286. A scholarly response to several of the major criticisms of secondary education by Arthur Bestor in several widely circulated periodicals during the mid-1950's.

Hanna, Paul R., ed., *Education: An Instrument of National Goals*. New York: McGraw-Hill Book Co., Inc., 1962. A compilation of papers presented at a conference at Stanford University during the summer of 1961 on the report of the President's Commission on National Goals. See especially the chapter by I. James Quillen titled "National Goals and the Secondary Schools."

"High School Drop-Outs," *National Education Association Research Bulletin*, 38:1 (February 1960). A brief nontechnical summary of the problem of the high school drop-out.

Lichter, Solomon O., Elsie B. Rapien, Frances M. Seibert, and Morris A. Sklansky, M.D., *The Drop-Outs*. New York: Free Press of Glencoe, 1962. See Chapter 10, "Conclusions," for a relatively nontechnical description of the potential drop-outs in the study described in this book. This chapter also contains brief suggestions for school and community action.

Liddle, Gordon P., "The Schools' Job with the Disaffected," *Educational Leadership*, 20:5 (February 1963), 292–293, 347. Implications—for the society in general and for the school in particular—of the problem of disaffected youth. See also in the same issue "The Dropout—Our Greatest Challenge" by Earl C. Kelley.

Melby, Ernest O., and Morton Puner, eds., *Freedom and Public Education*. New York: Frederick A. Praeger, Inc., 1953. Helpful in providing insight into the place of the school in the American society. A collection of articles, condensations, and excerpts from various sources written in answer to the most frequently voiced criticisms of the schools during the years immediately following World War II.

National Society for the Study of Education, *Adapting the Secondary School Program to the Needs of Youth*, Fifty-second Yearbook, Part I. Chicago: University of Chicago Press, 1953. A comprehensive program for the improvement of secondary education, contrasting sharply with the proposals of many of the recent critics.

Scott, C. W., C. M. Hill, and H. W. Burns, eds., *The Great Debate: Our Schools in Crisis*. Englewood Cliffs, N.J.: Prentice-Hall, Inc., 1959. A collection of pro and con writings by several authors covering the major criticisms of the middle and late 1950's. An earlier volume, *Public Education under Criticism* by Scott and Hill (Prentice-Hall, Inc., 1954), covers the late 1940's and early 1950's.

"Ten Criticisms of Public Education," *NEA Research Bulletin*, 35:4 (December 1957). Several of the ten categories of criticisms discussed represent long-term controversies in American public education.

Thayer, V. T., *The Role of the School in American Society*. New York: Dodd, Mead & Co., 1960. See especially Part I, "Formative Ideas in American Education," and Part II, "Changes in the Economic and Social Status of Youth."

# 2

# Purposes
# of American
# secondary education

Any culture is perpetuated and supported through the education of its young. Democratic social and political institutions require a system of public education that is geared to the needs of democracy. The needs of the individual are the first concern. The President's Commission on National Goals began the introduction to their report as follows: "The paramount goal of the United States was set long ago. It is to guard the rights of the individual, to ensure his development, and to enlarge his opportunity. It is set forth in the Declaration of Independence. . . ."[1] A little later the Commission continued this thought as they wrote "The status of the individual must remain our primary concern. All our institutions—political, social, economic—must further enhance the dignity of the citizen, promote the maximum development of his capabilities, stimulate their responsible exercise, and widen the range and effectiveness of opportunities for individual choice."[2] More specifically in relation to the function of education is this statement: "Ultimately, education serves all of our purposes—liberty, justice, and all our other

[1] John W. Gardner, "National Goals in Education," from *Goals for Americans* by The American Assembly, Columbia University, New York, N.Y. © 1960. Reprinted by permision of Prentice-Hall, Inc., Englewood Cliffs, New Jersey. P. 1.

[2] *Ibid.*, p. 3.

21

aims—but the one it serves most directly is equality of opportunity. We promise such equality, and education is the instrument by which we hope to make good the promise." [3]

The American Association of School Administrators has stated the general purposes of the secondary school as follows:

> The maximum development of all the mental, moral, emotional, and physical powers of the individual, to the end that he may enjoy a rich life through the realization of worthy and desirable personal goals, and
>
> The maximum development of the ability and desire in each individual to make the greatest possible contribution to all humanity through responsible participation in, and benefit from, the great privileges of American citizenship.[4]

Many statements have been devised of the general purposes of education in the United States. An examination of them reveals four common elements. First, there is the assertion that democracy cannot function without an informed electorate. This is probably the oldest educational purpose we have. It was the basic reason for the establishment of free, tax-supported schools in this country. Jefferson said it like this:

> If a nation expects to be ignorant and free in a state of civilization it expects what never was and never will be. . . . There is no safe deposit (for the function of government) but with the people themselves; nor can they be safe with them without information.[5]

James Madison wrote:

> A popular government without popular information or the means for acquiring it is but a prologue to a farce or a tragedy, or perhaps both. Knowledge will forever govern ignorance; and

3 *Ibid.*, p. 81.
4 American Association of School Administrators, *The High School in a Changing World*, Thirty-sixth Yearbook (Washington, D.C.: The National Education Association, 1958), p. 28.
5 Quoted in Elmer H. Wilds, *The Foundations of Modern Education* (New York: Farrar, Straus and Cudahy, Inc., 1936), p. 418. Reprinted by permission.

a people who mean to be their own governors must arm themselves with the power which knowledge gives.[6]

Jefferson and Madison were thinking mainly in terms of the need
for literacy. In their day the goal of a literate citizenry was a high
ideal. But citizens today need a great deal more than the skills of
reading and writing. The world has become a perplexing and complicated place in which to live. People depend on each other for
the necessities of life. Science has joined nations around the globe.
The problems of Africa, Europe, and Asia are American problems.
Older values are being questioned. People are perplexed by the
need to adapt traditional values to a complex new world, or to develop new values that make sense. To live with sanity in today's
world demands good judgment, emotional maturity, and the capacity to adapt. But sanity alone is not a reasonable goal; in a democracy citizens must strive to be alert thinkers, analysts of propaganda,
and understanders of issues. They must have the courage to meet
problems and the skill to solve them in cooperation with others.
Leaders cannot operate on a much higher plane of ethics and intelligence than that which commonly prevails in our culture. Thus
democracy demands far more of today's schools than the teaching of
reading and writing. Educational goals now encompass all of the
aspects of good citizenship training, including an understanding of
the issues presently facing the various levels of government and the
ability to identify and examine issues as they develop in the future.

A second common element in statements concerning the general
purposes of secondary education is the implementation of the ideal
of equality of opportunity, the minimizing of hereditary privilege.
This goal has perhaps superseded the citizenship goal in importance
in the eyes of many people.

A third aim, which is closely related to the second and may be
interpreted to mean the same thing, is the maximum development
of the individual in keeping with his potential. The concern of the
society for the dignity and worth of each individual carries over into
the purposes which the society assigns to its educational institutions.

A fourth element is the preparation of the individual to contribute to the social welfare to the greatest extent possible in keeping with his potential and his individual welfare. Statements of

---

[6] *Ibid.*, p. 419.

aims generally agree that the interests of the society will be best served if the interests of the individual are kept paramount.

Before moving to a more detailed consideration of the specific purposes of the American secondary school, we shall examine some of the major social forces which today affect educational goals and the means employed to achieve them.

## Social forces affecting secondary education

The school is one of several institutions designed to serve the people. It is an integral part of society, having close ties with other institutions as well as with the society itself. It is not only influential in its effect on all aspects of the society but is affected by any change in the society proper or any part thereof. Because of the interrelated nature of the society the role of the school cannot be discussed without an understanding of the basic character of the society.

One fundamental feature of our society is its capacity for continuous change at a rapidly accelerating rate. Some of the major elements of social change are of prime importance in our understanding of the role of the school, especially the secondary school.

*The relationship of the United States to the other nations of the world.* Perhaps the most far-reaching change that has occurred during recent years is the shift in political power following World War II. As a result the United States is one of the two major world powers, is clearly the leader of the free nations, and is engaged in a struggle to maintain its position among the nations of the world and its own way of life. It is presently faced with the challenges of the expansion of world communism. The nation is dedicated to the position that it must preserve not only its own freedom but that of other peoples.

For further study, the reader can turn to other books wholly devoted to this and related matters. We should note, however, that new sources of power, particularly nuclear fission and fusion, coupled with technological advances in transportation and communication have brought together widely different cultures and have made people, both within this nation and outside it, more dependent upon each other.

Such change is bound to have a profound effect on the schools.

After it became apparent that the Soviet Union was ahead of us in rocketry, many citizens began to expect the schools to strengthen their teaching of the scientific, mathematical, and technical skills necessary to enable the United States to overtake the Soviet Union in all phases of technological progress. The profession has accepted this challenge, as evidenced by the several extensive modifications in the methods and materials in the fields of mathematics and the sciences. Whether or not these particular modifications are to receive wide adoption and integration into the programs of our secondary schools cannot now be determined, but the fact that extensive adjustments will continue to be made seems well established.

Another expectation, presently at a lower level of urgency as far as the public is concerned but, nevertheless, of considerable importance, is greater emphasis on foreign language study. The increasing interdependence of peoples in our shrinking world will require a much higher percentage of citizens to be bilingual and multilingual. Unless educators can perfect some new means of accomplishing this objective by an intensive short-term process near the time of anticipated use, many secondary school students will be expected to devote more time to the study of languages, probably as an extension of a program begun in the elementary grades.

In connection with the nation's role of world leadership, the school has other obligations which have as yet received little fanfare in the media of national communication but which are of more lasting significance than technological proficiency. If the free nations are to maintain their freedom, it is essential that our foreign policy be carefully determined and carried out. The success of such an endeavor will be contingent upon an informed and dedicated citizenry, better informed and with greater commitment than exists at present. The school must accept more responsibility than it has in the past in this transformation. Americans must gain a better understanding of the needs and aspirations of the world's peoples. They must be willing to share their knowledge, their skills, and their spiritual and material wealth so that other nations may enjoy the benefits of the technological revolution. It is not enough that citizens who have intimate contacts with other cultures have the necessary skills and knowledges to establish and maintain mutually satisfying relationships. The citizen at the ballot box must also reflect understanding and dedication. This is the challenge to the social sciences, neglected thus far in the frenzy to update instruction, but destined to be subjected to a reorganization and redirection at least as profound as those now under way in the physical sciences and languages.

*The population explosion.* A second phenomenon that must be taken into account by the school is the rapid increase of population, another result of the technological and scientific revolution. In 1960 the world's population was about 3 billions and was increasing about 50 millions per year. At this rate there will be roughly 4 billion people on the face of the earth by 1975, and perhaps as many as 6 billions by the year 2000. The increase is, of course, the inevitable result of technical and scientific advances in medical care, housing, transportation, and the production, processing, storage, and distribution of food.

The United States has made its contribution to world population growth with an increase of 30 million people during the decade of the 1950's. During the 1960's the increase in the labor force in this country is estimated at 13½ millions, the largest increase during any ten-year period in history.[7]

Persons in the 14–17 age group will number over 14 millions in 1965, nearly 16 millions by 1970, and about 18 millions by 1980. This represents a doubling of this age group between 1955 and 1980.

The secondary school faces a challenge in how best to help students understand the many implications of the population explosion both at home and abroad. Its most serious challenge, however, will be the problem of how to cope with the increasing numbers who will expect to be accommodated by the school. If the same percentage of the age group attends high school as at present—and this percentage is not likely to diminish—the school plant will have to be greatly enlarged and the number of teachers will have to be increased appreciably. The only other alternatives are improved efficiency or a sharp reduction in the quality of secondary education. The schools are already feeling pressure and are destined to feel more as the population becomes greater. The pressure is in the direction of higher over-all pupil-teacher ratios, implemented for the most part by what is known as "large-group instruction." Unless the profession is ready with adequate research results demonstrating that the qual-

7 "Our Changing Population," *NEA Research Bulletin,* 39:3 (October 1961), 75–76.

ity of the educational product deteriorates as the pupil-teacher ratio is increased, the schools will not be able to resist the pressure for per capita cost reduction.

*In-migration.* Americans have become a very mobile people. About 20 per cent of them change residences each year. Fewer than 15 per cent spend their entire lives within the same county.[8]

There are several types of in-migration. The first type, the movement from rural areas to cities, began many years ago largely as a result of jobs created by industrialization. The trend has continued, perhaps as much a result of efficiency on the farms as of industrial expansion.

A more recent population movement, that from the cities to the suburbs, has resulted from several desires of families: to rear children in a less cosmopolitan environment, to have a new house, and to get away from the congestion and industrial dirt of the city. No doubt, the desire to "keep up with the Joneses" is also a motivating force in some instances. Facilitating factors for this movement are the general level of prosperity, including the ability to afford two automobiles, improved transportation facilities, and the ready market for urban property.

Two other kinds of population movement are the migration from the inland areas to the coastal areas and from the South to the North. Each is a part of the continuing process of industrial expansion.

Both the generalized population movement and the specific kinds of in-migration have profound implications for the schools. The effects of transiency among students—the problems of having to leave old friends and make new ones, of shattered patterns of scope and sequence in the various subjects, and of differing curricular emphases—are well-known. While not all schools have made the necessary effort to alleviate the problems, educators have a fairly complete understanding of the nature of the problems.

There are other important ways in which population shifts affect the schools. The population composition of all or parts of the community may undergo radical change over a period of time. The

---

[8] National Society for the Study of Education, *Social Forces Influencing American Education,* Sixtieth Yearbook, Part II (Chicago: University of Chicago Press, 1961), p. 97.

movements from the South to the North and from rural areas to the cities, coupled with the migration from the cities to the suburbs, have tended to lower the socio-economic levels in certain sections of the cities. The needs and aspiration levels of the students have changed correspondingly. It is not unusual to find high schools in certain sections of the cities in which the percentage of college-bound youth has been reduced sharply in a relatively short time. A school in this kind of community must review its curriculum annually and be prepared to make frequent modifications.

The population shift to the suburbs presents a different kind of problem for the schools. The new residents may outnumber the older, established families. The general effect on the population composition of the total community may be one of diversification. A wider range of socio-economic classes may be present, with the result that the ranges of academic ability, levels of achievement, and career plans are widened. At the same time there may be neighbor-hoods in which the population is homogeneous. On occasion such an area can be of sufficient size to encompass a considerable portion of the district served by the secondary school. The newcomers are likely to bring with them the drives, aspirations, values, and anxi-eties of those who are actively promoting their own upward social mobility. Pressures by middle-class parents on their children to suc-ceed in school are sometimes as harmful as the lack of regard for the value of education sometimes found among lower-class parents. "Not infrequently, parental concern leads to bribes, what some youths are calling 'academic payola,' to get the children to work harder in school. One New York suburb reported recently that several parents had offered their children a vacation 'on their own' in Florida at the semester break if they would work hard and achieve agreed-upon grades for the semester." [9]

*Economic growth.* The United States has been enjoying a period of unparalleled prosperity. The gross national product rose from about $350 billions in 1950 to $500 billions in 1960. Some predic-tions have placed it as high as $750 billions in 1970. The picture is

[9] Dan W. Dodson, "The Effects of Suburban Living," *Children and Youth in the 1960s,* prepared for the Golden Anniversary White House Conference on Chil-dren and Youth. Reprinted in Leonard Freedman and Cornelius P. Cotter, eds., *Issues of the Sixties* (Belmont, Calif.: Wadsworth Publishing Co., Inc., 1961) by permission of the National Committee for Children and Youth, copyright holders.

not completely rosy, however. Inflation has been constantly reducing the standard of living for those on fixed incomes, and encouraging demands for wage increases on the one hand and higher prices on the other. Each year a school program comparable to the previous year's efforts costs more. This is not easily explained, especially to persons whose incomes are not increasing as rapidly as living costs.

There are some paradoxes in the picture too. Poverty exists in the midst of plenty, unemployment in the midst of unprecedented economic activity. To the secondary school come the children of poverty-stricken as well as prosperous families. Unless some conditions are altered there may well be some young men now attending our secondary schools who will never be gainfully employed during their entire lifetimes. Although such problems cannot be solved by the schools alone, the school is not without obligation and is certainly being affected by these conditions.

*Automation: the expansion of machine power.* Closely associated with technological and scientific advance and economic growth is automation. The most serious effect of automation is job displacement of adult workers. Proposals advanced thus far for dealing with the problem include retraining and relocation. Neither is a proper function for secondary schools, at least as a part of the regular program. The school is concerned, however, with the transiency of the student population when large numbers of workers have to be relocated. It must also help the students to understand the social implications of automation, and it should look for ways to prepare youth to face the prospect of job displacement and retraining possibly more than once during their own lifetimes.

Another result of automation that is of concern to the school is the reduction of hours in the industrial work week for much of our labor force with the consequent increase in uncommitted time. Indications are that further reduction will occur. This reduction is not uniform across the labor force. Among the professions and in management, for example, the work week has been extended in many instances. The secondary school should re-evaluate its obligation to help young people take optimum advantage of their leisure time opportunities now and as they grow older.

*The expansion of knowledge.* Not least among the startling changes of the twentieth century has been the increase in knowledge. Civilization has moved from the horse and buggy to space satellites, from animal power to atomic energy, from hand power to automation. These and many other developments have resulted in a vast explosion of human knowledge. Facts and the vocabulary that conveys them have multiplied many times since 1900. In commenting on the effects of this tremendous expansion in sciences and technology, Lyman Bryson has remarked:

> Today no man needs go to the ends of the world in search of knowledge. He is overwhelmed at his own doorstep, bewildered by a vast accumulation of accessible knowledge which no individual could possibly master. He is frustrated by the realization that even if he had no work to do, took no time off for fun, and lived forever, still he could never comprehend more than a fraction of what there is to be known.[10]

Another aspect of this phenomenon is the manner in which our vocabularies are affected, illustrated as follows:

> The plays of Shakespeare have long been cited for masterly use of language. It is said that a total of 15,000 words composed the vocabulary used in these plays. This, it has been assumed, was a vocabulary not equalled by that of any other writer. Although this may be true of writers of that era, vocabulary usage has increased rapidly within the past century. The vocabulary used in the state papers of the late Woodrow Wilson contained more than 25,000 words, and educated men of affairs frequently use in their writings more than double the number of words found in Wilson's state papers.
>
> At the turn of the century the vocabulary of the average person was supposed to include about 1200–1500 words. Extensive vocabulary studies made in the 'twenties and early 'thirties placed the average word usage desirable for study at slightly over 5,000 words. Readers are familiar with the more comprehensive Thorndike and Horn 5,000 word and 10,000 word lists of most commonly used words. A study by Robert Seashore of Northwestern University in 1941 revealed a startling advance in vocabulary knowledge. He found that college students on the average knew 60,000 com-

10 From Lyman Bryson, *An Outline of Man's Knowledge of the Modern World*, p. 1. Copyright © 1960 by Catherine McGrattan Bryson, Executrix of the estate of Lyman Bryson. Reprinted by permission of Doubleday & Company, Inc., and published by McGraw-Hill Book Company, Inc.

mon words, 1500 technical words, and 95,000 derived words. A similar study by M. J. Van Wagener of the University of Minnesota indicates that the extensive knowledge of vocabulary found by Seashore for college students holds true as well for early adolescents. While the worth of some of the early vocabulary studies is subject to question, these studies do indicate a rapid growth in vocabulary usage and a growing awareness of the problems involved.[11]

The effects of the increase in knowledge are cumulative. Each new discovery opens the doors to many other discoveries. The breakthroughs are coming with increasing rapidity. It has been said that knowledge is now expanding to the extent that it doubles every ten years.

The expansion of knowledge has been fundamental to the other forces we have discussed. Without it scientific and technological advance would have been curtailed, as would industrial expansion and automation. The extent of in-migration would also have been greatly diminished.

Since the school is the major institution charged with the acculturation of the young, the explosion of knowledge is of vital interest and concern to all who teach or plan to teach.

The subjects traditionally included in the secondary school curriculum are being extensively reorganized both in content and teaching method. Teachers must devise better ways to keep themselves informed. They must be ready to abandon well-worn units, resources, and activities in order to make room for the inclusion in the curriculum of new insights based on new knowledge. The teacher's job during the next few decades will be harder than it has ever been before; it will also be more interesting, stimulating, and challenging.

We have briefly considered several social forces that affect the purposes of the secondary school in our society. Most of the criticisms of the secondary schools, especially in recent years, have been based on philosophical differences. Critics have rarely accused the educators of incompetency; they have questioned the philosophy upon which the secondary program is based. When a critic says, "You are

[11] Roland C. Faunce and Nelson L. Bossing, *Developing the Core Curriculum*, rev. ed. (Englewood Cliffs, N.J.: Prentice-Hall, Inc., © 1958), pp. 19–20. Reprinted by permission.

lowering standards, watering down courses, and pampering the students," he is not intending to say, "You do not know how to teach." He is saying, "You are emphasizing the wrong things, you are attempting to achieve the wrong goals, you have confused the trivia with that which is fundamental."

We were also involved in philosophical questions when we considered some of the social forces that exert a strong influence on the school. Obviously, it is difficult if not impossible to engage in anything beyond a most superficial discussion of educational activities and problems without becoming involved with questions of purpose, whether directly or by implication. Since educational purposes are so fundamental to an understanding of the teacher's role, it now seems essential that we consider the purposes of secondary education in the United States in more orderly fashion than we have done thus far.

## Specific statements of purposes

The earliest statement of purposes that can help us understand the detailed responsibilities of the secondary school was issued in 1918 by a group known as the Commission on the Reorganization of Secondary Education.[12] The Commission's list of the "Seven Cardinal Principles of Secondary Education," although not as detailed as later statements, does contain all of the elements required to give direction to a modern secondary school program. The principles as identified by the Commission are:

> health
> command of fundamental processes
> worthy home membership
> vocational efficiency
> civic participation
> worthy use of leisure time
> ethical character

A report by the Educational Policies Commission in 1938 titled *The Purposes of Education in American Democracy* [13] is one of the most comprehensive statements ever published on this topic. Edu-

---

[12] *Cardinal Principles of Secondary Education*, U.S. Bureau of Education, Bulletin 1918, No. 35.

[13] Educational Policies Commission, *The Purposes of Education in American Democracy* (Washington, D.C.: The National Education Association, 1938).

cational writers refer to this report often, and many consider it the basic document in its field. The fact that it is concerned with both elementary and secondary education does not reduce its usefulness.

The Commission organized the objectives of education into four broad categories: (1) self-realization, (2) human relationship, (3) economic efficiency, and (4) civic responsibility. Each of the categories is broken down into several competencies. The objectives of self-realization, for example, are detailed as follows:

> *The Inquiring Mind.* The educated person has an appetite for learning.
>
> *Speech.* The educated person can speak the mother tongue clearly.
>
> *Reading.* The educated person reads the mother tongue clearly.
>
> *Writing.* The educated person writes the mother tongue effectively.
>
> *Number.* The educated person solves his problems of counting and calculating.
>
> *Sight and Hearing.* The educated person is skilled in listening and observing.
>
> *Health Knowledge.* The educated person understands the basic facts concerning health and disease.
>
> *Health Habits.* The educated person protects his own health and that of his dependents.
>
> *Public Health.* The educated person works to improve the health of the community.
>
> *Recreation.* The educated person is participant and spectator in many sports and other pastimes.
>
> *Intellectual Interests.* The educated person has mental resources for the use of leisure.
>
> *Esthetic Interests.* The educated person appreciates beauty.
>
> *Character.* The educated person gives responsible direction to his own life.[14]

Each of the other three categories is detailed in the same manner. A discussion of each item in terms of its importance and certain other descriptive and clarifying information is included in the report. Although not sufficiently detailed to provide leads for means of evaluation, the Educational Policies statement can provide an imaginative faculty with a suitable frame of reference for evaluating the adequacy of their building or district program.

[14] *Ibid.,* p. 50.

A different approach was used by the Committee on Curriculum Planning and Development of the National Association of Secondary School Principals. The Committee identified ten imperative needs of youth and posed these as proper goals for secondary education.[15]

1. All youth need to develop salable skills and those understandings and attitudes that make the worker an intelligent and productive participant in economic life. To this end, most youth need supervised work experience as well as education in the skills and knowledge of their occupations.

2. All youth need to develop and maintain good health and physical fitness.

3. All youth need to understand the rights and duties of the citizen of a democratic society and to be diligent and competent in the performance of their obligations as members of the community and citizens of the state and nation.

4. All youth need to understand the significance of the family for the individual and society and the conditions conducive to successful family life.

5. All youth need to know how to purchase and use goods and services intelligently, understanding both the values received by the consumer and the economic consequences of their acts.

6. All youth need to understand the methods of science, the influence of science on human life, and the main scientific facts concerning the nature of the world and of man.

7. All youth need opportunities to develop their capacities to appreciate beauty in literature, art, music and nature.

8. All youth need to be able to use their leisure time well and to budget it wisely, balancing activities that yield satisfactions to the individual with those that are socially useful.

9. All youth need to develop respect for other persons, to grow in their insight into ethical values and principles, and to be able to live and work cooperatively with others.

10. All youth need to grow in their ability to think rationally,

15 Reprinted by permission from the National Association of Secondary-School Principals' publication *Planning for American Youth*, 1951. Copyright: Washington, D.C. See also the entire issue of the NASSP *Bulletin* for March, 1947, which was devoted to "The Imperative Needs of Youth of Secondary School Age." Ways in which the secondary schools across the nation were meeting each need are discussed in detail.

to express their thoughts clearly and to read and listen with understanding.[16]

These ten imperative needs have been widely discussed and have tended to become an ideological basis for general education in our secondary schools during the past two decades. One feature that distinguishes this statement from many others is the context in which it presents reading, writing, and arithmetic. To the degree that these skills are mentioned at all, they are presented as means to a larger end, such as rational thinking or knowledge of science. In contrast to this treatment, most statements of the responsibilities of the schools accent the "3 R's" as ends in themselves. In the manner of the Seven Cardinal Principles, they speak of the command or mastery of the fundamentals. It has been built into our folklore that these fundamentals are reading, writing, and arithmetic.

A different definition of "fundamentals" appears in a little book by Kelley titled *In Defense of Youth*. He defines the fundamentals as anything without which the organism cannot thrive. After pointing out that people can and do thrive without effective command of reading, writing, and arithmetic, he goes on to offer six fundamentals which the schools should help youth develop and utilize:

> 1. The first fundamental is other people. . . . This need is continuous throughout life, because the human potentiality for psychological growth is continuous.
> 2. In order to have other people we need good *communication* between at least one adult and the very young. . . . When the human environment looks facilitating, we tend to open up and to be receptive, that is more accessible to communications. If the human environment seems threatening, we tend to withdraw, to build barriers for our protection. . . .
> 3. In order to establish communications, to have other people, the human being must have other people in a *loving relationship*. If he is to develop into a person who can maintain human relationship, he must be a loving person. . . .
> 4. A fourth fundamental is that each person must have a *work-*

[16] The method of determining the purposes of secondary education by means of an analysis of the needs of youth has been dealt with extensively in a yearbook of the National Society for the Study of Education, *Adapting the Secondary School to the Needs of Youth*, Fifty-second Yearbook, Part I (Chicago: University of Chicago Press, 1953).

*able concept of self.* . . . One needs to think well enough of himself so that he can operate. . . . Nobody can do anything unless he thinks he can. . . .

    5. Every human being, in order to develop his full potential, must have *freedom.* . . . In order to have other people, the individual must behave in such a way that, while he has the choices of a free man, other people will not be repelled. This is freedom within the social scene. It is the product of cooperative living. . . .

    6. Every person needs the chance to be *creative.* . . . Creativity is the growing edge of learning and living and is essential to any life fulfillment.[17]

This reconstruction of the "fundamentals" seems to sharpen the issue that has been debated throughout the history of education: do schools exist only for intellectual training or do they face the larger task of developing more competent human beings?

A method of identifying educational purposes for secondary school youth somewhat different from the imperative needs approach has been proposed by Robert J. Havighurst, who uses the "developmental task" concept to provide direction to the activities of the school. According to Havighurst "a developmental task is a task which arises at or about a certain period in the life of the individual, successful achievement of which leads to his happiness and to success with later tasks, while failure leads to unhappiness in the individual, disapproval by the society, and difficulty with later tasks." [18]

Havighurst presents a list of developmental tasks for all age levels, from infancy through the years of later maturity. The tasks for adolescence are as follows: [19]

    1. Achieving new and more mature relations with age-mates of both sexes.

    2. Achieving a masculine or feminine social role.

    3. Accepting one's physique and using the body effectively.

---

[17] Earl C. Kelley, *In Defense of Youth* (Englewood Cliffs, N.J.: Prentice-Hall, Inc., © 1962), pp. 137–140. Reprinted by permission.

[18] Robert J. Havighurst, *Developmental Tasks and Education* (New York: Longmans Green & Co., Inc., 1952), p. 2. Courtesy of David McKay Company, Inc. See also Robert J. Havighurst, *Human Development and Education* (New York: Longmans, Green & Co., Inc., 1953).

[19] *Ibid.,* pp. 33–71.

4. Achieving emotional independence of parents and other adults.

5. Achieving assurance of economic independence.

6. Selecting and preparing for an occupation.

7. Preparing for marriage and family life.

8. Developing intellectual skills and concepts necessary for civic competence.

9. Desiring and achieving socially responsible behavior.

10. Acquiring a set of values and an ethical system as a guide to behavior.

Two things should be observed. The first is that this approach represents a compromise between two conflicting theories of education. One theory holds that freedom is necessary for nurture, the other advocates social restraints. The freedom advocates look first to the learner for clues as to purposes. The restraint advocates look to society and its needs. The developmental tasks idea is based on the thesis that the learner is already a part of the social order, and can be helped to define his tasks in the context of societal demands.

A second observation is that developmental tasks are conditioned by the interaction of the individual and his social environment. Thus they are conditioned by the combination of cultural values—ambitions, concepts, likes, dislikes, habits—which constitutes the prevailing climate of the individual's social class. Both the means of completing one's tasks and the criteria for measuring success will vary with one's social class. This fact offers a special challenge to teachers who commonly reflect middle-class values.

Developmental tasks are, by definition, the tasks at which the learner must not fail. He may live a satisfying life without command of the subjunctive, but he must develop emotional independence in order to become a mature, effective individual. This does not imply that intellectual development is unimportant. Indeed, certain intellectual skills are a means of achieving some of the developmental tasks of adolescence. But they are means, not ends in themselves. The basic drives of youth cannot be successfully disregarded by teachers who accept as a part of their job the fulfillment of the individual.

The approaches to educational purposes discussed thus far have been useful in providing direction to the secondary school program. They have been too general in nature, however, to have direct application to the work of the classroom teacher. The lack of immediate applicability is a major reason for the gap between statements of purposes and actual classroom practice.

This problem has been partially solved by an extensive project completed in 1957 under the sponsorship of the Russell Sage Foundation directed by Dr. Will French.[20] Dr. French and his associates used the framework of educational purposes established by the Educational Policies Commission, i.e., the objectives of self-realization, human relationship, economic efficiency, and civic responsibility, and expressed these in behavioral outcomes. The attempt was to identify and describe the desirable behavior contemplated under each of the four broad categories of purpose and then to provide several illustrations of observable activity on the part of the learner which would indicate progress toward the achievement of the objective. The effect of the application of this procedure on one of the categories, self-realization, is revealed by the following excerpt:

1. Growing toward self-realization. Our democratic society has as its basic reasons for existence the protection of individuals so that they may have opportunity for full development into their best selves and the encouragement to achieve it. It is logical, then, that public secondary education in such a society should first seek to facilitate this self-realization of each student. The cultivation of willingness and ability on the part of all students to attain the kinds and levels of behavior consonant with the native endowments of each and appropriate in our kind of society and culture, therefore, should be the first concern of a high school's program of general education.

1.1. Developing behaviors indicative of intellectual self-realization: Behavioral outcomes to be sought from general education because the living of a satisfying personal life requires intellectual development toward the level of one's capacity.

1.11 Improving his study habits, study skills, and other work habits.

1.111 Is skillful in securing information and in organizing, evaluating, and reporting results of study and research.

[20] Will French, et al., Behavioral Goals of General Education in the High School (New York: Russell Sage Foundation, 1957).

Illustrative Behaviors
(a) Decides on his purpose before planning action.
(b) Practices good study and other work habits when he has intricate thinking, reading, and planning to do.
(c) Consults some good periodicals if seeking information on political developments, foreign affairs, homemaking, scientific matters, book reviews, etc.
(d) Uses common sources of printed information efficiently; e.g., dictionary, encyclopedia, almanacs, telephone directory, *Who's Who, Readers' Guide,* and card catalog in library.
(e) Can read all parts of a newspaper for needed information; e.g., weather reports, radio programs, amusements, business news, editorials, local, state, national, and international news.
(f) Asks questions in such a way as to secure accurate information of public services, offices, or persons likely to have special information when in need of it.
(g) Uses books, maps, globes, charts, timetables, and graphs of all kinds to find needed information.
(h) Systematizes his work in order to accomplish the things he wants to do.
(i) Constructs line, bar, and circle graphs, diagrams, pictographs, and statistical tables to express quantitative relationships.
(j) Uses the typewriter or writes well enough to meet his needs.
(k) Reads and interprets the graphs, charts, tables, road and other maps encountered in newspapers, magazines, and other popular printed matter.
(l) Is able to draw relevant information from several sources, correlate it, make a defensible set of conclusions, and discard what is not relevant.
(m) Manifests a fair knowledge of the relative reliability of various sources of information: two or more newspapers, radio and TV commentators, consumer guides, government publications.
(n) Develops skills in noting and recording information in outline, notes, and summary statements.
(o) Uses a readily acceptable footnote and bibliographical form in identifying sources of information and ideas.
(p) Develops listening habits that enable him to gain intended meaning.[21]

Additional items from the list of "developing behaviors indicative

[21] *Ibid.,* pp. 92–93.

of intellectual self-realization," [22] with the illustrative behaviors are as follows:

> 1.112 Displays an inquiring mind; is intellectually curious and industrious.
>
> 1.113 Can learn independently and shows desire to do so.
>
> 1.114 Recognizes the importance of continuing to learn.
>
> 1.12 Improving in his ability to communicate ideas and to recognize and use good standards.
>
> 1.121 Commands and uses the basic skills of reading for information, ideas, opinions, stimulation, and leisure.
>
> 1.122 Expresses his ideas in speech, writing, or in some artistic form with increasing clarity and correctness.
>
> 1.123 Demonstrates his command of quantitative thinking.
>
> 1.124 Is developing some artistic and literary tastes and standards; exhibits creative capacity in some form of worthwhile intellectual activities.

Having considered some of the more detailed attempts to define the purposes of secondary education, including a highly specific statement of behavioral outcomes, let us now turn our attention to ways in which classroom activities may be related to purposes.

## The teacher's concern with purposes

It is difficult to conceive of any educational endeavor that is without purposes, whether at the district, building, or classroom level. Yet many schools have no written statements of purposes. Some schools have fairly comprehensive statements of purposes on file but seldom look at them. Other schools have statements that are so general that they cannot give much direction to individual teachers. Nevertheless, the educational program can be purposeful whether or not a written statement exists. The real purposes may not be those which are written nor even those which are enunciated by the teacher. The teacher may express a real concern for "teaching citizenship," yet give a low citizenship grade to a student who objects to the term project assigned by the teacher and offers a substitute proposal, or who reads a book on political parties during the time another stu-

---

[22] *Ibid.*, pp. 93–99.

dent is making an oral report to the class, or who carries on a quiet conversation with a neighbor during a free reading period about whether labor unions ought to be more carefully controlled. Such a teacher is not primarily interested in contributing to the development of his students' citizenship competencies. His real purposes are to operate a quiet classroom, to have the students conform to a pattern of deportment which he sets, and to keep all students working on the same activity at any given time. Each of the statements of purposes, both general and specific, which we discussed contemplated many behavioral outcomes which did not depend exclusively or even primarily on the ability to remember facts and information, yet teachers often give memory skill most of the weight when they assign grades.

A real concern with the total spectrum of the purposes of secondary education by each high school teacher would help to close the gap between purpose and practice. He can use the needs or developmental tasks approach or the "competencies" approach of the Educational Policies Commission. If he chooses the latter, he has the benefit of the detailing of behavioral outcomes as prepared by French and his associates. He may wish to work out the behavioral outcomes by himself or as a faculty project. Regardless of the particular approach he uses, he will probably be most successful if he translates each goal into terms of what the student may be expected to do or how the student may be expected to behave when he is making progress toward each particular goal.

There are other principles that we should keep in mind regarding purposes.

1. Since the function of education is in most cases one of helping people to satisfy their own needs, or accomplish their developmental tasks satisfactorily, or achieve certain competencies, the goals of the school should be viewed as ideals toward which students make progress. *Purposes must never be thought of as standards which separate the bright from the dull students, or the ambitious students from those who seem lazy. Some students will progress toward any given goal more rapidly than others and some will achieve or attain the goal more completely than others.*

2. Goals must be possible of attainment within the framework of the school. Activities carried on under the auspices of the school should provide experiences that seem likely to give rise to the behavioral outcomes contemplated by the purposes.

3. All activities in which the students engage under the auspices of the school must be related to one or more of the purposes; in fact, experiences should be selected on the basis of their potential contribution to one or more of the school's purposes.

4. Insofar as possible, purposes should contemplate measurable behavioral outcomes. Students' progress toward the achievement of purposes will be more readily measurable in relation to some purposes than others. In a few instances it will not be possible to secure more than fragmentary evidence. If teachers plan their evaluative techniques carefully, however, according to the particular behavior they desire to appraise, they can expect success in their evaluative efforts most of the time. The fact that many secondary teachers have been interested only in measuring students' memory of facts and ideas has delayed progress in the development of methods which could be readily used to measure other kinds of behavior.

5. Evaluation should be geared to the purposes of the school. Marks should be based on progress toward attainment of goals, preferably in relation to the individual student's ability (maturity level in relation to the specific goal) and his effort.

6. Purposes should be re-evaluated from time to time in relation to changes taking place in the society.

One principle determines the degree to which goals are attained: *Learning does not take place unless the learner wants to learn.* This is another way of saying that the goals of whatever particular kind of learning is being attempted must be accepted by the learner before he will learn. The teacher can have a comprehensive understanding of the purposes of education and a well-thought-out system of goals for his classes, yet learning can be at a very low level because the students do not consider what they understand to be the purposes the teacher has in mind as valid for them. This condition could be a result of a misunderstanding on the part of the students, i.e., they are not aware of the teacher's concept of the purpose of the learning, or it may be that the students reject the purposes. It is also possible that the students, or some of them, want to learn, but for reasons different from the ones the teacher has in mind. Whenever teachers use approval or disapproval, grades, honors, bribes, or other "extrinsic" rewards as an incentive to learning, they are encouraging the substitution of these for the "proper" goals.

If the purposes set by the school and the teacher are based on true needs (or developmental tasks), they will be the same as those set by the learners. The job of the school is to help the students understand their needs and translate them into purposes. Most high school students, for example, are concerned about their ability to earn their living as adults, but they may need some help in understanding the benefits of doing preliminary investigating of possible occupations while in high school. After the students have discussed some of the occupations with which they are familiar, perhaps as a result of a trip to an industry or business, and have had an opportunity to share with classmates ideas and information about possible vocational choices, they are likely to see how such experiences can be valuable to them as they progress toward economic independence.

We have noted that educational purposes grow out of the culture and that the purposes of education in a democratic society reflect the democratic ideals of individual freedom and opportunity. The central goal has been education for all, at least through grade twelve. Such a goal implies attention to the needs of all students, not just the intellectually elite and well adjusted. The government Panel on Education, which prepared the "Rockefeller Report," had this to say in relation to the "pursuit of excellence":

> First, we must not make the mistake of adopting a narrow or constricting view of excellence. Our conception of excellence must embrace many kinds of achievement at many levels. There is no single scale or simple set of categories in terms of which to measure excellence. There is excellence in abstract intellectual activity, in art, in music, in managerial activities, in craftsmanship, in human relations, in technical work.
>
> Second, we must not assume that native capacity is the sole ingredient in superior performance. Excellence . . . is a product of ability and motivation and character. And the more one observes high performance in the dust and heat of daily life, the more one is likely to be impressed with the contribution made by the latter two ingredients.
>
> Finally, we must recognize that judgments of differences in talent are not judgments of differences in human worth.[23]

We have made substantial progress toward this goal. No other nation has tried or achieved as much—by a wide margin! We can

[23] From *The Pursuit of Excellence: Education and the Future of America.* Copyright © 1958 by Rockefeller Brothers Fund, Inc. (as it appears in *Prospect for America,* © 1961). Reprinted by permission of Doubleday & Company, Inc.

be rightfully proud of our progress, however, only if we continue to strive for the complete fulfillment of our goal.

Thus far we have occupied ourselves with the nature of the school as a social institution, charged with responsibility for achievements deemed essential by the society. Now we shall turn to an examination of the central figure about whom all school matters should revolve, the learner, keeping in mind that no matter what society decrees that the school must do, the degree of success achieved depends upon the extent of harmony between the school's purposes and methods and the purposes and capabilities of the students.

## FOR FURTHER READING

Alberty, Harold B., and Elsie J. Alberty, *Reorganizing the High School Curriculum,* 3rd ed. New York: Macmillan Co., 1962. Chapter 2, "The American High School: Its Philosophy and Goals," consists of a scholarly summary of the various philosophic positions that may be held with respect to education. Following this section is a special treatment of the commitment of secondary schools to citizenship education for democracy.

American Association of School Administrators, *The High School in a Changing World,* Thirty-sixth Yearbook. Washington, D.C.: The National Education Association, 1958. Chapters 1 and 2 deal with educational purposes in relation to the changing American society.

Educational Policies Commission, *The Central Purpose of American Education.* Washington, D.C.: The National Education Association, 1961. The thesis that the development of the habits and skills of rational thinking should be the central purpose of education is set forth in this little pamphlet.

———, *Education for All American Youth, A Further Look.* Washington, D.C.: The National Education Association, 1952. A revision of the earlier *Education for All American Youth.* Presents in narrative form the challenges of our time for secondary schools.

———, *The Purposes of Education in American Democracy.* Washington, D.C.: The National Education Association, 1938. Probably the best known and most widely quoted statement on this topic.

Faunce, Roland C., and Nelson L. Bossing, *Developing the Core Curriculum,* rev. ed. Englewood Cliffs, N.J.: Prentice-Hall, Inc., 1958. Chapter 1, "Education Confronts New Challenges," consists of a review of changes in our modern culture which have an impact on the schools. Chapter 4 deals with philosophy and purposes.

Freedman, Leonard, and Cornelius P. Cotter, eds., *Issues of the Sixties.* Belmont, Calif.: Wadsworth Publishing Co., Inc., 1961. A collection of writings on ten issues. See especially the sections on "The Impact of Science and Technology" and "The Changing American Character."

French, Will, *et al., Behavorial Goals of General Education in the High School.* New York: Russell Sage Foundation, 1957. An excellent and comprehensive example of a means of making educational goals meaningful and useful.

*Goals for Americans,* The Report of the President's Commission on National Goals. Englewood Cliffs, N.J.: Prentice-Hall, Inc., 1960. Source material for the development and understanding of the purposes of education in contemporary United States. See especially the basic report (pp. 1–23) and the section on education in the second portion of the book (pp. 81–100).

Havighurst, Robert J., *Developmental Tasks and Education.* New York: David McKay Co., Inc., 1952. An explanation of the developmental tasks concept by its originator. A more detailed treatment may be found in Havighurst's *Human Development and Education* (McKay, 1953).

"The Imperative Needs of Youth of Secondary-School Age," *Bulletin of the National Association of Secondary School Principals* (March 1947). Each of the ten imperative needs is discussed in detail in terms of the rationale for its selection as essential and the manner in which schools meet the need. The latter is based on practices reported by schools across the nation.

Leonard, J. Paul, *Developing the Secondary School Curriculum,* rev. ed. New York: Holt, Rinehart and Winston, Inc., 1953. See especially Chapter 3, "The Determinants of the Curriculum."

McKean, Robert C., *Principles and Methods in Secondary Education.* Columbus, Ohio: Charles E. Merrill Books, Inc., 1962. Chapter 2, "Bases For Selecting and Organizing Content," contains a brief overview of the needs of society and of the needs of the community.

National Society for the Study of Education, *Social Forces Influencing American Education,* Sixtieth Yearbook, Part II. Chicago: University of Chicago Press, 1961. Excellent background material for understanding the role of the school in our society.

*Planning for American Youth,* rev. ed. Washington, D.C.: National Association of Secondary School Principals, 1951. A brief pictorial version of *Education for All American Youth.* Presents in graphic form the basic needs which American secondary schools must serve.

Rugg, Harold, and William Withers, *Social Foundations of Education.* Englewood Cliffs, N.J.: Prentice-Hall, Inc., 1955. Part V reviews the "Social and Psychological Problems in Changing America."

# 3

# The secondary school student

We have traced the rapid growth of secondary schools to the point where they now enroll about 87 per cent of American youth through age seventeen. We have examined the purposes of secondary schools and the characteristic needs of the youth whom these schools are intended to serve. We have noted that one outstanding fact about our youth is that there are so many of them.

Aside from their sheer numbers, we have also noted that youth have many needs in common. These needs—skills, knowledges, understandings, and values—form the basis of programs of general education in secondary schools.

It is fortunate that youth have much in common. Were this not the case, they could not profit from typical secondary schools, which seem to be set up on a premise that students are or can become identical. Teachers tend to give them all the same assignments in the same books, and expect them all to take the same tests covering the same material during the same span of time. While making some allowance for attitude and effort, teachers tend also to grade students in competition with their fellows, who may differ widely in intelligence, academic aptitude, and motivation. In short, although there are common needs and characteristics, young people differ in their readiness to learn. This fact of differing readiness accounts, at least in part, for the problem of drop-outs. But many more students are in school in body only; they have lost interest and would drop out if they could. Perhaps the greatest failure of the school lies in the inability or unwillingness of teachers to adjust instruction to individual differences.

## Individual differences

There has been a continuing interest in the phenomena of individual differences for at least the past fifty years. (Perhaps it should be added that more has been written and spoken than done about it.) Differences have created problems for as long as schools have existed. The high school of 1900 was probably not an effective experience for the 10 per cent of youth whom it served, but these selected young people managed to survive it or endure it because of their need to enter college. As more and more young people entered the secondary schools, the selective factor disappeared, and differences between students became more marked. Today, with almost 90 per cent of youth entering the high schools for at least a trial, the differences have forced our attention in a most dramatic way.

The same cultural changes that produced rapid increases in enrollment have accented individual differences in other ways. There was a time when life was simple and the few skills needed were common to most adults. The labor force was largely uneducated and unskilled. Girls were destined to become homemakers, with no political responsibility. Only a small number of professional or technical workers were needed, and even their training was brief and relatively simple by today's standards.

The twentieth century has witnessed a dramatic change. Today not only man-the-worker but man-the-citizen must present individualized abilities to the complex world in which he lives. People are dependent on the specialized contributions of others for their food and clothing. Technical developments in production, distribution, transportation, and communication have enormously changed their lives and complicated their problems of living. To live in a time of rapid change and interdependence calls for judgment and maturity. To be, in addition, alert, critical observers of the world with the ability to assess issues and make wise choices imposes a further challenge to individual powers. On this point Harold G. Shane has commented thus:

> In fine, a merely liberalizing education is not enough. The educated man also must experience a quality of personalized education which enables him to perform effectively as a specialist-cum-diversification—a man who not only has a specialty but also can see how to relate his expertness to other disciplines, to relevant logic systems, and to the dynamics of socially desirable change.[1]

It is impossible for anyone to know everything. Some selection must be made from the vast areas of established knowledge. In practice, that selection can only be made by the learner himself, as he seeks solutions to his problems.[2]

Thus recent changes in our culture have focused attention on the differences between one learner and another. Since such differences directly affect all learning and teaching, it is important for a prospective teacher to gain an understanding of some of them. Let us begin by making a visit to a high school classroom. The group is a world history class composed of tenth graders, twenty girls and thirteen boys.

First we look around the room and study the appearance of the students. We are immediately struck by the physical differences we see in them. Several of the girls are quite tall—in fact taller than most of the boys. Some are thin, some are normally developed, and three may be called fat. One girl appears to be about eleven years old (she is actually almost fifteen). The boys exhibit an even more startling range of physical size. Five seem to be little boys, five are about the height of the girls, and three are at least six feet tall. Several boys have acne on their faces. Although there is great similarity in the styles of clothing worn by the students, some of the sweaters and skirts are new and of good quality, some look a little like hand-me-downs; the boys wear sport shirts and either trousers or jeans, which also range from the stylish and new to the worn and rumpled. There is either a wide range of family income or of personal grooming—perhaps both.

1 Harold G. Shane, "The School and Individual Differences," in *Individualizing Instruction*, Sixty-first Yearbook, National Society for the Study of Education (Chicago: University of Chicago Press, 1962), p. 46. Reprinted by permission.

2 Elaboration of this point will appear in the section of Chapter 4 on individual perception.

As we listen to the class in action, we see some types of participants emerging: the hesitant speaker, the nervous giggler, the boy with the roving eye, the girl who knows every answer, the smooth self-salesman, the earnest bore, the gazer-out-of-windows, the teacher-baiter, the persistent wrong answerer. And there are eager and intelligent contributions made by several boys and girls, some who show evidence of having read the textbook, some with skill in using a map. No real discipline problems develop during our brief stay but we speculate that Miss Jones may one day have her hands full with the class clown, or the sullen giant with feet in two aisles, or the girl who is even now passing a note to the boy behind her. We wonder whether Miss Jones knows that there are several students who are not following what is going on at all. One of the latter is reading a comic book imbedded in his history text.

An assignment is made by Miss Jones, the bell rings, and the class leaves with about the normal amount of noise. There seems to be an overtone of release (or relief) in the conversations and postures of the departing students.

Miss Jones comes up smiling and announces that she has a free period and can talk to us about the class.

"I've had a real break in collecting some data about this class," she begins. "The counselor has made a special effort to supply some information I didn't have. I'm writing a paper for a graduate class, describing this one group of thirty-three kids. Would you like to hear what I have collected so far?"

We are indeed interested.

"Well, first of all, they are all in 10B but range in age from fourteen years and five months to seventeen years and one month. Five of the boys and four of the girls are sixteen or over; of these nine, one has lost a year from polio and eight have failed one grade in elementary school. Their I.Q.'s range from 81 to 132, with the average at 101.2. In reading they have an awful range of difference—the lowest reads at fourth grade level, and there are nineteen who score below their grade on the Iowa Test. Of course, there are three others who read at the college level and eleven whose score is tenth, eleventh, or twelfth grade level—but those poor kids who can't read —it is literally true that they cannot read their textbook for this course. I don't know what I'm going to do with them. I just don't know how to teach them to read.

"There was a test given them in the eighth grade with a section on history achievement. That was about a year and a half ago. At that time they ranged from third grade, sixth month all the way to eleventh grade, third month on history achievement. If we were to give the high school version of that test right now, we think we'd find at least five of these kids who are already above the average scores of college freshmen. But we'd also find twelve or fifteen who should be back in the seventh grade so far as history tests indicate.

"We have other data. Their health history is probably normal, but several need teeth filled, four are overweight, nine are underweight, thirteen wear glasses and only four of these have been rechecked within two years. Five boys played football this fall, and six are planning to try out for basketball. Of course, they're all in physical education but the teacher in gym tells me they aren't very much alike in coordination or game skills either.

"And their families—you should see the differences in them! Five are from broken homes and seven others have employed mothers. Three girls are from our wealthiest families, and seven girls and four boys are from welfare families. Four have one or both parents who were born in Europe, while six other kids came to our junior high school from the South. Then there is Erika, our exchange student from Norway—she's living with one of our teachers this year."

We thank Miss Jones and depart, not because she has run out of information but because she has some plans to make before she confronts another group of highly different individuals.

Miss Jones' class is typical of junior and senior high school classes almost everywhere. The range of differences has been substantiated by research studies for years. Such studies have revealed a somewhat staggering list of the factors of individual differences. Thus individuals differ in respect to a number of different skills and characteristics. A recent yearbook of the National Society For the Study of Education contains the following comment on this point:

> The phrase "individual differences" refers to the dissimilarities among the various members of a class or age group in any characteristic that can be identified. It is common to speak of the existence of individual differences in such things as problem-solving, reading ability, spelling ability, visual and auditory acuity, language skills, height and weight, dexterity, readiness to learn, interest, emotional stability, persistence, motivation, ability to

work alone, co-operativeness, and many other social, personal, intellectual, and academic characteristics.[3]

Various classifications of these factors of individual differences have been made. For the purposes of this chapter, we shall deal with physical differences, social maturity, interests, mental development, achievement, and cultural factors.

*Physical differences.* Physical differences are obvious. In the junior high school years it is not uncommon to observe height differences of eighteen inches and weight differences of one hundred pounds— between youngsters of the same age. Junior high school girls tend to be taller than boys, and are generally one and one half to two years ahead of their male age-mates in all aspects of physical development. The onset of puberty produces rapid change both internally and externally. The release of hormones brings about the beginnings of sexual maturation. Girls begin the menstrual cycle, and experience the filling out of hips and breasts. Boys find their voices deepening, their shoulders broadening, their beards growing. Body hair appears in both sexes.

But these changes do not occur at the same time for all children, nor proceed at the same tempo. Side by side in a seventh grade class sit one boy who is already man-sized and another who has yet to experience the first signs of puberty. Arm in arm down the hall walk a young woman who is biologically ready for motherhood and her girl-friend who is physically still a child. Large and small, fat and thin, long- and short-limbed, the junior high school boys and girls present a startling picture of physical differences. Equally startling but less obvious are the differences in growth and maturation of internal organs—heart, lungs, stomach, kidneys, liver, and glands.

The rapid spurt in the growth of external limbs and internal organs is not accompanied by a parallel development of strength. Growth in strength lags significantly behind increases in height and weight. In part, this fact accounts for the awkwardness we often observe in the early adolescent. There is further significance in this lag in strength; it results in extreme tiredness after protracted physical

[3] Theodore Clymer and Nolan C. Kearney, "Curricular and Instructional Provisions for Individual Differences," in *Individualizing Instruction,* Sixty-first Yearbook, National Society for the Study of Education (Chicago: University of Chicago Press, 1962), p. 267. Reprinted by permission.

effort. During the growth spurt, both boys and girls are likely to exhibit almost frenetic energy, followed by extreme fatigue. Since they are unaware of the cause of these feelings, they tend to be privately ashamed of being so tired. They may even conceal their fatigue or not be aware of it themselves if there is social pressure for continued activity, as in the case of competitive athletics.

During the entire period of adolescence, both boys and girls worry about their physical growth rate and its attendant phenomena. They become sensitive to unusual or delayed growth. Girls who feel too tall, boys who feel too short wonder why they have to be different from their peers. They may be disappointed in some features of their body, and they tend to be preoccupied with this phenomenon of physical growth. These worries often affect their behavior in significant ways.

Although the tempo of change slows down in later adolescence, the differences in timetables continue to be evident in senior high school. Even in the twelfth grade one can usually find some individuals, most often boys, who are just beginning their growth spurt.

Rapid growth resulting in unusual tallness carries with it a certain kind of social prestige for boys. The culture tends to reward height in boys, and to glorify it as a desirable characteristic. We often comment admiringly on how much a boy has grown, how he is now as tall (or taller) than his father. Both adults and youth perceive the early maturing boy as more handsome, more "manly." Mussen and Jones have commented on the effects of all this admiration of height in boys whose growth spurt comes early. They report that such early maturers describe themselves in fantasy themes as "self-confident, independent, and more capable of playing an adult role in interpersonal relationships." [4] Jones goes on to predict, on a basis of several related studies, that these self-confident feelings persist in adult years, long after the differences in growth have disappeared. She reports that these early-maturing boys continue in adulthood to be more willing and able to carry responsibility and that they make more successful vocational adjustments than the late maturers.[5]

Early-maturing girls, on the other hand, experience fewer social

[4] Paul H. Mussen and Mary C. Jones, "Self-conceptions, Motivations, and Interpersonal Attitudes of Late and Early Maturing Boys," *Child Development, Abstracts and Bibliography*, 31 (June 1957), 192.

[5] Mary C. Jones, "The Later Careers of Boys Who Were Early and Late Maturing," *Child Development*, 28:1 (March 1957), 113–128.

rewards than do the boys. They tend to become isolated from their own girl friends and from most of the boys of their own age.

Both boys and girls experience penalties as well as some rewards from early maturation. Adults appreciate the appearance of the early maturer, but expect more "adult" behavior from anyone who looks like an adult. The tall, well-developed boy or girl who looks two or three years older than his actual age may feel astonished and resentful when he fails to satisfy his parents' expectations. Teachers, too, may make the mistake of equating size with total maturation, and expect too much of the early maturer.

In the six-year high school, which accounts for more than 42 per cent of secondary schools in the United States, the students represent the entire range of development from childhood to adulthood. Unfortunately this fact has not always influenced choice of seats and facilities that students must share. In some schools the program, too, appears to have been planned without recognition of the wide range of physical differences of students. When a single building houses boys and girls from age twelve through age eighteen, it is appropriate to inquire what special provisions have been made for the two extremes of early and late adolescence. What access to gymnasiums, auditorium, laboratories, and shops have the junior high school students? How do their program of instruction and their classroom seats match the unique needs of these early adolescents?

*Social maturity.* There is a greater significance in this fact of physical differences than the need for seats that fit. The growth spurt in early adolescence is accompanied by, and reflected in, a wide assortment of other differences. Social maturity is one of these areas of difference. Girls become socially mature earlier than boys, and only in the last years of senior high school does this difference begin to disappear. The difference exists rather sharply between individuals of the same sex also. It assumes a special significance when one accepts Havighurst's thesis that the main developmental tasks of adolescence are emotional and social. As pointed out in a recent yearbook of the National Society for the Study of Education, the peer culture is an important influence on youth:

> Socialization, the process of social learning which is involved in becoming a member of a culture, begins at birth. In the early years the ways of culture are mediated to children largely by their par-

ents. Gradually in the elementary school years, and more markedly through junior and senior high school, the peer culture becomes a significant socializing agent. To a large degree, this socialization is a process in which each individual finds his own social role—finds it, gives it definition, enacts it, and develops it.[6]

Since the peer culture wields such important influence on growing up, it also significantly affects school learning. The differences in social maturity of the students in a given classroom can have a real impact on readiness to learn, as well as on ability to work with others. The attitude of early-maturing girls toward boys of their own age may be contemptuous or indifferent. In one seat is a small boy of thirteen who likes to watch cowboy movies on television. In the next seat is a young lady (also thirteen plus) who is "going steady" with an older boy who has dropped out of school. Social maturity affects attitudes toward materials of instruction, school routines, and assignments. It also influences attitudes toward teachers and parents. Above all, it directly influences the readiness to work with and to learn from one's peers. Social values and standards of behavior, which are involved in all these attitudes, change very rapidly during adolescence. In any given class the differences in such values may be dramatic.

The struggle for maturity involves some basic conflicts with adult codes. Indeed, the entire period of adolescence may be regarded as a succession of revolts and adjustments to the prevalent standards of behavior. As youth try to build an adequate self-concept, they frequently find themselves in rebellion against the expectations of adults. Friedenberg points out in *The Vanishing Adolescent* [7] that this rebellion is even more frustrating for youth when the adult figures against whom they must rebel are friendly, rather than authoritarian parents and teachers. Friedenberg defines the first and most fundamental task of adolescence as "clear and stable self-identification." He points out that such clear identification of self is impossible in our culture because of its numerous, subtle pressures for conformity.

6 Harold E. Jones and Mary C. Jones, "Individual Differences in Early Adolescence," in *Individualizing Instruction*, Sixty-first Yearbook, National Society for the Study of Education (Chicago: University of Chicago Press, 1962), pp. 134–135. Reprinted by permission.

7 Edgar Z. Friedenberg, *The Vanishing Adolescent* (New York: Dell Publishing Co., Inc., 1959).

Although some adolescents manage to survive their school experience without overt rebellion, they often do so at the cost of their own creativity and courage. Others rebel only occasionally, and finally learn their identity through their peer culture [8] or through jobs outside the school. Still others give up and quit school; it is these latter youth who never saw themselves as able to succeed in school, even though many of them have unusual abilities. Some of our most creative personalities are in this group who finally refuse to conform any longer to adult (school) standards and demands, no matter how kindly presented.

*Interests.* One perplexing aspect of early adolescence is the rapidly changing nature of children's interests. "Here today and gone tomorrow" appears to be the rule. This evanescence is a natural result of the exploratory impulse which characterizes this age-group. There is so much to be discovered, one hasn't time to linger very long with any particular interest.

With the earlier onset of puberty in girls, a difference appears in their interests as compared with those of the boys. Teachers who sponsor junior high school parties have discovered that the program must not only provide dancing for the girls and the older boys, but also group games for the younger boys. Collecting hobbies are still the rage among junior high boys. Their taste in literature is less sophisticated. Boys like mechanics, cars, sports, and science. Girls like sentimental fiction. While both sexes like movies and television, the girls prefer romance and the boys westerns, gangsters, and cartoons. Both sexes exhibit a lively interest in teen-age problems and in other people.

As boys and girls move on into senior high school, the differences in interests become less controlled by one's sex but even more complex than they were in junior high school. The problems of popularity and boy-and-girl relationships are more marked. Sophistication and personal grooming become important. The acceptance of one's own sex (I am a boy, I am a girl) brings with it a new array of interests.

[8] James S. Coleman reported a study of high school youth, which supports the view that group approval of one's peers is a much more powerful influence than learning as such. See "The Competition for Adolescent Energies," *Phi Delta Kappan*, 42:6 (March 1961), 231–236.

Vocational interests begin to show themselves. Vocational planning is a difficult task in today's complex world. Yet the senior high school boy and girl cannot escape this task, for it is an ever-present concern that affects many other areas of choice. Should a student accept a part-time job that seems to be related to his vocational plan? Should such a job be permitted to grow into one of such dimensions that part-time schooling is necessary? Should one try to make money while in school, or just test out one's tentative choice of a career? Should money be spent now or saved for further education? Should marriage plans be seriously entertained, or should such commitments be postponed until one's career is launched? Can one afford to take time for football? Join a club? Go steady? Answers to such questions will accentuate differences among students.

*Mental development.* Other kinds of differences are less obvious but just as dramatic as those we have been discussing. All teachers are interested in intellectual development, whether they see it as an end in itself or as a means of achieving developmental tasks. They are also interested in the educational achievement of their pupils. In respect to mental development and educational achievement, the differences between learners are of great significance.

When a random group of six-year-olds enters the first grade, two per cent of them will be below the average four-year-old in general mental development, and two per cent will be above the average eight-year-old. Disregarding the extreme two per cent at either end, there is a four year range in general intelligence. By the time this group has reached the age of twelve (seventh grade level), the range will have increased to almost eight years. *As long as all of the children of all of the people remain in school, the range continues to increase.* When the educational achievement of a typical sixth grade class is measured, we find a range of approximately eight years in reading comprehension, vocabulary, arithmetic reasoning, arithmetic computation, mechanics of English composition, and other forms of achievement. In almost any sixth grade class will be found a pupil with first or second grade reading ability and another with eleventh or twelfth grade reading ability. In any grade above the primary level will be found the complete range of elementary school achievement. [Italics added.] [9]

[9] Walter W. Cook, "The Gifted and the Retarded in Historical Perspective," *Phi Delta Kappan,* 39:6 (March 1958), 250. Reprinted by permission.

Any experienced teacher has observed this range of achievement. A typical sixth grade class of twenty-nine pupils was described by Cutts and Moseley as follows:

> The twenty-nine pupils show a range of more than $3\frac{1}{2}$ years in chronological age, 104 pounds in weight, 14 inches in height, 62 points in IQ, and 8 years 4 months in mental age. Their achievement, as measured by the Iowa Pupil Tests of Basic Skills, ranges from 4.3 to 9.9 in grade average (that is, the average of a child's sub-test scores expressed in terms of grade level), from 4.4 to 9.5 in reading, and from 3.5 to 11.4 in spelling. . . . A girl whose parents are on a high socio-economic level is seventh in intelligence (IQ 110) but first in the level of language usage (grade 9.9). A boy with the same IQ, whose family immigrated shortly before he was born, has a grade level of 5.7 in usage but 7.1 in reading and 6.7 in arithmetic problems. . . . The girl who has the next-to-highest IQ (124) now ranks sixth on the grade average.[10]

*Achievement.* Even more startling is the range in achievement to be found within a single individual. It is not uncommon to find a given pupil at the fourth grade level in spelling, the sixth grade level in arithmetic, the eighth grade level in geography, and the tenth grade level in literature. It seems clear that the grade-level classification which is almost universally used in our schools is unrealistic and almost meaningless. The problem is further complicated by the phenomenon of growth spurts, alternating with "plateaus" during which no significant growth can be observed. In short, today's achievement tests will not reflect tomorrow's differences. The factor of rapid and continuing change within each individual brings about marked and increasing differences between individuals. Lane and Beauchamp have pointed out the significance for classroom learning of such differences as:

sex
size
rate and tempo of growth
niceness of motor control
sensitivity of eyes and ears
skin pigmentation

[10] Norma E. Cutts and Nicholas Moseley, *Providing for Individual Differences in the Elementary School* (Englewood Cliffs, N.J.: Prentice-Hall, Inc., © 1960), pp. 1–2. Reprinted by permission.

strength
agility
reaction time
precision of movement
sense of balance
extent of peripheral vision
stamina
rate of recuperation from fatigue
shape of body and face
tensile strength of muscles, tendons, and bones
rate of coagulation of the blood
toughness of body membranes
pulse rate
size of feet
sharpness of persistence of visual imagery

They go on to say: "Since we readily recognize the fact that every individual is unique in these and many other physical qualities, we can see clearly that we must go to the limits of statistical infinity to find two people alike." [11]

Garrett Hardin, the biologist, in commenting on this matter of physical differences among healthy adult human beings, points out that variation ranges from two hundred per cent for "phosphate concentration in the blood" to forty-two hundred per cent for "minimum perceptible movement in peripheral vision." He goes on to ask some interesting questions regarding the expected behavior of "normal individuals" who vary widely in respect to the fourteen physical characteristics which he cites:

Should two "normal" men in whose veins the sex-hormone concentration differs by a factor of eleven behave the same? Should we give the same advice to two "normal" men when one of them gets drunk on an eighth as much alcohol as the other? Should we be surprised at a difference in the accident records of two men, both of whom have "normal" 20-20 vision, when one of them is forty-two times as good at detecting moving objects as the other? Plainly, the concept of "normality" is a thought-saving assumption

11 Howard Lane and Mary Beauchamp, *Human Relations in Teaching: The Dynamics of Helping Children Grow* (Englewood Cliffs, N.J.: Prentice-Hall, Inc., © 1955), pp. 127–129. Reprinted by permission.

that is capable of leading to unjust and even dangerous conclusions.[12]

This concept of normality has been fostered by the system of grade levels used by the schools. Parents, and often teachers, too, assume that it is normal for a seventh grade pupil to have seventh grade ability in all subjects. They tend to forget that the opposite is true: it is normal for our so-called seventh graders to exhibit at least a seven-year spread in their levels of achievement in various subjects. Goodlad reports that he has asked more than ten thousand parents and teachers in eleven states to indicate their knowledge of variability among fourth graders. He defined a fourth grade child as one enrolled in the fourth grade and who scores between 4.0 and 4.9 in each subject on a standardized achievement test taken at the end of January. Parents and teachers choose all the possible percentages for their answers, but only about 10 per cent reveal that they know the correct answer: namely, that less than 20 per cent of fourth grade children are fourth graders in achievement, by this definition.[13] This false assumption as to what constitutes "normal" achievement becomes even more damaging as the learner advances in school and differences in achievement become even more marked with each year of his education.

*Cultural factors.* Some of the differences among human beings are traceable to heredity. More of them are directly related to physical and emotional maturity. Still others are caused by such cultural factors as family background, socio-economic status, or the response to problems that the individual must confront. Included among these cultural factors are the kinds of schools and communities that students have experienced before reaching the secondary school. A junior high school in a large northern city serves a low socio-economic neighborhood characterized by constant movement of families. This school experiences over 100 per cent turnover during a school year. Many of the students have just arrived from rural schools in the deep South, and may have attended as many as ten

[12] Garrett Hardin, "Biology and Individual Differences," in *Individualizing Instruction,* Sixty-first Yearbook, National Society for the Study of Education (Chicago: University of Chicago Press, 1962), pp. 13–14. Reprinted by permission.

[13] John I. Goodlad, "Individual Differences and Vertical Organization of the School," in *Individualizing Instruction,* Sixty-first Yearbook, National Society for the Study of Education (Chicago: University of Chicago Press, 1962), p. 217.

schools before reaching the seventh grade. The cumulative total number of their actual months of schooling may be thirty to forty months in the rural South, or about three to four school years of ten months each.

A consolidated district in a Northern state maintains a six-year high school which receives about half its seventh graders each year from three local elementary schools, and half from twenty rural schools. The youngsters from the local schools may be significantly farther along in their academic skills than those coming in from rural schools. The latter have been inadequately financed for years, and suffer from obsolete textbooks, lack of enrichment materials and audio-visual aids, and poorly-trained teachers. Aside from this difference, the farm children continue throughout high school as a segment of the student body who ride the buses and are deprived of most of the social life which tends to unify the other half of the students.

Whatever the causes, the fact is that human beings are different, and that most of their differences increase with learning and growth. Differences in skills and in knowledge increase with effective learning. Life goals, interests and hobbies, commitment to new experiences, the self-concept—all these and many other differences among individuals continue to grow even more marked as they go on learning and living. There is simply no way to make people alike while they still live and learn. An interesting fact is that differences tend to become even more marked as schools improve. The better the educational program, the greater becomes the range of differences. In classrooms where there is a rich challenge to all pupils, it is generally true that observable gains occur among the slower learners; but even greater gains occur among the more rapid learners. Thus the range of difference becomes greater in situations where good teaching and learning can be found. Instead of bemoaning the fact of difference, teachers should accept it as fortunate, for in uniqueness lies the basis of social cooperation. Kelley and Rasey have pointed out this function of uniqueness:

> The opportunity to specialize, to perform separate functions better than any one cell could do them all and to perform these functions for others while others were doing different tasks for them, is the basis for all living tissue or organism above the level of the single cell. And so it is when people do things together.

Their uniqueness is what gives individuals value in social organization. If people were all alike, had the same abilities, there would be little value in association. None could learn from others; none could perform tasks which others could not do for themselves.[14]

*Socio-economic differences.* Children ought not to be penalized educationally by the accident of their birth into a particular social class. If their level of aspiration is limited by their family origin, it is the function of the school to raise it. If their concept of themselves is that they *cannot,* rather than *can,* perform their developmental tasks effectively, it is the task of good teachers to give them courage. A tragic fact about drop-outs is that they are typically low in self-concept. All too often, they also come from homes and neighborhoods that have low educational goals, limited vocational prospects, poor employability, and cultural habits that will prevent their moving up in the world. Even worse, these factors are likely to condemn them to a hopeless and perhaps antisocial existence in today's urban centers. The increasing accumulation of these unemployed youth has been called "social dynamite" by Conant. The society cannot afford to lose them from the schools, for there is no other constructive force that can help them become good citizens instead of police cases. If the schools, in their eagerness to raise standards, shove these youngsters out via the failure route, the schools will be depriving them and society of their only hope. There are few jobs awaiting the drop-out today—and there is no useful future for him.

The middle-class norms enforced by our secondary school culture are especially handicapping to lower-class youth. Both teachers and students tend to enforce certain standards of behavior, certain modes of dress and language. Only the conformists are really successful in adjusting to these standards. Adjustment is the slogan, and lower-class youth feel "out" of things. They do not own the school psychologically. Hollingshead pointed out in a classic study in 1949 [15] that the typical urban high school was under narrow social controls, creating in-groups and out-groups that were rather sharply defined.

[14] Earl C. Kelley and Marie I. Rasey, *Education and the Nature of Man* (New York: Harper & Row, Publishers, 1952), pp. 90–91. Reprinted by permission.

[15] August B. Hollingshead, *Elmtown's Youth* (New York: John Wiley & Sons, Inc., 1949).

A more recent study by Havighurst [16] reflects much the same basic phenomena in our modern urban complex. It seems clear that the schools can reject certain youngsters in ways other than academic failure.

*The fast and the slow.* Many educators today worry over the fate of the gifted youth, who are often trapped into a kind of mediocre monotony in classrooms where procedures and standards are geared to the slower students. They are also concerned about the students who cannot compete or meet higher (group) standards of one kind or another. This includes some youth who are physically or mentally handicapped. It includes many more who are normal, but deficient in skills.

Still other students are at a disadvantage in a classroom where group assignments and group achievement are standard procedure. These are the creative, often nonconforming youth who do not readily accept adult-imposed goals. They avoid or resist such imposition and either actually "fail" in their work or at least do not do well.

## Implications for teaching

All these students have the same problem: they suffer from the practice of an identical assignment, textbook, and test for each member of the class, and competitive marking. They pay for being different. Teachers know about individual differences, yet many teach as if they intended to reduce or eliminate difference by expecting the same performance from each student.

What happens in a school where differences are cherished instead of ignored? Dean Willard Olson has given an overview of a change that is taking place here and there:

> The democratization of educational opportunities has caused a gradual shift in attitudes toward individual differences in large numbers of people from suppression, to toleration, to cultivation. If one accepts capitalization on differences between individuals and building on strength *within* an individual as a desirable

[16] Robert J. Havighurst, *Growing Up in River City* (New York: John Wiley & Sons, Inc., 1962).

practice for schools, certain consequences follow. The curriculum becomes broad rather than narrow. The expected achievement is at the level of the child's ability rather than at the average norm, or standard for a group. Instructional materials with a range in difficulty are available for each class group. The marking or description of individual differences in achievement take on more the character of a nurturing than a punishing process. Reports to parents reflect the same characteristic. With a healthy respect for individual differences, child participation in planning becomes more acceptable and needful. Mechanical common assignments give way to more dynamic practices which permit seeking, self-selection and creative solution. Children may properly then occupy various roles in a group, have interests which differ, and be in the process of finding a place in a society which survives and prospers because individuals fit into its varied needs.

The time has come to accept individual differences in children as a reality, and to work with them without trying to blame them on anyone or to feel guilty that they exist. . . . Individual differences among people are a precious asset. A constructive program to meet them promises large returns.[17]

It will be noted that Dean Olson is drawing his examples from elementary schools. Some of these modifications in curriculum and teaching methods can be found, however, in junior and senior high schools today. As educators discover better ways of adapting to differences, they can go far beyond present practice toward helping youth to fulfill their individual potentials. Discovery of these better ways presents teachers with some challenges. Clymer and Kearney, quoted earlier, cite some of the needs of teachers that must be taken into account:

1. The need to know individual students

2. The need to recognize that not all teachers will adjust to individual differences in the same way

3. The need to provide generous time allotments

4. The need to plan carefully whatever is to be done in the classroom

5. The need to work effectively with the group as a whole

6. The need to move slowly into any type of adjustment to individual differences

[17] Willard C. Olson, "Individual Differences: A Precious Asset," *Educational Leadership*, 15:3 (December 1957), 142–143. Reprinted by permission.

7. The need to accept more noise and more confusion
8. The need to recognize failure and begin again
9. The need to accept less than 100 per cent adjustment to individual differences
10. The need to recognize that adjusting to individual differences calls for plain, hard work [18]

The secondary schools can and should welcome all youth, accept the fact of their differences, and capitalize on these differences by creating in the classroom a good society built on the uniqueness of its members.

Let us turn our attention next to the learning process, since sound teaching methods must be based upon what is known about learning.

## FOR FURTHER READING

Association for Supervision and Curriculum Development, *Fostering Mental Health in Our Schools*. Washington, D.C.: The Association Yearbook, 1950. Good brief treatment of characteristics of adolescents.

———, *Growing Up in an Anxious Age*. Washington, D.C.: The Association Yearbook, 1952. Discusses ways in which events in today's world affect adolescents.

———, *Human Variability and Learning*. Washington, D.C.: The Association Yearbook, 1961. Certain broad categories of human variability are identified and described briefly. Implications for teaching are discussed.

Ausubel, David P., *Theory and Problems of Adolescent Development*. New York: Grune & Stratton, Inc., 1954. Good presentation of basic theory regarding adolescent development.

Cutts, Norma E., and Nicholas Moseley, *Providing for Individual Differences in the Elementary School*. Englewood Cliffs, N.J.: Prentice-Hall, Inc., 1960. Good summary of data on various kinds of individual differences among elementary school pupils. Implications are spelled out for secondary school youth also.

Faunce, Roland C., and Morrel J. Clute, *Teaching and Learning in the Junior High School*. Belmont, Calif.: Wadsworth Publishing Co., Inc., 1961. Chapter 2, "Characteristics and Needs of the Early Adolescent." Sums up research on the nature of the junior high school student.

Friedenberg, Edgar Z., *The Vanishing Adolescent*. New York: Dell Pub-

[18] Clymer and Kearney, in *Individualizing Instruction*, p. 276.

lishing Co., Inc., 1959. A provocative analysis of the problems of adolescent rebellion in our conforming culture. Conclusion: adolescence is disappearing.

Goodman, Paul, *Growing Up Absurd*. New York: Random House, Inc., 1956. A keen analysis of the "spiritual emptiness" that adolescents perceive in our modern culture, and of the causes of disaffection in youth.

*Guides to Curriculum Building, Junior High School Level*. Cooperative Educational Planning Program, Problems Approach Bulletin No. 2, Curriculum Bulletin No. 12. Madison, Wisc., 1950. A tabular summary of developmental traits and their implications for the school throughout various growth levels.

Havighurst, Robert J., *Growing Up in River City*. New York: John Wiley & Sons, Inc., 1962. Effects of urban social controls on the process of struggling to adulthood.

Kelley, Earl C., *In Defense of Youth*. Englewood Cliffs, N.J.: Prentice-Hall, Inc., 1962. Part I, "It's Hard To Be Young in These Times," consists of six chapters dealing with the problems of adolescents in today's culture.

Kelley, Earl C., and Marie I. Rasey, *Education and the Nature of Man*. New York: Harper & Row, Publishers, 1952. Chapter 9, "Cooperation," sets forth a cogent argument for effective use of individual differences in any cooperative enterprise.

Lane, Howard, and Mary Beauchamp, *Human Relations in Teaching*. Englewood Cliffs, N.J.: Prentice-Hall, Inc., 1955. Special emphasis is given to the impact of individual differences on interpersonal relationships, both in and outside the classroom.

National Society for the Study of Education, *Adolescence,* Forty-third Yearbook. Chicago: University of Chicago Press, 1944. Various important facets and problems of the adolescent period are helpfully discussed.

———, *Individualizing Instruction,* Sixty-first Yearbook. Chicago: University of Chicago Press, 1962. An excellent collection of recent resumes of the facts regarding individual differences, and of the implications of these facts for curriculum development, promotion, and methods of teaching.

Olson, Willard C., "Individual Differences: A Precious Asset," *Educational Leadership,* 15:3 (December 1957), 142–143. A persuasive argument for exploiting individual differences in the elementary classroom as opposed to attempting to make all children alike.

———, *Psychological Foundations of the Curriculum*. Paris: UNESCO Educational Studies and Documents, 1957. See especially "Those Who Surprise Us," p. 28.

Remmers, H. H., and D. H. Radler, *The American Teen-Ager*. New York:

Bobbs-Merrill Co., Inc., 1957. Reports of Purdue Opinion polls regarding special fears and worries of adolescents.

Strang, Ruth, *The Adolescent Views Himself: A Psychology of Adolescence.* New York: McGraw-Hill Book Co., Inc., 1957. A highly readable account of the psychology of adolescence, illustrated by line drawings.

Wattenberg, William W., *The Adolescent Years.* New York: Harcourt, Brace & World, Inc., 1955. An excellent basic treatment of the theory of adolescent development, well supported by classroom illustrations.

# 4

# The learning process

The fact of individual difference is not new. It has been a source of perplexity to teachers for a long time. In today's schools it is not possible to ignore the fact of individual difference without experiencing a sense of continuing defeat and frustration. Teachers are increasingly asking themselves what can be done about the apathetic or hostile student, the nonconformist, the unmotivated, the slow or retarded, the "unready" student. These problem students, along with their more talented but often bored classmates, constitute a major challenge to our professional know-how. More and more teachers are turning to the field of educational psychology for some help on the problems of motivation. The complex question of how learning takes place is assuming new significance.

Teachers are sometimes reminded by their critics that Einstein could not have been certified to teach mathematics in the public schools. But experienced teachers are keenly aware that mastery of a subject conveys no magic in solving the real problems of teaching and learning. Secondary school teachers generally bring to their task a greater depth of preparation in their chosen subject fields than do elementary teachers. There are some exceptions, of course, but few of their teaching problems stem from inadequate knowledge of the subject. They are, instead, hampered by ignorance of the learning process or inability to bring about effective learning in their class-rooms.

When young people first enter the teaching profession, they are likely to be idealists about education. They feel a sense of pride and dedication as they reflect that they are at last real teachers. They assume that their students will want to learn, that they are basically good even though they are not alike. As time goes on, these young teachers must experience a reasonable amount of success in order to retain this initial faith and enthusiasm. If they do not succeed, if day after day they struggle vainly to interest their students in the subject matter which they themselves feel is valuable, they begin to lose faith in themselves and in their students. They may become cynical and look upon teaching as just another job. Or they may redouble extrinsic rewards and punishments and get their own satis-factions from the few talented students who succeed and survive. Loss of enthusiasm and idealism is a common phenomenon in sec-ondary school faculties. Some evidence of it can be detected in many conversations in the teachers' lounge or cafeteria. Comments such as these may be heard:

> I ask you, what do they teach kids in world history nowadays? I can't teach them any American history without their having some knowledge of European history. Why, my students this year say they never have even heard of the Renaissance. The whole first chapter of our text is based on the Renaissance and they should have learned it last year in world history. And they claim they never had it.

> So that smart alec Tom Jackson asked me in class what good studying plane geometry is going to do him. I said to him the most important thing about an educated person is his ability to think, and plane geometry teaches you how to think. And what do you think he said then? He said he was a thinker long before he enrolled in plane geometry! He got a D from me last month, that's the kind of great thinker he is.

> So I told them, for heaven's sake, how can you expect to im-prove your writing when you don't even remember the parts of speech? Do you suppose they ever learned them at all? Or do they just skip it in junior high English?

> Roscoe Anderson brought in this great big collection of rocks—there must have been fifty of them all together—and had the nerve

to ask me to help him label each one. When I reminded him I was busy he asked me for a book he could find the geological species and their names in. I should have given him a penalty hour right then but I just told him there was a unit on earth forms in next year's science syllabus.

That Mrs. Olson sent four kids to my art room yesterday to ask me to help them make a mural on westward migration—and not one of them ever had even Art I. I found out they didn't even know what cranial contours are.

So I just told the class, if they don't all do better on the final than they have so far, about half of them are going to repeat the course.

Frustration and hostility are reflected in such comments as these. Beyond the frustration and hostility, there is a naïveté regarding the learning process. Consider, for example, the assumptions that appear to underlie the comments:

1. Any content once learned should not be forgotten in one year.
2. There is an automatic transfer of learning from command of plane geometry to skill in critical thinking in nonmathematical areas.
3. Knowledge of the mechanics of grammar is essential for learning how to write correctly.
4. Students' present interests are of minor importance, compared with the orderly presentation of subject matter in logical sequence.
5. Creativity can only be tolerated after fundamental skills have been mastered.
6. Threats of failure are effective motivational techniques.

Research on the learning process has demonstrated that every one of these assumptions is false. These beliefs, and a hundred others which teachers often express or imply, are a kind of folklore abandoned by those who have studied the psychology of learning. Yet they persist, and do much damage to students, and they prevent teachers from developing effective learning situations.

Most teachers have had courses in educational psychology. They may even have had a reasonably good understanding of the learning process when they first received their certificates. It is possible that the pressures and frustrations of the teaching role have proved to be more powerful influences than knowledge of research. The climate of established opinion in a school faculty is also a potent force in reshaping the values of new teachers.

In other cases, the college courses in educational psychology may have been poorly presented and relatively unimpressive. Perhaps the courses were taught well but prematurely. Young people not yet immersed in the teaching role are often uninterested in theories of learning. They are being confronted with research answers to problems they do not yet have. (This same mistake may have been made throughout their high school careers also.) Whatever the cause, it appears that teachers who thoroughly understand the learning process are rare. It seems appropriate to review some fundamental ideas about learning before going on to discussions, in later chapters, of the teacher's roles and of effective methods.

One caution is in order. All educational issues are not to be resolved by a look at research. The psychologist does not pretend to assess the validity or the fallacy of goals. He simply says, in effect, "If these are your goals, here is what research indicates as promising means of attaining them." Until about 1900, psychology and philosophy were a single field of thought. They have become increasingly separated since the development of the behavioral sciences. Today the experimental psychologist tends to reject the responsibility for formulating the purposes of learning, but concentrates rather on the effective means of attaining whatever purposes are proposed. Educators must continue to develop values in the context of the needs of a democratic culture and the nature of the learners. To these logical considerations teachers must bring their own warm interest in children and youth, their convictions about what behaviors are "good," their personal commitment to the task of conserving and improving the culture. They must ultimately decide for themselves whether their goals are worthy. Research studies in psychology can help teachers determine which goals are attainable.

## Theories of learning

Many critics, and even some teachers, seem to hold theories about learning which have been long ago abandoned by psychologists. For example, it was once held that the mind of the learner was a storage tank into which the teacher poured prepared knowledge until the mind was full—and educated. Research on retention revealed one serious defect in this theory. There turned out to be so much leakage in the tank that it might more properly be thought of as a sieve.[1] In modern times no psychologist considers the mind-storage theory valid, but the secondary school curriculum and teaching methods often appear to reflect it. Emphasis on mastery of the textbook as an end product of each course is a case in point. Some teachers assume that a proper sequence of courses must be built on mastery of each course in its turn. The goal of memorizing consecutive segments of subject matter is still pursued by many teachers. The mind-storage theory has not disappeared from the schools, but only from the psychology books.

Teaching methods, too, continue to emphasize memorization instead of critical thinking or application. Teachers often talk about fact-learning as a means to some defensible larger goal. But students are not deceived by such talk. At examination time, which comes often in many schools, they find that teachers are still constructing tests and establishing grades largely on a basis of memorization of facts. As Burton has remarked, "The teacher whose aim for the pupil is to 'cover the text' or 'to cover the course of study' is far more common than we think." [2] An interesting historical treatment of the mind-storage concept appears in Ernest R. Hilgard's book, *Theories of Learning*.[3]

Another theory, quite different from the mind-storage idea, held that the mind was a kind of muscle that grew in size and strength as it was given hard exercise. Whereas the mind-storage theory emphasized stored-up knowledge, the "mental discipline" theory required the selection of those areas of subject matter which were thought most appropriate for building the mind. The subject matter became a means rather than an end in itself. Thus mathematics was treasured for its function in developing reasoning power, Latin and Greek for their contributions to discrimination and memory. Some subjects were assumed to be difficult for all learners;

[1] A good summary of the research on retention may be found in Howard L. Kingsley and Ralph Garry, *The Nature and Conditions of Learning*, rev. ed. (Englewood Cliffs, N.J.: Prentice-Hall, Inc., 1957), Chapter 12.

[2] William H. Burton, *The Guidance of Learning Activities*, 3rd ed. (New York: Appleton-Century-Crofts, Inc., 1962), p. 128.

[3] Ernest R. Hilgard, *Theories of Learning* (New York: Appleton-Century-Crofts, Inc., 1956), Chapter 1.

these were especially treasured, since hardness was supposedly a virtue in exercising muscles. Thus hardness became a goal in curriculum selection.

Now all teachers know that any particular subject is not equally hard for all learners. The case of the boy who has a gift for mathematics but cannot seem to learn a foreign language is so common that we no longer give it a second thought. Some honor students have lowered their grade-point averages by attempting to learn typing or industrial arts. Shorthand, history, music—any subject we can think of is easy for some and hard for others.

What, then, makes a subject hard or easy? The special aptitudes of the learner himself are certainly a part of the answer. At least two other factors operate: the interest that the learner feels for the subject, and his understanding of its use or application. In short, if a student has mathematical aptitude, is interested in mathematics, and sees its application to real life situations or problems, he will probably find mathematics easy.

But this description would disqualify mathematics from a mental discipline point of view. In its extreme (but logical) extension, the mental disciplinarian is looking for subjects which are hard—i.e., for which the learner has no aptitude, in which he is not interested, and for which he sees no real use. Thus the ideal subject must be difficult, uninteresting and useless in order to qualify as an appropriate mental discipline.

Perhaps few advocates of the mental discipline theory ever stated their case in this logical manner. In any event, the concepts on which the mental discipline philosophy was based have been generally exploded by psychologists. The work of Edward L. Thorndike and many others undermined the whole theory of mental discipline many years ago, by revealing that automatic transfer of training does not in fact occur. Yet the mental disciplinarians are still with us. Consider, for example, the following statement summing up the point of view of the Council for Basic Education: [4]

> . . . logic and experience suggest that certain subjects have generative power and others do not have generative power. . . . Among these subjects are those which deal with language, whether or not

[4] Incorporated as a "nonprofit educational organization pledged to the encouragement and maintenance of high academic standards in American public schools."

one's own; forms, figures, and numbers; the laws of nature; the past; and the shape and behavior of our common home, the earth. Apparently these master or generative subjects endow one with the ability to learn the minor or self-terminating subjects. They also endow one, of course, with the ability to learn the higher, more complex developments of the master subjects themselves.[5]

The "generative" subjects espoused for their disciplinary value by the Council are the same ones which James B. Conant advocates under the label of "homework subjects." He is referring to the usual academic subjects: English, foreign language, mathematics, science, and social science. In his book *The American High School Today,* Conant makes a number of uncritically approving references to "stiff academic programs," which he thinks are needed for the more able students. At one point he mentions that "these bright boys and girls are not working hard enough." In order to make them work harder, he would require them all to take more of these "homework subjects." [6] Thus the friends as well as the critics of public education are still reflecting the basic error of the old mental discipline school, which based the selection of required subjects on their assumed hardness and potency for training the mental faculties.

There is nothing wrong with the study of language, science, history, or mathematics. But these subjects have been built into the fabric of general education because they deal with universal needs, not because they are hard for all students and involve a lot of homework.

Secondary school teachers in these academic areas sometimes fall into the same trap as their lay critics. They set out to motivate the study of their own subjects by telling students that mathematics trains the mind or that foreign language study develops linguistic ability so that one can then easily learn any other language. They justify long homework assignments on the ground that hard work never hurts anyone, and that young people must *be kept out of mischief.*[7] They discourage students from pursuing side avenues of

[5] From *The Case for Basic Education,* p. 6, by James D. Koerner. Copyright © 1959 by Council for Basic Education. Reprinted with permission of Atlantic-Little, Brown and Company, Publishers.

[6] James B. Conant, *The American High School Today* (New York: McGraw-Hill Book Co., Inc., 1959).

[7] This in the same era when their elders are being treated to a shorter work-week and automated housekeeping!

interest, partly because they suspect that such pursuits are sly efforts to postpone or elude the main lesson and the "hard" assignments relating to it.

The earlier advocates of the mental discipline theory believed that the powers developed by the study of a subject could be then applied with automatic success to any new learning, even though it might be unrelated to that which did the training in the first place. This idea of "transfer of training" has been thoroughly exploded during the past fifty years. Transfer is achieved only by being first built into the learning method. Does the study of literature help develop a better system of values? Only if the process of forming and testing values is built into the classroom procedure. Can study of geometry develop powers of inductive and deductive reasoning? Only if direct efforts are made in that direction in the geometry classroom. Can such reasoning be then applied, for example, to the analysis of propaganda or social theory? Only if such materials are a part of the mathematics class. Can science teach us to be more intelligent consumers? Only if direct applications are systematically made in science classrooms. There is a real need in most secondary school classrooms for more and better applications of learning to life.[8]

*The "S-R bond."* The assumption of automatic transfer of training was discredited by the work of an entire generation of psychologists known as associationists or connectionists. Led by such men as Thorndike and James, this school of psychologists generally agreed that learning resulted from the presentation of certain stimuli, followed by predictable and measurable responses. This "S-R bond" (stimulus-response relationship) was the thesis of much research for almost a half-century beginning about 1900. The connectionists tended to look upon the learning process as a mechanical, almost physical response of the organism to its (contrived) environment from which the stimulus derives. The teacher (perhaps we should use the term "trainer") contrived the environment in such a way as to "stamp in" the desired bonds and stamp out the undesired ones. By various applications of rewards for success and penalties for failure, the desired responses were to be evoked, much in the same fashion as animals are trained.

---

8 For further discussion of the mental discipline theory, see Hilgard, *Theories of Learning,* Chapter 1.

Although the S-R bond is no longer the concern of most psychologists, certain basic elements of this philosophy have been built into the theory of programmed learning advocated by B. F. Skinner and others.[9] In spite of its general loss of favor in our own day, the connectionistic theory has had an enormous influence on education. Alberty has cited a number of common practices which may be attributed to the teaching and writing of Thorndike and his associates:

1. The daily recitation system with its emphasis upon the acquisition of facts and information.

2. Excessive reliance upon standardized tests as a basis of evaluation.

3. So-called objective marking systems in terms of normal curves.

4. The fixed curriculum determined by job or activity analysis, imposed upon the learner without giving attention to his needs and interests.

5. Excessive reliance upon repetitive drill as a basis for learning at the expense of the use of reflective thinking.

6. Teacher domination of the classroom at the expense of cooperative teacher-student planning.

7. Excessive emphasis upon external rewards and punishment as a basis for motivation.[10]

On the credit side, the connectionists were instrumental in discrediting the mental discipline theory with its false doctrine of automatic transfer of training. They were responsible for awakening a new interest in individual differences and observed behavior. Their emphasis on the environment for learning laid the basis for the later theory of the community school. And their approach to testing response (i.e. learning) became translated later into the concept of changed behavior as a criterion of effective learning.

*Organismic theory.* One of the most serious shortcomings of connectionist theory was its reduction of learning to the level of me-

---

[9] See for example, B. F. Skinner, "Teaching Machines," *Science,* 133:3331 (Oct. 24, 1958), 969–977, and A. A. Lumsdaine and Robert Glaser, *Teaching Machines and Programmed Learning* (Washington, D.C.: The National Education Association, 1960). Further discussion of programmed learning will be presented in Chapter 9.

[10] Harold B. Alberty and Elsie J. Alberty, *Reorganizing the High School Curriculum,* 3rd ed. (New York: Macmillan Co., 1962), p. 91. Reprinted by permission.

chanical and physical response. Whereas the connectionists believed that the learner was only the sum total of his various parts, more recent thinkers have held that the whole organism is much more than the sum of its parts. This "organismic" or Gestalt psychology advances the view that the learner does not respond mechanically in terms of simplified S-R bonds, but in a highly complex way as a constantly changing organism reacting as a whole to a constantly changing environment. Learning comes about in the process of interaction between a total organism and a total situation. Thus the process is neither mechanical nor easily predictable. It involves relationships, both within the organism itself and between the organism and the situation—which includes other learners. Meanings and associations become more vital than routine skills. Reflective thinking is more treasured than drilled responses. The learner constantly seeks meanings and interpretations; he tries to reconstruct experience and build new insights. He is no longer to be thought of as a mere recipient of stimuli or an instrument to be acted upon, but as a sentient, unique, complex being. He responds to his constantly changing environment as a total organism, of which every part affects the whole. He learns not only with his mind, but with his glands, nerves, muscles, internal organs, values, attitudes, fears, joys, anticipations. Because he reacts as a total person, he cannot successfully be dealt with as an arithmetic learner at one period and a language learner at another. Not only is he different from everyone else; he is different from what he himself was a few minutes earlier.

The organismic psychologists have given new meaning to the concept of individual differences. In their belief, it is the learner who is the object of the game, so to speak. It is he who is important, it is he whose reactions and behavior are to be studied. Instead of examining a mechanical response to a stimulus, teachers are challenged by the organismic thinkers to study a dynamic total organism who is being constantly affected by, and who is constantly affecting, his environment.[11]

---

[11] Leaders of the organismic school have been such psychologists as Lewis, Tolman, and Meier. More detailed analysis of this movement, and of the "experimentalists" who adapted organismic psychology to educational philosophy, may be found in Hilgard, *Theories of Learning*.

*Transactional theory.* In recent years, a number of psychologists have become dissatisfied with one aspect of organismic theory: its failure to explain the origin or source of the "whole" image which the human brain conjures up in response to external stimuli. Instead of the learner and his externality being separate entities which interact in each new learning situation, it seems to some investigators that the human organism and externality are parts of the same perceptual process. These theorists have become known as "transactional" psychologists because they hold that the individual acts *with* or *through* his environment and is an integral part of that environment. The process of translating the on-going energies of one's environment into his own perceptions, and of actually transforming the environment through this perceptual act, is called a "transaction." This term means a continuous process of transformation of energy from one form (for example light rays) into another form (such as neural impulses). It also suggests that the separation of man and his environment is not a valid concept, since man is continuously engaged in transforming and being transformed by his environment. "Real" perceptions are conceived by the transactionalists as relative instead of absolute predictions based on *past* experiences (repeated trials), which cause the individual to form some assumptions governing *future* action. Living is viewed as an evolving process, consisting of the inseparable elements of space, time, the environment, and the organism. Any particular learning act involves all these elements. As Hadley Cantril puts the matter:

> Each transaction of living involves numerous capacities and aspects of man's nature which operate together. Each occasion of life can occur only through an environment; is imbued with some purpose; requires action of some kind, and the registration of the consequences of action. Every action is based upon some awareness or perception, which in turn is determined by the assumptions brought to the occasion. All of these processes are interdependent. No one process could function without the others.[12]

The educational implications of transactional theory will be dealt with in a later section of this chapter, under the heading *"Each individual behaves in terms of his unique perceptions."* Readers

[12] Hadley Cantril, *The "Why" of Man's Experience* (New York: Macmillan Co., 1950), p. 59. Reprinted by permission.

who would like to learn more about transactional theory should read *Explorations in Transactional Psychology*.[13]

We have dealt all too briefly with the background of modern beliefs regarding the process of learning. In such a volume as this there is not space for a comprehensive treatment of these various theories about learning. One obvious hazard of brevity is over-simplification. Psychologists cannot be neatly categorized under certain labels. There has always been, in fact, wide disagreement among the experts as to the precise nature of learning. Not only has one school of thought emerged from and superseded another; even those psychologists who are generally classified as in agreement have expressed sharp differences in their concepts. Even today, not much is precisely known about cognitive processes such as the nature of insight. Disagreements increase when theory is translated into practice in the classroom. Cultural values held by educators affect their readiness to adopt new research findings. Old habits persist and practice tends to lag far behind theory. In any one secondary school today it would be possible to find practitioners of all the theories thus far discussed in this chapter, and some teachers will be holding two opposite views in confused reverence.

Yet there are some general principles on which psychologists tend to agree. In the succeeding part of this chapter an effort will be made to present some of these basic generalizations about the learning process on which there tends to be some agreement, and support from research. It is important to consider the basic elements in the learning process before we go on to "teaching and learning" in the classroom.

## Basic principles of learning

Most specialists in the field of learning theory agree with the organismic psychologists that learning consists of *the modification of behavior through experience*. Desired changes in behavior are considered the test of learning. If no change occurs, no learning has yet taken place. Arthur Gates has described this concept in the following language:

13 Franklin P. Kilpatrick, ed., *Explorations in Transactional Psychology* (New York: New York University Press, 1961).

Learning may be defined as the progressive change in behavior which is associated, on the one hand, with successive presentations of a situation, and on the other with repeated efforts of an individual to react to it effectively.[14]

Let us look briefly at some of the implications of this concept of learning as changed behavior, for it suggests a whole series of principles which affect the learning process.

1. *Learning is an individual experience.* When we speak of group experience, we really mean a number of individual experiences within a group. Other people's experiences are vitally important to the individual, but only when he can succeed in building them into his own experience. The experiences of others may be past, present, or future, but they are really only a part of the environment or situation with which the learner is interacting—the context in which his behavior will be tested.

The individual's experience may be direct (the "here-now-and-me" in action) or it may be vicarious (hearing or reading about the experience of others). If either kind of experience modifies the individual's behavior, it may be considered educative. Vicarious experience may fail to modify the learner's behavior because he cannot assimilate or reconstruct it; it may be either too remote from his previous experience and values; or he may lack the skill needed to understand it. On the other hand, direct experience is too limited to be very fruitful as the sole resource. Both kinds of experience, in some kind of sensible balance, are needed. Burton comments as follows on the contribution to reality of direct and vicarious experience:

> Few of us will be fortunate enough to "experience" directly the delta of the Nile, the geography of India, the contents of the world's art galleries, the life of the nomads of Asia Minor. Furthermore, no one can experience four thousand years of history, nor the actual life of Shakespeare, nor the Crossing of the Rubicon. . . . One can experience the first meeting of the Continental Congress, the storming of the Bastille, the westward march of the pioneers *vicariously* by reading, reflecting, dramatizing, seeing motion pictures, and constructing implements. The *vicarious* experience must be a truly active process; the learner must relive

---

[14] Arthur I. Gates *et al., Educational Psychology,* rev. ed. (New York: Macmillan Co., 1942), p. 299. Reprinted by permission.

the events as far as that is possible. He must *hear* the tramp of the rabble on the cobblestones of Paris, he must *see* the light in the old North Church, must *hear* the shot heard round the world, must *thrill* with Lewis and Clark at the sight of the Pacific.[15]

A common fault of vicarious experience, however, is that it is too unreal or unrelated to direct experience to be absorbed by the learner. In such a case it cannot modify his behavior in constructive ways. He may change his behavior in such ways as to avoid further similar experiences, but this outcome is not what the teacher seeks. Burton continues: "The failure to profit from vicarious experience because of its lack of any degree of reality is to be seen in much teaching of literature and history in secondary schools and colleges." [16]

In order for an individual to profit from either direct or vicarious experiences, he must build them into himself by analysis, association, and reflection. He must analyze their meaning, associate this with his own concepts and values, and reflect on whether and just how he can make use of them. Further discussion of this reflective process will be found in a later section of this chapter.

> I'm not very good in geography, either. They call it economic geography this year. We've been studying the imports of Chile all week, but I couldn't tell you what they are. Maybe the reason is I had to miss school yesterday because my uncle took me and his big trailer truck down state about 200 miles, and we brought almost ten tons of stock to the Chicago market.
>
> I even write out all the bills and send letters to the farmers about what their pigs and beef cattle brought at the stockyards. I only made three mistakes in seventeen letters last time, my aunt said—all commas. She's been through high school and reads them over. I wish I could write school themes that way. The last one I had to write was on "What a Daffodil Thinks of Spring," and I just couldn't get going.[17]

[15] William H. Burton, *The Guidance of Learning Activities*, p. 75. Copyright 1944 by Appleton-Century-Crofts. Reprinted by permission.

[16] *Ibid.*, p.76.

[17] Stephen M. Corey, "The Poor Scholar's Soliloquy," from *Childhood Education*, January 1944, Vol. 20, No. 5, pp. 219–220. Reprinted by permission of the Association for Childhood Education International, 3615 Wisconsin Avenue, N.W., Washington, D.C., 20016.

2. *The learner behaves as a total organism*. The learner is greater than the sum of his parts, and he is indivisible so far as his behavior is concerned. Not only his brain but his entire body affects his learning. As he approaches each new situation his readiness for learning is affected by a number of things. As a total person, he may be eager, curious, and active. Or he may be, again as a total person, listless, uninterested, and passive. He may even be hostile. He may be worried about a quarrel he has had at home, or self-conscious about the pimples on his face. He may be tired or suffering from upset stomach. He may have a memory loss because of his fears about examinations.

It is futile to select only the intellect for training; everything else about the learner comes with his intellect. One of his persistent problems is his need to react as a person to a daily series of unrelated subjects, teachers, and classmates, for this is the normal routine in a departmentalized secondary school.

> Phyllis approached every examination fearfully. She had a good daily recitation record in most of her classes, and she prepared carefully and at length for each examination—but she frequently failed on such written tests. She developed a series of physical symptoms as each examination drew near. She complained of indigestion, knots in her stomach, weakness in her knees, and headaches. On days when she had several examinations she became so ill that she had to be taken home.
>
> "Daddy," she wailed, "I know the answers but I feel so bad I can't remember a single thing when I get to class."

3. *Learning consists in the fulfillment of purpose*. All behavior is purposive, in the sense that it reveals the true purpose of the organism. The normal individual has purposes which he consciously or subconsciously seeks to fulfil. When his own purposes coincide with those of the teacher (usually as the result of good teaching), learning goes forward happily according to plan. Even if he can reasonably expect to fulfil his own purposes only occasionally in the classroom, he may tolerate what happens and, in effect, await that happy moment. If his previous experience has convinced him that the classroom is not a very promising place to satisfy his own purposes, he may react in any of several ways: (a) he may rebel and resist; (b) he may withdraw, either by truancy or by remaining in a state of somnolence; (c) he may set out to circumvent what is going

on through diversion tactics; (d) he may undertake to deceive or cheat; (e) he may simply endure what goes on and look forward to fulfilling his own purposes after school.

> In effect he is often saying to such teachers: "This is your idea. OK. Go ahead and make me do it." He still has his purposes, and he is still learning in terms of fulfillment of those purposes of his own; but he may have to do it outside the classroom, and he may have to thwart the teacher's goals as a means of achieving his own. Such negative or at least unplanned learning has always gone on whenever the school fails in its basic task of meeting the needs of the learner.[18]

This kind of learning occurs when the gap becomes too great between the purposes of the learner and those of the teacher. For example:

| | |
|---|---|
| The teacher reacts with sarcasm to a student's suggestion about class procedure. | The student learns not to question or evaluate his own work. |
| The teacher makes unreasonable assignments of homework. | The student learns whose work to copy. |
| The teacher corrects every error on a theme and thus uses a lot of red ink on each one. | The student learns that he can never learn to write. |
| The teacher dissects every poem in the anthology, seeking literal meaning. | The student learns to hate poetry. |
| The teacher corrects chalkboard work publicly. | The student learns to avoid the chalkboard. |
| The teacher emphasizes competition, is a "hard marker." | The student learns to cheat. |
| The teacher punishes students who work together. | The student learns that cooperation is improper. |

The secret of good teaching lies in the discovery and fulfillment of the constructive purpose of learners; and they do have such pur-

[18] Roland C. Faunce and Morrel J. Clute, *Teaching and Learning in the Junior High School* (Belmont, Calif.: Wadsworth Publishing Co., Inc., 1961), pp. 57–58.

poses. In contrast to the examples just noted, many classrooms present the happy spectacle of students and teachers pursuing constructive purposes with genuine satisfaction and achievement.

4. *Learning calls for action.* We have thus far pictured the learner as one who is pursuing constructive purposes as a means of modifying his own behavior as a total person, interacting with his environment. This is a dynamic, active process quite different from the concept of the learner as a passive receptor of external stimuli. Failure to interact leaves learning incomplete. In a real sense, learning is a present-tense business. That is, present action of some kind and on some level is called for if present purposes are to be satisfied and present behavior patterns modified.

Many school experiences are rationalized by the explanation that they prepare the learner for some future function. The teacher predicts, for example, that as a college freshman the learner will be asked to distinguish between a participle and a gerund; or that as an adult he will need to know the separate functions of the executive and legislative branches of government. Perhaps these predictions are valid, but present purposes are the first need of a genuine learning situation, and such purposes can be tested only by behavior, by action here and now. This present action may not take the same form as future action, but the action *must* occur if present learning is to be effective. Is the class studying a problem of any kind? Then what can be done about it? Are we reading a poem? Then what does it sound like and what does it do to us? Have we grasped a new principle of science? How can we use it? Have we found out what kind of man Napoleon was? What meaning has his value system for us, and how can we translate that meaning into our own lives?

In the areas of skill development the need for action is obvious. More subtle but equally significant is action of some kind in reference to concepts and newly discovered knowledge. Without provision for action, we fall back into the old mind-storage kind of teaching.

A twelfth grade government class was studying city government. As a means of better understanding, they made a trip by bus to the city hall, where they became fascinated, among their other experiences, by a conference with an officer of the city Planning Commission. This interested official was later invited to speak further to the class about the implications of the Commission's work for the neighborhoods in which the students lived. He asked them if they would like to help the Commission on an impending survey of this area. For the next two months the class was busy with a detailed survey and the construction of a housing-and-business map of the school's attendance area.

5. *Learning involves problem solving.* Without a problem to be attacked, there can be no direct learning. Teachers readily recognize this need in mathematics and industrial arts, where the problems are specific enough to serve as the framework of the curriculum. The problem in the workbook, however, may not be the learner's problem. His problem may coincide by chance with some problem confronted by classmates, but it is basically an individual problem that presents a challenge to individual learning. Skillful teachers have discovered ways to develop learning experiences that identify and use the problems confronted by the learner. Some less able teachers have never learned how to use the students' problems. In such classrooms the learner spends his efforts avoiding the learnings imposed by the teacher.

In Chapter 7 consideration will be given to the help teachers can give students who have personal-social problems that affect their success as learners.

6. *Reflective thinking is required for effective learning.* A crucial element in solving any problem is ability to think, to arrive at solutions through rational inquiry, to examine data and relate them to some previously established hypothesis. This ability is indispensable for effective democracy, which depends on the ability of citizens to solve problems instead of accepting uncritically solutions offered by leaders. Instead of regarding learning as a mechanical response to prearranged external stimuli, as the early connectionists did, psychologists now see learning as the application of intelligence to the solution of problems. Application involves certain processes, as Dewey pointed out many years ago in *Democracy and Education:* questioning of some unknown elements, interpretation of that which is already given or accepted, examination of new factors, development and testing of a hypothesis that agrees with the data.

Implicit in reflective thinking is the search for application or meaning of any new idea. This in turn calls for associating it with previously learned and accepted ideas and discovering relationships, if any. As the learner develops increased skill in this process he becomes more able to apply new learnings to other situations. This is transfer of learning, now actually built into the learning process. In today's complex world of rapid change, it is crucial that teachers provide for transfer of learning to new problem situations. Indeed, without such ability to transfer we should have to begin all over again in each new situation, without any benefit of past experience. As noted earlier, however, transfer does not occur automatically but must be built into the learning act. This is accomplished as the learner gains control of reflective thinking.

Teachers have assumed for years that this skill in reflective thinking was largely dependent on intelligence, as measured by I.Q. tests. In recent years it has been shown to be more truly an attribute of creativity. E. Paul Torrance, a leader in the current investigations of creativity, has summed up the abilities involved in creative thinking as "becoming aware of problems, thinking up possible solutions, and testing them." [19] Calvin W. Taylor identifies the characteristics of the creative person as follows:

> Ability to sense problems is an intellectual characteristic usually included in creativity. Ability to sense ambiguities, plus effective questioning ability may be important in creative activity. This ability may be described as curiosity in action.
>
> Motivational characteristics suggested are curiosity or inquiringness of mind, liking to think, liking to manipulate and toy with ideas, intellectual persistence, need for recognition of achievement, need for variety, effective work habits, high energy, and willingness to take long-range risks.[20]

Most of these traits have little or nothing in common with the factors measured in intelligence tests. Getzels and Jackson's re-

[19] E. Paul Torrance, *Guiding Creative Talent* (Englewood Cliffs, N.J.: Prentice-Hall, Inc., © 1962), p. 3. Reprinted by permission.

[20] Adapted from Calvin W. Taylor, "A Tentative Description of the Creative Individual," in *Human Variability and Learning*, Walter B. Waetjen, ed. (Washington, D.C.: Association for Supervision and Curriculum Development, 1961), pp. 62–79. By permission.

search [21] agrees with that of Torrance [22] and others that about 70 per cent of those whose performance on tests of creative thinking place them in the upper 20 per cent would be eliminated if only an intelligence or scholastic aptitude test had been used. This discrepancy is due, in part, to the fact that both I.Q. tests and traditional school practice have taken account of only a small fraction of the many facets of intelligence. Schools and intelligence tests have placed a high premium on "conforming thinking," as Guilford [23] has pointed out. This means that the tests predict academic performance of the kind most highly valued in the classroom. The essence of truly reflective thinking, on the other hand, is the creation of new meanings and relationships. It must, above all, begin with a genuine purpose.[24]

Since reflective thinking begins with a goal, plus certain barriers to its achievement, it is important that the problem be the learner's problem. This may or may not be the case, as regards the problems in the textbook or those posed by the teacher. Reflective thinking about a problem cannot proceed effectively until the thinker "owns" the problem, at least in a psychological sense. This is just another way of re-stating something discussed earlier: the purposes of the learner himself control his learning efforts.

> When he had spelled out number two, he found he had no idea of number one; fragments whereof afterward obtruded themselves into number three, which slided into number four, which grafted itself onto number two. So that whether twenty Romuluses made a Remus, or *hic haec hoc* was troy weight, or a verb always agreed with an ancient Briton, or three times four was Taurus a bull were open questions with him.[25]

[21] J. W. Getzels and P. W. Jackson, "The Highly Intelligent and the Highly Creative Adolescent: A Summary of Some Research Findings," in *The Third (1959) University of Utah Research Conference on the Identification of Creative Scientific Talent* (Salt Lake City: University of Utah Press, 1959).

[22] E. Paul Torrance, "Eight Partial Replications of the Getzels-Jackson Study," Research Memo BER 60-18 (Minneapolis: Bureau of Educational Research, University of Minnesota, 1960).

[23] J. P. Guilford, "Creativity," *American Psychologist,* 5:9 (September 1950), 444–454.

[24] The reader who wishes to explore this matter of reflective thinking further may enjoy H. Gordon Hullfish and Philip G. Smith, *Reflective Thinking* (New York: Dodd, Mead & Co., 1961).

[25] Charles Dickens, *Dombey and Son.*

7. *Each individual behaves in terms of his own unique percep-tions.* As the individual attacks a problem (pursues his purposes) what perceptions does he bring to bear on this essentially reflective process? For many years it has been recognized that behavior is influenced by perceptions, and that individuals do not perceive alike. In recent years research in this field of perception has established facts that directly affect the learning process:

> 1. Perception is not basically an optical phenomenon, but rather a response of a total organism to situations.
> 2. Perceptions are developed out of the experiences the individual has had.
> 3. Since each individual's experiences are different from those of other persons, his perceptions are also unique.
> 4. In order to share others' perceptions, one must systematically build "bridges" or seek common understandings.

It is not unusual for teachers to expect their students to get exactly the same meaning from a passage in a book, or to hear identically the same assignments, or to see the same thing in a picture or a film. No such common perceptions can be assured; they must be continuously built in, and tested. Teachers sometimes speak of "group experience" and imply that every member of a group has had the same experience and perceives it as do the other members. In this sense, there is no such thing as group experience.

Common experiences leading to shared perception are not impossible. They must, however, be "taught for" or sought in the classroom. A significant first step in this direction is for teachers to recognize the fact of unique perception and go on from that point. They will otherwise continue to make false assumptions about what is being perceived, and effective learning will not be achieved on such premises.[26]

8. *Learning (behavior) is a product of attitudes toward self.* A considerable body of research has confirmed the fact that the image of self is an important element in learning.[27] When an individual

[26] Readers who are interested in reading more about this phenomenon of perception might begin with a graphic little book by Earl C. Kelley, *Education for What Is Real* (New York: Harper & Row, Publishers, 1947).

[27] For a resume of the findings of research regarding self-concept, see the recent yearbook of the Association for Supervision and Curriculum Development,

sees himself as able to achieve a given goal, he has a significantly greater chance of success. When he sees himself as unlikely to achieve the goal, he is less likely to succeed; he is beaten before he starts. Thus the very effort required of him is impossible under this handicap of a poor self-concept. Everything that has been said thus far about the learning process hinges on the individual's image of himself. To strive, to seek meanings, to attack problems, to pursue purposes, all these efforts are predicated on some hope of success. In discussing this need for "can-ness" as a requirement for growth, Rasey and Menge have expressed the belief that this quality is the most basic personality need of all: "It is first essential that an individual see himself as a simple doer—as one who can. So long as he sees himself as one who cannot, he is lamed and blind to his own enhancement. He cannot try." [28] These investigators go on to point out that when teachers say of a child "he will not try," they should at least consider the possibility instead that "he cannot try," for this is often the literal truth.

What circumstances tend to destroy or diminish the self-concept of students? There are many influences in the home and community which can have this effect. Parents have often been guilty of destroying their children's self-image by comparing them with their more successful brothers and sisters, by making sarcastic or critical remarks in their presence, and by pressing compulsively toward unrealistic goals for them. Anderson reports that most retarded readers who have been referred to his clinic at the University of Michigan have had such treatment from their parents.

The system of symbol marks used by the schools has further reinforced the learner's belief that he cannot—cannot do arithmetic, cannot read, cannot write, cannot succeed in general at tasks imposed by the school. When school marks are regarded as rewards or punishments they constitute a serious barrier to a child's attempts to build an adequate self-concept. When the whole business assumes an aspect of competition, some students are going to refuse to compete because they already know they cannot win. Even those who

---

*Perceiving, Behaving, Becoming* (Washington, D.C.: The Association Yearbook, 1962). See also at the end of this chapter references to Combs, Jersild, Maslow, and Murphy.

28 Marie I. Rasey and J. Wilmer Menge, *What We Learn from Children* (New York: Harper & Row, Publishers, 1955), pp. 36–37.

can and do succeed are not really helped by the marking system, which presents them with no particular challenge. The rewards of achievement should be built into the task itself, not extrinsic to it.[29] There is reward in completing a difficult task, in helping others, in knowing that other people whom you value believe in and value you. The concept of self is central to the learning process.

> The ice came early and overnight. It was clear and smooth. The older children glided skillfully in and around each other. The small ones were running and sliding on their boot soles. We never dreamed that she would try this. Our adult knowledge that ice was last summer's fearsome water was not a hindrance to Heidi. To our surprise she ran and slid and came to a stop, still right side up. She turned and called to me, "Oh, Miss Rasey, I got so many things I can!" [30]

9. *Attitudes toward others and relationships with them affect learning.* Closely related to the attitudes toward self are attitudes toward others. Development of constructive attitudes is a primary goal of learning, for attitudes condition behavior. Teachers can build good attitudes toward others or help develop bad attitudes. They can encourage truth and loyalty or they can make cheating and tattling inevitable.

Group relationships are of great importance in our interdependent world. Schools should make it their business to capitalize the peer relationships and build them more effectively. The nature and tempo of learning are conditioned in many ways by group relationships. The status one has with his peers, their attitudes toward him, and his feelings about them directly affect his learning. Students learn from each other and help each other learn. Sometimes the requirements of group membership operate in such a way as to reduce one's effort in the classroom, lest one receive marks that are unacceptably high. Here and there are other lonely students who are compensating for their lack of group acceptance by redoubled effort for better marks; these isolates, too, are being influenced by relationships or their lack of them.

---

[29] Further discussion of symbol marks and possible alternatives to them will be found in Chapter 13.

[30] Rasey and Menge, *What We Learn from Children,* p. 36. Reprinted by permission.

Good classrooms should be models of effective group relationships. Group work on common problems is a fact of life and should be a characteristic of good teaching and learning. The use of small groups is, as a matter of fact, increasing in many good schools. This technique is further discussed in Chapter 8.

> In like manner, a feeling of belonging makes possible the security from which experimentation and creativity can occur. A feeling of belonging, however, comes from more than mutual trust and acceptance. It requires also that the child be given sufficient responsibility that he may have the feeling that people really count on him. Then one can feel that he is carrying his share of the load. It is at this point that a child in a classroom or in a family can say, "we." Not only can he then dare to try, but he can say "let's try" to others.[31]

10. *Learning (changed behavior) usually requires repeated efforts.* Behavior change is seldom built in a day. It is often a difficult process that promises success only after repeated effort and constant evaluation. Earlier concepts of learning emphasized rote memorizing and constant drill, frequently at the expense of meaning or purpose, reflective thinking, or problem solving. There is some of this outmoded reliance on blind drill in classrooms of our day. Many teachers, however, have tried to abandon meaningless drill and substitute more creative methods. In this effort they have sometimes overlooked the need for repetition of effort. Drill is more acceptable and meaningful when it represents pursuit of an accepted goal and offers some promise of success. "Practice does not make perfect" unless the learner accepts the goal and evaluates his degree of success. He must first see some real purpose in his efforts. He must evaluate his success or failure. And he must be able, with some help, to redirect his efforts in such a way as to make them more effective. Thus any desired change in behavior calls for a series of progressive efforts toward a goal, each effort subject to analysis and redirection. If the obstacles are great this process will not be an easy one nor a short one. Unless the learner really accepts the goal and hence sees a genuine purpose in his efforts, he will usually abandon the task.

---

[31] Association for Supervision and Curriculum Development, *Perceiving, Behaving, Becoming* (Washington, D.C.: The Association Yearbook, 1962), p. 148. Reprinted by permission.

This acceptance of the goal is sometimes referred to as motivation. The student must be motivated. If the goal is not his in the first place, the teacher may try to sell it to him by persuasion, by audio-visual gadgets, or by extrinsic rewards and punishments. A more acceptable meaning of motivation is the one developed throughout this chapter: a sense of purpose intrinsic to a problem one has to solve because it helps satisfy a real need. It is a different concept and a different approach that are involved when teachers develop learning experiences to fulfill needs, as opposed to deciding the experiences first and then trying to arouse an appetite for them.

*In conclusion.* We have presented ten closely related statements that appear to have been generally accepted today as principles of effective learning:

1. Learning is an individual experience.
2. The learner behaves as a total organism.
3. Learning consists in the fulfillment of purpose.
4. Learning calls for action.
5. Learning involves problem solving.
6. Reflective thinking is required for effective learning.
7. Each individual behaves in terms of his own unique perceptions.
8. Learning (behavior) is a product of attitudes toward self.
9. Attitudes toward others and relationships with them affect learning.
10. Learning (changed behavior) usually requires repeated efforts.

The reader may be reflecting at this point that these ten principles do not seem to apply to many of the activities of students in secondary schools. Let us turn in Chapter 5 to analysis of the various roles played by teachers and their use of the accepted principles of effective learning.

## FOR FURTHER READING

Alberty, Harold B., and Elsie J. Alberty, *Reorganizing the High School Curriculum,* 3rd ed. New York: Macmillan Co., 1962. Chapter 3, "Educational Values and Learning Theories," is an excellent summary of the relationship between philosophies of education and theories of learning.

Association for Supervision and Curriculum Development, *Learning More about Learning*. Washington, D.C.: The Association Yearbook, 1959. See especially the chapter by Arthur W. Combs, "Personality Theory and Its Implications for Curriculum Development," pp. 5–20.

———, *Perceiving, Behaving, Becoming*. Washington, D.C.: The Association Yearbook, 1962. Discusses the "fully functioning" person and how schools may develop such persons. Includes contributions by Arthur W. Combs, Earl C. Kelley, A. H. Maslow, and Carl R. Rogers.

Burton, William H., *The Guidance of Learning Activities*, 3rd. ed. New York: Appleton-Century-Crofts, Inc., 1962. This most recent edition adds many new illustrations and applications to an already useful book.

Combs, Arthur W., and Donald Snygg, *Individual Behavior; A Perceptual Approach to Behavior*. New York: Harper & Row, Publishers, 1959. Provides a broad framework for modern perceptual approaches to understanding behavior.

Faunce, Roland C., and Morrel J. Clute, *Teaching and Learning in the Junior High School*. Belmont, Calif.: Wadsworth Publishing Co., Inc., 1961. Chapter 3, "The Learning Process," briefly sums up modern theories of learning and their implications for junior high school teachers.

Hilgard, Ernest R., *Theories of Learning*. New York: Appleton-Century-Crofts, Inc., 1956. Scholarly analysis and comparison of past and present theories regarding the learning process.

Hullfish, H. Gordon, and Philip G. Smith, *Reflective Thinking*. New York: Dodd, Mead & Co., 1961. Purposes and procedures involved in the teaching and learning of the skills of reflective thinking.

Jersild, Arthur T., *In Search of Self*. New York: Bureau of Publications, Teachers College, Columbia University, 1952. Presents ways to help youth understand and accept themselves, especially through written compositions.

Kelley, Earl C., *Education for What Is Real*. New York: Harper & Row, Publishers, 1947. A brief description of the Hanover experiments in perception and their dynamic meaning for classroom learning.

———, and Marie I. Rasey, *Education and the Nature of Man*. New York: Harper & Row, Publishers, 1952. Chapter 4, "Man's Ways of Knowing" and Chapter 5, "Man and His Environment," sum up research in learning and perception. A later section of the book spells out implications for the classroom teacher.

Kilpatrick, Franklin P., ed., *Explorations in Transactional Psychology*. New York: New York University Press, 1961. Readings in transactional theory, including the nature of perception and its impact on learning.

Kingsley, Howard L., and Ralph Garry, *The Nature and Conditions of Learning*, rev. ed. Englewood Cliffs, N.J.: Prentice-Hall, Inc., 1957. Good basic treatment of modern theory regarding effective learning.

Lumsdaine, A. A., and Robert Glaser, eds., *Teaching Machines and Programmed Learning*. Washington, D.C.: The National Education Association, 1960. Revival of "S-R bond" theory as applied to various devices for programmed instruction.

Maslow, A. H., *Motivation and Personality*. New York: Harper & Row, Publishers, 1954. A report of recent studies relating to the self-image. Implications for school practices.

Murphy, Gardner, *et al.*, *Experimental Social Psychology*. New York: Harper & Row, Publishers, 1937. Describes the nature and causation of "social" learning.

McDonald, Frederick J., *Educational Psychology*. Belmont, Calif.: Wadsworth Publishing Co., Inc., 1959. See Chapters 4–13 for discussion of personality development and learning.

National Society for the Study of Education, *Learning and Instruction*, Forty-ninth Yearbook. Chicago: University of Chicago Press, 1950. Useful summary in nontechnical language of recent research about learning.

Peck, Robert F., and James V. Mitchell, Jr., *Mental Health*. Washington, D.C.: The National Education Association, 1962. A concise description of the relation of mental health to learning with implications for classroom management. No. 24 in the series "What Research Says to the Teacher."

Redl, Fritz, and William W. Wattenberg, *Mental Hygiene in Teaching*, 2nd ed. New York: Harcourt, Brace and World, 1959. Chapters 3 through 7 present fundamental facts about behavior, growth, personality, adjustment, and maturity.

Torrance, E. Paul, *Guiding Creative Talent*. Englewood Cliffs, N.J.: Prentice-Hall, Inc., 1962. An interesting resume of data on identification of creative traits, and evaluation of various procedures for working effectively with creative learners.

Trow, W. C., "What Research Says to the Teacher," in *The Learning Process*, American Educational Research Association and the Department of Classroom Teachers. Washington, D.C.: The National Education Association, 1954. A brief summary for classroom teachers of the basic principles of learning, as supported by recent research.

"What Research Says about Learning," *Phi Delta Kappan,* 39:6 (March 1958). Entire issue deals with recent research on the learning process.

# 5

# The role of the teacher

In the preceding chapter we explored the nature of the learning process, and presented ten principles of effective learning, defined as changed behavior. These ten principles can be summed up as follows:

> 1. Effective learning calls for a purposeful, persistent attack on some problem, requiring reflective thinking and leading to some kind of action.
>
> 2. The effectiveness of learning is conditioned by the unique manner in which the learner perceives the problem, how he relates to the group, and how he sees himself.

What does this approach to learning imply for the teacher? The fact is that few secondary school teachers perceive their role to be the facilitation of problem solving. They are more likely to view teaching as the presentation of a specialized body of subject matter—as "telling plus showing." Most teachers who have been certified for secondary schools originally became interested in teaching because of their keen interest in a particular subject-field. They took all the courses they could in this field. Their experience in college courses consisted chiefly of listening to lectures, taking notes, reading books, writing examinations, and presenting term papers to the instructor.

All these procedures seemed to fit a pattern. They all involved memorization and "acquisition" of concepts, facts, data, all related to an increasing command of or sophistication regarding some subject-field. Since people tend to teach as they were taught, the lecture and recitation methods are common in secondary schools.

## Traditional techniques of teachers

It is not always a simple matter for teachers to identify their own techniques in the classroom. Many of them sincerely believe that they are involving their students in a problem-solving process, when they are in fact maintaining direct or indirect control of the direction and sequence of each class session. Skilled observers have been able to identify "learner-centered" behavior of teachers, and to contrast these with "teacher-centered" actions or talk. Withall [1] reports one such study, in which the various categories of "teacher-style" were listed as follows:

1. The teacher is trying to *support* the child's ego.
2. The teacher is trying to *clarify*.
3. The teacher is trying to *structure* the situation.
4. The teacher is giving orders.
5. The teacher is criticizing.
6. The teacher is justifying his own beliefs.

Flanders [2] has developed a technique for "interaction analysis," which is aimed at systematizing and objectifying observation of what goes on in a classroom. His ten-point list is shown on page 96.

Although the process of interaction analysis was developed as a tool for the researcher, any teacher can benefit by attempting to analyze his own procedures and their impact on students. He may be surprised at the amount of classroom time he actually spends in controlling or manipulating the young people in his classroom.

Let us visit a high school history class for a brief observation. The lesson for the day is the series of military campaigns that culminated

[1] John Withall, in *Human Variability and Learning*, Walter B. Waetjen, ed. (Washington, D.C.: Association for Supervision and Curriculum Development, 1961), pp. 45–46.

[2] Ned A. Flanders, "Interaction Analysis in the Classroom: A Manual for Observers" (prepublication draft, School of Education, University of Michigan).

## CATEGORIES FOR INTERACTION ANALYSIS

| | | |
|---|---|---|
| TEACHER TALK | INDIRECT INFLUENCE | *1. *Accepts feeling:* accepts and clarifies the feeling tone of the students in a non-threatening manner. Feelings may be positive or negative. Predicting or recalling feelings are included.<br>2. *Praises or encourages:* praises or encourages student action or behavior. Jokes that release tension, not at the expense of another individual, nodding head or saying, "um hm?" or "go on" are included.<br>3. *Accepts or uses ideas of student:* clarifying, building, or developing ideas suggested by a student. As teacher brings more of his own ideas into play, shift to category five.<br>4. *Asks questions:* asking a question about content or procedure with the intent that a student answer. |
| | DIRECT INFLUENCE | 5. *Lecturing:* giving facts or opinions about content or procedures; expressing his own ideas, asking rhetorical questions.<br>6. *Giving directions:* directions, commands, or orders with which a student is expected to comply.<br>7. *Criticizing or justifying authority:* statements intended to change student behavior from nonacceptable to acceptable pattern; bawling someone out; stating why the teacher is doing what he is doing; extreme self-reference. |
| STUDENT TALK | | 8. *Student talk—response:* talk by students in response to teacher. Teacher initiates the contact or solicits student statement.<br>9. *Student talk—initiation:* talk by students which they initiate. If "calling on" student is only to indicate who may talk next, observer must decide whether student wanted to talk. If he did, use this category. |
| | | 10. *Silence or confusion:* pauses, short periods of silence and periods of confusion in which communication cannot be understood by the observer. |

* There is *no* scale implied by these numbers. Each number is classificatory; it designates a particular kind of communication event. To write these numbers down during observation is to enumerate, not to judge a position on a scale.

in American victory in the Revolutionary War. As we listen in, let us take note of the various roles played by the teacher:

*Teacher:* Today's assignment should take us through Chapter Six, whose title, you will remember, was "Washington Sees It Through." For Monday you will go on to Chapter Seven, "The Confederation and the Constitution." Please make a note to prepare to discuss the following questions, of those suggested on page 183: numbers 5, 6, 10, 11, and 12.

The teacher selects and assigns the task,

delimits the goals,

*Mary:* Will there be an outside reading assignment?

*Teacher:* Not for Monday. We will first get an understanding of this chapter in our book. I have several other assignments for library work which I will give you on Monday.

determines the resources,

Now let us go on from where we left off yesterday. John, please tell us what was happening to Washington's campaign when the bell rang yesterday?

chairs the recitation,

*John:* He had just beaten the British at Trenton and Princeton.

*Teacher:* Right. Now the whole war began to shift toward victory for us as a result of the British blunder of 1777. Andrea, please tell us about that famous blunder.

introduces the lesson,

communicates with students one-to-one,

*Andrea:* Didn't General Burgoyne surrender?

*Teacher:* Yes, but what was the blunder?

asks the questions,

*Andrea:* I don't remember.

*Teacher:* Who does remember?

*Blake:* Well, the fleet was supposed to sail up the Hudson and meet Burgoyne, but they didn't get their orders.

*Teacher:* In other words, General Howe failed to receive his instructions and sailed instead for Philadelphia. Who defeated Burgoyne's Army?

reconstructs the answers,

*Dolores:* General Gates.

*Mary:* I read in the book that Gates wasn't even there. Who really commanded the American army?

*Teacher:* It was Benedict Arnold, who later on became a traitor. Now we have seen the tide of victory turning to Washington. The loss of Burgoyne's army was a serious blow to British hopes. But so far the little American nation had been struggling along without any foreign allies. Now we see this changing as a result of Saratoga. What alliance am I referring to?

supplements the text-book,

sums up, and

supplies transition to next topic.

Let us leave the classroom at this point and go elsewhere in the building in search of more exciting teaching and learning. We shall surely find some teachers who involve their students more actively than this. There appears to be little resemblance to problem solving in this piecemeal reconstruction of textbook material. Indeed, it is not even a good example of the recitation method. At its best, a recitation period can be stimulating, provocative, and related to some real problems that students face. We shall even locate one or two stimulating class discussions in which most of the students are participating. We shall also see some instances of students working on projects in science or shop, and of free reading in English classes. Student reports of outside reading will also be noted in a few classrooms. And we shall also hear a considerable amount of lecturing.

The lecture at its worst consists, an old adage says, in transferring the notes of the teacher to the notebooks of the students without passing through the minds of either. It assumes that the task of a teacher is to tell the students. If the teacher is a lively lecturer with an engaging personality and a witty style the experience is a painless one for students. Indeed, many of them prefer this passive listening role to any role that would force them to assume some responsibility for their own learning. College students often urge greater use of the lecture method on the not-so-naïve ground that the instructor can thus capsulize all the pertinent information and save them a trip to the library.

*Telling and showing.* Lectures, like recitations, can be good, bad, or mediocre. If a teacher lectures in response to a request from the class; if he begins by relating the lecture to problems the class has developed; if he uses language which they can follow with understanding and interest; if he opens the subject for questions and discussion, his lecture may be helpful in much the same way as any resource—book, film, or demonstration—is helpful. But the fact remains that the lecture rests its case on the assumption that all students are equally ready or interested, all are hearing the same thing, and all can apply it in the solution of problems. There is the added assumption that all the students will remember the lecture. Even at its best, there seems little relationship between this passive listening role and the problem-attack required for effective learning. Teaching is not telling.

Yet telling and showing are all too common in the secondary school. Even the recitation method, as we have seen, tends to degenerate into a series of short lectures, interrupted by questions directed at individual students. The conventional concept of the teacher's role seems to be about as follows: his task is to "put his subject across." In pursuance of this goal, he assumes the chairmanship of the class. As chairman he assigns the lesson, announces the resources to be used, and limits the goals in terms of time available. He asks questions, switching about the class until he gets the "right" answers (i.e. the ones to be found in the textbook). He thus communicates with one student at a time and discourages communication between or among students. In order to construct a neat package for the day, he introduces the topic, rephrases or corrects answers, supplies transitions and summaries. He stands or sits at the front of the room where all can see him (and he can see all of the students). Since communication is usually on a one-to-one basis, there is no need for students to face each other or see more than the backs of various necks.

Whether he is lecturing or asking questions, the conventional teacher makes sure that the procedure is properly delimited, or held to the subject of the day.[3] Since he is regarded as a source of expert information, a sort of textbook-in-the-flesh, he must keep the lesson within the bounds of his own knowledge. Thus the one who knows the answers asks the questions and those who don't know are supposed to answer. But occasionally some "smart" students will play an interesting game with such a teacher, which consists of trying to catch him in a mistake. (There would cease to be any point to this

[3] Hughes reported a study of teaching acts in which 87.8 per cent of the teachers' words or acts were in this category of control. Cf. Marie M. Hughes, *Development of the Means for Assessing the Quality of Teaching in Elementary Schools* (Salt Lake City: University of Utah Press, 1961).

game if the teacher stopped pretending to be infallible.) When trapped into this game, some teachers become expert in ignoring or evading questions from certain students. Others have given up the practice of letting students ask questions. A few teachers have become so good at the game that they encourage it. With the enormous increase of knowledge in our time, no one can possibly pretend to know everything. It would be intellectually more honest to admit one's ignorance on some point and help students organize research on any honestly posed question.

The game of trap-the-teacher has nothing to contribute to the real business of learning. It doesn't help—indeed it hinders—the problem-solving process. It perpetuates the concept that only the teacher has any valid purposes for the class to pursue. Since the students did not share in setting up the goals or in planning the lesson, they assume that they have no responsibility for evaluating their own progress. It is taken for granted that it is the teacher's business to decide what is to be learned, and to make the students learn it. It follows that it is also his business to evaluate their performance. Their clues about their own progress consist of the marks they receive and the attitude of the teacher toward them. One of the most potent means of growth—reflective thinking about one's own strengths and weaknesses, successes and failures—is thus cut off from the learner and vested exclusively in the teacher.

Another important goal of education is growth in self-control, in desirable behavior toward others. Responsibility for this, too, is usually left exclusively to the teacher. Students are unlikely to assume any responsibility for controlling group behavior when they do not think of the class as their own. Thus the teacher may get all the experience in maintaining control. If he is skillful and interesting, "his" class discipline may not be a problem to anyone; still, he alone is having the important experience of group control. In cases where the class is poorly organized this problem of control may become a serious burden. It may, in fact, develop into the teacher's main concern and loom so large each day that not much else can go on except constant efforts to control the class. But whether "discipline" is good or bad, little progress is being made toward individual and group self-control.

The reader may at this point object that not all secondary school teachers are like the ones we have been describing. Even those who see themselves as purveyors of subject matter may do so creatively and skillfully. Some even manage to involve their students actively in the process. Some are warm human beings with a sense of humor and a good (effortless) command of class discipline.

We have been looking at some of the worst practices that result from the idea that teaching is telling. We have attempted to trace the kind of teaching that follows logically from that first premise. Most teachers do not pursue these roles to their logical conclusions. Even among those that see themselves basically as obligated to "give" their students the subject matter, many are skillful at selling it, or themselves, to students. But the motivation is all too often based on extrinsic rewards or punishments, such as marks and the threat of failure. Even though many of these teachers are liked and respected by their students, they are not achieving a high order of learning, for they have started with the wrong premise. They have assumed that subject matter is set out to be learned and that their chief function is to induce its learning. They have failed to begin with the learners' interests or concerns. They have, in short, confused means and ends.

## Roles played by effective teachers

Learning of any kind employs content. People do not learn without learning something. The content can (and should) become a means of attacking some problem that is real to the learner. He will use skills and knowledge in the problem-attack and learn them in the process. As he joins others in the common task of solving problems or pursuing interests, he will learn most efficiently if his teacher shares with him some of these roles that are so often pre-empted by the tell-and-show teacher. His learning will be significantly helped if he can share in:

> establishing goals for learning
> planning experiences that may achieve his goals
> making choices among various alternatives
> seeking and using resources
> engaging in and chairing discussions
> using reflective thinking
> making suggestions
> evaluating ideas

assessing his own progress and that of the class
practicing social controls

What does all this imply as to the role of an effective teacher? How would a teacher function who shared with his students such responsibilities as these? What roles would he play if he decided to cease the vain effort to purvey subject matter as an end in itself?

*Participant.* First of all, the teacher operates as a member of the group and makes contributions and suggestions regarding the topic or problem.

The ninth grade class in general mathematics was planning a visit to a local bank.

*Chairman:* I guess it's agreed, then, that we can make this trip either next Tuesday or Wednesday morning. Any preference?

*Amy:* Let's find out which is better for the people at the bank.

*Jack:* How would we find that out?

*Amy:* We could call and ask.

*Chairman:* That sounds OK. Mr. Jones, do you want to call them?

*Teacher:* I could, but a member of the class could do it just as well.

*Chairman:* Any volunteers?

*Floyd:* I go by the bank every noon. I'll ask, if you'll tell me who to see there.

*Amy:* See the president.

*Floyd:* He might be out to lunch.

*Chairman:* How about the cashier?

*Teacher:* He could probably give us permission to come. Speaking of permission, have we filled out an excursion slip yet in Mr. Peterson's office?

*Chairman:* I did that yesterday but left the date blank. I'll go in and finish filling it out when Floyd reports tomorrow.

*Teacher:* Good. What was it we had planned to see there in one hour?

*Marie:* I have the notes we made yesterday. Shall I read them? *(Several nods around the room)* Well, we were going to go as a class to the conference room and have the bookkeeper explain the deposit and withdrawal forms and how they are entered, and the cashier is supposed to tell us all about the system for clearing checks through the clearing house.

*Nora:* What's a clearing house?

*Chairman:* That's what we want to find out. Didn't you mention it, Mr. Jones?

*Teacher:* Yes, I think I did. It was stamped on the backs of those canceled checks Bill showed us.

*Bill:* I know all about it.

*Chairman:* Well, it won't hurt the rest of us to find out. What else were we going to do there, Marie?

*Marie:* I don't have all that written out. Each group has notes about their own plans. Jack is recorder of my group.

*Jack:* We were going to ask to see some foreign money at the Foreign Exchange window.

*Paul:* Our group is going to find out what happens to old torn money and how they get new bills.

*Cara:* We planned to find out how you borrow money.

*Teacher:* It sounds as though we will be pretty busy taking notes on all that. I suggest we keep in mind the general question of how a bank makes money as a business, in all these transactions, and what service it performs in a community.

*Chairman:* Any other questions? *(None)* Then let's postpone this until Floyd reports and go on to our own lesson on interest. Mr. Jones, will you take over now?

The teacher is the most mature member of the group, at least in years. His suggestions are listened to with attention because the class has learned that he usually has some helpful ideas. Yet they know they can sometimes ignore his advice if they have good reasons for doing so. They respect him for this, too. In this participating role he earns respect by the merit of his contributions and by the way he shares responsibilities. He is not assigning tasks, but helping in the attack on a real problem. He may assume some part of the group assignment himself.

The teacher is not, of course, a member of the class on the same basis as the students. This fact does not prevent his participation in discussion and planning. On some occasions he may even withhold his suggestions if he thinks the class has become too dependent on him. He may want to have the students puzzle their own way through to the solution of a problem. At early stages of teacher-pupil planning such withdrawal to the role of observer may be especially useful, as students are prone to revert to their older habits of dependency. As they grow in their skills and self-confidence and as able student leadership develops, such withdrawal by the teacher becomes less often necessary. In fact, to a sophisticated planning group this deliberate shift in roles by the teacher may even appear to be a shirking of the responsibilities of group membership. And of course the teacher is much more than a participant.

*Expediter.* The effective teacher plays the important role of expediting or facilitating plans developed by a class. He knows what resources will be helpful and where they can be found. He is well acquainted with the school library, the public library, and the city directory. He has accumulated many free but useful materials from both private and governmental sources which he has indexed for future use. He can borrow kits of books, pamphlets, exhibits, and reprints from the school library and have them readily available in the classroom. He is prepared to serve as liaison for the class with the principal's office or with various community agencies. He can help them locate speakers in the school and community. He interprets their work to other teachers, to administrators, and to parents as a means of aiding their future activities.

A group of teachers in the cafeteria became involved in a favorite topic.

"I'll be up late tonight correcting themes," said the English teacher. "I'm glad I don't assign them every day."

"My term papers in history have got to be returned tomorrow," chimed in another.

"You two should complain," said a mathematics teacher. "I have five sets of math papers to correct every night." He continued with a wink, "Now if we were only core teachers like Clara Johnson. I understand they don't assign anything and don't have any homework to do."

Miss Johnson chuckled without resentment, but also without much mirth. "You should just follow me around for one week," she said. "Monday night my core kids and I went bowling, and all but four of them were there. Tuesday after school I had three parent conferences, and I spent that evening telephoning the planning committee members to change the place of our weekly luncheon to the Kewpie Hamburger because they're washing walls at my house. Wednesday night I had a talk with the principal about a trip we're taking to the Art Institute, and Thursday evening I was where you were—at P.T.A. As for papers, I spent the weekend curled up with group reports. Anyone want to swap classes with me?" [4]

*Resource.* The good teacher is an indispensable resource to the class as a whole, to individuals pursuing personal projects, and to small sub-groups at work on various problems. He does not pretend to know all the answers, but he does not withhold that which he does know unless he thinks that ready answers will handicap students. He learns early to say, when asked a question that is beyond his realm of knowledge, "I don't know. Let's find out." This frank admission does not weaken his status in the class because he has never posed as an expert in all fields of human knowledge. His students know that he has a considerable amount of knowledge about some subjects, but when the enterprise is a cooperative one in which the teacher is a participant, they do not expect him to have all the answers on tap. They know he can help them find answers.

> The seniors in English had just listened to a rather lively, extempore panel on the pros and cons of capital punishment. Now they had scattered to their seats to pursue their own writing tasks. Some had gone to the file and pulled out unfinished pieces which they had been working on for several days. Others, stirred by the ideas expressed by the panel, were struggling with essays or poems on the problem of capital punishment. Four students had withdrawn to the conference room to work on the class magazine.
> The teacher moved about, giving help as various hands were raised. He sat down beside one student after another and conferred quietly about some problem of written expression. One student couldn't think of exactly the right word and wanted some suggestions. Another asked the teacher to repeat something he had said earlier about what items should be included in a "lead" sentence. Still others wanted to go over some corrections the teacher had made a day or so earlier in their written work. One boy, who had been idly chewing his pencil and contemplating the ceiling, seemed to need the teacher's advice, support, or perhaps friendly pressure in getting started.

[4] Roland C. Faunce and Nelson L. Bossing, *Developing the Core Curriculum,* rev. ed. (Englewood Cliffs, N.J.: Prentice-Hall, Inc., © 1958), pp. 214–215. Reprinted by permission.

The resource role takes a variety of forms, depending on what is going on in a class.[5] The teacher may lead a general discussion, demonstrate an experiment in science, read a poem in English, or explain an equation in mathematics. He may confer with individuals or supply some information to a small group that is working on some problem. Often he will be acting as a chairman of the class, at various stages of planning or in the evaluation process. At other times he will be operating in front of the class, but as resource person rather than as chairman. A resource person does not attempt to control the agenda of a group, but tries, rather, to give help when help is needed. The skillful teacher learns to avoid confusing these roles. The teacher who is committed to helping his students become responsible for their own learning tries to keep limits on his own chairmanship, to encourage his students to assume leadership, and to move as a teacher into other, more professional roles.

*Counselor.* Good teachers think of themselves as guidance workers. There are usually specialized counselors in a secondary school who are freed from teaching to enable them to do counseling. For a number of reasons, however, the basic counseling and guidance worker must be the classroom teacher.[6] A teacher who looks upon learning as modification of behavior must know his students. "Teaching students requires knowing them." This adage would not apply if we sought only to instill subject matter and measured our achievement by content-examinations. When we set out to modify behavior it becomes imperative that we know as much as possible about the behaver himself.

Guidance begins with acceptance, and a good teacher accepts each student. It is unreasonable to expect a teacher to like all students equally. Some of them seem hard to like, especially during adolescence. (It is these very students who need most to be liked!) Still it is reasonable to look to teachers for an accepting, cordial attitude toward all youth. If we hope for effective learning (changed behavior), and if teachers are to help in that process, students must perceive them as friends. As a teacher is able to move away from some of the directive roles mentioned at the beginning of this chapter, he will find it easier to be friendly toward his students. In-

---

[5] For further discussion see Chapters 10 and 11.
[6] This function of teaching is explored at greater length in Chapter 7.

stead of thinking of himself as the imparter of information, he will think of himself as a helper in the business of fulfilling purposes. He can achieve a significant release of pressure if the control of discipline can pass to the group, or at least become a minimal part of his role. It is possible to be a friend and counselor of youth when one has achieved a nonpunitive relationship with them. The effective teacher really likes to be with adolescents and is accepted by them as a person with whom they will readily discuss personal problems.

This concept of the teacher as friend has little acceptance among teachers who see themselves as controllers. Indeed, prospective teachers are often advised to avoid being too friendly. College supervisors have even been known to tell student teachers not to smile during the first week. "Be firm, be tough from the start," they say, "and don't relax this attitude until later on when you have established firm control." It is possible to find some teachers who are now approaching retirement, who have not yet "relaxed"! The trouble with this counsel to grimness is that first impressions of a teacher tend to set the stage—to win friends or to alienate—to lift the heart or to depress the spirit. Starting a new relationship on a note of hostility or threat is an unpromising beginning for one who seeks to be a friend and counselor to his students. Jeanette Veatch offers more constructive advice in her unpublished poem "Credo for a Teacher," which contains these lines:

> I love people—else I would not be
>     a teacher.
> My students are people, therefore I
>     will treat them as I would my friends.
> As I will be interested in how they
>     came to be what they are, I will ask
>     them about themselves.
> I will show them by my actions that
>     I am interested in them.

*Architect of setting for learning.* In the process of learning (changing behavior through problem solving), the setting and the interpersonal relationships are important. The teacher is the designer of the setting for the interaction. Dewey stated this challenge thus: "The only true education comes through the stimulation of the child's powers by the demands of the social situation in which he finds himself." [7] The "demands of the social situation" are a crucial factor in effective learning, which the teacher must analyze, plan, devise, or invent. He must ask himself some questions as he contemplates the classroom-plus-people that constitute the setting for learning:

> What would make the setting basically a social one?
>
> What challenges would be most fruitful for learning?
>
> What aspects of the setting would most effectively present such challenges?
>
> How can each individual be challenged by some aspect of the setting?
>
> How can the situation be so planned as to strengthen and support the learner?
>
> How can the situation challenge the learner without threatening him?
>
> How can the setting for learning leave some things yet undiscovered?
>
> How can the situation produce greater self-direction? Self-understanding?

Many other questions about the classroom setting will occur to a thoughtful teacher. There is, for example, the extent and nature of preplanning by the teacher: how can it be of such dimension and of such quality that it presents the learner with questions, problems, and a search for new truth instead of answers? Then there is the perplexing dimension of the student group itself. What relationships already exist? What restructuring of these relationships is desirable in our effort to present the learner with "stimulation of his powers"? And how can such restructuring be done without violating human feelings and concepts of what is right?

It is often assumed that teachers who seek to involve their students in planning have no need to do any planning themselves about what is to go on in the classroom. Such an assumption is false. The teacher who regards himself as an architect of a stimulating social setting must ask himself many questions and must plan skillfully and thoughtfully. Such planning goes on, not only before the class has

---

[7] John Dewey, *My Pedagogic Creed* (New York and Chicago: E. L. Kellogg and Co., 1897).

met, but throughout the year as each new day presents new stimuli to action, new quests to be launched, new problems to be pursued by the learner. The difference lies not in the amount of pre-planning by teachers. It lies rather in its nature and purpose.

The geography class had selected India for special study, as an outcome of a lively discussion of the current border war between China and India. The teacher's plan-book drew upon a number of sample units and a resource guide on Southeast Asia previously developed by teachers of the social science department. Some excerpts from her plans were as follows:

1. *Students' goals:* The ones they drew up in class yesterday are rather brief:
    a. To settle the question of whether India or China is violating another country's border.
    b. To understand what kind of place the war is being carried on in.
    c. To find out what kinds of countries India and China are.
2. *My goals:*
    a. To develop in them the ability to use data in arriving at answers.
    b. To help them understand the differences in the chief geographical areas of India.
    c. To give them some knowledge of the political history of India since 1947.
    d. To help them get some direct practice in investigating a problem, speaking, listening, writing reports, and working in small groups.
3. *Some questions that already have been raised:*
    a. What kind of life do Indians live?
    b. Who was Mahatma Gandhi?
    c. What kind of a leader is Nehru?
    d. Why does Krishna Menon always act so aggressive?
    e. How high are the Himalayas? How cold?
    f. Can anything be grown in the high border lands?
    g. If not, why fight over it?
    h. Is India pro-Communist?
    i. If so, why is China picking a fight with her?
    j. Can India afford a long war?
4. *Some possible small-group topics:*
    a. The Himalayas and Kashmir
    b. The Ganges Valley

    c. The desert
    d. The central plateau
    e. The subtropics
(or)
    a. The economy of India:
       How do the people live?
       What progress have they made?
       Can they afford a war?
    b. The religions of India:
       The Hindus
       The Moslems
       The Buddhists
       The Sikhs
       The Jains
    c. The people and their customs:
       Dress
       Recreation
       Houses
       Transportation
       Education
       The caste system
    d. Is India a true democracy?
       (central and state government)
    e. What was the influence of Gandhi? Is this waning?

5. *Some possible individual reports:* (These will emerge from small-group discussions by self-assignment.) Aside from those above, there may be individuals interested in such questions as:
    a. What is an Indian village like?
    b. What is life like in Bombay, Calcutta, New Delhi, Madras?
    c. What foods do Indians eat?
    d. What products does India import? Export?
    e. How does rainfall affect Indian life?
    f. How does temperature affect crops?
    g. What kind of army and air force does India have?
    h. How has the U.S. helped India since 1947?
    i. How has the Soviet Union helped India?
    j. What position do women have in India?

6. *Resources:*
   The library (ask for book truck)
   The public library
   The Indian Embassy in Washington
   The British Consulate
   Publications from Indian tourist agencies and Indian Airlines

Indian students at University?
Visitors returned from India?
Newspapers
News magazines
Photo magazines
Films
Film strips
Pictures
Movies and slides brought back by visitors
Interviews with people in community and at University who
   know India
Our own textbook, Chapters 17 and 18.

Instead of planning the presentation of the subject, the architect-teacher plans a "search and discovery" situation. Instead of planning how to present answers, he plans how to arouse questions. Instead of assuming an identical procedure for all members of the class, he plans a variety of avenues appropriate for different learners. Instead of anticipating all procedures and precluding any deviation from "his" plan, he leaves open a number of routes for his students to pursue. And, finally, he is less concerned with the sequence of the subject matter than he is with the sequence of skills and attitudes of the learner.

> And we teachers? We teach nothing. We can no more teach
> than we can learn a child. We are onlookers, while life teaches.
> We are attendants upon life, privileged now and then to become
> co-workers with life in arranging, ordering, and expediting ex-
> periences so that the learners may learn.[8]

*Sight-lifter.* Perhaps the most crucial factor in learning is the learner's own concept of self. If he sees himself as "one who can," he is enabled at least to make a beginning at the solution of problems or the pursuit of new truth. But if he has become convinced, by a long history of minor and major failures, that he hasn't the ability to do much of anything, he cannot even try. He will only go through motions until school releases him for other, more promising experiences.

Similarly, the concept of his world may be also so limited that it

---

[8] Marie I. Rasey, *Toward Maturity* (New York: Barnes & Noble, Inc., 1947), p. 231. Reprinted by permission.

presents him with few exciting vistas to seek out or pursue. Perhaps the most dramatic example of this limited perception may be found in the child of urban slums, whose parents have been unemployed (and unemployable) for as long as the child can remember; whose own world is limited to four or five dingy city blocks; and whose home is a dirty three-room apartment housing at least six persons. Yet one can find this need for higher horizons in children and youth of all cultures and circumstances.

Two visitors to a large junior high school in a run-down section of the city were appalled by some of the conditions they saw there. After lunch they found themselves conversing with Mrs. Robinoff, a rather matronly lady who told them she had taught for sixteen years at Franklin Junior High School.

"You seem to have a few problems here," observed one of the visitors.

"You name 'em and we've got 'em," Mrs. Robinoff said briskly. "Over half our kids come from families on welfare. Sixty per cent come from broken homes. Of these, half have no stepfather at all. At least half the male parents are unemployed—many of them out of work for several years."

"What about truancy and delinquency?" the visitors asked.

"Well, we have our share of delinquent youngsters," replied Mrs. Robinoff, "but you mustn't concentrate on those and overlook the majority who really are pretty good kids. As for being truant, what would you expect under their home conditions? Most of their mothers work. Many of them never finished the eighth grade. Some, not all, don't really care whether their kids go to school or not. (I really think these mothers are not typical, but there are some like that.)

"Did you know you could have a school with over 100 per cent turnover during a school year? Franklin has 110 per cent, or did last year. That's how rapidly people are moving about. By the time you locate a drop-out he has been back at school twice and dropped again.

"We made a public health survey in the homerooms a year ago and found, among other things, that 91 per cent of our students have dental cavities that need to be filled and very few of them can afford to go to a dentist. Our gym and shower rooms are the most important places in the building, since that is the only chance most of them get for a bath. There actually is no bath in many of these slum apartments, and if there is one it is shared by five or six people at least."

"But you still want to teach here?" asked one visitor in some surprise.

"Oh yes, I think I'd rather be at Franklin than at some suburban school for overprivileged kids. I've had some chances to transfer, but I don't know—there are rewards to be had here. Don't forget, for most of these kids Franklin is the only warm, comfortable, and approximately clean place in their lives. And the only place they can get a decent lunch. And the only place, it seems, where there are people who care what happens to them.

"In some schools I know about, you can't tell whether the kids need the teachers or not. Well, you can surely tell at Franklin. When you do help someone, the results are right there staring you in the face. And the things these kids say when they come back from high school to visit are wonderful. We have our problems and our failures too, but for most of these kids we teachers are their only hope of getting anywhere—and they know it!"

Thus the need is for a more adequate concept of self, coupled with a clearer understanding of how the "good life" is lived, and of how it can be lived, if only one develops the power to reach out and grasp. In this effort the school is the only hope for millions of children and youth. Fortunate are those learners who encounter one or more teachers who make them feel more able, who help them dream of meeting great challenges, and who give them the incentive to try.

This role calls first for acceptance of all youth, regardless of their present inadequacies. When a teacher applies his own standards to them, many of them look hopeless as well as helpless. They may be crude or profane in their speech, unable to read or write, hostile toward school and toward teachers, careless about personal hygiene (or downright dirty), and unwilling (or is it unable?) to make any effort to perform school assignments. It is these very characteristics which classify the boy or girl as one who is trapped in a hopeless milieu and unable to escape without help. Instead of saying of such youth that they just won't try, the teacher must first realize that they *cannot* try without first getting some incentive for growth toward a better life. The business of broadening horizons of such learners is of utmost importance for each individual, and for the society as well. Without such help it is unlikely that young people will ever contribute anything constructive to their world, or find any happiness in their own lives. Indeed, many of them will inevitably become inmates of prisons unless they get a vision of a better life and the belief that they themselves can achieve it.

But broader horizons are needed by youth who live in more fortunate social circumstances too. The very essence of the educational process, in all cultures and at all ages, is the development of aspirations and the courage to attain them. This effort will involve growth in areas of knowledge and skills. Whatever the subject under study, the teacher must seek to fulfil his role of sight-lifter for each individual.

> The adequate personality requires accurate, realistic information about himself and the world. . . . Effective behavior can begin only from reality. . . . As children become older and more sophisticated, learning continues with opportunities to explore more deeply the satisfactions of music and art, dance, sports, tools and models. A child may learn further about who he is as he reacts to the experiences of others as if they were his own. Vicarious learning, important in its meaning for the individual, occurs as boys and girls become personally involved with books and the many other media—television, recordings, films, and pictures—which portray people and events in other places and at other times. Interaction with peers; the opportunity to be with friends; time to talk through experiences, extend indirect learnings about self. . . . The boy or girl who depreciates his own ability, whose performance does not measure up to his capacity to learn, who so often is labelled the "underachiever," may need the evidence and the reassurance of new information about himself, information which says "he can." [9]

*In conclusion.* In this discussion of the various roles played by teachers, we have turned from popular but limited ideas of the teacher as purveyor of subject matter and enforcer of rules and standards to other, more fruitful concepts. We have emphasized that the teacher who uses subject matter as a tool for problem solving need not abdicate his professional responsibility. On the contrary, he turns to more exciting professional tasks, such as participant in planning, expediter and resource in problem solving, architect of social situations which challenge learning, and lifter of horizons for

[9] Association for Supervision and Curriculum Development, *Perceiving, Behaving, Becoming* (Washington, D.C.: The Association Yearbook, 1962), pp. 130–132. Reprinted by permission.

each individual in a class. At this point it may suffice to observe that problems of group control are minimal in classrooms where teachers succeed in building adequate incentives for learning.

Once more we must point out that each learner is different. This fact of life is what defeats teachers who:

1. Assume that the main task of the teacher is to package a certain predetermined amount and kind of content for delivery to the class.

2. Expect all members of the class to master this package in the same way and in the same period of time.

3. Reward or punish those who succeed or fail at this routine task.

The differences that exist (and increase) between individual learners contribute richness and challenge to the process of discovery, cooperative problem solving, and sharing of new ideas. It is the very fact of individual difference which makes group problem-attack possible, for without such differences a group would not exist or function. Discovery and sharing are premised on difference.

Good teaching is not easy. Taking account of individual differences is not easy. Accepting all learners is not easy. Lifting aspirations is a hard task. It would be so much easier if the teacher could content himself with the simple business of setting out subject matter to be mastered and then assessing the degree of its mastery by each member of a class. But such efforts, however easy, do not produce any learning in the basic sense of changed behavior. The effective teacher sets a higher goal for himself. Although he finds the role harder, he also finds it exciting, enriching, and challenging. He finds that he has actually had a hand in the most satisfying of all phenomena—the building of human lives.

In Chapter 6 we turn to another, related teaching role—that of helping boys and girls develop social controls.

## FOR FURTHER READING

Alexander, William M., and Samuel Ersoff, "Schools for Adolescents: Instructional Procedures," *Review of Educational Research*, 24:1 (February 1954), 54–65. Summary of findings of eighty-one research studies regarding teaching methods in secondary schools.

Cantor, Nathaniel, *The Teaching-Learning Process*. New York: Holt, Rinehart and Winston, Inc., 1953. Views of the teacher's role expressed by groups of teachers and interpreted by the author.

Faunce, Roland C., and Nelson L. Bossing, *Developing the Core Curriculum*, rev. ed. Englewood Cliffs, N.J.: Prentice-Hall, Inc., 1958. Chapter 9, "The Role of the Teacher," spells out roles sought by core teachers and suggests some intermediate steps along the way to these ideal roles.

Ojemann, Ralph H., *Personality Adjustment of Individual Children*. Washington, D.C.: The National Education Association, 1954. Several aspects of behavior are discussed with suggestions to the teacher for optimum success in guiding students in their learning. No. 5 in the series "What Research Says to the Teacher."

Rasey, Marie I., *This Is Teaching*. New York: Harper & Row, Publishers, 1950. The problem-centered seminar at the college level and its effects on the teacher's role.

Simpson, Ray H., *Improving Teaching-Learning Processes*. New York: David McKay Co., Inc., 1953. A good discussion of how the teacher's role shifts when problem-solving procedures are used in the classroom.

Spears, Harold, *Principles of Teaching*. Englewood Cliffs, N.J.: Prentice-Hall, Inc., 1951. Part III of this small book discusses the teaching process as teachers view it.

Stiles, Lindley J., "Methods of Teaching," in Walter S. Monroe, ed., *Encyclopedia of Educational Research,* rev. ed. New York: Macmillan Co., 1950. Reviews research under such categories as "teacher-centric, pupil-centric, and cooperative group" teaching.

———, and Mattie F. Dorsey, *Democratic Teaching in Secondary Schools*. Chicago: J. B. Lippincott Co., 1950. Part I contains a discussion of methods appropriate for developing skills of democratic citizenship.

Thelen, Herbert A., and Ralph W. Tyler, "Implications for Improving Instruction in the High School," in *Learning and Instruction*, Forty-ninth Yearbook, National Society for the Study of Education. Chicago: University of Chicago Press, 1950. Describes various phases of methodology appropriate for helping pupils pursue problem-solving activities.

Wiles, Kimball, *Teaching for Better Schools,* rev. ed. Englewood Cliffs, N.J.: Prentice-Hall, Inc., 1959. Chapter 15 discusses the process of becoming a "quality" teacher.

# 6  Maintaining classroom discipline

Good discipline is generally the product of a good learning situation in which the learners are too busy and interested to become behavior problems. References to discipline appear in many parts of this book. Why, then, a separate chapter about discipline? The fact is that the problem of maintaining classroom discipline is one of the most pervasive and pressing concerns of young teachers, and of teachers-to-be. Studies have revealed that prospective teachers worry more about the problems of control than about any other matter related to teaching. These fears often influence their behavior in such ways that they create their own disciplinary problems by revealing their insecurity. If they continue to dwell on the problem of classroom management, or are unsuccessful in achieving a normal kind of classroom morale, almost every other professional problem becomes pointless to them. There are some experienced teachers who continue to be frightened by the specter of anarchy. They seem to visualize the awful condition where their class is out of control, and this fear causes them to be more authoritarian than they would otherwise be.

## The meaning of discipline

The Oxford Universal Dictionary offers seven meanings for the noun "discipline": "(1) Instruction, teaching, learning; (2) a branch of instruction; (3) the training of scholars to proper conduct and action by instructing and exercising them in the same; (4) a trained condition; (5) the order maintained and observed among persons under control; (6) *Eccles.* the system by which order is maintained in a church; and (7) correction, chastisement." It is worthy of note that the most frequent interpretation of the word "discipline" among teachers is the last, and presumably the least, of the common dictionary meanings. The word has generally been subverted to mean "punishment," or at the very least, external controls. Yet the first meaning and the Latin word from which it is derived make "discipline" synonymous with learning. Since learning has earlier been defined as changed behavior, let us add that *discipline is the control of their own behavior by individuals, whether alone or in groups.*[1] This definition is in harmony with the classical meaning of the word and with the generally accepted principles of learning. It violates some common usage accepted by teachers, which will be examined as we proceed with this discussion.

Why has the very word "discipline" come to mean punishment? Why, in fact, are we so preoccupied with the subject of punishment, so fearful of youthful misbehavior? Some part of this is perennial and typical of all cultures in all ages. Socrates in 425 B.C. said: "Children now love luxury. They have bad manners, contempt for authority. They show disrespect for elders, and love chatter in place of exercise. Children are now tyrants, not the servants of their households." Throughout the ages, the elders have complained about youth. Most people love small children, but find it hard to express love for adolescents. As individuals, young people perplex and occasionally disgust their elders. In groups, young people may seem terrifying. And it is as group members that teachers see them most often. It is not surprising that we have become preoccupied with discipline as punishment or deterrent control.

Yet even the most fearful or authoritarian teacher would not argue that all adult citizens must be thus controlled or policed by someone in a position of authority. To enforce controls in this manner over some two hundred million Americans would call for

---

[1] Sheviakov and Redl have defined discipline as "the organization of one's impulses for the attainment of a goal." George V. Sheviakov and Fritz Redl, *Discipline for Today's Children and Youth,* rev. ed. (Washington, D.C.: The National Education Association, 1956), p. 4.

quite a police force! It is somehow assumed that self-control is learned on Commencement Night, after seventeen years of external controls.

The only functional kind of discipline in a democratic culture is self-discipline; and the only way in which self-discipline can be learned is by successful experiences in self-discipline. Thus we have defined discipline as "the control of one's own behavior."

## The criteria of good discipline

How can we recognize a classroom situation that is promoting good discipline, as we have defined it? Or one that is defeating or preventing such learning? Consider the following classroom situation:

*(Mrs. Jansen is commenting on the results of Friday's test in ninth grade mathematics.)*

*Teacher:* I think you should know that there were only two people in this class who heard the assignment on Thursday. These two people, Kenneth and Mary, had perfect papers. Four others had scores of sixty or over. The rest of you, twenty-four of you, didn't hear the homework assignment or else didn't care. You all failed a perfectly simple test you had all been warned on just what to prepare for.

The teacher selects two successful students, by name, and compares the class invidiously with them. Only two students seem to have "bought" the assignment. The rest of the class saw no reason to prepare for the test.

*Rennie:* Excuse me, Mrs. Jansen, but I didn't understand the assignment.

Some didn't follow the instructions.

*Louis:* I didn't have any time to prepare. Thursday night I had four hours of homework in English.

Some assigned other priorities.

*Jack:* Well, I guess I just didn't see any use in studying this stuff.

Still others didn't see any practical application of the assignment.

*Mrs. Jansen:* You mean you don't care whether you pass or not?

*Jack:* Oh I want to pass if I can—but what does it matter whether I know how to measure a room for papering or not?

*(Conversations have broken out all over the room. Mrs. Jansen picks up a ruler and bangs on her desk.)*

*Mrs. Jansen:* Quiet! When I want you to comment and criticize I'll ask you to. The next person that makes another crack will be sent to the office. In case you have forgotten, I am in charge of this class and I expect you to follow my assignments.

The teacher expects to play the role of sole leader in the situation.

*Mary:* Mrs. Jansen, in last year's math class four of us were tutors. This is not a crack, but couldn't we four help some others to get ready for tests?

At least one of the students offers to help the others.

*Mrs. Jansen:* What would you do that I can't do?

*Mary:* Oh I guess we couldn't do what you do, but some of us had these problems just last year and can remember what troubles we had and other students have.

*Mrs. Jansen:* I have no doubt you and some others I could name could help, as you call it, but I don't want any cheating on my exams in this class.

The teacher insists on being the only resource. She regards helping as immoral.

*Joan:* Who wants Mary's help?

*Mrs. Jansen:* What was that remark, Joan?

*Joan:* I said who wants Mary's help anyway? She always manages to get an A but that's because she does just what the teacher wants.

*(At this point the murmurs and chuckles in the class rise to a roar again, and a concerted clapping begins at the back of the room.)*

*Mrs. Jansen:* That's just about enough! Joan, you may go to the office, and see me after school today. The six people in the back row may come up to the front and take these vacant seats. If you people don't like offers of help from Mary and Kenneth we'll see how you take your next assignment from me. And whether you like it or not, I will not tolerate any further demonstrations or criticisms. I expect you to behave like young men and women. And that means accepting and performing your assignments without excuses and noisy clapping or conversation.

The teacher has started the class session by separating Mary and Kenneth from their peers, singling them out as her special pets. She now consolidates this barrier between individual students.

*Tony (to his neighbor, in a loud whisper):* A lot of help she ever gave me!

*Mrs. Jansen:* Tony, what did you say?

*Tony:* Nothing.

*Mrs. Jansen:* Don't tell me you said nothing! I heard part of what you said!

*Tony:* I said I don't expect to get any help from you.

*Mrs. Jansen:* Tony, you may go to the office immediately. When you get ready to apologize for that remark you may come back to class.

She also establishes the criteria for "good" behavior in the class.

The class does not exactly look upon the teacher as a resource or as a friend.

Perhaps we should leave this unhappy class to its future misery, which the teacher will fully share. She has laid the base for continued struggle against the group. She has committed herself to an unprofitable, but inevitable contest of wills. Her future class sessions are likely to consist of continuous scolding and resistance, punishment and rebellion, victories and defeats. All this seems to have little to do with any constructive teaching or learning.

What can we learn from Mrs. Jansen's mistakes? What criteria for effective discipline were demonstrated (in reverse) within ten minutes of this mathematics class?

1. *Effective discipline results when the students tend generally to accept the goals of instruction.* In some classes there is generally

good order, an atmosphere of "busyness," a dedication to some accepted purpose. Students are seldom ejected from such classes. The teacher does not find it necessary to engage in continual contests and quarrels. Most school administrators testify that a majority of those students "kicked" out of classes come from a few classrooms. What seem to be the common characteristics of these classes? They report that teachers who constantly have "discipline trouble" are the teachers who do not successfully motivate their students, who cannot seem to arouse in them any interest or purpose in performing their assignments. Perhaps the assignments in such classes remain the teacher's assignments and never become the students'.

2. *Effective discipline results when leadership for self-control develops in the members of the class.* As long as the sole person responsible for behavior is the teacher, discipline will remain ineffective. If the teacher controls with skill, poise, and a sense of humor, the class may proceed in orderly fashion but *without learning any of the basic skills of group control.* If, on the other hand, the teacher exerts his control capriciously, is emotionally unstable, inconsistent, partial or selective in his treatment of students, highhanded or domineering, the classroom may degenerate into alternating slavery and anarchy. The typical teacher does not represent either of these extremes each day, but if he undertakes to exercise exclusive control of discipline, he will on some unfortunate occasion violate some student's sense of dignity or right, and trouble will result. At his very best, the authoritarian teacher is depriving his students of their chance to develop self-control. Without this skill and habit, the individual is always dependent on external controls that our adult society cannot afford.

3. *Effective discipline results when class members depend on each other as important resources.* One does not readily cut himself off from those he needs. In groups where students are permitted, even expected to help each other in various projects, peer conflicts are usually at a minimum. Cooperation produces a climate of friendly interaction wherein individual differences are accepted, even treasured. On the other hand, fiercely competitive climates destroy interaction and cultivate dependence on external rewards and punishments. The successful students look to the teacher for approval and reward, and tend to view the unsuccessful with disdain or contempt. Teachers who equate cooperation with cheating are destroying an excellent resource for good classroom discipline.

4. *Effective discipline results when there is mutual acceptance among members of the class.* This criterion is closely related to the preceding one. When members of a class respect and accept their peers, they build a solid base for self- and group-control. They are willing to accept suggestions or criticism from those they respect. Real leadership can emerge from such a situation. But when the class is broken up into competing cliques, when it is disrupted by a continuing power struggle, even sensible suggestions "from the other side" are likely to be rejected or ridiculed because of their source. Teachers who pit students against other students are contributing, however unknowingly, to this power struggle between various groups in the class. It is peculiarly unfortunate when those selected for public favor by the teacher happen to be the very students who would be most able to give constructive leadership—if they were either left alone or helped to build good relationships with their classmates.

5. *Effective discipline results when the criteria for "good" behavior are accepted by the class.* In many classrooms students begin the year by sizing up each new teacher to discover what he expects in the way of acceptable behavior—or, negatively, how much they can get away with. Poor discipline results when students are confused by frequent shifts in the teacher's acceptance of various acts or remarks; or when the teacher's criteria are so inhuman or dictatorial that they tend to violate self-respect. Mediocre discipline can be observed in classes where the teacher's criteria for acceptable behavior are understood but only feebly or occasionally violated by some individuals. Really effective discipline, however, results from the establishment *by the class* of acceptable standards of conduct that make sense to them. Any subsequent evaluation of class discipline can be effective only when the members of the class accept the criteria. They are most likely to accept them, it seems clear, when they themselves have developed and adopted those criteria.

6. *Effective discipline results when the class members perceive the teacher, not basically as a controller of their behavior, but as a friend and resource for learning.* There is perhaps no more crucial criterion for class self-control than this matter of how students perceive the teacher. If they have always been conditioned to look upon class control as the teacher's business (and perhaps his main function), they are unlikely to be ready to assume this responsibility themselves. In spite of this reluctance, many classes are successfully

brought to the point where they are concerned about behavior of the group, aware of the criteria for good conduct, and able to enforce these without great difficulty. This achievement occurs quite readily in out-of-school groups where no adult is available to whom control can be surrendered. It also occurs in classrooms where teachers work systematically to establish their roles as friends and resource helpers. It never occurs in classes whose teachers continue to wield the sole control of behavior, and make it a matter of daily effort to retain this control.

## Classroom procedures that cause antisocial behavior

We have already identified certain criteria of good classroom discipline. These suggest, by reversal, some causes of poor behavior: failure of a class to accept the goals sought by the teacher; failure to develop any leadership in the class group itself; failure to use the resources of the class for mutual help; excessive competition, resulting in destruction of peer relationships; failure to develop acceptable standards of behavior with the aid of the class itself; and the students' perception of the teacher as assigner and policeman instead of friend and resource. Still other causes can be laid at the door of the teacher and his methods:

1. *Demands, standards, or expectations may be too high for students to meet.* When some students have a history of failure, they may not be able to make an effort. They may have already formed the habit of failure, and may see themselves as persons who cannot do school work, or at least that which is expected in this class. When the teacher's interpretation of higher standards consists of longer assignments, more difficult problems, and more punitive marking, there will be some students who will have little hope of success in class assignments. These individuals are likely to seek their success in other, less acceptable kinds of achievement in the classroom. They may become buffoons. They may become aggressive toward the teacher, or (more frequently) toward their classmates. They may bring comic books to class, or write notes behind the barricade of their open textbooks, or daydream in the effort to escape the demands of the teacher. They may go farther and become truants unless they can succeed at some assignment. If they must remain in school and meet what are to them unreasonable demands, they are quite likely to resort to copying and other forms of cheating.

There is evidence that this demanding attitude toward youth has become more prevalent and more insistent in recent years. The psychologist William Morse has stated:

> The Sputnik hangover in education has increased the discipline problem. Uniform pressure on pupils for academic involvement has further jeopardized the status of those who lack the capacity to accept such values. From the practice of "lifting" pupils whether or not they were ready for the tasks of the next class, we have over-reacted by failing more students when arbitrary standards are not met. Pupil hostility has increased. Unwittingly the schools themselves, by not recognizing these individual differences, have made discipline harder to maintain.[2]

2. *As a result of standard class assignments, some students may have too little or too unchallenging work.* It is an often overlooked fact that the common class assignment not only results in failure for some students, but also produces boredom in others. Boys and girls with high academic ability are usually able to finish such standard assignments long before the rest of the class, and look about them for something really interesting to do. Or they may be unchallenged by the rudimentary nature of the assignment, and either not bother to do it at all, or perform it in a superficial manner in a few minutes, and then amuse themselves by throwing up some road blocks in the path of the slower students who are not yet finished. Since the marking system is usually linked to the standardized assignment procedure, these "bright" students adopt the usual attitude that the mark is gauged to the amount and quality of the work, and they become experts at "earning" a mark with little effort. If a teacher assigns them extra work as a means of keeping them busy and out of mischief, it is perhaps natural for them to resent this as a penalty for their superior ability.

3. *Many students resent extreme authoritarianism on the part of a teacher.* Creative students are likely to develop cynical or hostile attitudes toward dictatorship. The teacher who tolerates no criticism or disagreement will encounter some able students who resent their passive, obedient roles and insist on raising issues or disagreement until they finally appear to the class in the role of rebels. There are

---

[2] William C. Morse, "School Discipline in the Next Decade," *Michigan Journal of Secondary Education,* 1:1 (Winter 1960), 5.

other students, less able or less articulate, who subconsciously resent tyranny and behave with aggression without precisely knowing why.

4. *Nearly all students react uneasily to anarchy.* Not often, but occasionally, teachers are observed who have confused democracy with *laissez-faire* government of the classroom, and who exercise little or no control over behavior. When the classroom climate degenerates into anarchy, everyone is unhappy. Since students themselves despair of rescuing such a lost situation and restoring order, they either remain silent and unhappy or join in the general disorder to maintain their status.

5. *Students generally resent inconsistency.* Much more common is the teacher who wavers back and forth from firmness to tolerance. Such a teacher may bang his fist on the desk, order people to be quiet, eject some students from the classroom, and generally act like an absolute monarch on one day; and the next day he may be all smiles and tolerate in the classroom the very behavior which he punished the previous day. This teacher is either unsure of his own philosophy, or too immature to react calmly to the inevitable challenges he must expect from some students. Young people are resilient enough to learn to adapt to almost any behavior that is consistent. When they don't know their limits (and have no chance to set up their own limits) they become uneasy and antagonistic.

6. *Teachers who overestimate the attention span of their students invite trouble.* In the junior high school, the span of attention is short. Boys and girls can pay close attention to any one presentation for brief periods of time. Their growing bodies demand activity. If the prevalent classroom procedure requires passive listening for too long a span, they will fidget, move their hands and feet, slump in tired fashion, shift in their seats, manufacture trips to the pencil sharpener, or get into physical hassles with their neighbors or with anyone who passes their seats. Not only is the teacher who disregards these signals inviting "discipline" trouble; he is also wasting everyone's time, for the students are not learning. In the senior high school the attention span is longer, but here also it can be easily overestimated. The experienced teacher has learned to vary his procedure and inject some activities that call for movement or change of pace.

7. *Students who do not understand the teacher often drift into misbehavior.* There are well-meaning teachers who use language that simply does not communicate to their students. There are a

few teachers who are so impersonal or preoccupied that their students never exactly feel that they are being spoken to. And there are, unfortunately, a few teachers who seem not to care whether students really hear them or not, who seem to be speaking for their own benefit. These teachers are inviting trouble. Students who do not or cannot hear instructions vainly ask for a repetition, or perhaps give up and find unacceptable ways to amuse themselves. At best, the teacher who does not communicate is asking for boredom and inactivity. These responses lead to misbehavior.

8. *Bad timing of classroom activities can produce poor discipline.* The class comes in from a lively songfest in music class or a basketball game in the gymnasium. They are just not ready to settle down. But the Latin teacher has a test for them or the English teacher wishes them to interpret Wordsworth's "Ode on Intimations of Immortality." A perceptive teacher is able to sense the mood of the group and has prepared some alternative activities that are more promising of success. A less able or experienced teacher may stubbornly buck the mood of the class and invite resistance, expressed by clowning, inattention, or outright hostility. Even a bit of humor or a brief change of pace may be all that is really required to settle the group.

9. *The classroom itself can be a factor in antisocial behavior.* Too many pupils huddled into a small room can scarcely move without bumping into someone else. (One bump deserves another.) Dark, dismal rooms are depressing. Noisy rooms are distracting. Plain, undecorated rooms are uninteresting. Overheated rooms produce lethargy. An able teacher may be able to overcome these physical conditions and manage to inspire a high level of learning. Nevertheless, there is little excuse for permitting these handicaps to persist when they are usually correctible. There are enough causes of disciplinary trouble without tolerating those that can be readily changed.

10. *The personality or mannerisms of the teacher may block rapport.* A high, squeaky or nasal voice, unusual or Bohemian dress, careless grooming or a dull preoccupation with self are handicaps to be overcome. A sense of humor is a great asset. The ability to laugh at oneself can offset many personality handicaps. High school youngsters can penetrate a false front readily; they resent a "phony" above all. Many a new teacher has taken a fall by trying to preserve his dignity or salvage his wounded pride. When decisions are made

to save face or to punish imaginary insults they are inevitably bad decisions. Any teacher who forms the habit of analyzing his own effectiveness is on the high road toward correcting personal mannerisms which block rapport with students.

## Some causes of misbehavior located outside the classroom

Many classroom management problems arise from conditions in the adolescent's life, which affect his attitudes in school or out. He cannot suddenly divorce himself from lifelong habits when he enters the classroom. If he has problems in his family or with his girl friend, he cannot file these away and then resume his worrying after class. If he has witnessed a family quarrel at the breakfast table, or been fired from his after-school job, or had a fight on the way to school, these incidents are quite likely to affect his attitudes in the classroom. If he has some worries about his own adequacy, his pimples, his height, the shape of his nose, or the length of his feet, his school work and his behavior in class may be affected by these worries.

The understanding teacher can do much to help young people live with their problems and even overcome them, if he first understands the nature of the problems and is patient in dealing with students. It is useless to say, as teachers often do, "nothing can be done about John; his problem is in his home and his family." Good teachers *can* help John by aiding him to acquire some understanding of himself and some hope for a better life. As pointed out in Chapter 2, adolescents are confronted by developmental tasks which they must accomplish in order to succeed—in school or out. When teachers understand which of these developmental tasks are involved in a particular behavior problem, they are on their way to giving some help and support. If, on the contrary, they assume the behavior is malicious and inexplicable, they may resort to punishment quite unrelated to the real cause of the symptom.

> The tenth grade English class was engaged in giving short oral reports on books they had been reading. When Mr. Jarvis called on Tim, the boy rather sullenly said "not prepared." Since this same response had been given by Tim on his previous book report, Mr. Jarvis was indignant.
> "And why are you not prepared?" he asked abruptly.

"Because I'm not, that's all," Tim replied with his eyes on his desk.

"Haven't you read your book?" persisted Mr. Jarvis, who was conscious that the whole class had become interested in this duel.

Tim shifted his feet, cracked his knuckles, finally looked up defiantly and said more loudly than necessary, "No! and I ain't goin' to!"

Mr. Jarvis felt his anger rising. "Well Tim," he said flatly, "I say you're going to *and* you can come in after school, *with your book* every night until you've finished it. I'll expect you here at 3:30 today."

"I won't be here!" snapped the boy defiantly.

"All right. You may go to the office right now, and see what the principal thinks about your attitude. Go on, the rest of us have work to do."

What caused Tim to refuse to report? There could have been dozens of causes, all of them interesting. The real reasons came out only gradually as the counselor patiently unraveled Tim's problems in the quiet of the office. The fact was that Tim had read the book chosen for his report, and had indeed been ready to report the previous day. He was really a shy, quiet boy who had never before defied any of his teachers. But before class that day a girl whom he secretly admired had teased him in front of another girl and two boys. Doris had started by asking him the name of the book he had read, and he told her it was Dickens' *Oliver Twist*. He was both surprised and embarrassed when she said:

"Yah, that figures. You're Jarvis's pet. He tried to get the whole class to read some book by Dickens and you're the only one he could scare into it. Tim's chicken, he reads Dickens, Tim's chicken, he reads Dickens." And the three listeners, giggling with appreciation, went on into the classroom, led by Tim's tormenter. What made the whole thing so devastating was Tim's secret admiration of the pert Doris. He had scarcely exchanged a word with her, but she was frequently present in his fantasies and he had often impressed her with brilliant (imaginary) conversations. Now he had obviously fallen in her estimation for some reason that escaped him. He had liked some parts of *Oliver Twist* but he saw now that he shouldn't have liked Dickens, and should have resisted Mr. Jarvis' suggestion. Still, he had no conscious intention to defy Mr. Jarvis or to refuse to report on the book. His own response to the teacher amazed and scared him, but it somehow exhilarated him, too. Once he had made the first refusal, he found no graceful way to back out of the situation. To his dismay, he found himself carried along by some uncontrollable impulse until he was playing an entirely unfamiliar role of resistance and defiance.

What could Mr. Jarvis have done in this situation? What advantage did he gain by making a public example out of Tim? It is perhaps too much to expect of Mr. Jarvis that he know immediately all the causes of any student's behavior in the classroom. It is more reasonable to suggest that he should understand that all behavior is caused, and that all behavior is logical to the behaver. He should have resolved to find out what Tim's problem was after class. There is seldom any benefit in public inquisition. Neither Tim nor the teacher can be expected to behave quite the same when they are playing to an audience. It is likely that Mr. Jarvis had more to gain than to lose by quietly ignoring Tim's first response and going on to another report. In doing so, however, he should not forget his own resolution to talk later with Tim and try to find out the cause of his failure to prepare.

Other causes are more obscure and often more serious than those in Tim's case. Conflicts with his father may drive a boy into quitting school in order to get a job and escape the home situation. Pressure by a mother for unrealistically high achievement may actually cause a girl or boy to resolve not to do well in school. Speech habits, including profanity and obscenity, may persist and find expression in the school setting. Parents who never finished school, or who had continual trouble in school themselves, may set an example for their children to follow.

Growing up is hard in the contemporary culture. The responsibilities that kept adolescents busy, and gave them a sense of participation in earlier, rural homes, no longer exist. There is no wood to be chopped, no path to be shoveled, no cow to be milked. Automated kitchens have simplified the preparation of food and dishwashing.

The acceptable age at which one marries and establishes his own home occurs several years after boys and girls are biologically ready for sex experiences. There is little help available to young people in understanding the strange, hard-to-control drives that come with adolescence. Giving this kind of help is still largely taboo in our society. The youth can neither understand nor handle gracefully his two conflicting urges to become independent of adults and to have a haven of love and security in time of trouble.

He is troubled also by the need to develop values that make sense. Here too are obvious conflicts between what he is told and what adults practice. The idealism characteristic of early adolescents may turn into cynicism in the later teens if no one gives them honest help in developing values.

The world of work is highly complex in our modern urban society. The perplexing problem of choosing a career at which one has a chance for success and happiness is always in the minds of youth, consciously or subconsciously. Whichever way they turn, they are confronted by choices which their parents and grandparents did not have, plus those which have always faced young people of every generation. The generally troubled international situation creates a climate of uncertainty for youth today. They respond, too, with resentment to the hostility with which the culture regards youth. There is actually no completely acceptable word for this period that comes between twelve and eighteen years of age. Most of the terms commonly used—"teen-agers"—"kids"—"adolescents"—have acquired a faint odor of opprobrium from the many criticisms of youth in our mass media of communication. All this has not escaped the attention of youth. It is part of the total person who comes to school. He brings not only his family with him as he enters, but also his whole pattern of experience, his neighborhood gang, his relationships with adults, his feelings about himself, his out-of-school interests and ambitions, his perplexities and his problems.

Thus the teacher is dealing every day with a whole complex of causes when he analyzes the behavior of his students. Fortunately, most of them learn to handle their problems without an undue amount of rebellion or trauma. Still, they are all affected in one way or another by their out-of-school life, with which it behooves the teacher to become acquainted. Some techniques for learning about the home and other out-of-school relationships will be presented in the next chapter as we discuss guidance methods. So far as discipline is concerned, the task of the teacher is to help his students develop such control of their own behavior that they can succeed in achieving their own goals. The help of community agencies such as the church and youth clubs will be useful in understanding the problem. The help of the parents is indispensable if a teacher is to proceed intelligently to help students.

First and foremost, however, the teacher must seek causes of behavior, listen patiently, try to convince young people that he can
really be helpful, and avoid snap judgments or acting without data.
A recent volume on school administration points out that the teacher's attitudes toward "offenses" defines poor behavior. "Normal
youth will whisper, giggle, move about, and be noisy—activities
which annoy some teachers but do not disturb others." [3] Most behavior problems can be solved if the teacher does not first aggravate
the symptom by making impatient or emotional responses, or by
trying at all costs to preserve the dignity of the teacher. Dignity that
takes great effort to preserve will be soon lost anyway.

## Questions often asked about classroom discipline

We have explored the causes of antisocial behavior, both in school
and out of school. Some miscellaneous questions are often asked
regarding specific situations or acts.

1. *Are noisy classes undisciplined?* This depends on the nature of
the activity going on and its appropriateness to learning. Many
teachers, and some principals, seem to regard a completely quiet
classroom as a well-disciplined one; it may instead be simply inert.
The quietest institution in any community is not the school but the
cemetery. There is not much going on in a cemetery—there isn't
supposed to be. But a school is a place where people behave (for
better or for worse), and where teachers seek to modify behavior in
constructive ways. If the activity of the class is work-centered, if it
is a group activity, if tools or musical instruments are needed, if
construction is called for, noise is not only necessary but an indication of production. A quiet factory is generally a closed factory.

If, on the other hand, quiet activities that require concentration
are the order of the day, noise is not appropriate. This criterion of
the requirement of the activity itself is one that usually makes sense
to students.

Experienced observers can readily detect the kind of noise that
does not stem from the activity, that in fact handicaps the activity.
This kind of noise usually means the class does not fully share the
teacher's goals.

---

[3] From Rudyard K. Bent and Lloyd E. McCann, *Administration of Secondary
Schools*, p. 233. Copyright 1960, McGraw-Hill Book Co., Inc. Used by permission.

2. *Can a teacher afford to be friendly with his students?* This issue has been debated fiercely and at length. It is usually assumed that a teacher loses his dignity by being friendly, or invites disorder by being so, or at least renders himself unable to enforce order. This depends on his motives and his status with students. If his motives stem from a sort of naked need to be liked, he may be giving such evidence of personal insecurity as to destroy the faith of students. If he seems to them to be a jolly sort of joker with no serious purposes, they will respond in kind and not pursue any serious purposes themselves—but they will give evidence of feeling uneasy about it. If the teacher alternates between being a buddy and a nervous tyrant, he will deepen their insecurity about what limits there are in the class. When they do not know the limits, they will be constantly trying to find them; and the base is laid for conflict.

But friends need not be helpless affection-seekers, or jolly jokers, or vacillators between acceptance and domination. Friends can be sincere, steady, consistent, and patient. Friends can be really interested in you, and your good friends are. Friends can have serious purposes of their own, and may even try to interest you in them; but they will not hate you if they fail. And older friends, adult friends, can be at one and the same time a rock on which to lean and a listening post. It seems that teachers who fear losing their status by being friendly did not have much status in the first place. Thus they haven't much to lose.

Adults should not seek to become peers of youth. A teacher who gossips and giggles with his students, or who tries to assume the status of a teen-ager in conversations, is simply not mature. The difference in age and status has not only the validity of being real, but it furnishes psychological support for adolescents. They need to be able to lean on adults at times, to draw strength from them. But this does not mean that the teacher must be unfriendly in order to remain a source of strength. On the contrary, he must develop rapport with students if he is to serve that function. He has the same obligation in this connection as a good parent—he should not (and cannot) cast off all his years and responsibilities in the effort to be a pal. But neither need he be aloof or hostile or objective. He should be able to understand the jargon of youth without adopting it as his own speech pattern. He should accept the individual without accepting all his behavior as good. He should be able to see a joke without becoming one himself.

3. *Should students ever be "kicked out" of class?* A weapon ever at the hand of the teacher is the threat to exclude students from the room. It is occasionally a dangerous weapon and should be used with discretion and for cause. In practice it is used far too often and has tended to create new problems instead of solving the original ones. High school administrators are often confronted with a line of sullen students in the outer office, sent there any given day from a few of the classrooms for offenses ranging from chewing gum to passing obscene pictures. Some assistant principals report that they spend nearly all their time dealing with the students excluded from a few classrooms, and thus never get time to work with the teachers who sent them out. This is a singularly unprofitable way to deal with discipline, since the students must generally be sent back into the same situation after a scolding or detention hour, and will probably be found back in the office a short time hence. We repeat, all behavior is caused and until someone has time and skill to delve into the causes and to help the student understand his own behavior, it will continue to be troublesome.

Being excluded from a class loses its point when teachers employ this weapon too frequently or for trivial misdemeanors. As a matter of fact, some youngsters are sent out of classes for quite unjustifiable reasons. Many an administrator is perplexed when he finds that the teacher was really at fault, but he must still appear to support the teacher against the student. The teacher may have misunderstood a remark, or wrongly assumed that it was directed at him, or taken umbrage over a series of events and finally "lowered the boom" on some astonished student for a relatively trivial offense. For veteran offenders, being sent out of an uninspired classroom may actually seem like a reward. Still, there are some situations when a teacher must exclude a student in order to give the class a chance to get on with its work, and provide himself an opportunity to work privately with the offender.

4. *Should individual counseling about behavior be carried on in private?* By all means. A teacher then gives himself a chance to learn the cause of a student's behavior without aggravating the situation further. The listening class furnishes an interested audience to which both student and teacher are playing. A student will go much farther than he might otherwise go, under the compulsion to show courage and impress the class. The teacher will often feel obliged to "make an example" of the offender when others are listening. This

is usually an unprofitable motive, but it is hard to be entirely free of this feeling when a class is watching your every move and enjoying the contest of wills. Neither teacher nor student will be at his best, or act naturally and sincerely, when an audience is present.

This need for privacy should not be used as a rationalization for sending students out of the room. Quiet conversation is possible at the student's seat while the class is at work. An increasing number of schools are providing conference rooms adjacent to the classroom, to which a teacher and student can retreat for conversation. In any case, it is usually possible to postpone the conversation until a free period or after school. This is worth some effort to arrange, for it promises much better results.

5. *Must not a teacher treat all offenders alike?* This notion that the punishment must always fit the crime has permeated the thinking of teachers for many years. It has done much harm. Since each individual is different, it naturally follows that his motives and his problems are different too. An inflexible rule for punishment can wreak havoc with some students who have briefly and accidentally slipped into error, and at the same time be completely unimpressive to the repeater. More important, if a teacher is to seek out and deal with the real causes of behavior, he must be prepared to act differently in each case. No matter how similar the act may appear to be, he will find the causes different for each individual. He cannot hope to deal with causes intelligently if he must fall back on standard prescriptions and punishments.[4]

But will not students resent the teacher's adapting punishments to causes? It is possible for a teacher to explain the differences in the ways he deals with similar acts if he takes students into his confidence. They can be helped to understand why a promise to do better is enough in one case, while in another a student's parents must come to school and confer about the correction of their child's behavior. They can come to realize that "objective" standards and rigid rules can be psychologically unfair. A public reprimand may produce tears in one student and mere disdain in another. Students are aware of such differences. They need only be brought to the realization that there may be several courses of action, all of them fair, but each of them different.

---

[4] An excellent summary of this point of view appears in Ruth Cunningham *et al.*, "Group Discipline," *NEA Journal,* 38:1 (January 1949), 34–35.

Pressure for standard rules and punishments is usually the symptom of a highly competitive classroom. In situations where students are not in ruthless competition with the rest of the class, the teacher is free to deal differently with individuals. He is not likely to be accused of being unfair when students understand that each individual has unique problems which must be dealt with if he is to be helped.

6. *Will my class ever reach the stage where it has solved all discipline problems?* By our definition, solution of discipline problems means that self-control has been achieved by all students in the class, so that the group can attain its goals. If we picture progress toward self-control as a continuum or as a road up a hill, it may be expected that a good teacher can eventually help a class reach a consistent "high" point. This usually means that they share the same goals, respect each other as resources, accept all members, and have assumed the obligation to enforce their own criteria for good behavior instead of looking to the teacher to play the enforcement role. Many classes fortunately reach this point, with the help of an insightful teacher.

But groups do retrogress. A class may slip a little down the continuum, on a given day. For any of many reasons, things may seem to be "coming unglued" some day. The teacher may have to move back into the role of judge and officer for awhile. A good teacher will not do this joyfully, for he knows that self-control is not learned without practice. As he takes the helm, so to speak, he will resolve to relinquish it again as soon as the group gets back to normal. The teacher will get much help in this from an experienced class as they try to evaluate what caused the controls to disintegrate. Such collapses of discipline will be few and far between if the students' purposes are involved, and if they have once experienced the satisfaction that comes from successful self-discipline. Such successes are contagious. A succession of them reinforces the ability of any group to re-establish order and leadership after a short period of retrogression.

7. *Are discipline problems an indication of need for the student to have psychiatric help?* Some few behavior problems are in this category, and the teacher must develop some skill in recognizing behavior that calls for specialized help. Wickman and others pointed out many years ago that mental hygienists approach behavior with a different sort of criteria than do teachers. In a classic comparison

study of the respective points of view of five hundred teachers and thirty professional mental hygienists regarding the "most serious" behavior problems of elementary pupils, Wickman found that these two groups of observers were looking for quite different kinds of behavior:

> The most striking difference between the teachers' and the mental hygienists' ratings is to be found in the comparative estimates of problems describing the withdrawing, recessive personality and behavior traits. Whereas teachers considered shyness, sensitiveness, unsociableness, fearfulness, dreaminess among the least serious of all problems, the mental hygienists ranked them together with unhappiness, depression, easy discouragement, resentfulness, cowardliness, suggestibility, and overcriticalness at the very top of the list as the most serious problems. These items in the mental hygienists' ratings completely replace the problems relating to sex, dishonesty, and disobedience which the teachers ranked as most serious.
>
> The items describing defiance to authority—impertinence, impudence, disobedience—which teachers considered very serious appear near the bottom of the mental hygienists' list.[5]

Teachers have become more sophisticated about the danger signs of mental illness since the date of the Wickman study. More recent studies show, however, that there is still room for improvement in teachers' attitudes toward behavior problems. Stouffer and Owens repeated the Wickman study, with some added refinements, in 1955. Their findings show that the problem child is still identified chiefly by annoying, disorderly, irresponsive, aggressive, untruthful, and disobedient behavior.[6]

8. *Is corporal punishment justified?* In earlier days corporal punishment was standard procedure. The birch rod or ruler was the indispensable tool of the teacher's trade. John Manning presented a terrifying summary of the sadism and stupidity of Nineteenth Century schoolmasters in an article in the December, 1959, issue of

---

[5] E. K. Wickman, *Teachers and Behavior Problems* (New York: Commonwealth Fund, 1938), p. 13.

[6] George A. W. Stouffer, Jr., and Jennie Owens, "Behavior Problems of Children as Identified by Today's Teachers and Compared with Those Reported by E. K. Wickman," *Journal of Educational Research*, 48:5 (1955), 321–331.

*Phi Delta Kappan.*[7] While most people now approve a more humanitarian means of punishment, there is still widespread support for corporal punishment among both parents and school people.[8] There is little evidence that striking, beating, or shaking students helps them to achieve valid educational goals. A good example of the point of view of mental hygienists toward physical punishment is one expressed by Redl and Wattenberg:

> The fact is that whippings, slappings, beltings, and paddlings can accomplish nothing that cannot be achieved better by some other method. The very conditions which physical punishment involves violate the known requisites for producing a psychologically justifiable result. Pain, whether produced quickly by a blow with a ruler or slowly by forcing a child to stand still in one place, invites anger, or panic, or bravado, which accomplish nothing. In addition, by using force, teachers set an example which preaches eloquently that deep down they believe might is right and that size or brawn mean more than logic or wisdom. Corporal punishment is a denial of everything an educator should stand for.[9]

*In conclusion.* One of the penalties of devoting a separate chapter to the subject of "maintaining classroom discipline" may be the creation of a distorted picture of typical classrooms. Fortunately, most teachers are not preoccupied every day with problems of student behavior. Standards and expectations do get established, and students generally adjust to them. Effective teachers make it their business to know their students, to analyze the relationships within the class, and to help students to gain increasing control of their behavior. As indicated in this chapter, effective discipline is most readily achieved in classrooms where:

1. students accept the goals of instruction,
2. they develop their own leadership for class control,
3. they depend on each other as resources for learning,

[7] John Manning, "Discipline in the Good Old Days," *Phi Delta Kappan*, 41:3 (December 1959), 94–99.

[8] See, for example, William W. Brickman, "Leadership, the Rod, and Education," *School and Society*, 81 (1955), 43–44.

[9] Fritz Redl and William W. Wattenberg, *Mental Hygiene in Teaching* (New York: Harcourt, Brace and World, Inc., 1951), p. 309. Reprinted by permission.

4. they accept each other,
5. they have an accepted code regarding constructive behavior,
6. they view the teacher basically as a friend and resource.

Effective teachers make it their business to know their students, to analyze relationships within the class, and to help students to gain increasing control over their own behavior.

The techniques required for gaining this professional knowledge, and for the broader application of such knowledge in guiding youth, will be discussed in the next chapter.

## FOR FURTHER READING

Alexander, William M., and Paul M. Halverson, *Effective Teaching in Secondary Schools*. New York: Holt, Rinehart and Winston, Inc., 1956. Chapter 6, "Classroom Discipline for Adolescents in a Democracy," is a good brief discussion of the close relationship between good discipline and good teaching.

Baruch, Dorothy, *New Ways in Discipline*. New York: McGraw-Hill Book Co., 1949. Contains much good advice regarding feelings of adults in their approach to discipline.

Grambs, Jean D., William J. Iverson, and Franklin K. Patterson, *Modern Methods in Secondary Education,* rev. ed., New York: Holt, Rinehart and Winston, Inc., 1958. See especially Chapters 12, 15, and 16 for basic treatment of individual and group "adjustment" problems.

Hymes, James L., Jr., *Behavior and Misbehavior—A Teacher's Guide to Action*. Englewood Cliffs, N.J.: Prentice-Hall, Inc., 1955. Much down-to-earth advice regarding what works and what does not work in improving child behavior.

Johnston, Edgar G., Mildred Peters, and William Evraiff, *The Role of the Teacher in Guidance*. Englewood Cliffs, N.J.: Prentice-Hall, Inc., 1959. Chapter 4, "The Teacher Takes a Closer Look at Some Children," discusses motivation of behavior of children and youth. Good examples drawn from the classroom.

Lane, Howard, and Mary Beauchamp, *Human Relations in Teaching*. Englewood Cliffs, N.J.: Prentice-Hall, Inc., 1955. Chapter 13 discusses in penetrating fashion "The Role of the Adult in the Child's Life." Many implications for discipline at the adolescent level.

Larson, Knute, and Melvin Karpas, *Effective Secondary School Discipline*. Englewood Cliffs, N.J.: Prentice-Hall, Inc., 1963. A description of an over-all program for improving discipline at the Cranston (Rhode Island) High School.

McKean, Robert C., *Principles and Methods in Secondary Education*. Columbus, Ohio: Charles E. Merrill Books, Inc., 1962. Chapter 9, "Classroom Control," deals with causation of behavior problems as analyzed by teachers.

*Michigan Journal of Secondary Education*, 1:1 (Winter 1960). The entire issue is devoted to various aspects of the discipline problem. See especially William Morse, "School Discipline in the Next Decade."

Nordberg, H. O., James M. Bradfield, and William C. Odell, *Secondary School Teaching*. New York: Macmillan Co., 1962. Chapter 10, "Discipline and Group Control," supplies guidelines for immediate problems and suggestions for long-range guidance.

*Phi Delta Kappan*, 41:3 (December 1959). The entire issue is devoted to discipline. See especially Manning, "Discipline in the Good Old Days."

Redl, Fritz, and William W. Wattenberg, *Mental Hygiene in Teaching*, 2nd ed. New York: Harcourt, Brace and World, Inc., 1959. Although this entire volume deals with discipline in a fundamental sense, Chapters 3 through 7 furnish a fine summary of the basic theory that should govern an approach to discipline.

Schulz, R. E., *Student Teaching in the Secondary Schools*. New York: Harcourt, Brace and World, Inc., 1959. Chapter 5, "Management of the Classroom," contains helpful advice about discipline, especially aimed at teachers-in-training.

Sheviakov, George V., and Fritz Redl, *Discipline for Today's Children and Youth*, rev. ed. Washington, D.C.: Association for Supervision and Curriculum Development, 1956. This pamphlet, originally published in 1944, has been found helpful by thousands of teachers. It gives advice that is psychologically sound and presented in highly readable language.

Stouffer, George A. W., Jr., and Jennie Owens, "Behavior Problems of Children as Identified by Today's Teachers and Compared with Those Reported by E. K. Wickman." *Journal of Educational Research*, 48:5 (1955), 321–331. Brings Wickman's study up to date by repeating it with a more recent sample of teachers.

Wickman, E. K., *Teachers and Behavior Problems*. New York: Commonwealth Fund, 1938. This study of some years ago is still a classic of its kind. Compares criteria of behavior as rated by teachers and mental hygienists.

# 7

# Guidance and the teacher

What is guidance? Much confusion exists regarding the program of guidance and counseling in secondary schools. Originally developed in an effort to help youth get jobs, the guidance movement acquired an aura of vocational selection and placement that still clings to it today, after nearly sixty years. References to "vocational guidance" and much of the discussion of guidance imply that its chief purpose is to help young people choose the right jobs and secure appropriate preparation for these jobs. The term "educational guidance" came to be applied to the latter goal, but was for some years linked to the vocational aspect. Still later, with the emergence of such goals as personal-social adjustment, civic training, and ethical and moral values, guidance was further subdivided into moral and social guidance.

## The modern concept of guidance

The development of the guidance movement has paralleled and reflected the broadening of educational goals referred to in Chapter 2 of this book. It has also reflected new concepts of the learning process discussed in Chapter 4. Most of all, efforts in guidance have been a response to the differences among individual learners, described in Chapter 3. As more and more youth have enrolled in secondary schools, it has become increasingly evident that the old curriculum did not adequately serve their varied needs. But changes in curriculum have always lagged behind changing needs. The guidance movement was born out of an effort to mitigate the worst effects of an inflexible curriculum, to fit students into more appropriate programs. In a sense, the modern guidance program grew out of the inadequacy of the schools.

Other influences have helped to shape the modern concept of guidance. The mental hygiene movement awakened both teachers and parents to the importance and complexity of emotional adjustment. Testing programs have entered the schools from industry and the military services, heightening awareness of the ways in which individuals differ. Tools for the guidance worker have been contributed by social work, industrial personnel services, research in psychology and child development. The realization that the learner attacks school or out-of-school problems as a total organism has helped teachers to move on from the narrow concept of vocational guidance toward a goal of assisting in total adjustment. One authority in the guidance field has defined it thus, in terms of its purpose:

> Viewing the life of the individual as a whole, guidance may be said to have as its purpose helping the individual to discover his needs, to assess his potentialities, gradually to develop life goals that are individually satisfying and socially desirable, to formulate plans of action in the service of these goals, and to proceed to their realization.[1]

Thus the concept of guidance has continued to become more comprehensive, until it now approximates the generally accepted concepts of education itself. The reader may have noted that the first six chapters of this book have emphasized the discovery and fulfillment of needs as a task basic to good education. The concept of learning set forth in Chapter 4 was based largely on the involvement of the learner in establishing and achieving socially desirable goals. In Chapters 5 and 6 the teacher is described as a friend of the learner who expedites both phases of this process: the development of goals

[1] From Arthur J. Jones, *Principles of Guidance,* 4th ed., pp. 77–78. Copyright 1951, McGraw-Hill Book Co., Inc., Used by permission.

and the achievement of them. More and more it has become evident that guidance as it is now conceived is simply a description of good teaching. On this point, Alexander and Halverson have contributed this statement:

> As we see it, teaching and guidance are not discrete functions. If teaching is conceived as direction of the traditional assign-study-recite-test type of activities, then identification of unique characteristics, interests, and abilities, and working with each individual in the light thereof may be rightly considered something separate and apart. But we do not so conceive of teaching, and instead believe that good teaching always involves understanding of individuals and working with them in the light of such understanding. Good teaching aims to help youth develop ways of thinking and behaving that will make them responsible, well-adjusted members of society. Guidance, even in the sense of specialized guidance services, aims at the same end. Hence we find it convenient to think of education as the process whereby individuals become increasingly able to solve their life problems; of teaching as the sum total of activities whereby teachers cause such education to take place; and of guidance as the way, contrasted to dictation, in which good teaching is carried on. Guidance, then, is really a description rather than just one procedure of good teaching.[2]

A recent yearbook of the Association for Supervision and Curriculum Development includes the following definition of guidance:

> With individual differences as our starting point, we view guidance as relating to all those things which adults do *consciously* to assist an individual child to live as fully and as effectively as he is able. . . . Guidance involves both helping the child adjust to a required pattern and adjusting the pattern to fit the child.[3]

Thus guidance is a term that simply represents the best teaching efforts. It describes teachers when they are really effective in:

2 William M. Alexander and Paul M. Halverson, *Effective Teaching in Secondary Schools* (New York: Holt, Rinehart and Winston, Inc., 1956), p. 320. Reprinted by permission.

3 Camilla M. Low, "Setting Our Sights," in *Guidance in the Curriculum,* Association for Supervision and Curriculum Development (Washington, D.C.: The Association Yearbook, 1955), p. 13. Reprinted by permission.

1. understanding the learner,
2. helping him understand himself,
3. helping him to establish goals for the good life, and
4. helping him to achieve those goals.

Another way of saying this was illustrated in Chapter 2, where the school was pictured as helping youth to achieve their developmental tasks and progress toward their own successful fulfillment. A school where no such efforts were made could hardly be called guidance-oriented. It would not be a very good school, either. Harold Alberty has stated this matter as follows:

> To the extent that the high school conceives its function as that of helping the adolescent meet his needs and solve his problems it organizes its curriculum for this purpose; and again the distinction between education and guidance tends to disappear.[4]

This statement, of course, applies just as emphatically to the junior high school. In secondary schools one must define teaching at its worst in order to distinguish it from guidance. If all teachers ignore their students' needs as they assign busy-work tasks they are scarcely playing a guidance role. If they impose authoritarian controls which prevent their students from ever learning the difficult skills of self-discipline, they are not effective guidance workers. In such a school, specialized counselors could not effectuate a guidance program either.

Yet there would be a kind of guidance going on, even in this situation. No matter whether teachers accept the title of guidance workers, they must function as such persons if they are with youth. A recent book on guidance includes the following significant reminder:

> . . . the teacher who wishes to be successful cannot overlook the backgrounds, needs, and problems of the pupils who make up his class. . . . Without consideration of these factors, teaching (i.e. the stimulation of learning) is bound to be ineffective. Even the most subject-matter-minded teacher must take them into account if he is to achieve his objectives. Whether he wishes or not, *every*

---

[4] Harold B. Alberty, *Reorganizing the High School Curriculum* (New York: Macmillan Co., 1953), p. 324. Reprinted by permission.

teacher is involved in guidance. His contribution may be negative. He may aggravate frustrations, weaken self-confidence, and make solution of the pupils' problems more difficult. His influence cannot be neutral.[5]

Thus the teacher is, for better or for worse, already a basic part of the guidance program. By the very way he operates each day he conveys to his students dreams of a better life or convictions that they can never attain it; he builds in them courage or fear, understanding or confusion, responsibility or resignation. When he helps them change their values or encourages them by a smile, he is exemplifying the ideals of the modern guidance program. A list of criteria for identifying teaching practices that promote effective guidance was included in a book on administration by one of the present authors:

> Teachers who use such techniques as the following are exemplifying good guidance methods in the regular classroom:
>
> 1. Studying the needs, interests, abilities, and problems of each individual in a class
> 2. Analyzing the relationships that exist between individuals and sub-groups in a class
> 3. Helping groups of students to discuss, analyze, and define problems of current interest that they need to solve for themselves
> 4. Guiding students in working on the solution of real-life problems
> 5. Deepening their insights and enriching their interest in the world about them
> 6. Helping students to evaluate their own growth
> 7. Guiding students in the techniques of group self-control
> 8. Giving students insight into their own behavior
> 9. Helping them to make increasingly wise choices among alternatives
> 10. Helping them to learn from their own mistakes
> 11. Helping them to respect themselves and others
> 12. Helping them to get along well with others.[6]

[5] Edgar G. Johnston, Mildred Peters, and William Evraiff, *The Role of the Teacher in Guidance* (Englewood Cliffs, N.J.: Prentice-Hall, Inc., © 1959), p. 5. Reprinted by permission.

[6] Roland C. Faunce, *Secondary School Administration* (New York: Harper & Row, Publishers, 1955), pp. 135–136. Reprinted by permission.

## The teacher as a counselor

It is commonly assumed that counselors are different functionaries from teachers—specially trained, higher salaried, and free from teaching duties. If any real counseling is going to be done, however, the classroom teacher must also become a counselor, preferably a skillful one.

Counseling has been defined by Carl Rogers as "a definitely structured permissive relationship which allows the client to gain an understanding of himself to a degree which enables him to take positive steps in the light of his new orientation." [7] A similar emphasis on the "nondirective" or permissive approach in counseling is found in Dugald Arbuckle's definition of it as "a process by means of which the counselee can come to understand himself so that he can solve his own problems." [8] Most definitions by modern authorities on counseling would agree with this central emphasis on self-understanding by the client, and on nondirective behavior on the part of the counselor. In a technical and specific sense, counseling refers to a one-to-one relationship or interview, as opposed to group guidance where more persons are involved. In a more common usage in the secondary schools, "counselor" and "counseling" have come to mean the whole guidance process, its direction and implementation. Our discussion of the "teacher-counselor" will include references to both concepts: the teacher in a one-to-one counseling role, and the teacher as a basic guidance worker, whether in the classroom or out of it. Since individual contacts frequently grow out of group situations, it seems useful to think of the "teacher-counselor" in all dimensions of the guidance task.

Can the teacher play this nondirective role which most authorities prescribe for good counseling? It appears to depend on what relationship he can build with his students. McDaniel and Shaftel define counseling as "a series of direct contacts with the individual aimed at offering him assistance in adjusting more effectively to himself and to his environment." They go on to warn that "this very broad definition places emphasis not so much upon the techniques em-

---

[7] Carl R. Rogers, *Counseling and Psychotherapy* (Boston: Houghton Mifflin Co., 1942), p. 18.

[8] Dugald S. Arbuckle, *Teacher Counseling* (Reading, Mass.: Addison-Wesley Publishing Co., Inc., 1950), p. 3.

ployed as upon the relationships which exist between counselor and client." [9] Translating this advice to the teacher-counselor, what kinds of relationships have been recommended as goals? In Chapter 5 the role of friend and counselor was emphasized as a constructive goal of good teachers. It was also pointed out that teachers can achieve this friendly relationship in classrooms where they have become resource helpers in problem solving instead of textbooks-in-the-flesh. In Chapter 6 the teacher's role in discipline was examined. Again, it was emphasized that teachers who strive to achieve self-discipline in their classes are able to free themselves from compulsive or punitive roles and become counselors instead of controllers of youth.

This same goal of good teaching is described in an excellent book titled *The Role of the Teacher in Guidance* by Johnston, Peters, and Evraiff:

> Students have to be able to perceive teachers in a certain light, and their perceptions are usually based on feeling tones. What the teacher says is probably not as significant as the attitudes he conveys. The teacher must be sensed as having genuine respect for the individual. He needs to be regarded as an accepting adult rather than a judgmental one. He has to be thought of as one who will understand the student. *Respect for the individual, acceptance, and understanding* are demonstrable to students not as techniques but by the way in which the teacher operates as a human being.[10]

But when can a busy teacher find time to talk with individual students? This depends, in part, on how available he makes himself. There are many opportunities for brief individual contacts every day. Good teachers see their students before school, after school, during the lunch period, in clubs and other student activities, at evening social affairs,[11] or just passing through the halls. Most secondary school teachers have a free period assigned each day for planning and counseling with students. In some schools this period is used by

9 Henry B. McDaniel and G. A. Shaftel, *Guidance in the Modern School* (New York: Holt, Rinehart and Winston, Inc., 1956), p. 120.

10 Johnston, Peters, and Evraiff, *Role of the Teacher in Guidance*, pp. 107–108. Reprinted by permission.

11 Further discussion of these contacts appears in Chapter 12.

teachers to relax in the lounge with their colleagues. There is surely nothing wrong with this practice unless it is carried to the extreme, when students can never find them or make appointments to talk about problems. Both kinds of activities can be scheduled by teachers who want to talk with their students as individuals.

Other opportunities grow out of classroom procedures. When individual work is going on, such as reading, writing, drawing, or constructing, the teacher can sit down for a quiet conversation with a student at his seat or in the conference room. In such a glassed-in space, a teacher can be physically separated from his class but visibly and functionally still with the class. At least two such conference rooms should be adjacent to each classroom. They offer many valuable contributions to good instruction, besides the provision of counseling space.

Teachers who use the device of small-group work at various times may find a further opportunity to talk with a student when help is not needed by the groups.

An illustration of a counseling interview, conducted by a teacher in the school cafeteria during lunch period, is reported by Johnston, Peters, and Evraiff:

> (The following interview took place in the cafeteria where I was on duty. The student seemed to approach me uneasily at first. As the conversation went on, I realized the boy had a definite problem and actually was seeking help and understanding. Thus this meeting certainly became an interview though not in a place conducive to a good interview situation.)
>
> *Student:* Hi, Mr. King.
>
> *Teacher:* Hello Jim, what's on your mind today?
>
> *Student:* Nothing much—I was just over there (pointing to a group of 8th grade girls seated at a table in the cafeteria. Most of the other kids had left the lunchroom). Boy! We really have some pretty sharp girls around here, haven't we? (Surprised by this remark from the student. Studious appearance—not the type usually interested in girls at this age and not the type the girls seem to go for. Sometimes we teachers don't know what our students are really interested in or concerned about.)
>
> *Teacher:* Yes, I would say that we have a lot of pretty girls.
>
> *Student:* That Jo Ann is the one I really go for.
>
> *Teacher:* You really like her, eh?
>
> *Student:* Ya, but she don't go for *me*. (Student looked down at feet while making this statement.)

*Teacher:* How do you know?

*Student:* She won't even talk to me. I say "Hi" to her and Sharon and they both say "Get out of here." (Long pause. Student was not looking at me. The long pause seemed more uncomfortable for me than for the student, but I felt he had something more he wanted to say.) She doesn't care if I live or die so what's the difference? (This last statement was full of emotion. I thought, "What a childish statement. He's not meeting the situation very realistically.")

*Teacher:* I don't believe she feels that way at all. (Teacher does not seem too understanding here of the student's problem or his feelings. In spite of this the student continues to reveal important feelings about himself.)

*Student:* Sure she does. She goes for Jack. You know him. I guess it's just me. (This seemed to be stated with the implication that Jack was not a good guy for her to know. Jack is 13, tall, strong, loud, an athlete, and very forward with the girls.)

*Teacher:* You feel you don't have a chance with Jo Ann?

*Student:* Nope, the sharp girls go for the big wheels around here. (Short pause.) What can you do about it? (Considerable pause.) (This question did not seem to be put to me but to the world at large.)

*Teacher:* Could you be using the wrong approach to these girls?

*Student:* I don't know. The other guys just stand around and whistle at them when they walk by. That's not the way to get a girl. Maybe I'm behind times, old-fashioned or something. You know—the guys stand outside of Barton's and whistle at the girls and say things to them especially in front of adults who are walking by. They call "Hi Grandma" to older women and "Pops" to the old men. I think sometimes girls have funny ideas about the guys they want to go out with.

*Teacher:* You mean you feel the girls tend to want to go out with the guys who aren't good?

*Student:* You don't know the number of girls we have who go out with bad guys at night in cars doing the wrong things. Your teen code didn't change that any. (This statement seemed to be made very challengingly.)

*Teacher:* Maybe these kids didn't have the proper guidance as they were growing up.

*Student:* Ya, take Jean. She didn't have any guidance. Only guidance she's had has been at school. Now she's teaching her younger sister all the things she learns in those cars at night. (At this point the student entered into a long account of the bad reputation his class has gotten as a result of the actions of kids like Jean.) Guidance is all right, but too much is junk! That's the way my Grandma is. Like when I stayed to watch Mr. Star fix his car the other night. I got home at 5 o'clock and she gave me a hard time. Since my mom works she thinks she's the boss around the house. She even tells my mother and dad what to do. (Considerable pause.) Everything was all right until my grandmother came to live with us. (Unfortunately, at this point the bell rang and I had to proceed to my next class. I felt that we were about to make some considerable progress. He asked if he might talk to me again, and I assured him that he could any time that I had free. We are to have lunch together this Friday.) [12]

This actual conversation was not offered as an example of the most skillful counseling techniques, but as an illustration of how much a teacher can learn when he listens. The base has been laid for giving this student some help through greater self-understanding. The teacher who really wants to help his students with their personal problems will create a time and place for further such talks. Out of these can come greater insight into attitudes and feelings that affect learning, and greater sensitivity and skill in helping students to learn.

*Studying the learner.* Both in his counseling role and in working with groups, the teacher-counselor collects much data about the individual. A recent book on the junior high school suggests the following list of types of data that may find their way into students' files:

1. Vital data: age, birthplace, home, number and sex of siblings, age and occupation of parents, educational level of parents, etc.

2. Health records: height, weight, history of disease, history of innoculations and vaccinations, dental conditions, eyes and ears, etc.

3. School record: Academic marks, achievement test scores, attendance and punctuality record.

4. Intelligence test scores.

5. Personal-social adjustment: to peers, to older persons, in home, school, community.

[12] Johnston, Peters, and Evraiff, *Role of the Teacher in Guidance*, pp. 109–111. Reprinted by permission.

6. Personal problems, fears.
7. Aptitude test results.
8. Personality test results.
9. Interests and hobbies.
10. Student activities: record of participation and leadership.
11. Vocational goals.
12. Employment record.
13. Image of self: personal goals, values, standards.
14. Anecdotal records.
15. Pupil- and parent-conference reports.
16. Record of participation in church and other community activities.
17. Samples of writing, art, etc., from various years.
18. Autobiography.
19. Insights about social or civic problems.
20. Special achievements.
21. Time budgets.[13]

To this list might well be added the vocational or college plans of senior high school students, data derived from sociograms depicting peer relationships, and recommendations of other teachers and specialized counselors regarding the student. All professionals who know the student will be contributing data to the file, as a means of developing a cumulative picture of past growth, present status, and possible future plans of each individual. The teacher-counselor must occasionally discard out-of-date or useless items. He will also be systematically contributing material to the file as a result of the developments in his class. For example, anecdotal records may be written as an outcome of observation of the student in significant classroom situations such as role-playing or small-group work.[14] The anecdote should be brief, succinct, and objective. It should describe what happened but exclude any judgments of the behavior. Trends in behavior, and probable causes can emerge from analysis of a series of skillfully written anecdotes.

Other kinds of materials emerge from work in the classroom. The student may reveal himself particularly well in a story or a poem he

---

[13] Roland C. Faunce and Morrel J. Clute, *Teaching and Learning in the Junior High School* (Belmont, Calif.: Wadsworth Publishing Co., Inc., 1961), pp. 224–225.
[14] Further discussion of these group techniques will appear in Chapter 8.

has written, or in his comments on something he has read. He may write short paragraphs analyzing himself and assessing his progress. He may respond in writing to such a question as "What would you do with three wishes?" Not only dreams but fears and problems have been revealed by this "wishing well" technique. Other projective writing assignments may result from viewing a picture or a film, or from incomplete sentences such as "The person I admire most is . . . ." Much can be learned about students from scripts they write for plays, reports of group projects, or evaluative logs. An example of such a log follows:

### WEEKLY CLASS LOG

Date _____

Class _____ Name _____

1. As I think about our work during the past week, it seems to me we have had some special successes and perhaps some failures:

2. I would like to see us make some changes in the way we are proceeding:

3. I have made some progress myself lately:

4. I could certainly use help on some things:

Further examples of evaluative techniques appear in Chapter 13, "Evaluating and Reporting Student Progress." These include self-appraisals, appraisals of others in the class, and assessment of progress in the class as a whole.

Other data that help us to understand students are letters to and from parents, statements about life plans, and questionnaires or inventories dealing with interests or hobbies, study habits, and job aspirations. Inventories have also been devised and used to learn more about radio, movie, and television interests and time spent in such activities; reading habits and interests; social activities; interest in current affairs; job preferences; behavior when confronted with a particular problem; sports interests; "people I like (or dislike)." An example of a simple, teacher-made inventory directed at just one activity follows:

## MY TELEVISION PREFERENCES

1. At home I get to choose TV programs (always) (often) (sometimes) (never). (Please circle proper word.)

2. When I have my choice, I tune in (Please check.)

|  | Always | Often | Sometimes | Never |
|---|---|---|---|---|
| Comedy | | | | |
| Newscasts | | | | |
| Romance stories | | | | |
| Adventure stories | | | | |
| Travel programs | | | | |
| Sportscasts | | | | |
| Educational features | | | | |
| Variety shows | | | | |
| Weathercasts | | | | |
| Pop music | | | | |
| Jazz programs | | | | |
| Record hops | | | | |
| Cartoons | | | | |
| Panels | | | | |
| Quiz shows | | | | |
| Feature movies | | | | |
| Westerns | | | | |
| Crime stories | | | | |
| Religious programs | | | | |
| Situation comedies | | | | |
| Historical programs | | | | |
| Style shows | | | | |
| Animal shows | | | | |

3. My three favorite shows, in this order, are
   a.
   b.
   c.

4. I watch TV about _____ hours each day, Monday through Friday. On week-ends I watch TV about _____ hours per day.

Many interest inventories are available from commercial sources. Examples are the Strong Vocational Interest Blanks,[15] the Bell Ad-

[15] Strong Vocational Interest Blank For Men (M) and for Women (W) (New York: The Psychological Corp.).

justment Inventory,[16] and the Kuder Preference Record.[17] In using these devices, or the "Agree-Disagree" type of attitude scale, teachers should remember that they are engaged in studying the individual learner. Average or mean scores from such inventories are likely to be meaningless. Even worse, the average response for a group tends to cover up the very information we are seeking—namely, what are the interests or attitudes of a particular individual.[18]

## The structure of the guidance plan

In the self-contained elementary school the study of individual learners is a reasonably manageable task for the "room" teacher. At most, he may have thirty-five or forty individuals on whom to collect data, but he usually has a whole year or even more with the same group. The departmentalized secondary school presents a different picture. The typical teacher in a senior high school has 150 to 200 different students each day. If he were to take seriously the challenge of learning "all" about each learner who confronts him in five or more classes per day, he would soon give up in despair. If he were lucky enough to have them in the same class for a full school year, he would probably learn their names and perhaps a little more identifying information about each student. He would also learn considerably more about a few of them; the ones who got into trouble for one reason or another, and the few who voluntarily sought him out after school. He could not reasonably be expected to study them all in depth, or to maintain and develop the cumulative file for them all as described thus far in this chapter.

*The homeroom plan.* The older class adviser system was devised, in part, to decentralize responsibilities relating to the guidance role and make the task more manageable. Unfortunately, as schools and classes grew larger there were just too many students for even the best class adviser to know well. In the late 1920's the homeroom plan was devised to provide more realistically for the guidance function.

---

[16] Bell Adjustment Inventory (New York: The Psychological Corp.).

[17] Kuder Preference Record (Chicago: Science Research Associates, Inc.).

[18] Chapter 13 will contain further discussion of tests and their uses, including intelligence tests, achievement tests, aptitude and personality adjustment scales.

The homeroom consisted of a section of 25 to 35 boys and girls, meeting extracurricularly for ten to sixty minutes daily for administrative and guidance purposes. Virtually all teachers had homerooms, since the entire student body was parceled out to the faculty in the same homeroom period. Early advocates had high hopes for the homeroom. H. C. McKown, for example, wrote in 1934 that "the homeroom creates a situation in which the pupil himself becomes the subject studied, worked with, and learned about. *He* and *his* activities, experiences, and interests compose the curriculum." [19] He thus justified the homeroom as the one place in the school where the students' own interests and concerns received attention.

For some years the homeroom plan seemed to flourish in both junior and senior high schools. In 1954 Lounsbury reported that 93 per cent of the 251 junior high schools included in his study had homerooms averaging 28 minutes in length.[20] Other studies indicate that the homeroom still persists in the junior high school, but has largely degenerated into an attendance-and-record room in those senior high schools which retain it. In spite of earlier hopes, the guidance function has not been notably effective in the homeroom.

One weakness in the homeroom plan is that it is added to the teacher's full teaching load. Thus, in addition to the 150 students he might confront in his classes each day, he now has thirty more in a homeroom. If these thirty do not happen to reappear in any of his classes, the teacher now has 180 different students. If he is to study test data, write anecdotal records, build up individual cumulative files, visit homes, confer with each student, and seek to understand him and counsel him effectively, his load must be reduced instead of increased. Where the homeroom plan has worked effectively as a guidance device, it has been a success because principals and teachers have worked vigorously together on the techniques of counseling and guidance, have had faith in the homeroom plan, and have resisted all efforts to reduce it to a routine administrative unit. This kind of effort is especially necessary as new teachers arrive who do not understand the purposes of the homeroom or accept its challenge.

---

[19] From Harry C. McKown, *Home Room Guidance,* p. 20. Copyright 1934, McGraw-Hill Book Co., Inc. Used by permission.

[20] John H. Lounsbury, "The Role and Status of the Junior High School" (Doctoral dissertation, George Peabody College, 1954), p. 134.

*The specialized counselor.* In the early 1940's the appointment of specialized counselors became popular in larger schools. These positions were generally filled by teachers who had been successful in dealing with students and who evinced some interest in the guidance techniques then becoming popular in industrial and military personnel work. Freed largely from teaching duties, these counselors were expected to receive advanced professional training and assume major responsibility in such areas as relaying occupational information; providing orientation to military service, jobs, and college; programming students; administering tests and interpreting test data to students and teachers. (They soon acquired other tasks in some schools—for example, dealing with discipline problems.) The movement spread to smaller schools and to nonurban schools, and today accredited high schools are expected to have trained counselors for every 250 to 300 students. Junior high schools, too, adopted the counselor plan but generally without adequate provision for manageable counselee loads. Goedeke's study in 1957 revealed that 54 per cent of the urban junior high schools had full-time counselors.[21] Smaller schools still appear to lag significantly in appointment of counselors, however. One study of 135 junior high schools in Michigan revealed that only 44 per cent of the schools enrolling less than 300 pupils had counselors, compared with about 70 per cent of the large junior high schools.[22]

There is evidence that the special counselors are better trained as well as more numerous than they were a generation ago. They more frequently see their task as one of leadership in developing guidance programs, to be implemented by the teaching staff. This means that they must perforce be interested in such matters as cooperative staff planning, in-service education, and the techniques of leadership. There is a real need for special counselors in every school, to provide for such tasks as:

> 1. Providing leadership in planning total-school guidance programs.
> 2. Providing leadership in in-service education of teacher-counselors in the various concepts and skills of the guidance role.

[21] M. Thomas Goedeke, "Operational and Supervisory Practices in Large City Guidance Programs" (Doctoral dissertation, George Washington University, 1957).
[22] Roland C. Faunce, "Administering the Junior High School," *Michigan Journal of Secondary Education,* 2:1 (Fall 1960), 36.

3. Helping the teacher to understand the behavior of individuals.

4. Helping to make information available about the requirements of colleges and the world of work.

5. Coordinating group and individualized classroom procedures.

6. Aiding in placement and follow-up.

7. Interpreting the guidance program and its goals to administrators and to the community.

It will be noted that most of these special counselor functions call for persons who can work with teachers rather than exclusively with students. The special counselors should be selected and trained with an eye to this major leadership function. Developing guidance programs really calls for changes in the attitudes and values of teacher-counselors. This is the complex and exciting responsibility faced by the special counselors. In meeting this challenge, they must do their best to build bridges between themselves and the teaching staff. This may call for special effort in an era when Federal assistance to specialized counselors, through the National Defense Education Act, has reinforced existing barriers separating counselors from teachers. They must demonstrate in every way the belief that teacher-counselors are the basic guidance workers. Like any other democratic leaders, they must earn their status by really being helpful to the teaching staff.

Above all, they must realize that they alone can do little about guidance. If they are in the most fortunate situation their counselee load may be as low as 250 students—too many for one worker to know or help. Even those students whom they do find time to meet and whom they may succeed in understanding must return to the very classroom milieu from which they were referred. Here they may encounter either further problems or help and understanding on the part of the teacher-counselor. Their success or failure will not be determined in the office of a special counselor, but back in the classroom, facing their problems and pursuing their goals. If they are lucky, they will return to a class staffed by a teacher who has developed such competencies as the following:

1. Understanding the growing, maturing child.

2. Understanding the forces in the community and the family that help mold the pupil's personality.

3. Understanding the influence of the peer group in shaping his attitudes and behavior as well as the part the learner plays in the interaction of himself with the matrix of his social environment.

4. Personal skill in the observation and analysis of pupil behavior in the milieu of these complex factors that enter into his growth and development as a person.

5. Ability to participate effectively in group processes, counseling pupil and parent.

6. Ability to define and solve school problems, which are regarded as basically a form of action research.[23]

The development of such competencies as these may be, and usually is, a tribute to the leader of an in-service education program for the staff. To this task the special counselor should address himself.

*The core program.* The core or block-time program originated and developed as one means of reducing the number of students for whom the teacher-counselor must be responsible. These classes employ a block of two or three periods daily, often obtained by a combination of English and social studies classes. In some schools science and mathematics are combined to form a block.

As originally conceived and developed during the 1930's, the core curriculum represented much more than a mere combination of subjects. Its approach to the secondary school curriculum was entirely different from the traditional (and still generally accepted) subject curriculum. It was expected that students and teacher in a core class would together plan their own curriculum through an attack on personal-social-economic-civic problems. They would use the materials and content from any and all appropriate subject fields as resources in problem solving. As a result of the longer time block usually assigned to core classes, time was also found for creative individual experiences, exploration of community resources, and guidance-oriented activities. The central purpose of the core curriculum was, however, the development, through problem-solving experiences, of the basic competencies needed by all citizens in a democratic society. As one authority put it:

[23] Adapted from Ira J. Gordon, *The Teacher as a Guidance Worker* (New York: Harper & Row, Publishers, 1956), pp. 10–12. By permission.

> The "core," then, as we are using the term, refers to that part of the curriculum which takes as its major job the development of personal and social responsibility and competency needed by all youth to serve the needs of a democratic society.[24]

Core programs flourished in both junior and senior high schools across the country during the 1930's and 1940's. Although curriculum authorities usually justified its extension in terms of integrating or unifying the curriculum around real problems of our culture, the main reason given by teachers and principals for adopting it was the advantage it offered for decentralizing guidance. The purpose assigned earlier to the homeroom was now advanced for the core program—i.e., the reduction of the number of different students for whom teachers must assume guidance responsibilities. One volume on the core curriculum summed up the purposes thus:

> . . . the core curriculum is designed to achieve better group and individual guidance, to help the pupil develop an all-important understanding of the democratic way of life, and develop skills in living democratically through experience, to give him an opportunity to assume some responsibility and choice in the learning process, and to provide a flexible time block in which a rich learning experience can take place.[25]

Although many senior high schools have experimented with core programs since 1930, it has remained substantially a junior high school development. Since the mid-1950's the number of senior high school programs has sharply diminished, largely as a result of the post-Sputnik emphasis on subject mastery. Meanwhile, the scheduling of the time block within which the core curriculum developed increased rapidly in junior high schools. Various surveys in the 1950's revealed that over half of the junior high schools were using the block-time schedule, usually obtained by a combination of English and social studies. Tompkins' study in 1955 found 57.3 per cent

---

24 J. Paul Leonard, *Developing the Secondary School Curriculum*, rev. ed. (New York: Holt, Rinehart and Winston, Inc., 1953), pp. 396–397. Reprinted by permission.

25 Roland C. Faunce and Nelson L. Bossing, *Developing the Core Curriculum*, rev. ed. (Englewood Cliffs, N.J.: Prentice-Hall, Inc., © 1958), p. 98. Reprinted by permission.

of junior high schools using block-time schedules, while 72.5 per cent of large junior high schools were so organized.[26]

The majority of these mushrooming block-time programs were in grades seven and eight. Perhaps a small minority of them were core programs as we have defined the term. Most were combinations of two subjects with a double period and one teacher. The overwhelming motive for adopting such scheduling was the belief, on the part of administrators and teachers, that it would facilitate guidance by reducing the total number of students for some teacher-counselors. The block-time teacher usually has only two or three sections instead of five. Some flexibility is needed in order to accommodate the curriculum to the needs of students. The block-time teacher enjoys some degree of such freedom. The curriculum itself tends to be organized around the problems and needs of the students, especially as the block-time class adopts some of the aspects of core. Finally, the in-service training of teachers for guidance is somewhat simplified. Unlike the earlier homeroom plan, one teacher can handle two or three sections of block-time classes, and this fact reduces also the total number of teacher-counselors on any particular school staff to be trained in the guidance role. Only teachers who are interested in developing competence in the guidance function may be selected for block-time teaching.

In some schools the block-time class remains with the same teacher for two or three years. The guidance role of the teacher-counselor is significantly enhanced by such continuity.

> He can learn a great deal about a group of youngsters in the longer period of time. He can relax a little and wait for some developments, that by their very nature, take time to manifest themselves. The group itself develops a family feeling and learns better how to interrelate, how to give its members support, how to use the resources of the group.[27]

The block-time teacher thus designated and trained as a teacher-counselor should be responsible for the cumulative record of each

[26] Ellsworth Tompkins, "The Daily Schedule in Junior High Schools," Report of the Committee on Junior High School Education, *Bulletin of the National Association of Secondary School Principals,* 40:220 (May 1956), 176–219.

[27] Faunce and Clute, *Teaching and Learning in the Junior High School,* pp. 223–224.

of his students. This file should, of course, be available to other teachers on request, as well as to special counselors and the principal. Copies of a few vital materials will be kept in a fireproof vault in the principal's office. It is important, however, that the personal file be in the custody of the teacher who will use it most often, and who will be responsible for its development. In schools employing the block-time schedule, this responsible person will be the block-time or core teacher.

*The sharing of information.* Other teachers who currently have students of the block-time group in their own classes will need to share as well as contribute information regarding their progress. Some schools have provided for this by grade-level staff meetings, preferably scheduled on school time. The special counselor often acts as chairman of such a grade-level group, whose function is to plan ways to improve the program of guidance (instruction) for the classes included in one grade level. They meet as often as once a week to perform such functions as the following:

1. Sharing information about pupils
2. Conducting case studies
3. Arriving at recommendations about guidance practices and specific suggestions for problem cases
4. Developing cumulative or developmental records
5. Learning to:
    write anecdotal records
    develop case studies
    make a sociogram
    use projective techniques
    conduct interviews with parents
    conduct counseling interviews
    use test results
6. Planning resource units
7. Developing new curriculum areas
8. Sharing results of experiments in teaching method
9. Planning contacts with parents
10. Evaluating the school's guidance efforts
11. Conducting such studies as:
    follow-up
    community surveys
    effects of curriculum change

out-of-school resources for guidance
trends in junior high school
trends in employment [28]

On occasion, the grade-level staff meeting may be expanded as other resources for guidance are drawn in. Case workers from the public welfare department, youth bureau, or juvenile court may be helpful on occasion. These sessions may assume the character of case studies if they are actually used for analysis of selected problem cases. Some schools are fortunate enough to have staff psychologists. Others have borrowed the services of psychiatrists on occasion. The visiting teacher and other personnel in special education may prove helpful as the group "gets down to cases."

*Teaching teams.* The grade-level staff will develop into a team for guidance and instruction as they continue to work together. In recent years there have been a considerable number of experiments in "team teaching" in both elementary and secondary schools. If the use of a staff team preserves and respects the continuity of relationship between a student and a teacher-counselor, it can enrich the guidance process. If, on the other hand, the purpose of team teaching is to herd students together into large groups for listening to lectures and TV programs, the plan can easily defeat the guidance program. Even in those situations where small seminars follow or accompany large-group instruction, the teacher-counselor needs continued contact with "his" groups if guidance relationships are to be developed and maintained. The guidance team we have been discussing does not resemble a hierarchy composed of master-teacher, ordinary teachers, and teaching aides. It is instead a partnership of equal colleagues who have come together to work on common problems. The key persons in the team are the teacher-counselors (who may be actually most of the members of the team in some schools). These teachers earn their status, not by their presentation skills, but by virtue of their counseling and guidance roles. To them should flow all the information and help available in or out of the school. Other teachers who have students for a single elective class may contribute valuable data about their progress. Some schools have developed forms for periodic reports by special-

28 *Ibid.,* p. 226.

class teachers to either core or homeroom teachers. Such forms might resemble the following one:

School_____ Date_____

Report on_____

To_____

From_____

    Class_____

1. This student has some special abilities:_____

_____

_____

2. I have discovered that he (she) is especially interested in_____

_____

_____

3. He (she) may have some problems on which help is needed:

_____

_____

4. He (she) has recently shown growth or achieved success in

_____

_____

5. His (her) mark at this point:_____

The teacher-counselor, whether homeroom or core teacher, will assume the responsibility for securing such reports at intervals from other teachers who have his students in their classes, school clubs, or other activities. As the reports are studied and added to the guidance files, a clearer picture develops of the problems, needs, and interests of each student. The teacher-counselor becomes progressively better equipped to talk intelligently with each student, and to conduct parent-teacher interviews regarding the student's progress. His increasing insight about the student also enables him to make suggestions to other teachers, and to plan various classroom experiences that promise to promote the student's growth.

*Guidance in the curriculum.* In Chapter 2 some analysis appeared of the "developmental tasks" approach to the study of needs of adolescents. These developmental tasks of adolescents may also be used as a set of criteria for evaluating the curriculum of a school.

For example, where, how, and to what extent are teachers helping young people to "select and prepare for an occupation"? Or to "desire and achieve socially responsible behavior"? What appears in the curriculum of the school relating directly to such goals? Which classes or which teaching units bear on the various developmental tasks?

Another curriculum approach designates these goals as "persistent life situations" and suggests a close look at the curriculum to discover what opportunities it offers learners for direct attack on such life situations. For example, "Working with Racial, Religious, and National Groups" is offered as a persistent life situation in our culture. The first goal contributing to growth in this area is suggested as "Understanding the Basic Characteristics and Purposes of a Group." Under this heading, it is proposed that an attack be made in some classrooms on

> *Extending ability to make accurate interpretations of existing attitudes toward other groups*—Considering evidence for classing all members of another group as having inferior or superior intellectual ability, as exhibiting common personality traits; finding how to detect propaganda for or against special groups; exploring special contributions of national groups—crafts, folklore, music, social or scientific advances; examining current news accounts referring to national characteristics of other countries; understanding in more depth similarities and points of difference in church services other than one's own; considering whether to abandon or to persuade parents to abandon customs that make one stand out as different.[29]

The implications of such approaches for individual and group guidance are immediately apparent. They represent a direct attack on real problems of our culture. The values by which youth live are the very subject for study.

The same statement might be made about the homeroom program referred to earlier in this chapter. As originally designed (and sometimes achieved), the homeroom gives students an opportunity to

[29] Florence B. Stratemeyer, Hamden L. Forkner, Margaret G. McKim, and A. Harry Passow, *Developing a Curriculum for Modern Living*, 2nd ed. (New York: Bureau of Publications, Teachers College, Columbia University, 1957), p. 263. Reprinted by permission.

read about, write about, and discuss such real problems of growing up as:

> boy and girl relationships
> family relationships
> opportunities in our school
> jobs and their requirements
> how can I assess myself?
> responsibilities of citizenship
> earning and saving money
> contributing to good school spirit
> making and keeping friends
> keeping healthy
> personal grooming
> how to study
> which college?
> our code for good behavior

The core program, with its freedom for planning and its longer time block, can go considerably beyond the homeroom in providing for guidance in the curriculum. Since it represents an attempt to organize learning around the real problems of youth in our culture, the core class can provide directly for a guidance-oriented curriculum. Consider the following list of units studied in various core classes:

1. Understanding myself and others
2. Getting along with people
3. Building better home and family life
4. Adjusting successfully to school
5. Getting and earning a living
6. Conserving natural resources
7. Building world peace
8. Understanding nuclear fission
9. Maintaining health
10. Analyzing propaganda
11. Learning to play
12. Taking my part in democratic government
13. Communicating with others
14. What can you believe?
15. Shall I go to college?
16. Knowing our community

17. Overcoming our prejudices
18. Knowing our Latin-American neighbors
19. Understanding Russia
20. Learning about the Far East
21. Buying insurance
22. Planning a home
23. Raising children
24. Understanding the American heritage
25. Understanding democracy and communism [30]

This list could be extended almost indefinitely as one examines the titles of units studied in core classes in schools across the country. The implications of such units for guidance are obvious. As students work together, they develop new insights about themselves and their culture, and they reveal themselves to each other and to the teacher-counselor. In block-time classes where there are some fixed areas of subject matter to be studied, there is less freedom to explore the current problems of youth. Yet even in such classes it is usually possible to inject the present tense—the "you-here-now" emphasis—through current events discussions and through occasional units injected into the curriculum.

Even in the strictly departmentalized school, it is possible for alert teachers to plan instruction in such ways as to create guidance-oriented writing and discussion. English teachers have learned much about students' problems and interests from their creative writing. They have also been able to use literature as a means of examining values and life goals. History teachers can help students understand and perhaps learn to live more effectively in today's troubled world. Mathematics teachers have guided their students toward becoming better consumers, and toward use of critical thinking in reference to nonmathematical problems of our culture. Science teachers have helped young people to seek evidence and to examine their own assumptions. All these goals may be guidance-oriented if teachers really want to understand and help youth.

Elective and specialized areas of the curriculum often bear directly on the guidance goals. In such courses as business education, industrial arts, home and family life, occupations, agriculture, personal-social problems, and consumer economics, young people are

---

[30] Faunce and Bossing, *Developing the Core Curriculum*, pp. 243–244. Reprinted by permission.

gaining increased understanding of themselves and of the require-ments of living. In many other courses teachers are contributing to better guidance as they use the traditional materials of the curricu-lum to help develop sound values, attitudes, and relationships. As pointed out earlier, guidance is a description of teaching at its best. Of course, the use of guidance-oriented content will not insure improved personal-social adjustment. It is possible for students to experience boredom or failure in courses labeled "family living" or "personal adjustment." The teacher must approach the class in a spirit of studying the learner, and adapting instruction to his prob-lems, interests, and needs. The teacher should remember the ques-tions of Elizabeth Brady as he undertakes each new class:

> Has he (the pupil) had a chance to learn what the school takes for granted—especially language, manners, ways of playing with others, obeying rules, concepts like "cooperation"? If not, what has he learned in these and related areas?
>
> What particular expectations and pressures has he had to meet thus far, particularly in his family and . . . group? To what spe-cial pressures has membership in a minority group subjected him?
>
> What values has he taken on? What does he consider success? What kind of self does he value? What does he expect of others?
>
> What concepts has he acquired about everyday realities—what a family is, or what a community is?
>
> What ways of expressing feelings has he developed? How does he feel about the things which happen to him?
>
> How has he learned to relate himself to others? What does he expect in his relations with others? [31]

Helping a student to discover his own needs, assess his own growth, and develop his own values and goals can thus become the objective of curriculum as well as of guidance, if teachers work toward such ends.

*In conclusion.* In this chapter we have examined a teaching role that might be described as teaching at its best. Guidance cannot be left to the specialized counselor, but must be built around classroom

---

[31] Elizabeth Hall Brady, "Children Bring Their Families to School," in *Foster-ing Mental Health in Our Schools*, Association for Supervision and Curriculum Development (Washington, D.C.: The Association Yearbook, 1950), pp. 27–28. Reprinted by permission.

teacher-counselors who accept and understand the learners, help them to understand themselves and others, and aid them in establishing and achieving constructive goals. Whether responsibility for guidance is assigned to homeroom or core teachers, or shared by grade-level teams, it must be assumed by teachers. Only thus can guidance be broadly implemented. This means that the total school must become guidance-oriented so that classroom procedures reflect guidance objectives.

In the chapters that follow we turn to the classroom to examine ways in which such objectives can be directly pursued.

## FOR FURTHER READING

Alberty, Harold B., and Elsie J. Alberty, *Reorganizing the High School Curriculum,* 3rd ed. New York: Macmillan Company, 1962. See especially pp. 377–387 for a cogent argument that a "sound program of guidance . . . is organically related to the curriculum."

Alexander, William M., and Paul M. Halverson, *Effective Teaching in Secondary Schools.* New York: Holt, Rinehart and Winston, Inc., 1956. Chapter 11 provides much practical help on "Studying the Characteristics of Individual Learners." Emphasizes the integral relationship of guidance and instruction.

Arbuckle, Dugald S., *Guidance and Counseling in the Classroom,* rev. ed. Boston: Allyn and Bacon, Inc., 1957. A good treatment of the basic identity between the teacher as a teacher and as a guidance worker.

Association for Supervision and Curriculum Development, *Guidance in the Curriculum.* Washington, D.C.: The Association Yearbook, 1955. Presents the point of view that guidance is teaching at its best. Good suggestions for relating guidance to the curriculum.

Cunningham, Ruth, *et al., Understanding Group Behavior of Boys and Girls.* New York: Bureau of Publications, Teachers College, Columbia University, 1951. Many examples from all school levels of ways of studying pupils in groups.

Faunce, Roland C., *Secondary School Administration.* New York: Harper & Row, Publishers, 1955. Chapter 7 discusses "The Guidance Program" as a way of improving instruction.

———, and Morrel J. Clute, *Teaching and Learning in the Junior High School.* Belmont, Calif.: Wadsworth Publishing Co., Inc., 1961. Chapter 9, "Guidance: Organization and Methods," suggests ways to use the block-time teacher as a teacher-counselor, and to share information among all teachers at given grade levels.

Gordon, Ira J., *The Teacher as a Guidance Worker.* New York: Harper & Row, Publishers, 1956. Good analysis of ways teachers must modify their traditional roles in order to perform effectively as guidance workers.

Grambs, Jean D., William J. Iverson, and Franklin K. Patterson, *Modern Methods in Secondary Education,* rev. ed. New York: Holt, Rinehart and Winston, Inc., 1958. Chapters 19, 20, and 21 discuss techniques of individual counseling, group guidance, and academic and vocational guidance. Emphasis on the teacher's role.

Johnston, Edgar G., Mildred Peters, and William Evraiff, *The Role of the Teacher in Guidance.* Englewood Cliffs, N.J.: Prentice-Hall, Inc., 1959. This entire volume places the teacher in a central position as regards the guidance function. See especially Chapters 5, 6, 7, and 8.

Kelley, Janet A., *Guidance and the Curriculum.* Englewood Cliffs, N.J.: Prentice-Hall, Inc., 1955. See Chapters 3, 4, 5, and 6 for illustrations of the guidance approach to curriculum and method.

McDaniel, Henry B., John E. Lallas, James A. Saum, and James L. Gilmore, *Readings in Guidance.* New York: Holt, Rinehart and Winston, Inc., 1959. See Chapter 6 for a useful discussion of observation of pupils, autobiographies, sociometric techniques, and cumulative records.

McKean, Robert C., *Principles and Methods in Secondary Education.* Columbus, Ohio: Charles E. Merrill Books, Inc., 1962. Chapter 11, "The Classroom Teacher and Guidance," spells out the implications of the guidance role for classroom teachers.

Peters, Herman J., and Gail F. Farwell, *Guidance, A Developmental Approach.* Chicago: Rand McNally & Co., 1959. Presents the guidance program as basically integral with good teaching. Many useful illustrations from the classroom.

Rasey, Marie I., and J. Wilmer Menge, *What We Learn from Children.* New York: Harper & Row, Publishers, 1955. Insights for the teacher-counselor, derived from a study of gifted children in a boarding school.

# 8 The classroom in action: learning in groups

Americans live in a social world. Perhaps more truly than ever before in the history of man, they find it necessary and inevitable to relate to other persons. Both work and play bring people together in groups of various kinds. It is no coincidence, therefore, that youth must confront such developmental tasks as "new relationships with age-mates of both sexes" and "desiring and achieving socially responsible behavior." The school which helps youth to live effectively in today's world must provide many opportunities for working with others in groups.

Unfortunately, many people are ineffective in this matter of group relationships. They find it difficult to engage in fruitful discussions, to persuade others and to be persuaded by them, to make choices and to arrive at consensus regarding a course of action. They play negative or unconstructive roles as members of a group. They shy away from assuming their share of responsibility as leaders, and find it easy to criticize those who do assume leadership. Most of these difficulties develop from attitudes and missing skills that might have been developed at an earlier age. Youth have a real need for group experiences in school.

In Chapter 4 we noted that group relationships affect learning. This is not only true of efforts to solve problems common to a group, but also of individual problems or processes. Students work-

170

ing in pairs or in small groups have made superior progress, for example, in writing paragraphs, solving algebra problems, and improving reading ability.[1] Thus even traditional goals of instruction may be hampered by the rather common insistence that students work alone. The skills of group work do not bloom by magic but must be learned. It is the schools' responsibility to provide opportunities for developing such skills. This requires both experience and critical analysis of one's successes and failures.

## The teaching of cooperative behavior

Students learn much from each other. When teachers encourage and facilitate peer relationships which bring about such mutual aid to learning, they promote the effectiveness of the whole learning process. They also make school more lifelike, more truly a real world where people plan together, work together, and play together.

Many teachers conduct their classes in such a way as to discourage group relationships. The traditional practices of assignment, recitation, and tests are based on a one-to-one relationship of student-to-teacher. The seating of the class often reflects this same polarization between any single student and the teacher. The students all face the front of the room, where the teacher takes his position. Questions and answers are directed at and received by one person. There is no interplay or circular discussion between the various members of the class. Help is not offered any student by another, nor is such helping considered honest or respectable. There are teachers who require their students to assert, at the end of an examination, that they have neither given nor received help on their papers. Talking to other students or sharing materials with them is sometimes considered a form of cheating. Such a view must be considered a strange anomaly in an interdependent society.

There is, of course, a legitimate function for some independent work. Tests of individual competence would not serve their purpose if they were actually written by teamwork. Creative arts often become unique, individual efforts. Other examples of individual work will be cited in the chapter which follows. There is much potentially valuable group effort linked to these individual projects,

---

[1] David H. Russell, *Children's Thinking* (Boston: Ginn and Co., 1956), pp. 266–267.

however, which teachers overlook or leave to out-of-school hours. Preparation for tests can be effectively done by groups. Plans for creative projects can be discussed, and their outcomes appreciated and evaluated by the class. Though much reading is silent and therefore independent, the appetite for literature can be stimulated and the standards of taste developed by class discussion.

Some teachers assume that one has only to number a class off into small groups and effective relationships will then automatically develop. They provide, in effect, only part of the needed program—namely the actual opportunity to relate to others. Beyond this, it is essential that students be helped to analyze their successes and failures, and reflect on how they can improve in such group efforts. Without critical reflection the situation may degenerate into anarchy. Alarmed by the resulting bedlam, the teacher may then shift abruptly to an even more rigid dictatorship than he had originally imposed. This frequent change from no control to strict authoritarianism confuses students, and makes them less capable of self-government.

Classroom democracy, like democracy anywhere, cannot be learned without being lived. Students must come to understand clearly what it is that they are experiencing, what demands or responsibilities it imposes on them, and how well they are playing their roles. Lack of skill in group planning may be due in large part to the fact that no one has ever systematically helped the students to develop such skills and to understand the process.

## Stages of group activity

The idea of group work is not new. Elementary and junior high school teachers have used the small-group device for many years, and for a variety of purposes. For several reasons its use is not as common in senior high school classrooms. Young people who seek to become high school teachers may not themselves have had much experience with group techniques in the classroom. The curriculum seems to them somewhat fixed and predetermined by state laws, by college entrance requirements, by skill levels demanded by future employers, or by tradition. There does not appear to be much opportunity for freedom to choose areas for study, or to plan ways to attack problems in the classroom. The extracurricular program is extensive, and teachers tend to assume that students will obtain their training in group planning through participating in after-school clubs, social organizations, and the student council.

It is sometimes assumed that group planning is useful only in core classes. If no core program exists in a high school, some teachers may conclude that there is no appropriate place in the classrooms for group planning or evaluation.

Perhaps we should look upon small-group activity as distributed along a continuum. The most limited or conventional activities would be placed at one end of this continuum, the most extensive activities at the other. One might move along this continuum with his students as they develop skill, self-confidence, and responsibility for effective planning of experiences. Consider, for example, the following range of planning experiences, which begins with the least ambitious activities and progresses from that point:

1. *Planning for an occasional special event*
   (A class party or trip to a play or film)
2. *Buzz groups for reacting*
   (Discussions in small, random-formed groups of a movie, panel, or special speaker)
3. *Studying ways to improve the classroom*
   (Committees for developing bulletin boards or hall exhibits)
4. *Choosing ways to present reports*
   (Grouping by topics drawn from the textbook, each group to report on "outside" investigations)
5. *Seeking and sharing resources*
   (Listing possible resources, exchanging books or other materials)
6. *Planning a program for parents*
   (Selecting highlights of a unit and arranging a program for a parent-night)
7. *Evaluating reports or programs*
   (In small groups, asking themselves how well the reports met preselected criteria)
8. *Choosing individual and group topics for study from prescribed unit in textbook*
   (Dividing up topics for individual investigation, then grouping by related topics for reporting)
9. *Evaluating behavior or group self-control*
   (Developing and applying standards of behavior)
10. *Planning for occasional supplementary programs or activities after "regular" work is done*

(Perhaps one period each week—club or current affairs program?)

11. *Choosing units for study from preselected themes or general areas*

("We must cover American history: what units should we include?")

12. *Choosing units for study that fit the criteria drawn up by the class*

(Freedom to plan not only content but process of study)

There may be some disagreement as to which activities are most difficult for the students to plan. Any teacher and any class could find some point on the continuum where successful (and fruitful) group experience is deemed possible. Classes that are really not ready for choice of problems for study may be able to choose methods of study and ways to report. Classes unready to evaluate their own behavior may be able to assess materials or debate public issues. And almost any class can fruitfully turn its attention to ways to improve the classroom. *Teachers usually minimize rather than exaggerate the readiness of students for group activity.*

*Getting acquainted.* In the preceding chapter many suggestions were made of methods for study of individuals by a teacher-counselor. In the same way, a teacher interested in group activity will study the class group and its subgroups. How do individuals relate to each other within the class? Who associates readily with whom when class dismisses? Who wants to sit with whom when such a choice presents itself? Do they make a different choice in terms of a different activity under way (for work in mathematics, or for planning a party)? What subgroups seem to control the class decisions? Which individuals are seldom chosen by anyone? Which are overtly rejected by most other class members? Which are almost always elected to any office? Which ones are so dependent on others' acceptance of them that they sulk or become hostile when they fail to gain such acceptance? Who is the class clown, and why does he behave this way? Who is always chosen librarian of the class? secretary or recorder? What cliques exist in the class, and how can these be absorbed in a common, class-planned activity?

As beginnings are made of small-group discussion and planning, certain other questions need to be answered by the teacher who systematically studies a class. For example, when the teacher leaves the room, do groups continue their work much as before, or do they disintegrate? (In short, how dependent are they on the teacher?) Is there evidence that all members share the goals of the group, or do some seem to be really in the wrong group? (And if so, have they actually changed their interests or was their initial choice made in terms of some extrinsic criterion such as friendship?) Do all members of a group exhibit respect for each other and remain friendly when they disagree? Do chairmen feel responsible to the group itself or to the teacher? Can the group carry on evaluation without name-calling or personal attack? Do they feel good about their group or would they be unlikely to choose it again? [2] These and many similar questions will help a teacher assess the readiness of a class group to move onward toward more meaningful planning.

A teacher cannot answer most of these questions without making at least a beginning at freedom to plan and work together in small groups. The sociogram may be useful even before that small beginning has been made. A bar graph or scattergram is used to plot individual answers to such a question as "Who are your three best friends in this class?" or "Who are three students with whom you would most like to work?" The responses reveal the most popular students, those seldom or never selected, and the social or friendship subgroups that exist in a class. It may also show the work groups that promise to have some cohesiveness. These are not always the same as the friendship groups.

Some teachers also use a negative-choice question, perhaps worded as follows: "If there are some members of the class with whom you would rather not work, who are they?" (Students may need to be reassured that it is normal for people to have such preferences.) These rejections offer some helpful further clues as to group relationships. The sociogram reveals some individual needs that must be dealt with in some way if a healthy group structure is to be achieved. An example of a sociogram plotted on graph paper is shown on page 176.

shown on page 176.

---

[2] Adapted from Roland C. Faunce and Morrel J. Clute, *Teaching and Learning in the Junior High School* (Belmont, Calif.: Wadsworth Publishing Co., Inc., 1961), pp. 187–188.

## SOCIOGRAM [3]

| | | 1 | 5 | 9 | 12 | 4 | 2 | 8 | 13 | 3 | 6 | 10 | 11 | 14 | 7 | 15 |
|---|---|---|---|---|---|---|---|---|---|---|---|---|---|---|---|---|
| Joe | 1 | | ⊕ | ⊕ | ⊕ | | | | | | | − | | | | |
| Tony | 5 | ⊕ | | ⊕ | ⊕ | | | | | | | − | | | | − |
| Herman | 9 | ⊕ | ⊕ | | ⊕ | − | | | | | | | − | | | |
| George | 12 | ⊕ | ⊕ | ⊕ | | | | | | | | − | | | | − |
| Sandra | 4 | | | | | | ⊕ | ⊕ | ⊕ | | | | | | | |
| Susie | 2 | − | | | + | ⊕ | | − | | | | | + | | | |
| Jane | 8 | | | | − | ⊕ | | | ⊕ | ⊕ | | − | | | | − |
| Ruth | 13 | | | | | ⊕ | | ⊕ | | | | | + | | | − |
| Mary | 3 | | | | + | | + | ⊕ | | | | | | | | |
| Jim | 6 | + | | − | + | | | | | | | ⊕ | | | | − |
| Peter | 10 | | | | + | | | | | | ⊕ | | | + | | |
| Mabel | 11 | | | | | + | | + | | | | | | ⊕ | | |
| Irene | 14 | | | | | + | + | | | | | | ⊕ | | | |
| Frank | 7 | | + | + | | | | | | | | | − | + | | |
| Bernice | 15 | + | | | | + | | + | | | | | | | | |

Symbols: ⊕ = Mutual choice, + = Choice, − = Reject

Choices or rejections recorded horizontally across the sociogram are those made by the individual; choices or rejections recorded vertically under the same number are those made by other students

3 Edgar G. Johnston, Mildred Peters and William Evariff, *The Role of the Teacher in Guidance* (Englewood Cliffs, N.J.: Prentice-Hall, Inc., © 1959), p. 166. Reprinted by permission.

regarding that individual. Bernice (number 15), rejected by five class members (Tony, George, Jane, Ruth, and Jim), is chosen by no one but expresses her own choice of Joe, Sandra, and Jane. Frank (number 7), is not rejected by anyone, nor is he chosen; he is an isolate at this point. Two well-defined cliques appear, one of four boys and one of five girls, which show patterns of mutual choice. Jim and Peter form a mutually chosen pair, which fact is fortunate for Peter (number 10), who has five rejections. A similar pair is composed of Mabel and Irene.

A teacher can discover relationships and needs from study of a sociogram. He may then plan ways to counsel members of the class and to structure subgroups in such ways as to help rejects become acceptable to the class, to bring isolates into a group, and to make constructive use of cliques in the work of the class—organizing committees and workgroups, and planning seating arrangements.[4] Such efforts to improve the quality of social relationships can pay rich dividends in learning. Youth who are isolated or rejected by their peers are handicapped, not only for effective learning but also for a good life. In addition to the sociogram, the "wishing well" test and the autobiographical theme referred to in Chapter 7 are useful techniques to employ in the study of group relationships.

Besides getting to know the class, a teacher interested in group relationship seeks to help class members also to know each other. A class may consist of representatives of various feeder schools who are nearly all strangers to each other. In later grades it is more common to find several who do know each other casually and a few who are intimate friends. Yet in the same class there are likely to be a few who know no one as yet. Introductions may be in order at the outset. One procedure is to set aside ten minutes to converse in pairs, then ask each student to introduce his partner and tell the most interesting things he has learned about him. Some classes play a game called "Guess who" in which a series of identifying details are told to the class without naming the subject. The class finally guesses the name. (This game may be played repeatedly as the year progresses.)

---

[4] Further discussion of the sociogram may be found in many books. See, for example, Ruth Cunningham et al., Understanding the Group Behavior of Boys and Girls (New York: Bureau of Publications, Teachers College, Columbia University, 1951), pp. 154–171.

To get beyond the mere knowledge of names, however, calls for play and work together in an informal setting. The class may plan a party, or a bowling or movie night. Working on various committees needed for planning such social functions will bring students into closer and more friendly contact. A buddy system may help the class remember such personal matters as birthdays, and keep track of people who are sick.

In the beginning it may be appropriate to place name-tags on the desk in front of each student. This will soon become unnecessary if socializing efforts are at all successful. A week-end in camp will carry a class group farther and faster than any other device for getting acquainted. When a camp experience seems impossible, the class may meet for a party in someone's recreation room or in the classroom or cafeteria. In fair weather a picnic is also a possibility.

The purposes of such a social affair are at least twofold: to reduce interpersonal barriers in order to facilitate *later* group planning, and to provide a function (in this case a social function), for which planning is *now* required. Social events are good for these purposes because the penalty for initial failure is not severe, and high interest tends to increase participation. It seems clear that the teacher should not, in his enthusiasm, assume this planning role himself. To do so would defeat his own purpose of introducing the class to the group planning process. Besides this fact, the class members can usually plan a better party themselves than can the teacher.

In these and other tentative beginnings of group planning the teacher is trying to build enthusiasm and confidence in the feelings of class members for the planning process. He does this by selecting an area where (1) success is likely, (2) interest is high, (3) failure will not be costly, and (4) the project is a brief one. As he watches the class plan and carry out a social function he asks himself some questions:

1. Which students are really pushing the plan?
2. Which students are going along "for the ride"?
3. Are they choosing leaders wisely?
4. Are they distributing responsibilities among all members?
5. Is there evidence of high interest?
6. Are they setting standards or criteria for success? (Will they know why they succeeded or failed when they analyze it?)

*Extending planning to the classroom.* Earlier in this chapter we listed several stages of group planning. Besides the planning of social functions, a number of classroom functions also lend themselves to student participation and small-group work by a class relatively unaccustomed to such responsibilities. These procedures should really involve students in discussion and ultimately in meaningful choices, on however limited a scale. In short, the task should not be a phony one.

Improvement of the classroom setting itself can be highly meaningful to students, but they should have real decisions to make in contrast to merely carrying out the teacher's ideas. If youngsters take turns erasing and washing chalkboards it should be because they volunteered to perform this service, perceiving a need—not to fill in as custodians at the teacher's request. As students look critically at their classroom, they may profitably ask themselves how it could be made more habitable. Some improvements must await action by the administration or the board of education. Others can be achieved by group action, almost immediately. Housekeeping duties are familiar tasks to students in laboratory classes. In shops, homemaking rooms, and science laboratories it is the established custom for students to organize for a final clean-up each day. Though such responsibilities have value, they generally lack the ingredient of group assessment of a situation, followed by planning and action to improve the room. Besides the common or routine tasks of arranging furniture after it has been moved, washing chalkboards, and picking up paper, students have planned and carried out many different improvements in their own room:

> developing bulletin board exhibits
> developing three-dimensional exhibits in corridor cases
> building a herbarium
> building and stocking an aquarium
> providing plants at windows
> landscaping yard outside classroom
> refinishing desks
> providing draperies
> providing blinds to darken classroom
> painting walls
> building dividers for storage of maps, etc.
> securing and hanging pictures on wall

The important point about all these cooperative efforts is not the actual improvement, however pleasant and useful that may be. The real purpose of the activity should be the improvement in skills of group planning and action. The teacher must assess the outcome carefully, not in terms of the physical product, but rather the leadership that has emerged, the quality of thinking that went on, and the various roles played by individuals during the project.

Miss Larsen left the principal's office in a somewhat melancholy mood. For the third time in as many years she had just been told that a collection of books for her English classroom was not in the budget. She was acutely aware that there were students in her classes who could not profit from the anthology used as a textbook. If only there were some way to secure two or three hundred books of various levels of difficulty and interest, she believed she might help individuals to form the reading habit.

During the period which followed, an opportunity presented itself to share her frustration with her American literature class. Sue Dolmich had reported on a short story by Hemingway, and closed her report by holding up a paperback copy of *The Old Man and the Sea.*

"I saw this at the drug store and just finished it last night," she said. "It is just wonderful, I think." Two other students held up paperbacks and started to talk enthusiastically almost in unison but about two different books.

"Wait a minute," Miss Larson interrupted them, "we can hear you better one at a time. John, what is your book?"

As he spoke, an idea dawned on Miss Larsen.

"How many of you have books of your own?" she asked as John sat down. About fifteen students raised their hands.

"If we had some good paperbacks right here in our room, would you be interested in trying some of them?" she asked. Several students said "Oh, yes." Others nodded.

"Well," Miss Larsen said slowly, "the school cannot afford to provide them, but I have about twenty good books that are bound in paper and in fair condition. I'll bring them tomorrow if we can figure out a place for them."

"Anyone can borrow my copy of *The Old Man and the Sea,*" said Sue. "In fact, I'll *give* it to Miss Larsen and she can loan it to anyone that wants it."

"How many of you have really good books you are through with and would like to contribute?" asked Miss Larsen. Hands went up, some with two or three fingers signaling.

"I count about thirty more books," Miss Larsen said, "but where can we put them in the room? And how can we be sure they are worth while for our classroom collection?"

Mae spoke firmly: "Oh you should be the judge of that, Miss Larsen. There are an awful lot of just terrible paperbacks at the drug store."

"We could take up a collection and buy a bookcase," suggested Frank.

"I have a better idea," offered Gerald. "At home we have two boards resting on glass bricks, and it works OK. That would be a lot cheaper."

"Shall we ask Gerald and Frank to look into the cost of the boards and bricks?" Miss Larsen inquired. "How many of you favor that idea?"

There was general agreement. And that was how the reading corner in Room 127 was first conceived. A candy sale provided funds for two attractive cedar planks and four glass bricks. The students worked out a different arrangement of their chairs to free some space at the rear of the room. A planning committee was elected to select or discard contributions, with Miss Larsen as "Chief Censor." The students went on a house-to-house canvass of the whole school area, asking housewives for books they no longer had any use for. Almost a thousand books were collected from this drive; about three hundred of them were judged suitable for the collection. Over half of these were in hard covers, and most of them in good condition. Later on the student library aides were induced to rebind about fifty books that were worn out. More planks and bricks had to be added as the collection stretched across the entire back of the room. All books were listed and carded, and card envelopes pasted in the back. As a triumphant climax to the project, a set of wicker furniture was contributed by one of the parents. Rules for the use of the library were developed by the class.

When they evaluated their efforts at the end of a month, all agreed that "Project Paperback" was a great success.

*Selecting goals.* Some teachers think of goals as already fixed for students by traditional requirements or by the textbook. It is true that considerable variation may be found in the extent of freedom for student selection of goals. In situations where students are invited for the first time to set up their goals for a class, they will often reflect the most traditional expectations and come up with a list such as this, for an English class:

> to learn rules of grammar
> to write correctly
> to speak correctly
> to understand literature
> to learn how to spell
> to turn in neat papers
> to take notes
> to diagram sentences

Such a class can be helped, however, to enlarge their views of what values can accrue from the study of English. One twelfth grade class came up with another kind of statement of goals:

> to learn how to get a job
> to express my thoughts so others will listen
> to make and keep friends
> to appreciate good books, movies, TV, radio shows
> to enlarge my vocabulary
> to write creatively
> to recognize propaganda
> to learn self-control
> to improve our class newspaper
> to know what employers and colleges demand in English skills

A seventh grade class called Unified Studies developed this list of class goals:

> to get good marks
> to pass to eighth grade
> to make friends and be a good sport
> to get along with the teacher
> to learn to work cooperatively
> to improve in writing down our thoughts
> to learn to speak better before a group
> to improve in reading aloud
> to learn to understand what we read
> to learn about the problems other people have all over the world
> to improve personal habits and appearance
> to learn to use the library
> to learn about our school and be active
> to study hard and really learn
> to improve our grammar
> to keep the room looking nice

to obey all rules and behave ourselves
to think before we speak and act
to improve in penmanship[5]

Such a list of goals can be used in many ways. The task of formulating it can contribute insight and skill in self-appraisal. If the list is kept before the class, on a bulletin board or in mimeographed form, it can serve as a frame of reference for oral evaluation and for individual self-appraisal. It is a useful beginning for a counseling interview. It can be helpful also when a class is trying to choose between various activities.

In elective classes where the subject matter is new to the students, some orientation will be needed before they are ready to formulate class goals. This may include talks by the teacher and by visitors from business or professional fields, films or film strips, and extensive class discussion. A list of goals may later be modified by a class as they acquire new insights or revise their values.

*Selecting a problem.* As a teacher undertakes to launch the process of problem solving, his specific approach will again be conditioned by the amount of freedom the class enjoys to select areas or problems for study. Many common fears about this matter of restrictions are either imaginary or self-imposed. Teachers often *assume* controls that do not exist. There may be no enforceable restrictions on the areas for study by a given class; teachers should look into this matter and not rest the objection on their first assumptions. In any case, they usually have more freedom than they assume.

Still, there are schools in which, at a given time, certain departmental agreements have been reached which at least restrict the choice of problems for study to selected areas. Thus the word "problem" tends to be defined in more than one way:

1. *Problem:* a topic in the textbook, restated as a question to be studied
2. *Problem:* a broadly stated question which careful study of an entire chapter of the textbook may help answer
3. *Problem:* an application of a principle in science or mathematics, already worked out in the textbook and ready for assignment to the class

[5] Louise Parrish and Yvonne Waskin, *Teacher-Pupil Planning* (New York: Harper & Row, Publishers, 1958), p. 31. Reprinted by permission.

4. *Problem:* a question developed by the class within the context of some broad theme already assigned to the class

5. *Problem:* a question on which the class seeks answers after some analysis of a social, civic, political, economic, or humanistic issue

6. *Problem:* a question arising from some difficulties in the students' relationships in or out of school

Although some aspects of the problem-solving procedure can be employed when the problems are already "given," this kind of "problem" does not lend itself to group choice. Unless there are *alternatives* to be considered, for example a choice of one out of two or more problems, students will lose most of the value that comes from group planning. On this score we may rule out the items numbered 1, 2, and 3 in the above sequence of definitions.

In any case, these types of problems are more likely to be real to writer and teacher than to the students. Unless the problems selected for study are real to students, they will not devote themselves to continued study or engage their own energies in pursuing the activity. As pointed out in Chapter 4, a problem must be a real one to the learner if he is to profit from it in the sense of gaining increased skill in problem solving. This condition is not an impossible one to achieve; items 4, 5, and 6 lend themselves to a real problem-solving process, by offering alternatives for choice.

When a class approaches the choice of a problem, some criteria are needed. These, too, must be group-developed if the resulting choice is to affect the group. Without any explicit criteria the choice tends to become a haphazard one, much influenced by the interests of a few leaders in the class. The need for establishing criteria can be readily explained to a class. Rosalind Zapf reports the use of the following introduction by a teacher of a ninth grade class:

> Since we are ready to suggest problems to investigate, we need to decide how we are going to know whether or not the problems that are suggested are worth taking time to work on. When you go into a store to buy a coat, you consider a number of things before you buy it. You may say to yourself, "Is this the kind of coat I need? Is it warm enough? Is it well made? Do I like it? Is it the right color? Is it different from my last one? Can I afford it?" If the answers to these questions are satisfactory, you are likely to buy the coat, but if not you do not buy it.

Such questions are called *criteria*. They are standards by which we decide whether to buy or not buy. For our choice of problems for study, we need standards or criteria, also; otherwise we may select a topic which will have little or no value for us. What are some of the things you think we ought to consider in choosing a problem?"[6]

This ninth grade class was free of any predetermined limitations such as those imposed by a textbook or course of study. With minor adaptations, however, this same introduction could be made to reflect a general area within which choices of problems are to be made. For example, a history teacher who felt obliged to "cover" the text might say:

As you all know, our subject for the year is world history. This is a big field to cover and I suppose you won't all remember the same things when we get through. It is a very interesting process, though, to discover what happened "yesterday" and long ago, and it helps us to understand today's problems. Perhaps you might like to select some special problem we have today for special study, looking into its history for some light on how it became a problem, or perhaps a discovery or invention. For example, there is the house you live in. What kind of house did your grandfather live in? Or his grandfather? Or the first man? And what factors brought about changes in housing? In other words, how do we happen to have the kinds of houses we now live in, and why did man once live in caves or in mud huts or in log cabins? This is just an example. Our world is full of interesting things that have gone through similar changes since the beginning of recorded history.

Now, if you wanted to choose such a problem or topic for special study, how would you go about it? What would you use as criteria or standards for your choice of a topic?

One class developed a set of criteria for selecting a problem which finally took the following form:

### CRITERIA FOR SELECTING A TOPIC

1. It should be one that will be of value to us now and/or later. This means:

---

[6] Rosalind Zapf, *Democratic Processes in the Secondary Classroom* (Englewood Cliffs, N.J.: Prentice-Hall, Inc., © 1959), pp. 163–164. Reprinted by permission.

a. it should help us to understand the world in which we live, or
b. it should help us to understand ourselves, or
c. it should help us to understand adult life and its problems, or
d. it should help us to understand the connection between life in the past, our present life, and life in the future.

2. It should be something we really want to know about.
3. It should be something we haven't studied before. . . .
4. It should be broad enough so that many may work on it, but not so broad that it cannot be completed.
5. It should be one for which materials are available.
6. It should be one that will help us achieve our goals.[7]

The teacher has some criteria, too, for what problems the class should be working on. He will neither withhold his suggestions nor impose them when they obviously appear unacceptable to the class. He will, in such cases, hold his ideas in reserve until an appropriate time develops to suggest them again. (It is easier to be patient when one has the same class for at least a full school year.)

Teachers have no monopoly on the "right" problems for study. In some cases, teachers have been so conditioned by their own training that they try to impose ideas on the class. It would be better not to launch the problem-solving process in the first place than attempt later on to steer it back into the course of study. One teacher lumped all the students' suggestions into one problem: "What are the social, economic, and political forces that have shaped democracy?" This might be a good theme for a four-year course in college, but leaves something to be desired as a problem for short-term study in a high school class. It is highly probable that the more specific problems proposed by the students were better problems for them to attack.

Teachers get impatient with the narrow or limited problems sometimes proposed by youngsters. Even after the application of criteria, such problems as the following may seem inadequate or trivial to a teacher:

Winter sports: What can they do for us?
How do you get to be a deep-sea diver?

7 *Ibid.*, p. 165. Reprinted by permission.

Should eighth grade girls wear cosmetics?
What is the moon like?
Why study history?

Teachers who are depressed over the triviality of such questions should remember two facts: (1) One must begin with students' interests and concerns, and then help them to broaden and deepen these concerns by study; and (2) the *process* of problem solving is vastly more important than the specific subject matter learned. With time, skill, and enthusiasm, a good teacher can help a class build a very respectable course of study from somewhat humble beginnings.

Some classes may be unable to achieve consensus on a single problem for study. At least two courses of action are possible: (1) to adopt a broad problem area and break it down into specific problems for each of which there are takers; (2) to permit free choice of problems which meet the criteria, and not seek any common link between groups except a common time span for pursuing their various problems. Both methods have been successfully used by experienced teachers. The separate-problem plan may be more appropriate for younger students and for less structured subjects such as art, occupations, or core classes.

*Organizing the groups.* At least a minimum kind of organization will be needed by each group. A chairman and a recorder are necessary, and perhaps also a librarian to take charge of materials. Each group should be given help in developing a plan of work, which will guide its attack on its problem. The elements in such a plan of work are suggested by the following form used by a high school social studies teacher:

### GROUP PLAN OF WORK

Statement of group problem:

_____

_____

Questions we want to answer:

_____

_____

Which member(s) will be responsible for which questions?

_____

_____

What resources do we now plan to use?

_____

_____

What help will we need from outside our group?

_____

_____

Approximate date for reporting to the class:

_____

Plans regarding format of our report:

_____

_____

*Finding resources.* The nature of the specific problem will suggest the type and scope of resources needed. There are the teacher, the other class members, the room library, the school library. There are books, pamphlets, articles, newspaper clippings, pictures, graphs and tables, films, film strips, recordings, tapes, and TV programs. In the community are libraries, museums, youth agencies, fire and police departments, banks, hospitals, stores, factories, offices, and many adult citizens with special contributions to make. There are state and national agencies from whom help may be requested, as well as international organizations. There are chambers of commerce and foreign consulates. There are natural resources and urban projects and government planning agencies. A rich reservoir of resources awaits the lively work-group in search of answers.[8]

*Sharing and reporting.* According to agreement, the various groups will be scheduled to share their findings (and sometimes their recommendations) with the class on a scheduled date. The groups may need much help in preparing an interesting report. They must remember that no one in the class is quite as interested in their topic as they are, since the others chose a different one. A variety

8 More extensive treatment of resources for learning appears in Chapter 10.

of techniques for lively reporting may be used. According to the nature of the content, it may be appropriate to use a panel, debate, symposium, or outside speaker. Drama of some kind may be helpful. Radio and TV techniques sometimes contribute interest. Pictures, exhibits, film strips, glass slides or transparencies may be appropriate. The opaque and overhead projectors are useful tools. A written report, duplicated for the class, may help in various ways:

1. As a discussion guide, or
2. As a supplement to oral reports, or
3. As the basic report, releasing the oral report for commentary or dramatic highlights.

*Evaluating group efforts.* Throughout the group planning and research, the teacher will have been helping the groups evaluate their efforts. They will respond at a rather early stage to such questions as:

What task has each member of the group assumed?

How can the plan of work be made more specific, or more complete?

How much time should the group allow for sharing research results and planning the report?

As the groups proceed with their work, they may ask themselves some further questions:

What unexpected difficulties are we having?

What help do we need?

How could we make better use of our time?

As the teacher observes the various groups in action, he will ask himself some other questions about their procedures and behavior:

1. Are most of them interested in what the group is doing? or, Is their project still one member's idea?
2. Do they start work promptly? or, Does the chairman or teacher finally have to call them to order?
3. Do they have a systematic plan? or, Can't they remember what they had agreed to do next?
4. Do all members take part? or, Are there idlers or subgroups for conversation?

   5. Do they listen to each other? or,
      Do they compete for attention?
   6. Do they assume some responsibilities between meetings? **or,**
      Are they jealous of infringement on "their own time"?
   7. Do they act as one group? or,
      Are they split into cliques? 9

The teacher will find ways to translate such questions as these into inquiries for the groups to handle as they assess their progress. Weekly logs or evaluations in brief form may be requested from each member of a group and written in response to such items as:

For me, the high points of our group work this past week have been:

Our low point as a group was reached when:

I myself made some contributions to the group:

I could improve as a member of my group by:

Summaries of these individual logs can be duplicated for class or small-group use in their regular periods of evaluation. Thus individuals will be assessing their own progress in writing, work-groups will spend some time each week in oral evaluation of their progress, and some general class discussions will be devoted to the over-all progress of the entire class. At the end of a unit, such questions as the following might guide the class in its evaluation:

In what ways have we benefited from this unit of study?
What have we learned about the subject that we didn't know before?
In what ways will this new understanding be useful to us?
What does this new knowledge mean to us?
What skills have we developed or improved?
What have I learned about myself?
To what extent am I satisfied with my accomplishment? 10

As indicated in an earlier chapter, activity without critical analysis may be aimless. It is important that each student understand as clearly as possible just what has occurred and what effect it has had

---

9 Faunce and Clute, *Teaching and Learning in the Junior High School,* p. 180.
10 *Ibid.,* p. 170.

on him. There needs to be constant assessment by the student if the experience is expected actually to modify his own future behavior. He must be involved in a continuous search for meanings, relationships, and applications.

Not all the outcomes of a learning experience will be immediately apparent. Some results may appear months or years afterward. This realization should not deter teachers from developing a solid basis for self-assessment in the classroom, for without criteria or goals no effective later assessment can be made.

Some self-assessment efforts have failed because the goals were too narrow or limited to permit success by all members of a class. If the apparent goals of a class are concerned with learning facts about the Peloponnesian Wars, some students may be forced to pretend, to cheat, to put up a good front, or to abandon hope and just drift. None of these alternatives offers a good basis for self-evaluation. Students cannot afford to engage in self-assessment unless they can see themselves as successful in terms of some of the goals of the class. This in turn implies that those goals will be broad and varied enough to permit some success by each student.

There will be some failures, of course. Even these can be helpful if they are analyzed by the class with a view to correcting faults and avoiding these particular failures next time. Successful experiences that are never analyzed do not help students particularly to develop decisions or resolutions to the point of how to repeat them. The *feeling of success* is of great importance, since it builds courage for further effort in group work; but experiences must be evaluated if students are to hope for clear understanding of that which success requires. The importance of the evaluation process cannot be overemphasized.

When students understand what is happening in a class, and its values for their learning, parents are likely to understand also. This may be especially important when the classroom procedure does not closely resemble that which parents recall having experienced when they were in school. This is another excellent reason for effective evaluation. The student who understands and can defend what goes on in school is our best public relations agent. This point will be more thoroughly developed in Chapter 14.

*Development of roles of group membership.* When learning is problem-centered, a concept of leadership emerges. The leader is no longer thought of as the student who most readily conforms to adult demands or who has the best memory for facts. In problem-solving activities the leadership tends to become situational, in the sense that it shifts from one member to another in terms of what the situation demands. Thus it is not confined to the few students whom teachers sometimes think of as "natural" leaders. It is not the product of hereditary traits or social prestige, but of function. If the problem-solving process is effective, it will provide a wide variety of functions, thus enabling most of the members to find an area in which they can exercise leadership. The leader role tends to be disseminated throughout the group as students increasingly assume responsibility for their own learning.

Alexander and Halverson have suggested the following roles for this "leader-member," who will hopefully be every member of a group on one occasion or another:

> —he gives facts and opinions
> —he seeks facts and opinions
> —he clarifies and summarizes discussion
> —he tends to human relationships [11]

Other constructive roles will appear as groups continue their work. While each member will assume some responsibility for the group's problem and work on it between meetings, the tasks may be differentiated in terms of skills, contacts, and interests of each member. One may be more gifted than the others in drawing or construction activities. Another may have some creative ideas about interpretation through music or drama. Another may have useful contacts in the community.

There should be an official group record; the task of the secretary is one demanding orderly, systematic, and responsible recording of what has occurred and what plans have been made. Other members may develop skill in referring to the record, checking the plan of work, and in general helping the group recall just where it is and where it is going.

There are group members who have more ideas than the others. This gift of ideas will be more generally the property of all members

[11] William M. Alexander and Paul M. Halverson, *Effective Teaching in Secondary Schools* (New York: Holt, Rinehart and Winston, Inc., 1956), adapted from headings, pp. 192–195. By permission.

if the goals of a class are broad. Students should be encouraged to propose their ideas, even if subsequent reflection causes the group to postpone or lay the suggestion aside.

When disagreement develops, it is helpful for a group to have at least one harmonizer-analyst, who seeks the basic elements of agreement in opposite positions and suggests compromise.

A valuable role in any group is the "bringer-in" who exhibits concern that all members contribute and participate. If he is effective he can appeal to individuals to enter the discussion or assume some special responsibility without giving offense.

The constructive humorist can release a group from tension by injecting a witty remark that produces a general laugh without hurting anyone's feelings. This role calls for skill and self-restraint, since it can turn a group from its goals when it is used too often or unwisely.

There are negative or nonconstructive roles also, which can be avoided as group members become more mature and more competent in self-evaluation. There is the class clown, who may be motivated to divert the group from its purpose by a variety of personal needs: to cover embarrassment, to relieve boredom, or to secure group acceptance.

There is the earnest helpless student who is always appealing to authority, asking what the teacher wants, or trying to settle an issue by citing opinions of an authority.

There is the dominator, who gives no one else an opportunity to talk and can tolerate no disagreement. There is the persistent debater or hairsplitter who seems to care less about facts or truth than about winning an argument—on either side! There is the aggressive or angry member who resorts to name-calling as a substitute for reasoning. There is the negative member who is constitutionally opposed to anyone's ideas but has no suggestions of his own to make. And there is the "goof-off," who has lost interest in the group's problems and takes no part in its work. He may also try to interfere with it by irrelevant comments or by being noisy or mischievous.

All these, and perhaps some other negative roles will appear in groups at some time or other. Some of them can be resolved only by persistent counseling by the teacher. Most of them, however, will gradually yield to group pressure if the group has chosen a problem in which the members are really interested. This choice of a problem is therefore of crucial importance if progress is to be made and members are to play mainly constructive roles.

Clarification of the roles played by group members can be brought about by general class discussion, by posters or humorous cartoons in the classroom, and by role-playing skits. In the latter device the teacher selects certain roles and asks students to play them, spontaneously and without advance notice. The class then analyzes the various roles seen in this "group" and what causes people to play these different roles.

The teacher who experiments with small-group work on problems selected by the class is usually concerned about the success of the groups. The following criteria may be suggestive of values he looks for and strives to achieve:

1. *A completely accepted goal*

    1.1  Do all group members understand the group's goals?

    1.2  Is the purpose or goal genuine to all members of the group?

    1.3  Do group members feel that they are solving the group problem?

    1.4  Do they try the solutions experimentally (or)

    1.5  Do they at least talk about the solutions enthusiastically?

2. *Ability to keep and use a written plan as a definitive record of progress*

    2.1  Does the group operate within a group-adopted, written plan?

    2.2  Does the group use written records effectively?

3. *Enthusiastic participation*

    3.1  Do members begin group sessions promptly?

    3.2  Do they use their time efficiently?

    3.3  Do all members take part in some way?

    3.4  Do members discuss the group's work enthusiastically between sessions?

    3.5  Do members assume responsibilities for their share of the group's project between meetings?

4. *Concern by all for the growth of each individual*

    4.1  Do they listen with respect to each other?

    4.2  Do they encourage contributions from each other?

5. *Leadership disseminated throughout the group*

5.1 Does the real leadership reside in the group, not the teacher?

5.2 Can the group achieve order and progress without domination?

5.3 Are various leadership roles assumed in turn by all members instead of always residing in the chairman or in one or two others?

6. *Habit and skill of critical self-evaluation*

6.1 Can the group accept self-criticism?

6.2 Can the group accept criticism by the teacher?

6.3 Can members evaluate each other's roles without conflict?

7. *Understanding and skill in various group processes*

7.1 Can the group usually achieve consensus?

7.2 Can the group pull itself together after failure or confusion?

7.3 Do members understand the various roles in group work?

7.4 Do they tend to avoid negative roles?

7.5 Do they identify their own roles honestly? [12]

*The planning cycle.* As groups report findings and evaluate their efforts, the class then faces the question of what problem or problems to pursue next. If they are not too limited by requirements of a textbook or course of study, they may again develop a list of possible problems, check them against the criteria, and launch another unit. The new unit may grow out of the preceding one, or it may be suggested by a class experience such as a field trip. Not all classes will pursue their planning in exactly the same way. In general, however, classes which are relatively free from an imposed subject-matter sequence may develop some such cycle of planning as the following:

1. The problem is selected as the culmination of:

   (a) An exploratory experience suggested by either the teacher or the pupils, or

   (b) Another related or lead-up unit, or

[12] Adapted from an unpublished report of Education Workshop, Wayne State University, Detroit, 1950.

      (c) A class problem census in which every effort is made to get all voices heard and to get at the real problems and interests of the group, and

      (d) A careful checking of the problems against a list of class-developed "Criteria for the selection of a problem for study."

2. The area is clearly stated and defined.

3. Areas of study are decided upon in terms of:
    (a) Tentative solutions,
    (b) Natural research division,
    (c) Individual and group interests.

4. Needed information is listed.

5. Resources for getting information are listed.

6. Information is secured, selected, and organized.

7. Information is analyzed and interpreted.

8. Tentative conclusions are stated and tested.

9. A report to the total class is planned and presented.

10. The entire process is evaluated, including the validity of the conclusions.

11. New avenues of exploration toward further problem study are pursued.[13]

These eleven steps were developed as a description of problem solving in a relatively unstructured core class. This means, in effect, that no specific sequence of required subject matter confronts the class. The core class may have a general obligation to pursue units within a theme-for-the-year, or to draw upon three or four broad resource areas for their problems. The fact still remains that such classes enjoy greater freedom to employ problem-solving procedures than do most subject-oriented classes employing textbooks.

As pointed out earlier in this chapter, however, there are many points on this continuum of group problem solving, and even the most restricted class can secure planning experiences occasionally, or in reference to some aspects of their work. Any class can help establish goals, or form small groups for formulating questions, or engage in self-evaluation. Almost any class can help improve the classroom itself. Suggesting and securing resources beyond the textbook is a fairly common group procedure.

---

[13] Roland C. Faunce and Nelson L. Bossing, *Developing the Core Curriculum,* rev. ed. (Englewood Cliffs, N.J.: Prentice-Hall, Inc., © 1958), pp. 156–157. Reprinted by permission.

Many teachers object to such efforts, however, as a waste of time. They say they must cover the subject matter (shouldn't they instead try to *uncover* it?), and they just don't have time to involve students in group planning or evaluation. There is more than one way to waste time. Rushing through a textbook may be a waste of time if no real learning (modified behavior) results. Writing tests on content that will be totally forgotten within six months may be a waste of time. Indeed, any teaching procedures that do not modify the student's values and attitudes toward self and others are usually a dreadful waste of time.

It is true that group relationships are not developed in a day. Any method of involving the learner in basic decisions affecting himself takes some time. It is the belief of the authors that no more important challenge confronts education than that of helping young people develop more adequate relationships and attitudes toward themselves and others. The time devoted to this kind of teaching and learning is not wasted. And it cannot be done by memorizing the "right" attitudes from a book. It requires direct experience and critical reflection on the meaning of the experience.

## The value of small groups

Planning with students can be carried on in the total class. Indeed, most of the basic decisions must be made by all students if the class is not to degenerate into a confederacy of independent small groups. The most "group-minded" teacher will be working with the entire class a good share of the time, and part of this time will be spent in teacher-student planning. If students are to relate to each other as well as to the teacher, the geography of class seating should be a circle or a hollow square instead of rows facing the teacher.

There are some functions that lend themselves well to small groups of four to ten students. Participation in discussion is increased, or at least made possible, when there are fewer participants dividing the same amount of time. When consensus is needed on plans, it is more readily possible to secure agreement in small groups. Individuals are more likely to assume responsibility as members of small groups, since the nonparticipant is more conspicuous than in a class of thirty-five students. Morale can be built and friendships strengthened by continued work in the same small group.

Leadership can be better observed, and can find more opportunity to blossom in a continuing small group.

*Other group experiences.* We have been discussing the small group formed by interest in a problem, and confronted with the obligation to pursue and report research on the problem. There are other ways to use group experience fruitfully. Most readers will recall having been members of project-pairs or committees in science or homemaking classes. Team sports are popular in physical education.[14] The social activities of a class have been described earlier. Small groups are often used for brief periods and for specific activities, such as reviewing for a test, giving reactions to a speaker, or discussing books, films, plays, or TV programs. Class trips or community surveys call for committees of students. Fund drives, service projects, and the planning of assembly programs call for planning committees.

A class newspaper or magazine is an excellent project from which to learn how to relate to others. Besides the journalism class or school paper staff, which is in some schools the best illustration of group relationships, many core classes and English classes publish their own paper or magazine as a vehicle for creative writing. The numerous decisions required for publishing even an occasional, mimeographed paper form a natural occasion for working with others.

Many classes use student committees for a variety of administrative purposes. Alexander and Halverson have suggested five such committees for a classroom:

> *Physical Facilities Committee*
> (Cleanliness, equipment needs survey, heat, ventilation, etc., utilization plans, recommendations for new equipment, renovation, etc.)
>
> *Interclass Plans and Activities*
> (Joint ventures such as parties and field trips, sharing of materials of instruction, intervisitation of classes)
>
> *Total School Plans and Activities*
> (All-school ventures such as student council, activity ticket, etc.,

[14] The intramural program and other nonclass activities involving group relationships are discussed in Chapter 12.

recommendations for total school improvement, school service projects)

*Community Improvement Planning*
(Surveys, service projects, recommendations for community betterment)

*Pupil Welfare Committee*
(Illness of class members, cards, flowers, etc., awareness of "hidden costs" and providing for them, tutoring assistance to pupils in need of help with their school work) [15]

In addition to the administrative function, small groups are a useful means of adapting certain learning procedures and materials to various levels of skill. The teaching of reading, for example, has been facilitated by use of three or more textbooks on different levels, each adapted to different vocabulary powers. Small groups within the classroom have been formed for the use of these different readers. In a similar way, varied levels of reading materials are now available in science and social studies, as well as in several other fields. Small groups are also sometimes formed for carrying on various projects which differ in their challenge or difficulty. This is a familiar technique in science and in mathematics, as well as in homemaking, industrial arts, and business education classes.

Such small groups within the classroom should be temporary and flexible. There should be adequate opportunity for students to move from one group to another as their interests and abilities suggest, and for them to work with all students on classwide projects. Teachers have generally discovered that interest-grouping within the classroom is a more promising approach than grouping by ability, in terms of effective learning.

*In conclusion.* The procedures used for group learning require a completely different role for the teacher from that of subject-purveyor and sole evaluator. The teacher studies the class and the relationships that obtain within it. He sets the stage for the planning process. He helps students establish criteria and choose problems for study. He moves about the room, wherever he is most needed at the moment, helping iron out difficulties and assisting each group in its

[15] Alexander and Halverson, *Effective Teaching in Secondary Schools,* **p. 256.** **Reprinted** by permission.

search for materials. He acts as a resource person himself when it will not handicap a group to tap the handiest resource. He helps to expedite plans and guides the evaluation process. He helps develop skills in discussion, reading, and writing in connection with the work of groups. He takes the helm when he must to restore order, always seeking at the same time to develop in the students criteria for self-control and a desire to achieve it. He inspires by his enthusiasm but is also capable of withdrawing to the observer's role when good leadership develops in the group. He expedites the plans of the class and avoids dictation. Above all, he helps students to understand the significance of their own efforts.

In short, the teacher ideally operates as a mature leader in the indispensable process of group planning, group action, and group evaluation. As he performs this role with skill and insight, his students will grow in courage and competence in this important task of working with others.

Although people are always relating to other people in groups of some kind, they are still unique individuals engaged in a constant search for values. In the next chapter we turn to the individual experiences that are also provided for in an effective classrooom.

## FOR FURTHER READING

Alexander, William M., and Paul M. Halverson, *Effective Teaching in Secondary Schools*. New York: Holt, Rinehart and Winston, Inc., 1956. Fundamental principles of group planning are amply illustrated by classroom examples. See Chapters 7, 8, and 9.

Cunningham, Ruth, *et al.*, *Understanding Group Behavior of Boys and Girls*. New York: Bureau of Publications, Teachers College, Columbia University, 1951. Discussion of the sociogram and many other techniques for study of group relationships.

Detroit Citizenship Education Study, *Problem Solving*. Detroit: Wayne State University Press, 1948. Graphic presentation of sequential steps in problem-solving activities by groups.

Faunce, Roland C., and Nelson L. Bossing, *Developing the Core Curriculum*, rev. ed. Englewood Cliffs, N.J.: Prentice-Hall, Inc., 1958. Chapter 6, "The Core Class in Action," contains many illustrations of group planning and evaluation in core classes.

———, and Morrel J. Clute, *Teaching and Learning in the Junior High School*. Belmont, Calif.: Wadsworth Publishing Co., Inc., 1961. Chapter

7, "Learning Through Group Experience," gives many classroom examples of formulating criteria for selection of problems, group attack on problems, reporting to class, evaluating outcomes. Some discussion also of less formal group relationships and ways to improve them.

Hock, Louise E., and Thomas J. Hill, *The General Education Class in the Secondary School.* New York: Holt, Rinehart and Winston, Inc., 1960. Chapters in Part II deal with such topics as problem solving, individual roles in groups, and evaluation.

Johnston, Edgar G., Mildred Peters, and William Evraiff, *The Role of the Teacher in Guidance.* Englewood Cliffs, N.J.: Prentice-Hall, Inc., 1959. Chapter 10 suggests many techniques a teacher may use for the study of classroom groups at work.

Kelley, Earl C., *The Workshop Way of Learning.* New York: Harper & Row, Publishers, 1951. A description of a college workshop for teachers, which contains many pertinent principles of group endeavor that apply also to the secondary school classroom.

Lurry, Lucile, and Elsie J. Alberty, *Developing a High School Core Program.* New York: Macmillan Co., 1957. Chapters 4, 5, and 6 discuss problem areas, resources, and methods in core classes. Many examples of specific techniques for group work.

Miel, Alice, *et al., Cooperative Procedures in Learning.* New York: Bureau of Publications, Teachers College, Columbia University, 1952. Illustrations of goals, methods, problems, and ways to develop skills in cooperative procedures.

Miles, Matthew B., *Learning to Work in Groups.* New York: Bureau of Publications, Teachers College, Columbia University, 1959. Chapter 2, "Effective Group Behavior," is especially helpful for teachers.

National Society for the Study of Education, *The Dynamics of Instructional Groups,* Fifty-ninth Yearbook. Chicago: University of Chicago Press, 1960. A comprehensive and scholarly treatment of this topic from various points of view. An excellent synthesis of what is known and what this knowledge suggests to the teacher.

Noar, Gertrude, *Freedom to Live and Learn.* Philadelphia: Franklin Pub. & Supply Co., Inc., 1948. Brief description of the core program in action in Gillespie Junior High School in Philadelphia.

Parrish, Louise, and Yvonne Waskin, *Teacher-Pupil Planning.* New York: Harper & Row, Publishers, 1958. This small book is entirely devoted to the techniques of cooperative planning and group work in the classroom.

Smith, Louis M., *Group Processes in Elementary and Secondary Schools.* Washington, D.C.: The National Education Association, 1959. The results of research in group dynamics are discussed and related to the functioning of groups in the classroom. No. 19 in the series "What Research Says to the Teacher."

Strang, Ruth, *Group Work in Education,* rev. ed. New York: Harper & Row, Publishers, 1958. Good discussion of the principles and procedures of group work. Note especially Chapter 6, "Group Work in the Classroom."

Toops, Myrtle, *Working in the Core Program in Burris Laboratory School.* Muncie, Ind.: Ball State Teachers College, 1955. Pamphlet describing steps taken by classes in the core program as they plan their work.

Wiles, Kimball, *Teaching for Better Schools,* rev. ed. Englewood Cliffs, N.J.: Prentice-Hall, Inc., 1959. Part III contains such useful chapters as "The Development of a Class Group" and "A Way of Working with a Group."

Zapf, Rosalind, *Democratic Processes in the Secondary Classroom.* Englewood Cliffs, N.J.: Prentice-Hall, Inc., 1959. An excellent basic presentation of group planning. See especially Chapter 3, "Working in Small Groups," and Chapter 5, "A Problem To Work On."

# 9 The classroom in action: individual experiences

All learning is essentially an individual experience. We have noted, however, that many fruitful learning experiences can take place when the individual is functioning as a member of a group. The use of small groups in the classroom offers greater flexibility for adapting the curriculum to the interests of the individual, since his interests are taken into account in the formation and choice of groups. As a teacher moves about, observing such groups at work, he discovers individual strengths and weaknesses, since they stand out more readily in a small group. And the variety of roles played by individuals in small groups offers numerous opportunities for individual success or growth.

## The individual within the group

Each group faces a challenge to make effective use of the interests and abilities of each member. Students know a good deal about each other because of the orientation period that the class as a whole has experienced. Some individuals who are extroverts and perhaps accustomed to leadership may become leaders almost immediately. For others it may take some time before the group discovers ways of capitalizing their hobbies and special abilities. If students in small groups are encouraged to use each member effectively, and if their problem is real to all members, their efforts to provide for individual interests and skills will usually be successful.

The planning process in small groups offers many different roles for individuals to play, as pointed out in the preceding chapter:

| | |
|---|---|
| listener | idea-giver |
| do-nothing | fence-sitter |
| information-giver | shy guy |
| belittler | peacemaker |
| leader | wisecracker |
| blocker | summarizer |
| know-it-all | complainer |
| questioner | objector [1] |

As students' roles are observed by the teacher, a basis is developed for helping them move to more constructive roles and away from the "hindering roles." Through individual conferences the teacher can often develop insight by the student into his own problems of behavior as a group member. Other students in the group can reinforce this process as they become more sophisticated in the use of group procedures. In some cases it may be helpful to arrange for a student's transfer to another group more closely aligned with his interest.

Other kinds of individual problems call for the teacher's help:

For example, there is the frequent case of the youth who sees a question and wants to answer it quickly, or have it answered superficially, rather than plan why and how it might be answered adequately. A little less familiar but more difficult is the pupil who feels that planning how to solve problems is a waste of time: "Why doesn't the teacher tell us?" Such individuals as these can usually be dealt with in the group situation and by their peers. The most difficult cases are those pupils who have always been "told" and simply do not understand how to go about thinking through ways and means of solving problems. These are the pupils who need conferences in which the teacher asks questions to probe for their ideas about how to solve problems, however elementary, with which they are thoroughly familiar. The teacher

1 Rosalind Zapf, *Democratic Processes in the Secondary Classroom* (Englewood Cliffs, N.J.: Prentice-Hall, Inc., © 1959), p. 112. Reprinted by permission.

then draws parallels with procedures being used in the class, using illustrations repeatedly.[2]

Some students need individual help in taking notes, organizing them, and drawing their own conclusions from their research. (They may have been copying paragraphs verbatim out of encyclopedias for years.) Others may need to develop criteria for recognizing the validity of an authority. (Whatever is in print must be true!) Various skills are called for as members of a small group undertake a problem:

reading, including reading of technical or advanced materials
map-making and map-reading
developing and using charts and tables
taking and organizing notes
skills in bibliography
using the telephone
command of interview skills
library skills
knowledge of community
skill in art or photography
building models or dioramas [3]

It will be noted that some of these study skills are needed, at a minimum level, by any group member who operates effectively. Others are specialized or technical skills which one or two group members may develop.

Other kinds of individual skills are called for as a group undertakes to report findings to the class:

| | |
|---|---|
| oral report | drama, role-playing |
| panel, symposium | leading discussion |
| debate | radio, television |
| pantomime | photography |
| musical composition | art work |
| poem | models |
| editorial, essay | maps |
| narrative prose | charts, graphs [4] |

[2] William M. Alexander and Paul M. Halverson, *Effective Teaching in Secondary Schools* (New York: Holt, Rinehart and Winston, Inc., 1956), pp. 352–353. Reprinted by permission.

[3] Roland C. Faunce and Morrel J. Clute, *Teaching and Learning in the Junior High School* (Belmont, Calif.: Wadsworth Publishing Co., Inc., 1961), p. 196.

[4] *Ibid.*, p. 197.

As groups are challenged to vary their reporting procedures, to create new and interesting devices for communication to the class, opportunities increase for use of different kinds of individual talents. Again, the teacher is provided a ready-made occasion for giving help to certain individuals who have communication problems.

Doris came into my room during planning period and asked whether she could talk with me.

"You certainly may," I said. "What would you like to talk about?"

Doris twisted a ring on her finger. "It's our report," she finally blurted out. "I'm s'posed to get up there and tell about what a rural school is like and I'd just rather die!"

"You attended a rural school, didn't you?" I asked.

"Yes, I never was in any other school until this year."

"Did you like it there?"

"It was OK I guess. But I like Lincoln better."

"What was it like in your other school?"

"Well, for one thing, there were only twenty-one of us in the whole school. And we heard all the other grades recite because we were all in the same room."

"Anything else?"

"Oh I've found out a lot about the one-room school from an article in a magazine. There's an awful lot of them still, and that surprised my group. And it said it took a special kind of teacher to teach in a school like that. And a lot of other stuff, but I just can't talk about it to the class. I never could."

I patted her hand. "You know, I think they'd be really interested in that report. You're the only one with first hand experience in such a school."

"I know that," moaned Doris, "but I just get all mixed up when I am in front like that."

"Could you tell us about it if you didn't have to stand up in front of us?" I asked.

"Maybe, but everybody stands up when they report," Doris objected.

"Well, let's talk to your group about it today. Maybe we can figure out a plan so they'll all just sit where they are and give their reports. You'll do all right, I feel sure."

Doris brightened up a bit. "Well, I'll try if I can do it from my seat."

Some communication problems involve more than shyness or timidity. Serious speech handicaps may call for some help from a speech correctionist. Some problems are persistent and yield only gradually to even the most enlightened efforts of a teacher. Yet understanding and patience are essential, whatever the nature of the problem.

As small groups carry on evaluation of their work, some valuable skills may develop in certain members:

> recalling facts
> organizing facts
> understanding implications of facts
> applying the if-then principle
> testing generalizations
> using records effectively
> looking at one's self objectively
> assessing causes
> projecting probable results
> being able to stick to a task [5]

There will be group members who possess few of these evaluative skills. In some classes these roles may remain goals for the students to reach. As groups persist in their work, however, they will develop increasing control of the evaluative process, and individuals will emerge who give leadership to this task in various ways.

Other kinds of individual roles become helpful as classes plan special projects. Oscar can operate a film-strip projector. Ned knows a farmer who would be glad to have the class visit his farm and ask questions. Amy's mother works in the city planning office and can secure an audience for the class with members of the staff. Maurice is experienced in camping and fishing. Carol writes interesting poems. Wilma has made puppets and practiced ventriloquism. Bill knows a lot about baseball. Jack makes balsa-wood models.

Teachers sometimes say: "But this class of mine isn't interested in anything." What they usually mean is: "These kids aren't interested in what I want the class to learn." As the base of class activity is broadened, it becomes respectable to display interest in that which was previously thought of as an out-of-school activity. Not always will a class uncover a ventriloquist or a song-composer in

[5] *Ibid.*, p. 197.

their midst. Some of the individual skills may be unspectacular, but still useful. And the interests in sports, hobbies, television, movies, or animals are almost always present, merely awaiting discovery. They will emerge as (1) the group gets better acquainted, and (2) the range of acceptable activities becomes broader, so that new roles develop for various individuals. Both teacher and students should make it their business to find out and then seek to use the interests of each individual.

## The development of skills

*Speech activities.* In most senior high schools an elective program is offered students in the specialized skills of speech, as well as one or more general speech classes. Unfortunately, students who tend to elect such subjects are not those who need the most help in oral communication. Some secondary schools include or have some access to specialized speech teachers, but this is not a typical situation. In most schools the only practice and guidance available to the "ordinary" student is in English classes or (in most junior high schools) in core or block-time classes. Speech is, of course, a commonly practiced skill in almost all classes. The English teacher, the general speech teacher, or the core teacher is usually expected to give students help in improving their oral communication.

Such help is not always available, and when it is available it is not always very helpful. The class may be too busy to find any time for improving speech. In most core classes, or in any class where group problem solving is systematically practiced, improvement in oral discussion skills is an obvious outcome. Students experienced in the small-group technique usually show good command of discussion and oral-reporting skills. They have had considerable experience in engaging in discussion and in chairing it. They often learn how to present issues, report information, clarify meaning, and formulate questions and answers, as on a panel. They may become skilled in conducting interviews, in using the telephone, in making introductions, and in practicing parliamentary procedure. Their experience in reporting to the class will have given them further experience in such specialized speech skills as role-playing, narration, debating, reading poetry, and presenting radio or television programs.

Speech skills have an application in other classes and in out-of-school situations. The individual who possesses some skills should be encouraged to develop more specialized abilities such as:

> interpreting verse orally
> giving humorous or dramatic readings
> taking part in plays
> acting as master of ceremonies
> debating and oratory
> selling
> producing television shows

Opportunities for pursuing such specialized speech interests are available in large high schools, either in elective courses or in the student activities program.

A less commonly achieved goal is that of giving special help to individuals who lack the skill or the confidence to communicate with others at even a minimum level of competence. Thelen has described an imaginary "Skill Development Laboratory" in which students practice their speech in alcoves equipped with tape recorders and are assisted by older students acting as tutors.[6] This use of recording equipment for self-diagnosis and correction of speech habits is increasing. Some studies have shown this individual self-study to be superior to a classwide approach to speech problems, and feasible in a comprehensive high school.[7] Most teachers have access to tape recorders. In schools in which recording equipment is limited, the student who needs help will have to get individual coaching from a skillful, understanding classroom teacher. In many cases, perhaps most, the basic problem is the learner's attitude toward self. He usually needs self-confidence more than anything else. He may be lucky enough to encounter a teacher who can build his self-esteem. If he is still luckier, he may find friendly classmates who encourage him instead of laughing at his efforts, and classrooms where everyone's interests and skills are cultivated.

*Art and music.* Individuals who are talented in art or music can find elective programs in which to sharpen their talents in most

[6] Herbert A. Thelen, *Education and the Human Quest* (New York: Harper & Row, Publishers, 1960), pp. 184–185.

[7] See, for example, Ruth Golden, "Effectiveness of Instructional Tapes for Changing Regional Speech Patterns" (Doctoral dissertation, Wayne State University, 1963).

senior high schools. The work of specialized music groups at the high school level is often astonishingly good. Fine art work, too, is done in any large high school with adequately equipped art rooms and good art teachers.

In the junior high school, two challenges confront the so-called exploratory program in music and art: (1) to help individuals discover special interests or talents in these fields, which they should pursue in senior high school, and (2) to give *every student* an opportunity to appreciate and enjoy art and music as a medium of expression. J. L. Mursell has said:

> Music is one of the most universal human needs. The impulse to create and enjoy it exists among men everywhere, and has existed always. . . . while men remain the beings they are, they will continue to need music.[8]

The same claim can be convincingly made for art, which preceded written language and therefore history as a means of communication. Much personal enrichment and success-feeling are potentially available in music and art.

Teachers have failed to develop an appetite for music and art in many individuals who need these media of expression. Part of the fault lies with music and art departments which have one eye on public presentation, and which therefore select the talented students for special emphasis and concentrated production. Any really good program in music and art would have at least an equal emphasis on enjoyment of these media by all students, along with opportunities for the gifted ones to specialize. Part of the failure is due also to excessive departmentalization and the attitude of many teachers that art and music should be confined to the periods assigned to such activities.

Art and music are communication media that should pervade all subjects and all activities aimed at effective communication. Students can sing and hear records in history class as well as in a music class. Groups preparing to report to a core class should make use of illustrations, posters, costumes, models, and scenery. Scrapbooks and bulletin boards offer individuals a challenge for creative expression. The class magazine can employ art design.

[8] Quoted in Arthur E. Ward, *Music Education for High Schools* (New York: American Book Co., 1941), p. 2.

One class made a systematic study of the ways in which the cultures of other lands had influenced our American folk music. This study led them to listen to many records and to sing folk songs themselves. The music teacher became the chief resource of the class during this study. Another class was making a tape recording of their study of American education, and enlisted the help of the music teacher in selecting and recording the musical introduction and "bridges." Still another class held a parody contest as a feature of their weekly program and invited a jury of "experts" from the *a cappella* choir to judge the musical quality of the various presentations.[9]

It will be noted in these examples that the music teacher served a resource role. Many teachers who have not specialized in music feel insecure about directing musical activities in their own classes. The secondary school should be so organized as to make collaboration and team effort between teachers not only possible but easy and natural. Art teachers also have often helped students develop projects in other classes. One history teacher reports:

Three girls in my eleventh grade American history class stayed after school one night until six o'clock, circling the classroom walls with a mural drawn on wrapping paper. It depicted the various stages in costumes of women in America, beginning in colonial times. It was to serve as reinforcement for their report to our class the next day. Miss Allan the art teacher had helped them learn how to draw the illustrations and design the various panels.

Many students who have limited academic talents can draw, paint, or letter. Other individuals enjoy music and can sing well. If the classroom procedures are broadly planned, such talents can be discovered and capitalized. Recognition and success can be arrived at through a wide variety of talents and interests. Students who have no great gifts in art or music can nonetheless be helped to appreciate and enjoy these activities.

Appreciation of any art form is a highly subjective matter. Tastes and values vary widely, but can be developed if teachers begin where students are. It is hard to develop appreciation of "good music" if teachers define the word "good" so narrowly that students' present tastes are completely rejected.

*Reading.* Literature, too, is an art form and subject to varying individual tastes. One objective of teaching reading is to heighten the appetite for more reading of good books. This objective is often defeated by limiting all students to the same books. By the criterion of appreciation, defined as appetite for more of the same, the one-book approach is doomed to failure. Thirty students are simply not going to appreciate equally the same story or poem.

This limitation of a whole class to one literature assignment is sometimes justified on the grounds that it enables a teacher to maintain standards. It may, in fact, defeat standards of appreciation because it is premised on the false assumption that all students *can* read the same piece and *will* like it if they read it. On this score, Fred Wilhelms offers some observations:

> By contrast, the literature teacher who lives by human *goals* has a host of media at his command. He wishes, let us say, to use literature to deepen the youngsters' understanding of themselves and others, of the subtle motives that drive mankind, of the human condition itself. His materials range at least from the insightful masterpieces of Shakespeare and Dostoevsky to those "westerns" that combine true characterization and motivation with an exciting story. And if he is reasonably facile, they can all be brought to bear within one class. . . . It is not so simple a matter as "watering down" standard content or lowering standards. It is driving so zealously for fundamental objectives that we are willing to search endlessly for media that will work. And that depends, at bottom, on seeing content as means to an end, not as the end itself.[10]

If most graduates never voluntarily read the authors they were forced to read in school, efforts to teach appreciation have failed. Does this mean that teachers have no obligation to improve students' tastes in reading? On the contrary, classrooms should contain many good books on various vocabulary levels, appealing to a wide

---

[10] Fred T. Wilhelms, "The Curriculum and Individual Differences," in *Individualizing Instruction,* Sixty-first Yearbook, National Society for the Study of Education (Chicago: University of Chicago Press, 1962), pp. 68–69.

variety of interests. Teachers and students should plan to spend some time discussing their reading, and whetting the appetites of others by giving a few samples orally. Discussions of what is good or what is poor should aid students to develop criteria for judging effective writing. If bulletin board exhibits feature new and interesting books, if the classroom library contains books that students like to read, and if time is devoted to silent reading as well as critical discussions of what is read, most students will develop the habit of reading. But they will seldom be reading the same book at the same time. It is also unlikely that they will all like the same books, or poems, or stories equally. Adults seldom arrive at such consensus.

A classroom collection of books is a must, if there is to be an individualized approach to reading. It need not be costly. Instead of buying a single anthology, the school or the students may buy several sets of ten or twelve books each. One teacher of literature asks each student to take out a library card and put the six books which the card entitles him to borrow into a rotating classroom collection. Another teacher encourages students to buy paperbacks chosen from a classroom list and contribute the books to the class after they have read them. County, state, and municipal libraries loan substantial collections of books for a period of time. Many school libraries have book trucks on which a rolling classroom library can be assembled and taken to a room for specified periods. Some teachers have augmented their collection by asking parents to donate books. Boards of education are increasingly disposed to spend regular sums of money for classroom libraries, as they discover that the cost of books is not only small but a wise investment for improved instruction.

When a teacher accepts the fact that individual tastes and reading levels differ, not only will the classroom climate reflect this realization, but his own operation with individual students will reveal it:

1. He will suggest books that may be interesting or helpful to small groups.
2. He will make similar suggestions to individuals, and hand them books to look over.
3. He will provide time for browsing in the classroom reading corner.
4. He will study individuals' reading scores on standardized tests.

5. He will analyze individuals' reading interests, from interest inventories in the files.

6. He will listen to some students' oral reading and help them discover errors and deficiencies.

7. He will encourage students' visits to the classroom library before and after school.

8. He will stress success, not failure.

9. He will talk enthusiastically about books or stories he himself has enjoyed.

10. He will help students develop criteria for recognizing good writing.

11. He will teach students how and when to scan, how and when to read reflectively.

12. He will talk to parents about ways to encourage home reading—time, place, and materials for it.

13. He will use visual or dramatic means to whet the appetite —films, plays, television.

14. He will encourage students to keep a critical record or diary of what they read.

15. He will measure his own success by progress made by each individual, not by material "covered" by the class.

Teachers in secondary schools have seldom had training in teaching the beginner to read. A special problem is presented by the retarded reader who is several years "behind" the rest of a class in vocabulary and reading rate. The techniques of helping such slow readers are not necessarily complicated. The problem is aggravated, however, in classrooms where the only books are too difficult for some students to read at all, and where all students are expected to read the same materials during the same time period. If no time is allowed for individualized reading during a class period, the retarded reader will continue to receive no help and will be likely to give up all hope of success.

In some classrooms, however, such a student may be given books he can read and time to read to the teacher while others are pursuing their own reading. Two or three short periods with a teacher each week can be helpful if both student and teacher really believe success can happen. As the student progresses, he may need less time with the teacher. In schools where a reading clinic or remedial teacher is available, the retarded reader may get some special help at regular intervals. The crucial need is for the student to believe he can learn to read. He should not be subjected to ridicule or to any situation where his failure is published to the class.

Other teachers besides those responsible for literature can be helpful in teaching reading. Not only history, science, and mathematics teachers, but also those in such special fields as business education and industrial arts can contribute to improvement of students' reading skills. At the very least, all teachers have an obligation to develop command of the specialized vocabulary and concepts unique to their own specializations.

*Writing.* Encouragement is helpful for those students who need to learn to write. Fear of failure or ridicule limits the student to the stereotyped, required minimum or induces him to copy passages from an encyclopedia to present as "his" written report. Why do students feel they cannot write? Some of them have been told they could not, by their parents and teachers. Many more have learned it by looking at papers returned to them, with every error dramatically red-penciled. And, of course, there is the report card mark, which is a convincing persuader. Teachers who hope to build self-confidence as a basis for voluntary writing must not tear apart the students' work. They must use praise more often than censure. They need not correct every error on every paper. Many good teachers concentrate their corrections on a few kinds of errors each time, and try to find a good word to say about the writing, too. The teacher's main purpose at the start should be to develop in the student a lively interest in writing of one kind or another, and a conviction that he *can* write. Improvement in the finer points of word choice and paragraph organization can come after a student becomes really interested in writing.

Not only the English or core teacher, but *all* teachers who have contacts with a student should be concerned about his improvement in writing. There are numerous opportunities in a science or social studies class to help students develop writing skills. Not only through tests and term papers, but also through class projects such as newsletters, business letters, and project-interpretations for school exhibits can teachers of all subjects help students move to higher levels of written expression.

A class newspaper or magazine offers an excellent vehicle for developing an interest in writing. When things are going to be read by others, they should be correct. Besides, it is fun to plan a paper, organize the space, obtain contributions, and produce the issue to be sold or handed out to other students. There can be a place for humor, sports, editorials, and news commentary, even though the magazine format seems to lend itself better to creative writing and art work. If a printed paper is too costly, the mimeograph machine can be used. There are jobs for all—editors, sports writers, humorists, artists, poets, essayists, short story authors. There are tasks for typists, cartoonists, business managers, proofreaders, interviewers, reporters, salesmen. There are real responsibilities to be assumed. There are deadlines to be met. The whole class must be proud of each issue, so it must be as good as they can make it. Some students may carry a major part of the responsibilities, but there can be a job for everyone. Less talented students should be able to get an occasional piece published, too. The incentive of publication may be exactly what they need.

The school paper may also offer an opportunity for the creative writer to publish short pieces. National magazines such as *The Junior Scholastic* and *The Scholastic* publish outstanding work of high school students. One such poem carries in it a message for all adults who assume youth have no problems:

> You see youth as a joyous thing
> About which love and laughter cling. . . .
> You see youth as a joyous elf
> Who sings sweet songs to please himself. . . .
>
> But I, I see him otherwise—
> An unknown fear within his eyes. . . .
> He goes about in still alarm,
> With shrouded future in his arm,
> With longings that can find no tongue,
> I see him thus, for I am young.[11]

One junior high school teacher discovered, quite by accident, that all but five of her students had brothers in the service, whose present stations were scattered all around the world. She suggested a series of letters to their servicemen, and worked with them to plan a series of emphases for these letters that promised to raise them a bit above

[11] Charles Brown, high school student, Pawhuska, Oklahoma. Quoted in Edgar G. Johnston, *Administering the Guidance Program,* (Minneapolis, Minn.: Educational Publishers, Inc., 1942), p. 84.

the family-gossip level. She also obtained the names of correspondents for the five who had no relatives in the service. To her surprise, the students wanted to read each other's letters and make suggestions for improving their word choice, spelling, and capitalization. Most of the servicemen caught the idea and started responding with interesting letters describing far-off places and people. Similar letter-writing projects have been launched with "pen-pals" of the students' own age in other countries.

The teacher whose main purpose is to develop in each student a readiness to write will not give standard theme assignments. He will encourage creativity and the courage to express ideas that are different in ways that are different. He will seek out the shy or timid students and help them take the first experimental step toward writing *their* thoughts and feelings in their own best way.

*Science and mathematics.* The secondary school has offered both required and elective courses in science and mathematics for many years. Since the middle 1950's there has been a considerable increase in the number of students electing such courses throughout the three or four years of senior high school. New concepts and a new vocabulary have changed the face if not the entire body of these fields. In today's scientific world it has become increasingly evident that some students should pursue specialized study of mathematics and science throughout high school and college, and go on to the numerous careers in industry, business, or government which today demand such competencies. Most high schools have increased their elective offerings in both science and mathematics.

Less agreement seems to exist on the exact role of science and mathematics in general education. What concepts and skills in these areas are needed by all citizens? More specifically, what kind of a curriculum in these subjects can meet the varying needs of both slow and fast learners, of both boys and girls, of both junior high school and senior high school youth? As the language and concepts of mathematics undergo radical change, is it equally appropriate to introduce such changes into both required and elective courses? Should science and mathematics remain outside the stream of general education, or is there a way to build them into the core curriculum or the grade-level unit taught by a team of teachers?

Both general and specialized opportunities in mathematics and science are needed if individual needs are to be met. Those who have the interest and capacity should be able to go as far in these fields as they can in the high school years. The specialized courses should be so individualized that talented students are enabled to go far beyond other students and perhaps beyond their teachers, too. Through use of individualized contracts or programmed learning, through individualized laboratory experiments, and through use of out-of-school resources, some students in any secondary school should be able to develop into specialists investigating concepts far beyond the usual textbooks or laboratory manuals. It should be possible to free such talented students from other classes to make a block of time available for work in the laboratory or mathematics workroom. If a university campus or an industrial laboratory happens to be nearby, advanced courses or apprenticeships are possibilities.

What about the mainstream of general education? What can be done to help less talented youth to live competently in today's scientific world? We have entered a period of history characterized, perhaps dominated by developments in science. Discoveries and predictions of discoveries fill our newspapers and magazines. Scientific development has outstripped our capacity to plan its use and evaluate its effects. As youth grow up in a culture dedicated to conquest of space, abolition of disease, and discovery of new food and fuel resources, they must know vastly more than their fathers needed to know about science. If the classroom faithfully reflects these phenomena of our culture, such knowledge will not need to be imposed by adults but will be acquired as a means of solving problems in which students have expressed interest. Such problems exist all around us, shout their challenge on television and radio, and are eagerly discussed out of school by both adults and youth. Is the conquest of disease responsible for today's exploding population? Is the rapid increase in world population exhausting our food resources? What can be done to conserve and replenish those resources? What is the role of synthetics in the constant search for new resources? Of conversion of sea water? What new sources of fuel and power are to be discovered in nuclear and solar energy? What can be done to improve the health of all men everywhere? What developments in communication and transportation can help us? How does a computer work? What present and potential uses has it? These and many other questions and problems confront us today, both as adults and youth. They may be expressed in more simple or more technical language. They may involve rudimentary or complex ideas. The fact is that science is changing the world, and people must understand and adjust to change.

Throughout mathematical and scientific investigation the twin questions of "how" and "why" persistently face teachers. It is no longer enough to accept phenomena; teachers must understand them. Older classroom practices will not do. Teachers cannot supply students with answers, to be memorized and regurgitated. Teachers must encourage students to ask always: "How did this occur? Why did it occur? Under what conditions would it occur again?"

The following objectives of scientific thinking were spelled out for junior high school youth, but they at least suggest a direction for this area of general education at all levels:

1. They need to gather facts and to think clearly about their meaning and their relationships.

2. They need to differentiate between facts and opinion, between truth and fiction.

3. They need to develop a wholesome curiosity about the nature of the earth and living things.

4. They need to understand the importance of natural resources and their conservation.

5. They need to grow in their understanding of biological structures and functional processes of growth.

6. They need to practice healthful and safe habits of living.

7. They need to adjust their ways of living to the world of applied science and invention.

8. They need to understand that cooperative living is imperative in a scientific world.[12]

These same goals could have been stated (in perhaps other terms) by any group of junior high school students who are lucky enough to be in a science class that faithfully reflects the world about them. The goals offer many clues for problem solving and practice of scientific thinking. Teachers must not use such statements as rationales for using standard content for every student in a class. To do so would prevent the attainment of the goals. Each individual differs significantly from every other in almost every trait or skill involved in the learning process. He may share the general goals

[12] *The Bulletin of the National Association of Secondary School Principals,* 35:182 (December 1951), p. 17.

with others, but he approaches the problems of science or mathematics in his own unique way and at his own pace. On this point Wilhelms has remarked:

> If what we seek is genuine attention to the individual, we shall have to turn our back on the obvious and provide *room* for radical differences in mode of approach. In general education, especially, we shall have to assume that only goals are universal, that content and method must be infinitely varied. It is impossible and undesirable to plan all the necessary variations in advance. What *can* be planned is a structure and organization which make it easier to see individual needs, and, through use of large blocks of one sort or another, to make provision for them.[13]

Wilhelms' reference to "large blocks" suggests the core curriculum or a grade-level team approach. In the core program a block of time is used for study of the persisting problems of all citizens, with the science and mathematics teachers either themselves working with a science-mathematics block of two periods or serving as resource teachers to help when needed by a core class. Grade-level teams would involve the science and mathematics teachers, along with all other general education teachers at a given grade level, in cooperative planning and teaching of units directed at the fields of science or mathematics. It is important to preserve a continuous relationship with the same groups in such a team plan.[14]

Whatever the plan, there must be numerous opportunities for individuals to work on problems real to them and geared to their achievement level. This means that materials for reading must be varied, that laboratories should be available to small groups and to individuals, that projects will be carried on continuously by individuals and occasionally shared with others. Both in general classrooms and in science laboratories there should be individual work-stations and storage for projects that are being carried on. Perhaps a science teacher should be freed for a half day or more at each grade level to come into core classes and help students pursue a science problem, or to assist individuals and small groups in a well-equipped laboratory. Such a "consultant" would be a very busy person in a school that was really adapted to individual interests

---

[13] Wilhelms, in *Individualizing Instruction,* p. 73.
[14] This problem is discussed further in Chapter 15.

and needs. He would be a resource person in classroom discussions of science principles or concepts. He would help develop aquaria and in other ways improve the climate of each classroom for science. He would be pursued by eager individuals who had questions or needed help in setting up experiments. Before, during, and after school hours he would be consulted by individuals who were at different stages of investigation in science. He would perhaps be working after school and on Saturdays with special-ability science groups, with science clubs, and with individuals preparing projects for science fairs. He would also help groups and classes arrange field trips to nearby laboratories or natural resources, and bring in scientists from the community to speak to classes. Throughout his efforts he would remember that each individual has unique interests and powers. He must be able to pursue those individual interests at his own pace in order to have something to share or contribute.

## Other provisions for individual growth

*The elective program.* The elective program of the secondary school is often cited as a means of paying attention to individual differences. We have referred to it already in our discussion of speech, science, and mathematics classes for the talented. Beginning especially at grade nine, the typical secondary school makes available an elective program in foreign languages, mathematics, science, speech, business education, industrial arts, art, music, homemaking, and vocational subjects. A large urban high school may offer an astonishing range of specialized electives ranging from silvercraft to Greek, and from television production to machine lathe.

In advanced courses of these elective sequences, it is highly probable that the factor of selection has operated to bring together a group having somewhat similar interests and competencies. This by no means insures that individual needs will be effectively met in such classes. It is still possible, in fact, to defeat the goal of individualization, even in elective courses. If all students are expected to learn the same things at the same pace, individual needs will be violated and much potential growth will not be attained. In first-year elective courses there is a high rate of failure because of unrealistic demands of teachers and unwise choices by students. This waste of human resources could be avoided by good counseling and by a probation period during which a student might withdraw from an elective course without a recorded failure.

Because interested students form the bulk of advanced elective courses, teachers of such courses often permit individuals to proceed at their own pace in such fields as industrial arts, typing, shorthand, accounting, art, and vocational skills courses. Foreign language laboratories also offer individuals an opportunity to advance at their own tempo in oral mastery. It is perhaps true, also, that a somewhat greater variety of activities is offered students in such subjects as arts and crafts, homemaking, and industrial arts. To the extent, however, that elective courses are focused on *types* of differences (common to a class) instead of *individual* differences, they may easily miss their mark. If teachers in elective curricula assume, as they sometimes do, that their students are all alike and can proceed through standard content at a standard pace, they may actually make it more difficult for the school as a whole to take account of individual differences.

*Student activities.* In many a school, the only significant opportunity for pursuing individual interests is in extraclass activities such as clubs, the school paper, athletics, dramatics, and social experiences. This program will be discussed at length in Chapter 12. Interests and hobbies have a real place in the classroom too. When students talk or write they need a topic. The special hobbies or interests they pursue out of school are natural topics for oral reports, special programs, exhibits, bulletin boards, and "themes." Hobby interests also furnish a convenient channel for getting acquainted. The guidance program must enable teachers to discover these personal interests if they are to help students become better adjusted to school. Boys and girls must begin where they are, and where-they-are includes those interests which they voluntarily pursue on their own time.

*Work experience.* Many boys and girls have part-time jobs. Various surveys indicate that from one third to one half of all high school students earn wages in occasional or regular jobs. Only about 10 per cent of these jobs are systematically related to school experiences.[15] These school-related jobs are mostly part of the Smith-

[15] Mary Smith and Ray Bryan, "Work Experience," *Review of Educational Research,* 26:4 (October 1956), 404–410.

Hughes or George-Deen cooperative programs for apprentice training.

Teachers who are interested in individual interests cannot afford to overlook the work experience of youth. While many of these jobs do not contribute training skills for the specific occupation of the student's future, they make a number of contributions to his development. They help him learn something about the world of work and its conditions, the importance of promptness and responsibility, the demand on a job for such skills as making change or answering a telephone. At the very least, they teach him what it is like to earn his own money. At the best, a job can be so school-related as to provide a high motivation for what goes on in school. In any case, a job held by a student helps make him what he presently is, and that fact makes it of interest to teachers.

Probably many more students should be helped to find part-time jobs. In 1942 the American Youth Commission completed a major study of youth problems with the following recommendation:

> In many cases and not for financial reasons, pupils in the upper years of high school and junior college should divide their time equally between school attendance and wage employment. Half-time work in private employment, with half-time devoted to instruction in the schools, would be an especially appropriate type of program for the twelfth, thirteenth and fourteenth grades.[16]

This recommendatioin is even more relevant to youth's needs today. Most of the one million youth who leave school each year will be unemployed for months or employed only at intervals. Job upgrading programs are currently being launched in urban school systems to attempt to draw a segment of these drop-outs back to school for job training. Similar programs are needed, on a much broader scale, for both out-of-school and in-school youth.

In addition to providing extended opportunities for part-time jobs and training for these jobs, the school should make a greater effort to relate what goes on in the classrooms to the work experience of students. Alexander and Saylor have suggested the following questions which teachers should ask themselves about this matter of work experience:

---

[16] American Youth Commission, *Youth and the Future* (Washington, D.C.: American Council on Education, 1942), p. 124.

1. Are other persons interested in developing a work experience program? What is the interest of parents, employers, and labor organizations in more work experience for boys and girls? Is there some school-community group which is interested in undertaking or sponsoring a study of work experiences?

2. What work are boys and girls already doing in the community? Could they do some jobs better if they had related training in school? Could some classes give special attention to some of the jobs that many youth hold outside school as baby-sitters, newspaper boys, grocery clerks, and so forth?

3. What jobs are pupils doing in school that point to work in the community? How can pupils who do good work on their school jobs be helped to get broader experience in the community?

4. What jobs in the community can be done by high school boys and girls on a part-time basis? Which of these have educational value? How can continuing inventories be maintained of these job opportunities?

5. How can boys and girls working on school-sponsored community jobs be supervised? What cooperative arrangements can be made for the school schedules of boys and girls who work at these jobs and for the teachers who supervise them? What credit for graduation can be given for work experience? What financial support is available for the program? [17]

*Independent study.* Various plans for individual contracts or unit lessons have been tried in schools since at least 1888. The best known of these were the Winnetka and Dalton plans, which had in common the provision for independent work by each pupil for some part of his day. As he completed his unit-lesson or contract, he was given a mastery test to reveal whether or not he was ready to proceed to another lesson. The contract idea has survived in some subjects. With modifications, it appears in typing and accounting classes, as well as in some shop and drafting courses.

Recent developments may bring about a renaissance of individual contract plans as an alternative to classwide lessons. One such development is programmed learning, presented either by teaching machines or by "programmed" books. These devices are varied in their form and complexity, but they are aimed at (1) presenting to

---

[17] William M. Alexander and J. Galen Saylor, *Modern Secondary Education* (New York: Holt, Rinehart and Winston, Inc., 1959), p. 544.

an individual some material to be learned or tasks to be performed, (2) providing for some activity on the part of the student, and (3) correcting his errors or influencing his responses. Skinner and others have developed several different teaching machines based on the stimulus-response psychology discussed in Chapter 4. In general, these devices are most effective when the content to be learned is fixed. There is evidence that such fixed content can be memorized by an individual via teaching machines more efficiently than by group methods. Certain kinds of intellectual skills, such as spelling and capitalization or arithmetic processes, can also be learned efficiently through programmed learning. There is less evidence of its effectiveness in teaching the skills of problem solving or inductive thinking. In the areas of highest creativity or discovery-learning, the teaching machine seems most ill-suited. In general, the greater flexibility or creativity demanded by a given goal of learning, the less appropriate is the fixed program.[18] Conversely, the more rigid or fixed the skill or body of content to be learned, the better is the prospect of acquiring it by programmed learning.

Some claims of the advocates of programmed learning appear to be valid.[19] One of these is that the program makes it possible for an individual to proceed at his own pace, instead of being either overwhelmed or bored by material assigned to an entire class. Another advantage is that it frees the teacher from conducting drill activities and enables him to assume more creative roles. Some observers maintain that programmed learning will ultimately force teachers to abandon comparison-marking of students, since comparison will become impossible when individuals are not engaged in similar learning-tasks.

Other claims seem dubious. Some advocates say teachers will be able to handle larger classes, and thus fewer teachers will be needed. It is more probable that the systematic use of programmed learning would limit class size, since programs must be selected, adapted, and

[18] A teaching machine is a device for projecting a program to the learner. The program itself, which can be used apart from the machine, is the basic element in this approach to individualization. The book type of programmed learning appears presently to be the more versatile as well as the less expensive of the two general forms of projection.

[19] See, for example, A. A. Lumsdaine and Robert Glaser, eds., *Teaching Machines and Programmed Learning* (Washington, D.C.: The National Education Association, 1960).

evaluated in terms of each individual's progress. In any case, the assumption that all experiences can or should be thus programmed is unacceptable to educators who believe in group interaction and social learning.

Some limitations are inherent in programmed learning. It is based on a psychology stressing the automatic response to a selected stimulus. It is thus a form of training rather than of education, since it forecasts the desired response and inhibits all others. It eliminates the adventure of learning, the creative process of seeking insights and solving problems, and reduces learning to a preselected track and a sequence of experiences toward that which the writer of the program has determined to be the goal. In short, programmed learning takes the planning role away from both students and teacher. Finally, the goals relating to human adjustment and relationships cannot be achieved by preselected programs. Cooperation cannot be placed in a test tube nor learned by solo use of an auto-tutor. Freedom to move at one's own pace is not enough. Individualization demands also the freedom to plan, to attack problems, to select materials, to evaluate one's progress in relating to others. There is the further objection that teaching machines may tend to become ends in themselves, rather than means to better teaching.

The programmed book shares some of this hazard of becoming an end in itself. In some versions of the programmed book, however, there is provision for analysis of failures and progressive awareness of success. The Crowder scrambled-book, for example, makes at least some contribution to the skills of (solo) problem solving. The student moves by direction to various pages of the book, where he will find further instructions or explanation of his previous errors.[20] It appears possible that some types of programmed learning may persist and prove useful in the process of individualizing instruction.

*Study halls.* Individual preparation has traditionally been provided for in secondary school schedules through assignment of students to one or more study halls each day. In these periods, augmented by homework, the student is expected to prepare his daily lessons. In most junior high schools, the study hall has given way to

---

[20] See Lawrence M. Stolorow, *Teaching by Machine* (Washington, D.C.: U.S. Department of Health, Education and Welfare, 1961), pp. 37–38.

use of part of each period for supervised study under the direction of the teacher concerned with the subject under study.

*The Trump Plan.* Various alternatives to the six-, seven-, or eight-period day for high schools have been tried experimentally. One of these, often called the "Trump Plan," [21] provides for a division of the students' day and week to provide for three different types of groupings: (1) large groups of 100 or more students for lectures or television viewing, 40 per cent or about twelve hours each week; (2) seminar groups of twelve to fifteen students, discussing concepts and developing group skills, 20 per cent or about six hours weekly; and (3) independent study in laboratories or individual stations, 40 per cent or about twelve hours weekly. The costly provision of tutors for individuals engaged in independent study, and of leaders for small seminar groups, is made economically feasible by the large-group instruction. Unfortunately, the latter forces the teacher to use the lecture system or the show-and-tell techniques of television, neither of which lends itself to participation by students or inter-action between students and teacher. There is a further problem of developing continuity of a teacher with a group of students, if the small seminar groups are frequently changed. Perhaps more basic is the objection that changes in the schedule do not result in any changes in teachers' philosophy of instruction. Individualization demands a new approach to goals, assignments, and evaluation. Time for "independent study" may or may not facilitate individual-ization.

*Acceleration.* Secondary school educators are again being urged to promote some talented students more rapidly and graduate them at an earlier age. It is being argued, as it was during the 1940's, that only thus can schools provide the needed leaders and specialists for industry and government during their younger and more vigorous years. Besides, say the proponents of this acceleration, "Some students are ready for college by age fourteen; others not until eighteen.

[21] Named for J. Lloyd Trump, Director of the Commission on the Experimental Study of the Utilization of the Staff in the Secondary School, a commission of the National Association of Secondary School Principals aided by the Ford Foundation. See J. Lloyd Trump and Dorsey Baynham, *Focus on Change: Guide to Better Schools* (Chicago: Rand McNally & Co., 1961).

Why hold back the talented individuals and make them go through the lock step of the secondary school?"

It is quite true that some students could move from junior high school to college, so far as their academic skills and knowledge are concerned. If their ultimate success depended only on their academic talents, some individuals would be ready for college at age twelve. But much more is sought in secondary schools than merely knowledge and skills of reading and computing. If secondary education is a process of growing up with others, of developing responsibility and maturity, can these processes be hastened? Is there any shortcut to social maturity? Those who fail in college do not generally do so from lack of academic skills, but rather from immaturity or irresponsibility. The high school years are a precious asset for this hard task of growing up.

In any case, *acceleration* by grade is not necessary if teachers succeed in avoiding a lock step. All students need not study the same assignments at the same time. Students need not be marked competitively. The materials of instruction need not be the same for all students regardless of reading level. Students need not all take the same tests on the same day. Teachers can and must make provision for individual differences through *enrichment* of individual learning.

*Ability grouping.*[22] Another device in widespread use is often justified as a means of providing for individual differences. This is *segregating* students into sections formed by certain criteria for judging their ability to succeed in a given subject. Both in its earlier period of popularity (during the 1920's) and today, these criteria for grouping included school marks, recommendations of previous teachers, scores on achievement tests, reading test scores, and I.Q. (based usually on scores on group intelligence tests).

Research has been both voluminous and carefully done for at least forty years on the successes and failures of ability grouping. The results of this research may be summed up as follows: (1) There is little or no evidence that ability grouping results in better teaching or learning; and (2) administrators, teachers, and most parents favor

[22] This discussion of ability grouping first appeared in an article by one of the authors of this book in the *Teachers College Record*, Indiana State Teachers College, Terre Haute, 34:2 (November 1962), pp. 64–69.

ability grouping as a step toward better teaching and learning. The contradiction presented by these two research findings is an interesting phenomenon.

A recent summary of research findings of studies made during the 1930's was compiled by Della-Dora. The following generalizations were substantiated amply by the research of the 1930's, and have been corroborated by most recent research also:

> 1. Teachers, parents, pupils, and administrators associated with ability grouping generally favored it.
> 2. Pupils grouped according to "ability" as measured by group intelligence tests and/or standardized achievement tests, generally did *not* achieve greater subject-matter mastery than did their counterparts in regular (heterogeneously grouped) classrooms. . . .
> 3. Pupils grouped according to I.Q. and/or achievement test results still exhibited a wide range of differences both in measured ability and in actual performance. . . .
> 4. Initial differences in both measured ability and actual performance increased with time in "homogeneous" groups. . . . *Within a relatively short span of time all groups became more heterogeneous.*[23]

When one evaluates the effects of grouping of any kind, it is necessary to ask what goals were sought by the adoption of a grouping practice. Is the plan supposed to make the teaching task easier? Is it a means of separating the gifted for special attention? Or of selecting some children for remedial help? Is grouping designed to alleviate the worst effects of competition for marks? Or to make a start on the business of individualizing instruction? Or is it a reflection of some current philosophies that aim at creation of a favored (intellectual) elite which is to be rewarded by superior status?

Evaluation of ability grouping must be made in relation to purposes advanced by various educators as appropriate for the secondary school.

1. *Does ability grouping produce greater mastery or progress toward traditional goals of instruction?* In general, the answer to this question must be no, as teachers look carefully at their own research. If we omit the elective program of the secondary school from our

---

[23] Delmo Della-Dora, *One Hundred Years of Grouping Practices* (Detroit: Wayne County Board of Education, 1960), pp. 5–6.

consideration and look at grouping practices in required courses at all levels, it is a safe generalization that there is no significant improvement in progress of pupils toward traditional goals *from grouping alone*. Indeed, most advocates of such grouping are aware of this fact and inform teachers that their procedures with their classes (after they are grouped) must be significantly different in order to effect instructional gains. The obvious question: was it grouping that helped, when gains were observed, or the changes in method which followed after grouping? The question must remain an academic one if teachers continue to operate in the same old way after the grouping has been done.

2. *Does ability grouping help to promote social adjustment, democratic behavior in small groups, or ability to make choices and evaluate progress?* On the contrary, ability grouping begins with subject-matter mastery, adjustment to adult expectations, and academic success in general. These goals are reflected in the very means by which groups are originally established. It does not represent a broadening of educational goals or a departure from older concepts of mastery, competition for marks, emphasis on memory and on drill, etc. Use of ability grouping assumes these aspects of education to be both inevitable and desirable. Since some proponents of such grouping believe that teaching methods and philosophy cannot be changed, they argue that the students will get hurt less if they are in roughly similar ability groups.

3. *Does ability grouping encourage youngsters to learn democracy through its practice?* If most of the leaders are sequestered in one group, the processes of democracy may prove difficult. Teachers who are struggling to teach democratic skills in the slowest of the slow groups well know how difficult it is.

4. *Does ability grouping help to unify the social structure of a school?* The opposite effect is usually noted. Since middle and upper income pupils tend, because of their cultural advantage, to be found in "faster" or "superior" groups, this separation tends to stratify the school and deprive youngsters of the needed experience of social interaction with all sorts of people. They may, however, take part in extracurricular activities that are not segregated according to academic ability.

5. *Does ability grouping give greater confidence and success to the slow student?* The evidence is somewhat confused here. Some studies indicate that slow learners are relieved to be rid of their

competition. Others report that slow learners resent the stigma of being classified as "dummies," and that they are well aware of being thus classified, no matter what precautions are taken to avoid the stigma effect. Teachers report much confusion about standards for marking and promotion of such pupils. Can they "earn" and receive an "A"? If so, what is the effect of this at graduation time? In an effort to be consistent, some high schools have started issuing "certificates of attendance" to such slow learners or, in some cases, a different colored diploma. These devices would appear to establish the social stigma permanently.

It should be remarked in passing that an inflexible grouping plan can condemn a "late bloomer" to the slow group, and perhaps even dictate his future in some schools. Serious violations of the democratic ethic result when teachers stick to their first and often erroneous convictions about a pupil.

6. *Does ability grouping mitigate the worst effects of competition?* Initially this may occur. Studies show, however, that within a short time a new continuum of competitors becomes established in all groups, and generally teaching methods, including marking practices, encourage competition. In the "fast" or high groups, some youngsters now find that they are praised or otherwise rewarded by the teacher less frequently. In the "slow" and average sections, a new spread develops between fast and slow learners, new praise-patterns emerge, and their effects on individual incentive are dubious.

Is competition really appropriate as a factor in learning? It would appear to be malapropos to some of the most basic educational goals. For example, through competition do students learn the skills of cooperation? Or appreciation of music or poetry? Or capacity for love? Or freedom from prejudice? Or fair play, honesty, patience, responsibility?

If such goals as these are to be the real targets as teachers help youngsters to grow up in a social setting, should not the whole approach to instruction be chosen accordingly? And if teachers succeed in this effort to any degree, will they not help to make it progressively more clear that grouping by academic ability is either irrelevant or inimical to their real task?

Many authorities agree that sectioning pupils by academic ability is unnecessary if instruction can be flexibly geared to the learners' needs and interests by other means. Emphasis on marks and competition can be diminished. Individuals who are gifted in some way can be encouraged to pursue their individual talents to the utmost without being segregated from their fellows. Slow learners can be given special help in subgroups within the regular classroom. As teachers develop the knack of varied procedures, they find time to move about from group to group and individual to individual, helping wherever help is most needed. They abandon the single textbook approach and collect classroom libraries of considerable variety, both of interest and word power. They have other resources available, too, for individual questing and discovery. They use help from other teachers on the team, and they discover that children can help one another when they are not artificially separated. Children with unusual academic aptitudes can learn some significant values through giving such help to their classmates.

All these individualizing techniques, and many more, are in use by ingenious teachers already. As we turn our attention to the further development of such stimulating methods, we shall discover what rewards they offer. Without the use of individualized and small-group learning, ability grouping will fail anyway. With its use, there is no need for ability grouping in general education.

*In conclusion.* In this chapter some analysis has been made of the means by which individual growth can be encouraged. Many special roles challenge the learner, both as a member of a classroom group and as an individual. In required courses in general education he can sharpen his skills and deepen his insights in such areas as speech, art, music, literature, and creative writing. Science and mathematics offer other kinds of individualized experiences. Both the elective courses and the student-activities program can contribute to individual growth. Work experience offers still another valuable resource. School leaders are presently committed to the search for means of individualizing instruction, as seen in the experimentation with ability grouping, acceleration, and programmed learning. These administrative devices appear to have little impact unless accompanied by real changes in teaching method. Our greatest need is to rediscover the individual and gear our teaching efforts to his unique needs, interests, and goals.

In the next chapter we turn to the problem of finding and using resources for learning.

## FOR FURTHER READING

Alexander, William M., and Paul M. Halverson, *Effective Teaching in Secondary Schools.* New York: Holt, Rinehart and Winston, Inc., 1956. Chapters 11 and 12, "Studying the Characteristics of Individual Learners" and "Providing for the Individual Learner," are helpful to teachers who strive to find ways to deal with learners as individuals.

Association for Supervision and Curriculum Development, *Creating a Good Environment for Learning.* Washington, D.C.: The Association Yearbook, 1954. See Chapter 4 for a report of how individual exploration can grow out of a group project.

———, *Fostering Mental Health in Our Schools.* Washington, D.C.: The Association Yearbook, 1950. Chapter 5, "Individuality Develops," gives many helpful ideas for building individual exploration around emerging needs.

Blair, Glenn Myers, *Diagnostic and Remedial Teaching in Secondary Schools.* New York: Macmillan Co., 1947. Detailed suggestions about procedures for diagnosing difficulties and for remedial work.

Della-Dora, Delmo, *One Hundred Years of Grouping Practices.* Detroit: Wayne County Board of Education, 1960. Sums up a century of research on effects of sectioning pupils by ability.

Faunce, Roland C., and Nelson L. Bossing, *Developing the Core Curriculum,* rev. ed. Englewood Cliffs, N.J.: Prentice-Hall, Inc., 1958. Chapter 7, "Enriching Individual Learning," discusses individualized experiences in speech, writing, reading, art, music, science, hobbies, and citizenship.

Faunce, Roland C., and Morrel J. Clute, *Teaching and Learning in the Junior High School.* Belmont, Calif.: Wadsworth Publishing Co., Inc., 1961. Chapter 8, "Learning through Individual Exploration," explores ways to challenge individual exploration in core classes, speech, art, music, literature, creative writing, science, and other subject areas.

Grambs, Jean D., William J. Iverson, and Franklin K. Patterson, *Modern Methods in Secondary Education,* rev. ed. New York: Holt, Rinehart and Winston, Inc., 1958. Chapter 13, "Slow and Fast Learners," discusses the problem of individualizing instruction in terms of rapidity of learning, as well as in other factors of difference.

Keough, Jack, and Robert E. De Haan, *Identifying Children with Special Needs,* Vol. I, and *Helping Children with Special Needs,* Vol. II. Chicago: Science Research Associates, 1955. These pamphlets contain some helpful suggestions for teachers who are trying to identify and serve individual needs.

Metropolitan School Study Council, *The Slow Learner in the Average Classroom*. New York: The Council, 1954. This pamphlet gives many suggestions regarding methods of helping the slow learner.

National Society for the Study of Education, *The Education of Exceptional Children*, Forty-ninth Yearbook, Part II. Chicago: University of Chicago Press, 1950. A useful general reference on one type of individual difference.

———, *Individualizing Instruction*, Sixty-first Yearbook. Chicago: University of Chicago Press, 1962. See especially Fred T. Wilhelms, "The Curriculum and Individual Differences."

Rothney, John, *The High School Student—A Book of Cases*. New York: Holt, Rinehart and Winston, Inc., 1953. Methods of studying pupils with special problems of personality.

Taba, Hilda, and Deborah Elkins, *With Focus on Human Relations, A Story of an Eighth Grade*. Washington, D.C.: The American Council on Education, 1950. An interesting account of how individual exploration and self-realization can emerge from group projects.

Wiles, Kimball, *Teaching for Better Schools*, rev. ed. Englewood Cliffs, N.J.: Prentice-Hall, Inc., 1959. Chapters 8, 9, and 10 are most helpful in reference to creating classroom climates where individual differences are respected and provided for.

Wrightstone, J. Wayne, *Class Organization for Instruction*. Washington, D.C.: The National Education Association, 1957. Concise discussion of research findings on grouping, with the implications for grouping within the classroom, and of instructional adaptations to fit the pattern of grouping adopted. No. 13 in the series "What Research Says to the Teacher."

# 10

# Resources for instruction

## The teacher as a resource

The teacher is usually able to give help in locating sources, in supplementing and synthesizing information gathered from several sources, and in providing immediate answers or correcting initial errors of fact, *when such answering will stimulate instead of stultify further research.*

It should be noted that we are discussing only one kind of resource at this point: that of information or its interpretation. In a broad sense every teacher serves as a resource in dozens of ways as students organize an attack on problems or areas for investigation. We have referred to this kind of resource role as facilitator or expediter of the process. In this chapter we are speaking of a more specific resource-role concerned with supplying data or relating facts to problems under investigation. Teachers should perform this role only occasionally and only after asking themselves this question: Will my contribution really help in the problem-solving process, or will it discourage my students from seeking answers for themselves?

Teachers should do less talking and more listening. Secondary teachers are all specialists in one or more subjects, which they selected as their majors or minors because of their interest and initial competence in these subjects. They find an almost over-

whelming temptation to tell what they know at the earliest opportunity. Teachers equipped with a specialized knowledge of history,
mathematics, or literature may easily drift into the role of textbook-
in-the-flesh. Students readily accept this role for their teachers, because they have always perceived teaching as "telling" or because it
relieves them of some responsibility for seeking answers elsewhere.
Thus, they are deprived of the essence of learning—the process of
finding and relating data to a real problem, which they have themselves formulated. The speech teacher may be so fascinated by his
special knowledge of the anatomy of speech that he spends all the
class time talking of these matters and leaves no time for students
to speak. The English teacher who talks endlessly of the mechanics
of grammar and who finds little time to let students write is a familiar figure in many schools. The history teacher who wrote his
thesis on the Napoleonic era may have so much interesting information to convey on that subject that students have no time (or
need) to explore resources on any other topic of history.

Not all teachers lecture that much. It is fairly common practice,
however, for teachers to supply information already available in
the text, or in other books in the library. This answering is not
always in terms of any questions students have asked. It may become
a habit to volunteer information. In either case, it would be helpful
for the teacher to ask himself what the probable effect of these ready
answers will be on the *process of search and discovery* that must
characterize good problem solving.

There are situations where it is highly appropriate to supply
some facts or to correct misinformation on the spot. As a teacher
grows more skillful in asking stimulating questions in place of making statements, information may be given in a manner that spurs
students to further investigation. As students come to know their
teacher well as a participant in class problem solving, he will find
that he cannot honestly refuse to help without hindering his relationship with the group. He cannot say to them "I don't know"
when they know he does! One does not treat his friends thus.

Even in such situations, however, the teacher need not pose as
the only resource, or even as a constant one. An immediate answer
to a question can and should be so phrased as to open up a new
question or a whole avenue of investigation not previously noted
by the class. As such investigations follow and grow more broad in
their scope, the teacher will soon find that he does not know the

answers himself. He will be free of the limited and often stultifying role of answer man, and can join his students in searching for data and in arriving at new insights.

## Students as resources

Not only teachers, but also students serve the resource role. In Chapter 4, in the discussion of the learning process, it was noted that attitudes toward others and relationships with them affect learning. Students have always learned from each other, even in the most competitive, single-standard classrooms. When they are not permitted to help each other in the class, they do so in study hall or at home. Many a "slow" student has found that he can understand an explanation given by a classmate, when he had been baffled by the teacher's explanation.

> I was trying to guide Henry through the intricacies of a long division problem. At my other shoulder stood Jackie, restless with pent-up eagerness. At last he could stand it no longer.
> "Oh Miss Rasey, let me help him," he blurted out. "I just learned it yesterday and you must have had it a thousand years ago." [1]

In classrooms where cooperation is respectable, students can become quite skillful as resources in the process of learning. They are also resources in various fields of knowledge, since each has had unique experiences that can contribute to someone else's learning at some appropriate point. If the scope of study is broad, these personal experiences can be tapped and will prove useful. One student may be an authority on baseball, another on wild life. Unless the classroom procedure is flexible, these areas of high interest may never emerge and some students will be thought of as "not interested in anything."

## Resources within the school

It seems appropriate to examine, first of all, some of the resources for learning that exist within the school itself. The classroom, the library, and the materials used for classroom and homework assign-

---

[1] Reported to the authors by Marie I. Rasey.

ments will be considered first, followed by some discussion of audio-visual aids to instruction.

*The classroom as a resource.* A teacher who values creative, problem-solving activities more than lectures and recitations will need a classroom suited to his purposes. Classrooms in older secondary schools are about twenty by thirty feet in size and accommodate thirty to forty students in fixed seats. (Listening does not require much space.) For many years, while these narrow quarters were thought sufficient for senior high school general classrooms, elementary and junior high schools have been built with a different concept of instruction. It is common for elementary schools built even thirty years ago to have large rooms in which activity space is available in addition to the area needed for pupils' desks. In the high schools, more space has always been provided for laboratory areas such as those used for science, art, homemaking, and industrial arts. Thus those subjects which have been thought of as most appropriately "learned by doing" have had space provided for student activity.

This laboratory concept is today extending itself to the general or academic classroom also. If a teacher expects to employ problem-solving procedures, small groups, dramatization, or construction activities, a room of six hundred square feet is not adequate. If facilities are to be provided for conferences, storage of individual projects, and exhibits of students' work, a larger general classroom is indicated. Alexander and Halverson have suggested the following interesting contrast between the lecture-recitation kind of room and the "laboratory type" more suitable for problem solving:

### CHARACTERISTICS OF LECTURE-RECITATION AND LABORATORY-TYPE CLASSROOMS

| *Lecture Recitation* | *Laboratory Type* |
|---|---|
| 1. Uniformity in size and shape | 1. Diversity in size and shape depending on nature of instruction |
| 2. Rigidity in seating arrangement | 2. Flexibility in arrangement of pupil stations and their use, depending on needs and activities of learners |

3. Lack of opportunity for movement around room by pupils

4. Paucity of materials and equipment, mostly uniform for each pupil

5. Adaptable primarily to listening, reciting, and uniform activities for total group

6. Forces teacher into "telling" or "listening" role

7. Emphasis on acquisition of facts and skills as ends in themselves

8. Use of blackboard for drill on facts and skills

9. Class time assigned arbitrarily by teacher for recitation and study

3. Considerable movement and activity, less sitting

4. Varied materials and equipment, depending on need and activity of individual pupils

5. Geared to "doing things" and to various kinds of activities by individual pupils and small groups

6. Allows teacher to "do things" together with pupils, to act as assistant, as expert, or as co-learner

7. Primary emphasis on facts and skills as they relate to solution of problems

8. Use of blackboard for making a record of problems, purposes, plans for action, or summaries of decisions and responsibilities.

9. Class time used flexibly, depending on group and individual needs and activities [2]

Teachers interested in developing an active kind of learning need laboratory-type classrooms. It is true that some ingenious and resourceful teachers have managed to carry on flexible teaching in inflexible quarters. More often, the physical features of the classroom establish the climate and set the limits of student activity. If students are to use the room itself as a resource for learning, it must reflect this role in its size, equipment, and flexibility. Let us examine briefly the kind of learning space which can best serve as a resource for active learning.

The general classroom should be large enough to accommodate many activities. For a section of thirty students this probably implies

[2] William M. Alexander and Paul M. Halverson, *Effective Teaching in Secondary Schools* (New York: Holt, Rinehart and Winston, Inc., 1956), p. 73. By permission.

a minimum of thirty square feet per student, or about nine hundred square feet. Each classroom should have two small conference rooms adjacent to it for small-group or committee meetings, for privacy in making a tape recording or in counseling an individual student, and for use on occasion as the teacher's office. Partial glass partitions may be used to incorporate these conference rooms into the general classroom and still provide privacy.

In the large classroom, part of the center space is used for movable tables and chairs that can readily be arranged in a variety of ways to facilitate different kinds of class procedures. For example, when a general class discussion is in progress the tables might form a hollow square. For small-group meetings, the tables might be moved into positions of relative privacy, perhaps separated by movable room dividers such as bookcases or tackboards. One or two groups may use the conference rooms, thus increasing the available space for separating groups in the larger room.

Adequate storage space is needed for projects and materials. There should be cupboards for large and small projects, shelves and drawers for supplies, cubicles for large flat items such as posters or maps, and files for students' written work. Classroom libraries will require shelf space for three hundred to five hundred books. A periodical rack is needed. Bulletin board and chalkboard space should be adequate for the type of class the room is to accommodate. Lighted exhibit spaces facing the corridor invite a class to interpret its work to the school and community.

Dark curtains are needed for showing films in the room. Electrical outlets on all walls make possible the use of recorders, projectors, electric tools, radio, and television. Television conduits make it possible for closed-circuit programs to originate in the classroom.

An aquarium is a useful addition to any general classroom, not only those used for science classes. Flowering plants add another resource for learning. Simple hand tools and a vise make available other kinds of activity. Running water and gas should be available in the work-counter, making the room more flexible for art and for science experiments or demonstrations.

First-floor classrooms should face out to the school yard and have separate exits. The portion of the lawn outside each classroom might be developed and maintained by students. Another kind of "facing out" is achieved by including a good daily newspaper, news magazines, a radio, and a television set in the classroom.

What, in summary, are the characteristics of a room which will itself serve as a resource for learning?

1. Its space is adequate.
2. Its furniture arrangement is flexible.
3. Adequate storage and exhibit space is provided.
4. It is colorful, interesting in its decor, homelike.
5. It provides space for doing, making, constructing.
6. Films, TV, and other visual aids can be used in it.
7. Books, magazines, clipping files, maps, globes, and natural resources are immediately available.
8. The room is light and without glare.
9. It is acoustically treated.
10. It accommodates counseling and small-group activities.

New schools are increasingly providing general classrooms of this laboratory-type. The cost is not as great as usually assumed, and is in any case a sound investment. Most of the features described can be provided at lower cost than traditional buildings that look like monuments but do not provide adequate classrooms.

What about the teacher who moves into a school in which few of these provisions are available? Must he abandon all hope of using the classroom as a resource?

On the contrary. An ingenious teacher can improvise learning resources in an older classroom. The most serious handicap may be the size of the room, but even this problem can be dealt with in some degree. Removal of the teacher's desk and rostrum may provide some needed space without serious sacrifice. A standing file is a more useful piece of equipment than a desk, takes up less space, and costs less money. Movable seats are not prohibitively expensive and can make the room more flexible. In most schools a place can be found for one or two small groups to work at times outside the room—in halls, empty classrooms, or the library. This helps considerably in finding space for those who remain in the classroom.

Bookshelves can be built with two boards and four bricks. Cupboards can be made of brightly painted orange crates. Bulletin boards can be cheaply made in the school shop from Celotex or pegboard panels. Extra tables and chairs can be obtained from somewhere in the school or community. Murals can be painted on wrapping paper. The library can be enriched by free materials from industry and government sources. Students have often provided their own classroom draperies, pictures, and collections of books. In one classroom the boys stayed after school for three weeks, sanding and varnishing the tables whose tops had become marred over the years. In another school a biology class planted a flower garden and reseeded the lawn outside their windows. Other classes have built and planted window boxes for flowers, developed dioramas for corridor exhibits, raised funds to buy a piano or a television set for the room, and painted walls to improve lighting and appearance. One ambitious teacher painted a space map on the ceiling as a means of helping his students become acquainted with the planets and stars.

Some teachers must share rooms with other teachers because of overcrowded conditions or bad scheduling. Effective teamwork between teachers who share a room may enable them cooperatively to develop, store, and use materials and equipment. It is important for the classroom to become more than a mere assembly point for students and teacher. If learning is to become effective, the room must become a challenging situation for those who live in it, even briefly. The "homeless" teacher should make every possible effort to obtain a room he can develop into a rich resource for learning.

A small, dark, overcrowded, and poorly equipped classroom is a limitation that is not easily overcome. But a teacher who really wants his room to serve the resource role can improve it with the help of students and parents. School administrators should be told about such an improvement project, since their help can be of crucial importance. Teachers should make sure that inadequate classrooms are not built into schools that are being planned now.

*Classroom libraries.* Both general and specialized classrooms need books and other printed materials. For a class of thirty students it is probable that three hundred to five hundred books are needed. These books should include both resource materials in areas under study, and literature for individual enjoyment. There should be a wide range of vocabulary level and conceptual difficulty represented in this collection, as well as a wide range of interests. Fortunately, books are now being published in considerable numbers which fit this description. Junior high school students can have access to many books that are written on an elementary vocabulary level but deal with stories or topics of adolescent and adult interest.

Many school libraries are becoming materials centers. This means, among other things, that books and pamphlets are catalogued in the library and made available for loan on a classroom basis. Book trucks on casters are loaded with the titles selected by a teacher and moved to the room to serve as a bookcase. At periodic intervals the collection is exchanged, in whole or in part, for some other titles. Multiple copies are purchased of books that are most in demand. Part of a given collection may be built around a unit or problem area under study at that moment by the class. For example, such a list of problem areas as the following may be reflected in library resources:

Problem Areas for General Education
in the Secondary School:

1. Self-Understanding
2. Healthful Living
3. Home and Family Living
4. Personal-Social Relations
5. Education and School Living
6. Vocational Preparation
7. Living in the Community
8. Democratic Government
9. Economic Understanding
10. Relationships with Minority Groups
11. Intercultural Understanding
12. Finding Values by Which To Live [3]

This list of problem areas was devised for general education. More specialized areas such as the elective science and mathematics programs would also be represented in the materials from which classroom collections are drawn. The teacher has a special responsibility to help locate resource materials that illuminate both sides of controversies and issues. The skills of critical thinking and discussion can be learned in the process of exploring such controversies. Without valid resource materials, such discussions can become unprofitable conflicts of unsupported personal opinions. Since few textbooks supply this kind of resource material, there is a real need to build it into the classroom library.

Nationally, school libraries have generally approximated a stand-

[3] Abstracted from Jean Victoria Marani, "A Technique for Determining Problem Areas for General Education in the Secondary School," (Doctoral dissertation, The Ohio State University, 1958), pp. 312–326.

ard of five books per student, although standards of the American Library Association range from ten books per student in small schools to three books per student in very large high schools. One survey for 1953–54 showed an average of 6.29 volumes per student in high school libraries.[4] The recent increase in the number of low-cost books, including paperbacks, has undoubtedly increased this figure somewhat. The trend toward classroom libraries is not an alternative to the centralized library, but rather an effective means of getting materials out from the "center" to the user.

In many schools where centralized libraries are limited, the classroom collections have been built up by other means. Students have bought supplementary books instead of textbooks, or in addition to these. Parents and students have contributed books. Units such as those distributed by Scholastic Book Services [5] have been subscribed for by the school, along with the paperback library which accompanies each unit.

*Departmental libraries.* Other kinds of decentralized libraries will be found in most secondary schools. Collections of books and other materials may be maintained by the science or industrial arts department and borrowed by various teachers as need arises. Some of these libraries are available also for direct student use. In the Rutgers Plan for teaching literature a large collection is maintained for every two English classes, housed in a nearby room and supervised by a teaching aide. Paperback versions of good books are finding their way increasingly into such collections. In the Rutgers Plan, which has become known by various other titles in particular school systems, a remarkable increase in the amount of student reading has been noted.[6]

*The school library.* Many reference books cannot efficiently be duplicated for each classroom. In the school library a student becomes versed in the use of the *Reader's Guide to Periodical Litera-*

4 Nora E. Beust and E. M. Foster, "Statistics of Public School Libraries, 1953–54," in U.S. Office of Education, *Biennial Survey of Education in the United States, 1952–54* (Government Printing Office, 1957), Chapter 6.

5 Scholastic Literature Units, Scholastic Book Services, 50 W. 44th St., New York, N.Y.

6 Paul B. Diederich, "The Rutgers Plan for Cutting Class Size in Two," *The English Journal,* 49:4 (April 1960), 229–266.

*ture,* the card index, encyclopedias, and specialized reference books. Students should receive an orientation experience in the school library, and perhaps also use the librarian as a resource person in their own classroom. To this end, teamwork is needed between teachers and librarians. One report of such teamwork was written by the librarian and two core teachers at the Ohio State University School. They summarized their concept of the essential unity of their respective assignments in the following words:

> The librarian's participation is needed in helping teachers and students achieve the aims of the reading program, in the location and development of materials, in the guidance of reading, and in special instruction. . . . When teacher and librarian discard preconceived ideas of a difference in responsibilities, and each freely undertakes whatever is necessary for the success of the reading program, then results are assured.[7]

The materials center is being broadened in many schools to include audio-visual materials and demonstrations or teaching tools, which are discussed at a later point in this chapter.

*The textbook.* In spite of much debate and many reservations expressed regarding the basic textbook, this device remains the chief resource for instruction in many classrooms. The objections to this use of the textbook are rather serious:

1. The single textbook for all students cannot be adapted to various reading levels within a class. Thus it is usually too difficult for some students and too simple to challenge others.

2. The single textbook cannot adapt to all individual interests. It must remain a kind of summary or collation of those items the author thinks basic.

3. The single textbook does not usually present all sides of an issue or challenge students to engage in study of controversial issues.

4. The single textbook tends to be the only resource that is consulted because it is so handy. It thus discourages search and investigation.

[7] L. Jane Stewart, Frieda M. Heller, and Elsie J. Alberty, *Improving Reading in the Junior High School* (New York: Appleton-Century-Crofts, Inc., © 1957), pp. 65–66. Reprinted by permission.

5. Perhaps worst of all, the single basic text tends to establish the scope and sequence of instruction. Instead of its being used as a resource, it tends to become the curriculum, and the goal-determiner for teachers seeking an easy way to solve the problem of planning.

On the other hand, the basic text is alleged by some teachers to have some advantages:

1. The textbook is relatively cheap, close at hand, and convenient.

2. It insures that all students will have access to some resource.

3. It gives students a common ground for discussion, since they are all assumed to have read the same material.

4. In the absence of adequate classroom libraries, there would be no resource material for all students except for the textbook.

5. The textbook need not determine the sequence of instruction. It may instead be used like any other resource.

6. Textbooks have improved in quality, both in language and format.

7. Textbooks can be planned in such a way as to be graded in difficulty and sequential in content. The use of such a series thus reduces repetition and omission of significant content.

This last item is perhaps the chief reason for the retention of the basic textbook series in many schools. It appears to some educators that there is no other device for obtaining a sequential coverage of knowledges and skills thought to be needed for general education. Unfortunately, reliance on this approach to sequence ignores the facts of individual difference, spelled out throughout this book. There seems little merit in developing a sequence of learning that never happened! Scope and sequence that depend on a textbook series that is unreadable by a large number of students are fantasies.

It is true that textbooks are more attractive today than formerly. The best of them have interesting illustrations, dramatic use of color, good type, and (in some instances) good writing. The same things might be said of other resource books. If textbooks were used as just one of many resources; if assignments in the text came *after* instead of *before* the search for data in other books; and if planning proceeded independently of the text, through study of problems arrived at by student-teacher planning, the worst abuses of the single basic textbook might be obviated. The fact remains that many students cannot read a book thought appropriate for a given grade level, and must find their information in other sources. By the same token, many students will find the language and concepts of the textbook too elementary to be of interest; these advanced readers need other, more challenging materials. In required courses, at least, there seems to be no sound reason for requiring all students to read the same book.

It is not easy in some schools for a teacher to abolish use of a single textbook.[8] If the school purchases books for students, the control of the policies may be in the hands of central administrators or the board of education. If students pay for books, their parents may expect to have the books used in the classroom. With skillful interpretation by the teacher, however, it is usually possible to substitute a variety of resources for a single one, or at least to deal with the textbook as one resource instead of a complete guide. It is easier to get rid of the single textbook approach after an adequate classroom library has been developed. Also a teacher must learn to organize instruction around problems or units independent of the approach used in the textbook, if the text is to serve the function of a resource instead of a syllabus. Burton has commented on this point as follows:

> *Second,* the teacher should consciously break away from the "mastery-of-the-text" concept and give explicit attention to the total range of learning outcomes. Teachers should define explicitly the actual behavior patterns, meanings, attitudes, facts, and skills toward which learning may be guided. Teachers far too often do not know any objectives other than "cover the text" or "follow the course of study." [9]

Thus the appropriate use of a textbook is conditioned by the teacher's own approach to instructional planning. If his goals are broad and his materials are rich, he will go far beyond the textbook and depart also from its exact arrangement of topics. Further discus-

[8] The total value of new textbooks sold in the United States in 1956 was estimated at $277,000,000, according to *1956 Annual Survey of the Textbook-Publishing Industry,* American Textbook Publishers Institute, 1957.

[9] William H. Burton, *The Guidance of Learning Activities,* 3rd ed. (New York: Appleton-Century-Crofts, Inc., © 1962), p. 96. Reprinted by permission.

sion of this planning activity will appear in the chapter which follows.

*Workbooks.* One particular type of textbook is the consumable and inexpensive workbook. Usually bound in cheap, paperback covers and intended to be "used up" each time around, these aids to homework are sold at the rate of nearly thirty million dollars worth each year. The popularity of the workbook arises chiefly from the ease with which it lends itself to individual drill by the student. Like any drill procedure, however, the workbook can be and often is overworked. When drill becomes an end in itself and is not related by either teacher or student to the basic concepts or problems under study, it loses its value. In such cases the student comes to regard the workbook answers as the goal, and he may simply fill them in by copying from some other student's workbook. This procedure may have social value or give practice in use of the telephone, but it contributes little to reflective thinking or development of new insights. The workbook appears to have become separated from the main stream of instruction and to have degenerated in far too many cases into a kind of meaningless busy work.

*Homework.* Closely related to the problem of resource use is that of homework. There has been much debate and also a considerable amount of research on the subject of homework. There are the uncritical advocates of more homework for all students, and especially for the more able ones. On the other end of the continuum are the equally uncritical enemies of homework. Those who advocate it are currently on the popular side, if one can judge from the amount of homework assigned in senior high schools. Various studies indicate that the amount assigned or expected of students approximates at least two hours per day. In recent years the amount of homework assigned has increased and extended into the junior high school. Even elementary teachers are now assigning homework in many schools.

Typical of the arguments for more homework are these:

1. It helps students learn the skills of independent study, useful for success in college.
2. It teaches self-reliance.
3. It enriches and supplements classroom instruction.

4. It reinforces classroom learning.

5. It helps students develop leisure habits and interests that are promising for later life.

Other assertions are that homework improves students' school marks (which is debatable), and that it helps keep youth busy and out of mischief (which is a dubious justification). The critics of homework base their attack chiefly on its excesses, or on its unrelatedness to school learning:

1. Homework deprives youth of family life or of normal social pleasures which are themselves educative.

2. Homework is usually designed to be asocial, or aimed at separation from one's fellows.

3. Homework is often unrelated to what goes on in the classroom; it therefore tends to become busy work.

4. Homework is carried on under the most unpromising study conditions in many homes. It may develop poor study habits.

5. Homework forces the teacher to spend all his time checking answers and leaves no time for his basic task of helping students learn *how* and *why*.

6. Homework separates the learner from his teacher, thus depriving him of systematic help.

It might be added that the usual assumption regarding homework assignments is that they derive from teacher and/or textbook. It is seldom mentioned that students who really become involved in a problem-solving process will pursue the problem with enthusiasm outside of school, too. Those who develop interest in reading will read at home. Those who become enthusiastic about writing will pursue this activity at home. In short, homework, properly conceived and self-assigned, is a kind of test of the effectiveness of the teacher. If he is successful in "motivating" his students, homework will go on without specific assignments. If he is unsuccessful in this effort, the homework he then feels he must assign may tend to lose value and become busy work or (worse) a disciplinary procedure.

It seems likely that most secondary schools will continue to have homework expectations. It behooves teachers, therefore, to evaluate it and improve it. Specifically, they should plan it in such a way as to avoid creating unbearable burdens on students. Strang makes certain further suggestions for improving homework practices:

More school time should be devoted to the guidance of learning.

Students should be encouraged to do more reading and studying of the kind that will have continuing value in later life.

Students should be allowed more initiative and choice in the matters of what and how and when and with whom to study.

Homework should be more individualized, meaningful, and useful; students should uncover new problems in school which they solve at home.

Approval should be accorded to homework that is well planned and successfully completed.[10]

A teacher who wishes to make homework meaningful must help students seek and find resources for it. The typical home library is ill-provided with such resources, and the public library may not be very helpful for some kinds of home study. Teachers who overlook this lack of resources may inadvertently force students to copy from encyclopedias or to rely exclusively on their textbooks; students also often copy each other's work.

*Audio-visual aids.* Good teachers have used audio-visual aids for many years. Maps, charts, and graphs serve a variety of functions, not only in geography and mathematics but in nearly all subjects. Three-dimensional objects and models are helpful in reinforcing understanding by supplying additional media for perception. In combination with charts, these realia may, for example, picture vividly a manufacturing process or the evolution of costumes. A bicycle wheel helps teach the relationship of circumference to diameter. A product exhibit helps identify a foreign culture and its economic basis.

Photographs, cartoons, and other drawings serve teachers in dozens of ways—reminding a class of its list of goals, inspiring students to write stories or poems, orienting them to occupations or processes in industry, business, or government, getting them acquainted with people of another culture—the list could be endless.

More expensive but also more versatile are film slides and glass slides. Not only are slides available commercially on almost any topic, but many amateur photographers have collections of them,

---

10 Ruth M. Strang, "Homework and Guided Study," in *Encyclopedia of Educational Research,* Chester W. Harris, ed. (New York: Macmillan Co., 1960), p. 678.

taken in the course of their travels. In most classrooms today there are students who can locate such visual resources in their own homes.

The 16 mm. sound film is a common tool in secondary schools. Large school systems are building extensive film libraries. Other schools can rent films from extension services of public universities, or from other sources in government or industry. Unfortunately, rental arrangements often result in such delay that the film, when it finally arrives, has no longer any relevance to the topics currently being studied. Many of the weaknesses in the use of films stem from their unavailability at the time when the need exists.

Other types of projectors are useful, too—the opaque and overhead projectors for presenting flat pictures, drawings, notes, and diagrams; the film-strip projector for a consecutive series of photographs; and the microprojector for reproducing microscope slides on a screen.

Both disk and tape recordings are valuable in music, speech, literature, geography, history, human relations, science, and the study of controversial issues in government. The making of recordings by students themselves can be helpful in evaluating individual growth or in preparing presentations to an audience. Most schools now have tape recorders readily available for classroom use.

For a quick overview of the various types of audio-visual aids, the following list is a useful beginning. The reader may add to the list from his own knowledge. New devices are constantly emerging. The list is intended to be a suggestion of the scope of these aids, not a comprehensive classification of them. Many of these aids can be made by students, with significant value in new learning.

1. *Models* and *replicas:*
   Schools, stores, banks, post offices
   Facsimiles of historical documents
   Houses, tools, weapons, boats, inventions, planes
   Cutaway models of human body or of machinery
   Automobile and aviation trainers
   Planetarium
   Terrain models
   Three-dimensional mock-ups
   Puppets, dolls
2. *Actual objects:*
   Clothing
   Cars, bicycles, furniture

Animals, fish, invertebrates
Agricultural products
Manufacturing products
Business forms
Rocks, plants
Geometric forms: sphere, square, etc.
Aquarium
Specimens
Demonstrations
Clocks, calendars, rulers, etc.
Exhibits

3. *Audio-visual reproductions:*
Moving pictures
Film strips
Film slides
Glass slides
Radio and television programs
Maps, globes
Charts, graphs, diagrams
Photographs
Drawings, paintings
Posters
Disk recordings
Tape recordings
Chalkboards
Bulletin boards
Microscopes
Opaque and overhead projectors
Two-dimensional mock-ups
Stereographs (three-dimensional pictures)
Microprojectors
Comic strips
Exploded drawings
Cellophane drawings [11]

Schools are increasingly including audio-visual materials and equipment in their resources for classroom and building use. In spite of their growing sophistication in use of these aids, teachers are frequently disappointed in their uneven effects on students. Some stu-

[11] For a comprehensive treatment of the types and uses of audio-visual aids, see Edgar Dale, *Audio-Visual Methods in Teaching*, rev. ed. (New York: Holt, Rinehart and Winston, Inc., 1954).

dents are highly enthusiastic, some are blasé or seemingly unaffected. Some students do not even seem to have watched the same film or heard the same recording as the rest, though they sat through it.

The facts about perception, discussed in Chapter 4, must be taken into account. Each learner brings his own unique perceptions to the lesson and sees what his experience has prepared him to see. If teachers expect a common impact they must plan for it, and prepare students for watching or listening. Teachers must time the use of an audio-visual aid so that it is perceived by students as related to their questions or problems.

Even when used with skill by teachers, audio-visual aids make different impacts on different learners. They are simply reinforcement or enrichment for learning by other means and not the sole medium of instruction. Teachers who overdo their use diminish their effect.

*Educational television.* The same caution must be applied also to educational television. Not all students will (or can) see or hear the same things. Since the program is planned by an outsider, it is aimed at a mythical "average" listener. If it hits its mark for some, it will miss it for others. Careful planning and limited use of television may increase its effectiveness for most students.

Educational television received its first major boost in 1952 when 242 channels were set aside for educational use by the Federal Communications Commission. (This number had been increased to 267 channels by 1961.) During the 1950's and 1960's these channels were in demand by school systems and colleges. Meanwhile, closed-circuit television also made its appearance, introducing the added element of local telecasts through coaxial cables by a school to its own classrooms.

Aided by Ford Foundation money and encouraged by preliminary research findings, school systems across the country have experimented with television teaching, both with live and kinescoped programs. Hagerstown, Maryland, one of the pioneers, was televising by closed circuit to almost 17,000 pupils each day in 1961. The Midwest Program on Airborne Television Instruction was sending programs from two DC-6 planes over Lafayette, Indiana, to one-half million pupils in 1,164 school systems of six states by 1962. At least forty urban school systems were by that date committed also to closed-circuit television for some classes.

There appears to be little doubt that students can learn the lessons conventionally included in the curriculum by television. The Fund for the Advancement of Education (often referred to as the Ford Foundation) has spearheaded most of the research on the effectiveness of television teaching.[12] Their reports, and reports of research from other sources,[13] show television to be at least as effective as conventional teaching in classes ranging from music to mathematics and from spelling to history. The increased cost of such instruction by television has been justified by editorial writers as an experiment in mass instruction, which could ultimately be cheaper through its replacement of some teachers. This claim is rejected by educational leaders in television teaching. Some maintain that television enables school systems to use teachers more efficiently, since schools may select the best presenters of each subject area and expose them to hundreds of students at once. It is further argued that less able teachers have an opportunity to improve their skills by observing their colleagues at work. Meanwhile, as in the case of most curriculum innovations, proponents maintain that the lesson planning and teamwork by teachers involved in the experiments have stepped up the quality of teaching and improved the curriculum. They also suggest that commercially produced video tapes and kinescopes can ultimately enrich this medium by bringing to classes the finest talent in the world. Because of restrictions and cost, such kinescopes are not yet generally available for use in educational television.

Opponents of educational television have not been exactly silent, though their voices have not been heard through the popular mass media. Those who believe that "teaching requires knowing the learner" are dubious about a technique that features presentation of facts and concepts by lecture and demonstration. They urge a re-emphasis on development of new attitudes and changed behavior. They point out that little impact can be made toward that task by "show and tell" procedures. They fear that attention to individual differences will be minimized as increased emphasis is placed on large-group instruction. And they resent the establishing of a status

12 Ford Foundation, *Teaching by Television* (New York: Fund for the Advancement of Education, 1961).

13 See, for example, Arthur D. Morse, *Schools of Tomorrow Today* (Garden City, N.Y.: Doubleday & Co., Inc., 1960).

hierarchy among teachers that is based on their specialized skills in dramatic presentation.

"But," reply the advocates of television, "research has shown that students do learn the usually expected facts and skills as well by ETV as by conventional teaching."

"Exactly," respond the critics, "but all that proves is that you can do the wrong thing better by television. You will reinforce by such methods most of what is wrong with education. You will give permanent status (and perhaps higher salaries) to teachers who can do well the very things they should not do in the first place."

Thus the pros and cons of ETV are being argued everywhere, while experimentation goes forward and both private and public funds are being invested in new installations. Perhaps the real uses of television await discovery, and may require years of fumbling and false directions before they are incorporated into practice. Inlow comments on this issue in a recent book and suggests seven criteria to be applied to each new television experiment:

1. Which areas of learning respond best to a telling-listening-showing situation? . . .

2. Which important outcomes of learning cannot be accomplished by telling, listening, showing? Can independence, altruism, citizenship, research skills, emotional control, effective speaking habits, analytical thought, or problem-solving be achieved through these means, and if so, to what degree?

3. When telling, listening, showing are effective learning media, what is the proper balance in any curriculum area between the impersonal, large audience and the more personal, small group approach?

4. How can teachers not in the prestigious, on-camera category be made to feel professional? . . .

5. Can non-certified teachers or teacher-helpers be employed effectively and specifically in what ways—as monitors or proctors?

6. Will television teaching be as effective when the glamor wears off as it seems to be at present?

7. And last, is evaluative research adequate when based primarily on achievement testing? [14]

---

[14] Gail M. Inlow, *Maturity in High School Teaching* (Englewood Cliffs, N.J.: Prentice-Hall, Inc., © 1963), pp. 115–116. Reprinted by permission.

The Michigan Committee on Educational Television recently examined the basic functions of teaching by television, using their own state philosophy of public education [15] as a frame of reference. Their report contains the following statements of belief, and questions regarding educational television:

> *Educational Values:* The publication, "A Statement of Basic Philosophy Regarding Public Education in Michigan" contains a section entitled, "We Hold These Values." Using appropriate statements from this list as guide posts, we can see that direct instruction by educational television is consistent with some values and in conflict with others.
>
> WE ACCEPT THE FACT THAT EVERYONE IS UNIQUE. Each person has his own individual needs and abilities and can make his own special contribution.
>
> Since each person is unique, would it not be difficult for educational television, which is a mass communication medium, to provide for differences among children and between classrooom groups?
>
> Can a body of information be selected which would be suitable for all children in all Michigan communities?
>
> If so, who would determine the content and method of presentation of the material to be telecast?
>
> How could it be scheduled to arrive at a time which would be appropriate for classroom groups and individual learners?
>
> WE BELIEVE THAT AMERICAN CITIZENS ARE BORN FREE AND EQUAL. Our ideal is to provide a comprehensive, contemporary educational program for each individual, regardless of the school district in which he might live.
>
> Has educational television an important contribution to make in improving the range of learning experiences available to youngsters in a financially deprived or geographically isolated school district?
>
> Would such use of television be appropriate for the total class groups for a large portion of each school day or only for individuals and small groups with unique needs?
>
> Are there other devices such as the sound film or teaching machines which could accomplish the same purposes more effectively and efficiently?

[15] Michigan Department of Public Instruction, *A Statement of Basic Philosophy Regarding Public Education in Michigan,* Bulletin 364 (Lansing: The Department of Public Instruction, 1960).

WE BELIEVE THAT CLOSE COOPERATION BETWEEN HOME AND SCHOOL IS ESSENTIAL. To best serve the child, the home and school must aim at the same goals and should maintain a two way system of reporting and conferring regarding the growth and development of the child. . . . Parents have the obligation and responsibility to understand the basic educational values of their school and help determine these values.

Is ETV flexible enough, even when programs are locally originated, to alter its goals in the light of results from parents' or educators' discussion of children's needs?

Can parents help determine or influence the educational values which, in turn, will affect the content and presentation of televised instruction when programs originate in another locality?

WE BELIEVE IN THE USE OF ALL AVAILABLE INFORMATION AND RESOURCES TO HELP IN DETERMINING WHAT THE EDUCATION OF EACH CHILD SHOULD BE. This requires that we look to each child before determining what kinds of experience will have value for him. Education must continually depend upon scientific inquiry to judge the appropriateness of a curriculum to the individual and the effectiveness of methods and materials employed.

If we accept the scientific approach, which requires that we look to each child before determining what kinds of learning experience will have value for him, can we also subscribe to the idea that education consists of passing on via TV a body of subject matter to all children?

How can ETV be used to help teach the skills, attitudes and understandings appropriate to each learner?

WE BELIEVE IN THE FREEDOMS ESSENTIAL TO THE PERPETUATION OF A DEMOCRATIC SOCIETY. Foremost of these freedoms, we believe, must be freedom of mind.

Are there aspects of national and local activities which, if telecast, could stimulate thought and awaken interest in the ideals of democracy?

Is there a danger in the use of a powerful medium like ETV, particularly in a large network situation, that indoctrination could take place?

WE BELIEVE IN EDUCATION FOR IMAGINATIVE, LOGICAL AND CRITICAL THINKING. We do not believe that one learns to think by being told to do so, but only by actually thinking. One must be given the opportunity to solve problems—social, academic, economic, personal—that demand creative and critical thought.

Can TV contribute to developing problem solving skills?

Since viewing television is passive, is there any likelihood of pupils having less opportunity for creative activities and critical thinking? [16]

Some of the most thoughtful advocates of television teaching recognize the limitations of the medium and urge careful preteaching and follow-up, as in the case of any audio-visual aid. An excellent statement of basic considerations for learning has been presented by Harold E. Wigren:

> 1. The learner—not the teacher—is the central figure in any learning situation, whether that situation be in the classroom or on television. The objective, therefore, is learning, not teaching.
>
> 2. The learner should be considered a rational participator rather than a passive receptor of impressions. He must be involved in the learning situation if he is to use it for his own betterment and if change of behavior is to result.
>
> 3. Mere exposure does not guarantee learning. Unless something occurs within the learner, he will be able neither to remember nor to use what he has presumably learned.
>
> 4. In the final analysis, each student selects what he learns. He makes his selections in terms of his own needs, interests, and purposes. . . .
>
> 5. Because the learner does the selection of learning experiences, he must be given opportunity to make decisions as he progresses through the learning experience.[17]

Wigren went on in the same address to stress such basic principles as the uniqueness of individual perception, the essential need for interaction in learning, and the role of discovery and exploration in learning. Educational television built into a total experience such as Wigren was describing might be a quite different resource from the mass viewing thus far experimented with in the secondary schools. The obstacles to use of television at the right time and for the right purposes may be someday overcome.

---

[16] Subcommittee on Educational Television, *Report to State Curriculum Planning Committee* (August 25, 1960), pp. 4–5.

[17] "Learning: Some Basic Considerations" (address to MPATI Evaluation Session, Ann Arbor, Mich., November 14, 1961).

*Language laboratories.* In the preceding chapter reference was made to the use of tape recorders for improving speech skills in English. An extension of this device is rapidly growing in popularity among foreign language teachers. Individual booths equipped with microphones and head-sets enable each student to listen to a tape recording in a foreign language and to practice his own oral command of it by imitating the recording, and then listening to his own efforts. In some installations he can also communicate with and receive individual instruction from the teacher at the control panel. The less costly installations permit only one tape, or at most two or three at one time. In more expensive laboratories, each student can hear a different tape if desired.[18]

More than one thousand language laboratories are already in use, and most new buildings are now including one or more such facilities. Their advantages for the oral-aural method of teaching a language are obvious. Each student can hear the language pronounced by a native. He can practice his own pronunciation as an individual learner instead of awaiting his turn as in a conventional class. He can meanwhile be individually monitored and corrected by the teacher. He can work continuously at his own level and pace without disturbing others. In spite of its cost, the language laboratory seems destined to continue in popularity as a result of its proven contribution to students' oral command of a foreign language.

The basic problems relating to teachers' ability to adapt their methods and handle the equipment skillfully are being generally solved. The laboratory should be adjacent to the language classroom, or even structurally a part of it, if a teacher is expected to use it conveniently. For example, he should be able to supervise a few students in the booths while other activities are going on in the classroom. At other times, of course, the entire class would be using the laboratory.

## Resources of the community

If learning is to become lifelike, it must escape the narrow confines of the classroom and make use of the rich resources of the

18 A good description of the various types of language laboratories may be found in Edward M. Stock, *The Language Laboratory and Modern Language Teaching* (New York: Oxford University Press, 1960).

community. Perhaps the most obvious resource from the community is the parent or other citizen who has some unique experience or knowledge to contribute. For many years alert teachers have tapped this resource. They have found people generally happy to come into the classroom and help the group on some problem or topic. Mr. Jones has just returned from the East and has some interesting colored slides of life in rural Japan. Mrs. Smith edits the newsletter of the League of Women Voters and has made a study of certain political issues now under debate. Mr. Simpson is an executive in a corporation and has some interesting information on automobile manufacturing and sales. The Reverend Mr. Black has made a special study of the great religions of the world and can compare them objectively.

Other contributions may be less spectacular but equally helpful at a certain stage of work by a class. Parents have presented recipes, folk songs, or costumes of a foreign culture; they have shown students their collections, or told them about their jobs, or discussed community problems as members of a panel. Parents have helped classes learn nearly everything from weaving a basket to developing a city budget.

Using such resource persons effectively calls for careful planning. It is perhaps obvious that knowledge of some subject does not alone qualify a person to convey or report his knowledge. A list of persons who (1) have a special contribution to make and (2) can do it well should be developed by the staff of a secondary school for the use of teachers and students. Resource files of this kind have been built up in many schools, and often contain hundreds of names. Addresses, telephone numbers, and a brief description of the type of contribution the person is qualified to give make the resource file a useful tool.

The file might well contain other community resources. Not only persons, but agencies and places can contribute to learning at some level and at an appropriate time. Students have visited and received help from a wide variety of community resources:

| | |
|---|---|
| banks, offices, stores | libraries |
| factories | government offices |
| farms | historical landmarks |
| railway stations | power dams |
| airports | conservation projects, parks |

radio stations
television studios
newspaper plants
telephone offices
post offices
theaters
city halls
museums
art institutes

experimental gardens
scientific laboratories
mines, oil fields
employment service offices
chambers of commerce
health departments
courts
hospitals
housing projects

This list could be extended almost indefinitely if it were to be particularized in terms of specific communities, and of special problems or needs of various classes. The resource file can be helpful to teachers, not only in locating the right community resource but in alerting them to the possibilities that are waiting to be used by school classes.

A survey of the community is a valuable learning experience for students, and can enrich the resource file also. As different problems arise, occasions are presented for a class to organize and carry out a survey of community resources, as well as of problems and needs. What exactly is the function of the city planning commission? Where do we get our water? How do we protect its purity? Can we be assured of its continued supply? What are the functions of the various divisions of the Police Department? What are future plans regarding expressways? Parks and other recreation areas? Schools? What social services are performed by churches? What is the average income of our community? What types of housing are there? What controls exist to prevent deterioration of residential areas? What health problems do we face as a community? Where are there areas that threaten public health or safety, or that are just plain ugly? These and dozens of other questions arise in classes which use problem-solving methods. They suggest at least a visit to places or agencies outside the classroom, and, in some instances, a full-scale survey that may take several weeks to complete. Such surveys not only help students to gain new understanding of community problems and needs, they also teach valuable skills such as:

conducting polls
writing letters
using the telephone
interviewing

meeting new persons
organizing trips
planning the survey
taking notes
selecting and organizing ideas
drawing conclusions
reporting findings
planning recommendations

When students leave the building for an hour's field trip or for a more extended project, careful planning by the class will help guard against mishaps and insure maximum learning from the experience. Permission slips should be signed by parents. The building administrator should also approve the trip, if only to enable him to interpret its purpose to other teachers and to parents. Some consideration should be given by the class to such matters as what they hope to learn, what questions will best produce that learning, what kind of behavior will insure the success of the venture, and what courtesy demands of visitors. Individual responsibilities, including certain leadership roles, should be planned in advance. Follow-up of the trip should include discussion and analysis of what was seen or heard, its meaning or applications, and what conclusions or recommendations can be drawn from these new experiences. There should also be an evaluation of the trip, both as a learning resource and as an experience in class self-control. Most schools have rules or policies relating to at least some of these factors of the field trip.

Out of experiences on field trips or community surveys have developed many service projects by students. In general, these projects come about through:

1. Observing a problem or need that exists in some aspect of community life.

2. Deciding what needs to be done about the problem.

3. Identifying what students themselves could contribute to the solution of the problem.

4. Planning and carrying out the proposed service project.

5. Evaluating the outcomes.

A small creek flowed past the grounds, partly on school property and partly on an old, abandoned railroad right of way. The science classes had for several years gone on hikes along this creek to collect small specimens, to study erosion, and to measure the flow-rate. One spring a discussion in science class brought out the fact that the creek channel would be much more useful if some planting were done along the banks. Permission was readily obtained from the railroad and contributions to the project flowed in from parents and from civic groups. The class made several trips to woods some miles distant and brought back shrubs, flowers, and small trees which they had obtained permission to dig out. Neatly lettered wood signs were placed beside each plant as it was identified. Thus was born our community's nature trail, which is still being used and enjoyed by both children and adults.[19]

Examples of projects undertaken by students for serving and improving their own community could be multiplied. Over twenty-five years ago Hanna reported a list of several hundred community services performed by youth. The list ranged from projects designed to improve health, safety, and beauty to increasing family income and writing a local history.[20] In urban communities, students have aided public agencies in conducting polls, mapping neighborhood areas, getting out the vote, controlling rats and other pests. They have beautified the community by planting trees and flowers, and by conducting clean-up and paint-up campaigns. They have petitioned for and obtained traffic lights and needed city ordinances. They have aided needy families, conducted salvage drives, and campaigned for community improvements of all kinds. No one can survey the overall story of services to the community by youth without a feeling of pride and exhilaration.[21]

Not only do these service projects produce tangible outcomes which are assets to any community; they also provide an outlet for the altruism of young people and lend reality to the learning process. Resources for learning go beyond printed materials, speakers, and audio-visual aids. Resources also await discovery and use in

[19] Roland C. Faunce and Morrel J. Clute, *Teaching and Learning in the Junior High School* (Belmont, Calif.: Wadsworth Publishing Co., Inc., 1961), p. 289.

[20] Paul R. Hanna, *Youth Serves the Community* (New York: Appleton-Century-Crofts, Inc., 1936).

[21] For numerous examples of actual community services performed by youth, see Edward G. Olsen, ed., *The Modern Community School* (New York: Appleton-Century-Crofts, Inc., 1953).

the form of real problems to be solved, real needs to be met, and real services that will help make the community a better place to live. This is the thesis of the "community school."

*In conclusion.* In this chapter we have examined the resources for learning that exist or can be developed in the classroom, in the school, and in the community. The classroom itself can be a place that challenges and facilitates learning if ingenious teachers seek resources and plan their arrangement with skill. Students engaged in problem-solving activities will find resources in the school library, in the audio-visual materials center, and in the staff and the facilities of the total school. They will also find valuable help outside the school from private and public agencies and from persons in their own community and outside it.

Effective use of such resources calls for good planning. The chapter that follows will take a look at the whole process of instructional planning.

## FOR FURTHER READING

Alexander, William M., and Paul M. Halverson, *Effective Teaching in Secondary Schools.* New York: Holt, Rinehart and Winston, Inc., 1956. Chapter 3, "The Classroom as a Learning Laboratory," contains good suggestions for making the classroom itself a major resource for learning. Chapter 10 includes a good check-list for field trips.

Association for Supervision and Curriculum Development, *Creating a Good Environment for Learning.* Washington, D.C.: The Association Yearbook, 1954. This entire yearbook provides helpful suggestions for building resources into the actual learning environment.

Burton, William H., *The Guidance of Learning Activities,* 3rd ed. New York: Appleton-Century-Crofts, Inc., 1962. This most recent edition adds many new illustrations and applications to an already useful book.

Dale, Edgar, *Audio-Visual Methods in Teaching,* rev. ed. New York: Holt, Rinehart and Winston, Inc., 1954. Basic and comprehensive reference on all types of audio-visual aids and their uses.

Englehardt, N. L., Jr., "Laboratories for Learning," *School Executive,* 74:3 (November 1954), 63–66. Graphic presentation of ways to design classrooms that are themselves resources for learning.

Faunce, Roland C., and Nelson L. Bossing, *Developing the Core Curriculum,* rev. ed. Englewood Cliffs, N.J.: Prentice-Hall, Inc., 1958. Chapter 10 suggests many resources in school and outside that can enrich learning. Emphasis is on process of pupil discovery of such resources.

Faunce, Roland C., and Morrel J. Clute, *Teaching and Learning in the Junior High School*. Belmont, Calif.: Wadsworth Publishing Co., Inc., 1961. Chapter 12 suggests many ways to use the community as a resource for learning.

*Free and Inexpensive Learning Materials*, 11th ed. Nashville, Tenn.: Division of Surveys and Field Services, George Peabody College for Teachers, 1962. A useful, alphabetized listing of inexpensive classroom materials and their sources.

Grambs, Jean D., William J. Iverson, and Franklin K. Patterson, *Modern Methods in Secondary Education*, rev. ed. New York: Holt, Rinehart and Winston, Inc., 1958. Chapters 7 and 8 include some excellent suggestions for classroom materials and community resources.

Klausmeier, H. J., *Teaching in the Secondary School*. New York: Harper & Row, Publishers, 1958. Chapter 11 presents a useful, short summary of the uses of audio-visual materials.

McKean, Robert C., *Principles and Methods in Secondary Education*. Columbus, Ohio: Charles E. Merrill Books, Inc., 1962. Chapter 6, "Selecting and Using Instructional Materials," discusses ways to put the textbook "into perspective." Good suggestions also for supplementary materials.

Metropolitan School Study Council, *Fifty Teachers to a Classroom*. New York: Macmillan Co., 1950. Enriching classroom learning by the use of resource persons is the theme of this attractive pamphlet.

Miel, Alice, *et al.*, *Cooperative Procedures in Learning*. New York: Bureau of Publications, Teachers College, Columbia University, 1952. Chapter 5 contains suggestions for discovering enriched resources.

Mills, H. H., and Harl R. Douglass, *Teaching in High School*, 2nd ed. New York: Ronald Press Co., 1957. Chapters 15 and 19 discuss uses of instructional materials and community resources.

Olsen, Edward G., ed., *The Modern Community School*. New York: Appleton-Century-Crofts, Inc., 1953. This entire volume is a useful handbook on ways to use community resources for effective learning.

*Sources of Free and Inexpensive Educational Materials*. Chicago: Field Enterprises, Inc., 1955. A useful list of places to write for supplementary materials.

Stock, Edward M., *The Language Laboratory and Modern Language Teaching*. New York: Oxford University Press, 1960. Contains a good description of the various types of language laboratories now in use.

Wendt, Paul R., *Audio-Visual Instruction*. Washington, D.C.: The National Education Association, 1957. The author considers the place of audio-visual materials in the classroom in the light of available research data. No. 14 in the series "What Research Says to the Teacher."

# 11

# Planning
# for classroom
# instruction

The use of many resources for learning demands systematic planning. Teachers who depart from the basic textbook are sometimes accused of having no lesson plans. A few teachers may justify this accusation, but in general the reverse is likely to be true. The easiest, and least fruitful approach to teaching is complete reliance on the textbook. When one uses a textbook not only as the chief resource, but also as the determiner of goals, scope, and sequence of learning, there is not much room left for any further planning by the teacher. The same thing may be said, perhaps in a slightly less degree, of those who faithfully follow a course of study or syllabus.

Curriculum guides are of various kinds. Their stated purpose is usually that of supplying a "minimum" common experience for a class, beyond which each teacher is encouraged to diversify pupil experiences in terms of readiness or skill levels of individuals. Some teachers, however, will settle for the minimum as the plan for the class. This is likely to be especially true of those teachers who are unaccustomed to planning and who therefore tend to lean on the suggestions of authors of anything that is in print. This is the hazard of curriculum guides; they may become a crutch for the dependent teacher.

266

## Why plan?

Freedom from preplanning by others constitutes a challenge to planning by teachers. The use of multiple resources also helps create the challenge to plan. The more use teachers make of rich and varied resources such as were discussed in the preceding chapter, the greater is their need for systematic planning. Finally, the degree to which teachers involve their students in planning affects both the amount and nature of the planning. The more the teacher seeks to give his students some experience in identifying their own goals and procedures, the less he has to rely on preplanning by others and the greater is his consequent challenge to engage in planning. But he should be planning *with* students, not just *for* them, and the nature of the plans is also affected by student involvement. This point will be discussed more fully later in this chapter.

To the question "Why plan?" we have, in substance, replied:

1. We must plan carefully if we expect to escape the tyranny of the textbook and the syllabus.
2. We must plan systematically if we expect to use varied resources for learning.
3. We must plan creatively if we hope to involve our students in formulation of goals and choice of procedures.

Any good teaching reveals good planning. Lesson planning is not popular or easy, but it is an essential part of effective teaching. Confronting a class without any plans is not a promising procedure for teachers who wish to be professionals.

*Use of resources.* In preceding chapters we have discussed the materials and resources of instructional planning. Among these resources are the students themselves, whose interests, problems, needs, and competencies deserve careful study. Good teaching will involve plans to convert these learners into resources for the group. The classroom itself has also been discussed as a resource. Good teaching calls for planning to equip the classroom in such a way as to make it a rich resource, and to use it in that fashion. Other facilities and materials throughout the school and community are available to the alert teacher: persons, materials, tools, equipment, and special facilities. Little use can be made of these resources without systematic inventory and planning. Use of resources not only suggests planning; it demands it.

*Definition of purposes.* The whole process of planning is affected by purposes of teaching and learning. Throughout this book we have defined learning as the modification of behavior. Teachers who accept this definition will ask themselves such questions as these: *What behaviors* do we seek to change? *In what ways* do we want to change behavior? Such questions directly structure purposes, which in turn must be the starting point of planning.

In Chapter 2 the "behavioral goals" of education, as spelled out by French and others, were discussed. This approach to instructional purposes requires teachers to answer certain questions as they begin to plan:

1. What traits, skills, characteristics, or attitudes would an *educated person possess?*

2. How would he behave if he had acquired these traits, skills, characteristics, or attitudes?

3. What can teachers do with students to *bring about these desired behaviors?*

All planning is based on purposes of some kind. When the only obvious purpose is command of selected subject matter, teachers are obliged to select it on some basis, and their criteria for selection compels them to ask: Why this material? Why these activities? Teachers who seek to use subject matter as a means to the end of changing the behavior of learners in desirable ways must begin by defining these behavioral goals.

## Types of approaches to planning

*The unit method.* One approach to the achieving of greater flexibility of instruction is the unit method. Its goal is to achieve relationship between various knowledges, skills, and concepts by grouping them around some larger topic or problem. Alexander and Halverson define the "unit of work" thus:

. . . a unit of work is a major division of instruction, built around some single idea, theme, problem, or purpose, and including such subject matter and activities as are related and important to learners in developing the idea, theme, problem, or purpose.[1]

The idea of the unit method might be illustrated as follows, using the field of American history as an example. Most textbooks in history follow a chronological approach. This requires that all the separate events occurring during a given time period are studied in a single chapter or section of the textbook, even though their only relationship to each other may be their having occurred simultaneously. Some recurring topics, such as tariff laws, will be studied perhaps a half-dozen times during the year but with little relationship to each other. Meanings and relationships are lost in the attempt to preserve strict chronology of all events. A unit in American history, on the other hand, might be developed around such a topic as "The Negro in America." The unit might draw on the textbook and on numerous other resources to give understanding of the history of the Negro since slaves were first brought to this country in 1619, as background for discussion of cultural and political achievements of Negro citizens in the Twentieth Century, and of problems of integration and civil rights which confront the nation. Thus the unit method brings many events and issues together around one problem or topic, instead of scattering them over ten months of school and three and one-half centuries of history.[2]

A literature class may undertake a unit on "courage," or "the development of values" and use literature from many time periods as a resource in arriving at understanding of these concepts. A science unit may deal with "protecting our water supply," or "should we stop nuclear testing?" A government class may study a unit on "financing our schools." In any case, the logic of the unit resides in the learner's perception of it as a significant problem. He must see relationships between various parts of the unit, and between the unit and a problem he accepts as having some validity.

In Chapter 4 there was discussion of the learning principle that the learner behaves (learns) as a total organism. This means that he

[1] William M. Alexander and Paul M. Halverson, *Effective Teaching in Secondary Schools* (New York: Holt, Rinehart and Winston, Inc., 1956), p. 434. By permission.

[2] Some history texts group several chronologically connected chapters under one heading and label them a unit, such as "Unit 9: The Era of Jackson." This practice appears to be a distortion of the meaning of the unit method in history.

attacks the learning situation as a whole person who cannot be segmented into separate subject compartments as most senior high school curricula are. This idea of the wholeness of the learner has gained widespread acceptance and accounts for the growing interest in the unit method. Although teachers often violate this concept in their curriculum planning, there is increasing effort to use the unit method, especially among those teachers who achieve some freedom from textbooks.

Throughout this book, emphasis has been placed on recognition of and allowance for individual differences. A unit should be broad enough, and flexible enough to permit each (different) learner to perceive its significance for *him*, and to find experiences in it designed for *his* successful learning. The unit method, properly used, can make a significant contribution to this challenge of meeting individual differences. Brink has commented on this fact in discussing recent research on adapting the curriculum to the individual:

> Instructional procedures that provide for the selection of a wide variety of learning materials, for organization in large units, and for flexible methods of teaching facilitate adaptation to individual differences within the classroom.[3]

The unit method not only permits adaptation to individual differences; it meets most of the criteria of effective teaching, generally supported by research. One excellent summary of these criteria appears in *Reorganizing the High School Curriculum,* by Harold and Elsie Alberty. The list is headed "Some characteristics of an effective generalized teaching-learning procedure":

> 1. The concept of the complete act of thought provides the key to an effective classroom procedure. This concept involves: perplexity, confusion, or doubt, leading to a definition of the problem, the setting up of one or more hypotheses or tentative plans of action; investigation; analysis, interpretation, testing the various hypotheses with the necessary elaboration, modification, or refinement of the most fruitful hypothesis; and action based upon adequate data.
>
> 2. The complete act of thought describes not only the way an

---

[3] William G. Brink, "Secondary Education: Programs," in *Encyclopedia of Educational Research* (New York: Macmillan Co., 1960), p. 1266.

individual goes about resolving a difficulty, but also describes the way a group with a common problem operates in order to find a solution to its problem.

3. An effective teaching procedure recognizes the unity of various learning products, e.g., ideals, attitudes, understandings, appreciations, skills, and treats them as integral parts of the learning situation.

4. The ideals of democracy, the dynamic nature of the individual, the basic principles of motivation suggest that an effective teaching procedure gives a large place to cooperative purposing, planning, working, and evaluating.

5. An effective teaching procedure should take into account the wide range of individual differences which characterizes all groups, however common their purposes may be.

6. An effective teaching procedure should be sufficiently flexible to deal with a wide variety of learning situations.

7. An effective teaching procedure should facilitate the use of a wide variety of resources, such as reference materials, films, and recordings as integral parts of the learning experiences.

8. An effective teaching procedure draws freely upon material from appropriate fields of knowledge.[4]

Thus the unit method may be said to provide for effective learning. Paraphrasing the Alberty criteria, the good teaching unit should:

1. Employ problem-solving.
2. Be directed at unified goals.
3. Involve student-teacher planning.
4. Provide for individual differences by use of variety of resources.
5. Draw upon and integrate various fields of knowledge.

The unit will usually be so planned as to provide for several weeks of study, though there are some units that are shorter than this. Procedures in planning a unit vary somewhat, but most of them consist of the following parts:

1. *Statement of purposes:* reflecting both teachers' and students' purposes.

4 Harold B. Alberty and Elsie J. Alberty, *Reorganizing the High School Curriculum,* 3rd ed. (New York: Macmillan Co., 1962), pp. 331–332.

2. *Learning experiences or activities:* initiatory, developmental, culminating.

3. *Evaluation of unit:* by what means? with what instruments?

4. List of *materials* and *resources* to be used: in the classroom, in the school, in the community, or elsewhere.

*The lesson plan.* The lesson plan is a daily device. Even when it is drawn up for a week in advance, it is basically a plan for each day. In many schools, such daily plans are required of teachers in advance, for the use of substitute teachers.

If the unit method is in use, the lesson plan may well follow the organization of the unit and include, in outline or brief form, the purposes for the day, the activities, materials, and evaluative procedures to be used. Obviously, not all the purposes or procedures of the unit will be reproduced in a daily plan. It is more likely to present a brief version of some selected elements of the unit. Since other classroom experiences go on most days, not related to the unit under study, these activities also will appear in the lesson plan so far as they can be predicted.

A teacher's lesson plan is different in another significant respect from the teaching-learning unit. Students often participate in the actual planning of a unit. It is therefore a product of teacher-pupil planning. The lesson plan, on the other hand, is the teacher's own road map for each day. It may well reflect the drives or purposes of the group; indeed, it is to be hoped that it will. But it is a record of the teacher's expectations regarding what may take place during a given meeting of a class.

In classes where lecture and recitation procedures are used and the textbook is faithfully followed, the daily lesson plan is of little use. At most, it then becomes a brief notation of the pages "covered" and of the exercises or problems due each day. A homework assignment might also appear. In classes where procedures and resources are varied, the lesson plan assumes greater importance. It is a help to any substitute teacher; it is a guide to the teacher who prepared it, lending system and order to what is attempted and insuring efficient use of time. Yet, like the unit, the lesson plan is not sacred or unalterable. A good teacher is always prepared to discard or postpone some items planned if other, more significant developments occur.

Nordberg, Bradfield, and Odell make four suggestions regarding lesson plans:

1. Keep them simple. Don't make essays out of them. Don't attempt to cover too much ground.
2. Use the same form consistently, once you have decided upon the form. Of course, improvements in the form are in order.
3. Whatever form is utilized, include a space for teacher self-evaluation.
4. Make the lesson plan an integral part of the unit.[5]

Many teachers find that a simple outline for daily lesson plans saves time. For example, some such form as the following may be useful:

DATE_____ CLASS_____
TOPIC, PROBLEM _____
_____

PURPOSES_____
_____
_____

PROCEDURES_____
_____
_____
_____
_____

RESOURCES, EQUIPMENT, MATERIALS_____
_____
_____
_____
_____

FUTURE PLANS_____
_____

REMINDERS_____
_____

[5] H. O. Nordberg, James M. Bradfield, and William C. Odell, *Secondary School Teaching* (New York: Macmillan Co., 1962), p. 103.

In Chapter 5 an illustration was presented of a unit plan which reflected both student-teacher planning and the ideas separately prepared for presentation by the teacher. This plan was developed for a unit which might require a substantial part of class time for several weeks. A daily lesson plan for one of these class periods might look something like this:

DATE: Tuesday, Apr. 15    CLASS: Geography (2nd pd.)

TOPIC: "The Himalayas: Are they worth fighting for?"

PURPOSES: To understand the geography of the Himalayas, their contribution to Indian economy, their historical function as a barrier, why the Chinese seem able to overcome this barrier.

PROCEDURES: 1. Ask for report on this morning's newscast re the fighting in the eastern Himalayas. Douglas, supplemented by Georgia and Anne. (Ask for volunteers to check out any new developments Wed. A.M.)

2. Report by Group B on height of various peaks, temperatures, how people earn their living, etc. Encourage group to think about

(a) Traditional pacifism of India, Nepal, Sikkim.

(b) Comparison, standard of living in pastoral valleys of Himalayas and on Gangetic plain. (Compare also, our own standard of living?)

(c) Must Nehru be considered pro-Communist, or has he been trapped in his sincere effort to stay in the middle?

3. Show whole class physical map of S.E. Asia and explain briefly effects of mountain ridge on rainfall in Assam and Kashmir, sources of Indus, Jumna, Ganges, and Brahmaputra rivers, temperatures on plain, etc.

4. Brief progress reports, Group A on Buddhism, Group C on dress and customs.

RESOURCES: Map of India, map of S.E. Asia, Chapter 28 in text, materials on India from consulate. (Check on doll collection to be brought in by Carol.)

FUTURE PLANS: Progress reports, all groups. For Wednesday, Group D?

REMINDERS: Visit of graduate student from India—mention clothing drive—ask class about books-for-India idea? On Wed. ask them to lay out three or four questions for Friday's weekly evaluation.

Plans will not be alike from class to class, from one subject to another, or from one day to the next. Nor should they be. The extent of student involvement in planning will affect the lesson plan, as the illustration indicates. Some teachers make greater use of lecture and recitation procedures, others of group reports and discussion, still others of construction or dramatic activities. Some lesson plans will be shorter than the example given above; others need to be longer. The basic things to remember are that (1) good planning will help to promote good teaching and learning, and (2) students must share in planning if they are to identify with the lesson and grow in responsibility.

*The resource unit.* In common practice, unit teaching confronts a handicap in the form of the established textbooks and curriculum guides, which do not commonly lend themselves well to unit teaching. Instead of "teaching in wholes," many teachers find themselves following textbooks in which the relationship of topics is not meaningful to the student. As one remedy for this problem, the resource unit has emerged during the past two decades. Alberty has defined a resource unit thus:

> A resource unit is a systematic and comprehensive survey, analysis, and organization of the possible resources (e.g. personnel, problems, issues, activities, bibliographies) and suggestions as to their use, which a teacher might utilize in planning, developing, and evaluating a proposed learning unit in the classroom.[6]

A resource unit is much more comprehensive than a teaching-learning unit. Whereas the latter is usually developed by one teacher and his students as a guide to the study of a single broad topic or problem, the resource unit is the product of planning by a group of teachers representing more than one subject area, probably at one grade level. It deals with a broad area including many possible problems or topics. One resource unit would contain materials and possible activities for a series of different teaching-learning units. It is therefore a sort of reservoir out of which a teacher and his class might draw many suggestions for a particular teaching-learning unit. Whereas students in a class may participate in the planning of a teaching-learning unit, most resource units are developed by teach-

6 Alberty and Alberty, *Reorganizing the High School Curriculum*, p. 422. Professor Harold Alberty has pioneered the development of the resource unit concept in the United States.

ers, well in advance of the classroom situation. If the resource unit is planned flexibly and bound in loose-leaf form or arranged as a card file, it is possible for activities and materials to be added to it periodically from the teaching and learning experiences of various classes; hence it can eventually reflect the teacher-student planning that characterizes classroom units drawn from it. The experiences of successive groups of students with related learning units can be used to enrich a resource unit:

1. Students can furnish new aspects of the problem area that will cause revision of the initial statement with which the resource unit opens.

2. Students' statements of their objectives for learning units can modify the general objectives of the resource unit itself.

3. Students will devise new experiences that deserve a place in the resource unit, for the subsequent use of other groups of learners.

4. Students will discover new materials that should be added to the bibliography.

Resource unit development goes on most naturally in situations where there is some freedom from textbooks and courses of study. Core teachers have made a great contribution to resource units, and to the methodology which supports their use, perhaps because they are not required to follow course outlines and have the incentive for experimenting with the integrated curriculum.

Many resource units have been published, either in printed or mimeographed form.[7] Although such units are helpful to any faculty group engaged in planning resource units, the fact remains that any

[7] Examples are the thirty resource units in the *Problems in American Life* series developed by the National Association of Secondary School Principals and the National Council for the Social Studies, 1201 16th St., N.W., Washington 6, D.C.

See also the resource unit by Harold Hand, *Living in the Atomic Age* (Urbana: University of Illinois Press, 1946); *Santa Barbara County Curriculum Guide for Teachers in Secondary Schools,* Vol. IV (Santa Barbara, Calif.: Schauer Printing Studio, 1941); *Introduction to the Unified Studies Program* (Merriam, Kan.: Shawnee-Mission District High Schools, 1959, mimeographed); Harold Alberty *et al., Helping Teenagers Explore Values* (Columbus, Ohio: The Ohio State University, 1956).

resource unit is most effective when it is used by the teachers who developed it. Time and funds are needed for such local resource unit planning.

The resource unit usually begins with a brief statement of a problem area and its significance. Persistent questions which students are asking about the problem area are reflected in this preliminary statement.

Next comes a list of objectives sought by teachers and by students relating to the selected problem area. The list of objectives is subject to repeated revision as the resource unit is tested by various groups.

The third section is a list of learning experiences that might be classified as *initiatory, developmental,* and *culminating* and *evaluative* activities. They are broad in scope. They include experiences in reading, writing, speaking, listening, and observing. They might also include planning, acting, singing, playing, surveying, constructing, creating, discussing, summarizing, and evaluating. These varied activities serve as a reservoir on which teachers in English, social studies, science, art, music, health, and mathematics might draw for learning units related to the general problem area. They are also used by core or common learnings teachers.

A final section of the resource unit consists of a bibliography of materials useful in study of the problem area. This list, like the others, is subject to constant revision by the contributions of students and teachers as they work on learning units drawn from the resource unit.

Thus the resource unit is developed as a flexible, open-ended source of activities and materials for learning units. It consists of four sections:

1. A statement of the problem area and its significance.
2. A list of objectives of teachers and students in studying the problem area.
3. A list of learning experiences that have helped and will help students in studying the problem area.
4. A list of materials useful in studying the problem area.

It should be noted that freedom of choice is essential if there is to be any assurance that the problem chosen will be a real one to most of the students. If it is not real to them, it will be unlikely to engage their interest for a long enough period to provide a basis for a learning unit. The techniques of the problem census are of vital importance here, since a good start is half the battle.[8]

Whether the choice is limited or not, the listing and selection of problems by students can furnish valuable leads for resource unit areas. Persistent problems have a tendency to cluster around certain general areas, which invite the development of resource units by teachers. Some problems selected by students will lead to other related problems. For example, one class pursued a learning unit on vandalism in the schools, which opened up into another unit on juvenile delinquency. This problem, in turn, led the class to study education, police protection, housing, and community recreation. Teachers at a given grade level, confronted with such clusters of related problems, will have little difficulty in selecting a problem area for a resource unit. As they plan together, they will be constantly reviewing what has happened in each class as a clue to what is likely to develop next. This "backward-then-forward look" can establish a scope and sequence of real experience.

What are some of the problems that have formed the basis for developing resource units? One group of ninth and tenth grade teachers planned resource units on:

1. Entering a new school
2. Understanding and respecting other members of our democratic society
3. Conserving natural resources
4. Food and health
5. Choosing an occupation
6. Getting along better with people [9]

The Minneapolis Public Schools published *A Primer for Common Learnings* some years ago, which listed the following resource units among those persistently used in secondary schools:

Conflicts between Ideals and Practices
Driver Education and Training
Home and Family Living

[8] These techniques of the problem census, including criteria for selection of problems for study, are discussed in Chapter 8.

[9] *Planning and Working Together* (Lansing, Mich.: Superintendent of Public Instruction, 1945), pp. 62–111.

Minneapolis City Government
Natural Resources for Minnesota
Orientation Unit for Seventh Grade
World in Which We Work [10]

It has been noted that the core or common learnings teachers have pioneered the development of resource units. The following list of units represents some of the persistent problems of concern to students in core classes:

1. Understanding myself and others
2. Getting along with people
3. Building better home and family life
4. Adjusting successfully to school
5. Getting and earning a living
6. Conserving natural resources
7. Building world peace
8. Understanding nuclear fission
9. Maintaining health
10. Analyzing propaganda
11. Learning to play
12. Taking my part in democratic government
13. Communicating with others
14. What can you believe?
15. Shall I go to college?
16. Knowing our community
17. Overcoming our prejudices
18. Knowing our Latin-American neighbors
19. Understanding Russia
20. Learning about the Far East
21. Buying insurance
22. Planning a home
23. Raising children
24. Understanding the American heritage
25. Understanding democracy and Communism [11]

[10] *A Primer for Common Learnings* (Division of Secondary Education, Minneapolis Public Schools, 1948), pp. 23–25.

[11] Roland C. Faunce and Nelson L. Bossing, *Developing the Core Curriculum*, rev. ed. (Englewood Cliffs, N.J.: Prentice-Hall, Inc., © 1958), pp. 243–244. Reprinted by permission.

Resource units are most efficiently developed by teams of teachers, including representatives of several subject-fields. For example, the list of units quoted above includes some with a social studies and language arts identification. It also, however, includes some units which would lean heavily on science teachers for their development (numbers 6, 8, 9) and some units with which mathematics teachers would readily identify (8, 21). Science and mathematics activities, as well as those in art and music, language arts and social science, homemaking and industrial arts, would also be planned to contribute in significant ways to all the units.

Teachers sometimes ask whether resource units can be drawn on by those who are responsible for developing sequential skills, as in mathematics or shorthand. They argue that it would be a pure coincidence if the mathematics experiences listed in a resource unit on consumer buying would happen to fit into the learning of the Pythagorean theorem in a tenth grade geometry class. As noted earlier, teachers in all classes will be directing some activities that are separate from those in the unit. An example of this is a drill activity needed to strengthen a particular skill. Another example may be the development of a new concept which emerges from something previously learned and which lays the base for some subsequent concepts. It is quite possible that mathematics teachers may feel more compelled to adhere to the internal structure of their subject than do some other teachers.

It should be remembered, however, that meaning and relationships affect all learning. There would be little benefit in adhering strictly to a structure or sequence for teaching concepts of geometry if no learning resulted. A well-developed resource unit should include some useful activities and materials which will help give relatedness and significance to mathematics, in terms of its contribution to the solution of human problems. The goals of mathematics can be built into general education if the resource-unit team includes mathematics teachers. The same thing can be said of other specialized areas.

Space does not permit including an entire resource unit in such a book as this, but a few illustrations from one unit will help to show the variety of contributions such a unit can make. The resource unit chosen is "Doctor, Lawyer, Spaceman? (A Resource Unit on Vocational Exploration)." It was originally developed by teachers under the direction of Professor Clara Chiara at Western Michigan University.[12]

The unit opens with an introduction that emphasizes the need for freedom of choosing one's occupation, and the obligation such freedom imposes to understand and appreciate the requirements and challenges of various vocations. The "Philosophy" section, which follows, lays some stress on the importance of goals. The teachers' objectives are:

1. To help the student realize that there is a place for each individual in our democratic and economic life.

2. To bring about the realization that each individual may make a valuable contribution to society.

3. To awaken in each student a consciousness that our contributions may be made in many fields, and that each field is a necessary complement of the others.

4. To help the student to see that there is a dignity to life and labor and that the unskilled as well as the skilled may make valuable contributions to their homes, their communities, and their nation.

5. To help all of the students to a knowledge that each individual has value because he is an individual and that in performing our tasks faithfully and well we contribute to each other's well-being.

More specific teacher objectives are also listed:

1. To help the student realize that tomorrow will be his day.

2. To help the student to see some of tomorrow's potentials that are contingent upon today's planning.

3. To awaken in the student the consciousness that today's studies will help him plan for tomorrow.

4. To help the student develop a wholesome attitude toward work, and to stimulate a desire to try his hand in money-making activities while he is yet in school.

5. To stimulate the individual to accept and participate in his role as a contributing citizen while he is yet a student.

6. To help the student see that a large measure of his contribution to his family and his community will come through his economic activity.

12 Clara Chiara et al., "Doctor, Lawyer, Spaceman?" (Kalamazoo: Mich.: Western Michigan University, 1958, mimeographed).

7. To stimulate the student to prepare to accept his responsibility toward the moral, social, and economic welfare of his home, his community, and his nation.

8. To encourage investigation of one's aptitudes and desires relative to different kinds of employment.

9. To get ideas concerning job opportunities.

10. To acquaint students with the requirements in various fields.

11. To provide carefully selected guidance material relative to possible careers.

Students' objectives, too, are listed. Many of these, we may assume, will have been noted in most learning units drawn out of larger resource units. Students expect to develop ability to:

1. Evaluate one's self in the light of career demands.
2. Use library facilities to broaden one's knowledge.
3. Communicate orally and in writing.
4. Study effectively.
5. Think and observe critically.
6. Understand career terminology.
7. Plan purposefully.
8. Locate materials.
9. Read graphs and charts.
10. Use index, appendix, table of contents.
11. Plan and make decisions.
12. Read more and better material.
13. Interpret, write, speak.
14. Use bibliographies.
15. Use catalogs.
16. Use reference materials.
17. Work in groups.
18. Take notes.

The next eight pages of the published unit present a definition of the scope of the unit. The authors suggest that the classroom teacher is a crucial agent in efforts to help students choose appropriate vocations in a rapidly changing world. They discuss frankly the complexity of this choice and recommend that teachers seize upon any and all concerns—the desire for a car, the diminishing demand for unskilled labor, the growth of automation, the increase in mobility, etc., as thresholds for examining vocational alternatives. They warn against presentation of specific job classifications and urge instead the broad fields approach:

> ". . . working to feed people; to supply daily needs; to protect people; to transport people; to improve people's material life; to inform; to entertain; to shelter; to heal; to help; to govern."
>
> From the philosophy of the worker in a democratic society through a study of his motivation for working; automation, adult education and re-education; recreation and hobbies; vocations for the handicapped; mobility of the American; compensation and business relationships of the worker; psychology applied to the employment field . . . from this list it can be seen that the specific vocation is the minor detail in this unit.

One hundred learning activities are then suggested, representing a wide variety of experiences in several different subject-fields. It may be useful to note a few of these, classified in terms of their contribution to commonly accepted subjects and categories.[13]

> *Writing activities:*
> Write for materials (many sources listed).
> Write skits on "July 4, 1976" based on study of trends already evident.
> Write a dramatic skit on an era in the life of some person selected by the class.
> Write a brief story of a drifter's life.
> Write essays on "What I Should Like To Be."
> Write an imaginary history of your life from the age of fourteen to forty, describing the successive steps you took in preparing for and progressing in your vocation.
>
> *Speech activities:*
> Plan (and carry out) a series of interviews with adults in various unusual but practical fields.
> Plan (and produce) an assembly program for fun based on the TV program "What's My Line?"
> Ask ten adults the following questions: "Are you doing the kind of work you would like to do?" . . .
> Interview persons in the profession you are interested in studying.
> Plan (and carry out) an interview between two members of your

---

[13] The authors of the unit did not classify them in such categories. They have been arbitrarily labeled as they are quoted as a means of illustrating the scope and broad contribution of a team-planned unit.

class, one acting as an employer and the other as an applicant for a position.

Prepare a talk about your chosen vocation and try to "sell" it to other members of the class.

*Mathematics activities:*

What percentage of the class plan to go on to college and prepare for a vocation?

Compare rents and costs of living in a rural district and in a city.

Prepare a graph showing the effect of education on the average income of an individual throughout his lifetime. What implications should this have?

Plan a budget which will cover your expenses through college or training school.

*Science activities:*

Plan a day camp emphasizing the outdoor, camping, pioneer or naturalist type occupations.

Make a survey of (science) hobbies practiced by students.

Make a glossary of terms used in study of various (science) careers.

*History and Geography activities:*

Study about famous people who realized fame through a hobby, viz. Margaret Mitchell, Grandma Moses, the Wright Brothers, Henry Ford.

Show by examples that it is more difficult to choose a vocation today than in your great-grandfather's time.

Make a list of twenty-five workers who helped to make your breakfast possible this morning.

Study the history of your chosen occupation.

Write the history of your grandfather's preparation for his vocation.

*Art and Music activities:*

Make bulletin board displays of different kinds of work.

Make a diorama or shadow box depicting your chosen kind of work.

Develop cartoons portraying various aspects of occupations.

Study folk dances and songs of several foreign countries to see how often vocation is the pride of the singer or dancer.

Make a chart showing the most desirable steps to take in preparing for the occupation you are studying.

Make posters to "sell" your chosen kind of work.

*Field trips:*

Tour a local newspaper or TV station.

Plan a series of trips to local places of business.

Make arrangements to watch the people at work who are doing the kind of work you are interested in doing.

Talk with an employer or personnel manager, and ask him what qualities he likes to see in his workers.

Visit local businesses and industries. Note the general work and the various skilled occupations.

*Surveys:*

of youth organizations in the community.

of hobbies found in the community.

of recreational facilities in the community and state.

of different kinds of retailers listed in the classified business directory.

Only a few of the one hundred suggested activities have been quoted here. Many others deal with specific sources to which students might write for material, literature on vocations to be critically read and contents noted, lists of scholarships and samples of aptitude tests, films of various occupations, speakers to be brought into the class, suggestions for constructing a vocational ladder, etc. The section on activities closes with a one-page "Outline for Study of an Occupation," which lists ten or twelve suggested questions to be asked under each of three headings: (1) conditions within the occupation, (2) requirements of the occupation, and (3) rewards obtainable.

The final twenty-eight [14] pages of this resource unit consist of bibliographies of materials, arranged in the following manner:

Bibliography for student reading

Teachers' references

Films and filmstrips

Teaching aids (free)

Teaching aids (not free)

Tests for evaluation of unit

The advantages of the resource unit are numerous. It is useful as a means of restoring unity or relationship among the various subjects in a departmentalized secondary school. It fills the void that

---

[14] This particular resource unit is fifty-four typewritten pages long. There are many which are longer than this, including especially those developed by larger groups of teachers.

occurs when teachers attempt to break away from exclusive reliance on textbooks. It enriches the available resources in all classes. It provides an occasion for team planning, with its resulting stimulation of ideas for better teaching and learning. It supplies incentive for increasing the resources available in the school library or materials center.

In spite of these significant advantages, only a few secondary schools have launched any systematic program for developing resource units. Such obstacles as the following may have to be overcome if this valuable device is to enjoy widespread use:

1. Senior high schools in urban areas have become so firmly departmentalized that it simply does not occur to anyone to worry about the over-all impact of various learning situations which the student samples every day.

2. Planning resource units calls for interdepartmental organization of some kind, and for leadership to develop it.

3. Such planning takes time, which should be scheduled into the teachers' day if adequate results are expected.

4. Perhaps most significant of all, teachers tend to follow established and traditional procedures. The resource unit represents a break from tradition.

All these obstacles can be and should be overcome if a school wishes to use resource units. In the junior high schools much interdepartmental planning is being undertaken. Common planning periods are being scheduled for teachers at the same grade levels. Summer workshops and in-service classes have undertaken such planning. It appears that what is needed in most schools is a way to get started. In schools where resource units have been tried, they have often proved so useful that teachers have asked for more time to continue their development.

*The resource file.* Whether or not a faculty group has undertaken development of resource units, any alert teacher can collect resource materials to enrich and supplement the textbook. Such a file of materials can be collected from many sources: state and federal governments, business and industrial firms, chambers of commerce and other civic organizations, colleges and universities, teachers' organizations, publishing firms, newspapers, magazines, travel agencies, labor unions, and personal friends. A teacher in search of materials will be on everyone's mailing list. He may throw away half of what he receives but he will still enrich his teaching resources steadily by such free or inexpensive materials as:

> newspaper clippings
> articles and pictures from magazines
> pamphlets
> cartoons, jokes
> reprints
> posters
> product-exhibits
> charts
> tables
> graphs
> maps
> letters
> lists of materials
> advertisements
> book reviews
> scrapbooks
> reports of past classes
> tape recordings
> free filmstrips
> slides
> replicas of historic documents

Much of this material can be kept in a vertical file. Pieces that are too bulky or irregular in shape to place in an ordinary $9'' \times 12''$ folder may be stored in a large drawer or on a closet shelf. Both continuous addition and periodic pruning are indicated if (1) the resource file is to be kept up-to-date, and (2) it is to remain of high quality and interest.

The resource file may also contain stocks of certain duplicated items which have often proved useful to previous classes. One teacher had fifty to one hundred copies of each of the following items in one drawer of his resource file:

> List of names, addresses, and telephone numbers of foreign consulates located in the city
> List of all chambers of commerce in the state which supply free material
> Two unfinished stories for students to complete

Four case studies illustrating use of personal values in making decisions

Several unpublished but outstanding poems written by high school students

Outline of procedures for conducting an investigation of a problem

Suggestions for judging oral reports

Outline of common errors in writing

List of sources of free materials

Criteria for judging quality of a television program

Although such resource files are usually developed by individual teachers for their personal use, they will be much richer and more helpful if they are shared. A team of teachers working together at a given grade level or in the same department can cooperatively develop a really impressive resource file available to all. Such partnership in the development and use of a resource file will not only produce better resources, but also promote their more effective use.

*Team teaching.* A great deal of interest has arisen in recent years in team teaching. One writer [15] estimated that by January, 1962, one thousand secondary schools in the United States were using teaching teams on a somewhat regular basis and that the team approach was being given occasional use in as many as four thousand schools. According to *Life,* one quarter of the junior and senior high schools in the country were experimenting with some form of team teaching by March, 1963.[16]

The greatest stimulus to team teaching grew out of studies carried on by The Commission on the Experimental Study of the Utilization of the Staff in the Secondary School. The National Association of Secondary School Principals, with the aid of a foundation grant, sponsored the Commission. According to the chairman of the Commission, the studies were motivated by the realization that demands for better services for young people and greater efforts on their part on the one hand, and demands for reduction of school costs on the

[15] Ira J. Singer, "Survey of Staff Utilization Practices in Six States," *The Bulletin of the National Association of Secondary-School Principals,* 46:270 (January 1962), 1–13.

[16] *Life,* 54:12 (March 22, 1963), 79.

other could not be met with the present limited supply of teachers and probable funds available for education.[17]

Team teaching is not new, either in concept or practice. Teachers have always worked together in one way or another. Probably the first organized attempt at team teaching took place in connection with the core curriculum, which began about 1930. In one version two teachers having a common group of students for four subjects (English-social science; mathematics-science) and a common daily planning period met two or more times a week to discuss student progress and to plan means of improvement of this portion of the students' school day. Although there were occasions when the two groups of students were combined for a common experience, this was not a major focus as it is in today's team plan.

There are many different ways in which a teaching team may be formed. Brownell and Taylor have described a variety of types of elementary and secondary team models within which several variations may exist. At one end of the continuum is a team composed of several teachers from several academic disciplines who have the same students one period each.[18] At the other end of the continuum these authors visualize a team consisting of two or more teachers with other noncertificated personnel from one subject area. In one school the science, mathematics, English, and history teams each consist of two experienced teachers, two beginning teachers, and one instructional assistant.[19]

Advocates of team teaching are currently making the following claims for it:

> One basic learning goal is the development of individual competency in independent study; another is the ability to make decisions and discuss important matters in groups. Conventional school organization makes groupings of optimum size (not more than 15) under the direction of a teacher impossible. By using the

17 Lloyd S. Michael, "New Directions to Quality Education in Secondary Schools," *Bulletin of the National Association of Secondary School Principals,* 45:261 (January 1961), 11–18.

18 John A. Brownell and Harris A. Taylor, "Theoretical Perspectives for Teaching Teams," *Phi Delta Kappan,* 43:4 (January 1962), 154.

19 Ridgewood High School, Norridge, Illinois. See "High Schools 1962, Profiles of Significant Schools" (New York: Educational Facilities Laboratories, Inc., December, 1961), p. 15.

teaching team and placing students in large groups part of the time, the small-group ideal may be realized.

Many of the activities performed by teachers, e.g., lecturing, demonstrating, making group assignments, viewing films and TV with students, can be done as well in large as in small groups. The teaching team facilitates the necessary flexibility in group size.

Team teaching with its use of a team or teacher leader provides a natural basis for recognizing the schools' best teachers, by financial and/or other means.

The use of teaching teams with the concomitant large-group, small-group flexibility facilitates the extension of time available for preparation and other professional activities of teachers.

The team arrangement encourages (even forces) cooperative planning by teachers.

It provides more time for teachers to work with individual students.

It enables the teaching staff to make the best use of individual faculty members' talents and competencies.

It provides for more adequate supervision of beginning teachers by placing the beginner in close association with one or more experienced staff members.

Those who oppose team teaching cite what they consider to be disadvantages or shortcomings:

Team teaching is a fad, emphasizing change for the sake of change. Many schools introduce it in order to "get on the bandwagon."

Team teaching as presently conceived and popularized is tied to the belief that students may well spend a portion of their time in groups of one hundred or two hundred. This is an unwarranted and unnecessary increase in group size.

The nature of team organization with its emphasis on the use of large groups in order to provide time for teachers to prepare and to work with small groups and individuals may focus too much concern on memorization of content with a consequent loss of emphasis on other essential learning.

The large-group emphasis tends to increase the amount of time the teacher spends talking (lecturing) to the students. As an educational device lecturing is at the low end of the scale in efficiency.

Since team teaching as presently conceived and structured is a fairly recent phenomenon, the evidence regarding its success or failure will probably not be in for many years, if ever. It probably will be found to be approximately equivalent to conventional methods. As we pointed out in Chapter 1, secondary schools are far from perfect. Team teaching does not of itself seem to solve any of the basic shortcomings of contemporary education. On the other hand an intelligent, informed, and dedicated faculty organized on a team basis could certainly achieve more than a poor staff organized on either a team or conventional basis. This is another way of saying that the central figure in any educational process is the teacher. If the teacher is competent, young people will learn.

## Evaluating planning

What are the characteristics of a school where excellent instructional planning is being practiced? What are the criteria of good planning?

1. *Freedom and flexibility are essential.* Without freedom to experiment, to depart from established routines, there is no incentive to plan. There is also little chance to adapt instruction to the needs of the learners.

2. *There are clear-cut purposes shared by most of the staff.* The purposes must be shared if they are to serve as a basis for planning. No administrator has a monopoly on good ideas. Staff members must have an opportunity (and a challenge) to help develop the school's purposes.

3. *Respect for the individual is a cornerstone of effective planning.* Not only democratic theory, but efficient operation demands maximum respect for the individual. Each teacher should come to school each day with the sincere conviction that his ideas matter.

4. *There must be machinery for total school planning.* Departmental segregation creates competition and prevents any systematic look at the total learner, or at the total school.

5. *There must be a time for planning.* In the long run, little effective planning will occur on an after-school basis. That which is worth doing is worth scheduling. This is closely related to the criterion which follows.

6. *Funds for staff planning are essential.* Staff time is money, and modest appropriations for summer workshops and in-service courses are necessary for good planning. Funds are needed for library materials, for resource persons, for duplicating, and for travel.

7. *Perhaps most important of all, plans should reflect concern for growth of individual learners, and their differences.* Plans that deal with classes as though the individuals within them were all alike do not result in actual learning. At worst they may discourage learning by establishing unrealistic expectations.

It is this factor of individual differences which most crucially affects planning. Recognition of these differences, and of their significance for learning, will pay no dividends in the classroom unless we have planned *different procedures,* and provided *different materials,* and finally planned to *evaluate differently.* The wide range of skill in reading must be reflected in the materials the teacher uses. Teachers must constantly ask themselves some questions as they plan:

1. What materials, resources, activities have we planned to use that will be challenging to the most skillful readers? The most retarded readers? The able students who have certain specific reading problems?

2. What procedures have we planned that will develop self-confidence in those who are shy in group situations?

3. What procedures have we included that will appeal instantly to the mechanics-minded, or practical students? And what about the poetic ones, the abstract thinkers, and the creative nonconformists?

4. How have we planned so that leadership roles will be assumed by those who most need the experience?

5. Have we planned so that satisfactions and rewards that are intrinsic in the task can be shared by all students?

6. How have we planned to help students understand and accept the fact of difference, in themselves and in others?

7. How have we provided for the most active, energetic, lively members of our class?

8. How have we planned to arouse the most apathetic students?

9. What plans have we made for individual projects that may be entirely "different"? For small-group projects?

10. Do our plans provide for learning by other means besides the printed page? (audio-visual media, demonstration, group discussion, construction, dramatization)

11. Have we planned ways to encourage divergent thinking?

12. Have we planned evaluation means more varied than content tests?

13. Do our plans leave room for the various skills brought into the classroom by each individual?

14. Do our plans take account of varying home backgrounds?

15. Do our plans provide for mutual help instead of competition?

16. Do our plans foster learning *how to learn* by each student?

Other questions will suggest themselves to the thoughtful teacher who seeks to take account of individual differences in his planning.

Our analysis of various kinds of curriculum organization omitted one area that is really part of the total curriculum. This is the program of student activities, sometimes referred to as the extracurricular program. In Chapter 12 we turn to analysis of the teacher's role in organizing and sponsoring such activities.

## FOR FURTHER READING

Alberty, Harold B., and Elsie J. Alberty, *Reorganizing the High School Curriculum,* 3rd ed. New York: Macmillan Co., 1962. Chapter 11 includes a good example of a learning unit. Chapter 12 includes a comprehensive explanation and an actual example of a resource unit.

Alberty, Harold B., *et al., Helping Teenagers Explore Values.* Columbus, Ohio: The Ohio State University, 1956. An example of a resource unit, developed and used at The Ohio State University School.

Alexander, William M., and Paul M. Halverson, *Effective Teaching in Secondary Schools.* New York: Holt, Rinehart and Winston, Inc., 1956. Chapters 14 and 15 include criteria for a good "unit of work," and explanation of day-to-day planning. Lists of sources of materials are included in Chapter 15.

Association for Supervision and Curriculum Development, *Creating a Good Environment for Learning.* Washington, D.C.: The Association Yearbook, 1954. Chapters 4 and 5 give illustrations of unit development by student-teacher planning.

Bureau of Curriculum Research, *The Unit in Curriculum Development and Instruction.* New York City Board of Education, 1956. A good guide to unit planning.

Faunce, Roland C., and Nelson L. Bossing, *Developing the Core Curriculum,* rev. ed. Englewood Cliffs, N.J.: Prentice-Hall, Inc., 1958. Chapter 10 includes discussion of the resource unit and the resource file.

Grambs, Jean D., William J. Iverson, and Franklin K. Patterson, *Modern Methods in Secondary Education,* rev. ed. New York: Holt, Rinehart and Winston, Inc., 1958. Chapter 6 defines and illustrates a learning unit, gives its stages of development, and shows how the unit affects day-to-day planning.

Kettlecamp, Gilbert C., *Teaching Adolescents.* Boston: D. C. Heath and Co., 1954. Sample units are included in the appendix.

Leonard, J. Paul, *Developing the Secondary School Curriculum.* New York: Holt, Rinehart and Winston, Inc., 1953. There are examples of units of work in Chapters 15, 16, and 17.

McKean, Robert C., *Principles and Methods in Secondary Education.* Columbus, Ohio: Charles E. Merrill Books, Inc., 1962. Chapter 5 deals with long-range planning of teaching units and resource units, as well as short-range planning of daily lessons.

Mills, H. H., and Harl R. Douglass, *Teaching in High School,* 2nd ed. New York: Ronald Press Co., 1957. Five chapters are devoted to unit and lesson planning.

Nordberg, H. O., James M. Bradfield, and William C. Odell, *Secondary School Teaching.* New York: Macmillan Co., 1962. Chapter 5 consists of a good brief explanation of unit planning. A sample unit on "Protection of the Community's Health" is included.

Romine, Stephen A., *Building the High School Curriculum.* New York: Ronald Press Co., 1954. Chapter 11 contains much helpful material under the title "Building and Using Units and Courses of Study."

Steeves, Frank L., *Fundamentals of Teaching in Secondary Schools.* New York: Odyssey Press, Inc., 1962. Chapter 4, "The Essentials of Unit Planning," argues for specific preplanning and illustrates a complete unit plan.

Strickland, Ruth G., *How To Build a Unit of Work,* U.S. Office of Education, Bulletin No. 5. Washington, D.C.: Government Printing Office, 1946. A step-by-step description of the procedure used in developing units.

# 12

# Student activities

During the twentieth century the concept of the curriculum has changed significantly. It was once assumed that the curriculum referred only to those experiences that were carried on in the classrooms under the direct supervision of teachers. Any other activities, such as athletics, which went on after school hours, were logically enough thought of as extracurricular. This may once have been a useful phrase to distinguish the total learning situation from narrowly conceived and formally conducted classroom experiences.

Today the curriculum has come to be defined as the sum total of all the activities and experiences provided by the community through the school for the education of children and youth. As the curriculum tends to live up to the implications of this definition, the separation of student activities from parallel classroom experiences becomes less valid. As the curriculum becomes increasingly a means of aiding learners to meet problems involved in growing up, it is accordingly thought of as embracing all activities carried on by the school. One of the pioneers in the theory of student activities, Elbert K. Fretwell, put the issue thus: "It is the business of the school to organize the whole situation so that there is a favorable opportunity for everyone, teachers as well as pupils, to practice the qualities of the good citizen here and now with results satisfying to the one doing the practicing." He also offered a second thesis that "extra-curricular activities should grow out of curricular activities and return to them to enrich them." [1]

1 Elbert K. Fretwell, *Extra-Curricular Activities in Secondary Schools* (Boston: Houghton Mifflin Co., 1931), p. 2.

Although Fretwell was using the phrase "extra-curricular," he was already laying the base in 1931 for the drawing together of the classroom and extraclass experiences as related parts of a single process.

During the three or more decades since Fretwell wrote his thesis, the acceptance of activities as legitimate and necessary educational means has progressed significantly. Most activities came into the school by the back door. They were generally organized outside the school by the students themselves, in earlier years. At first resisted by the schools, these activities and organizations showed a remarkable vitality and persisted on the fringe of the schools in spite of opposition. Gradually administrators and teachers accepted them and brought them under school sponsorship in order to control abuses that sometimes developed. Finally, in recent decades, these activities became necessary phases of a good school. Their extent and quality are examined by any informed group who are engaged in evaluating a secondary school.[2]

Yet the public is not sure that student activities are really basic to the curriculum. Consider the following examples:

> A young married couple had been permitted to return to high school, but to classes only. They were barred from all activities, organizations, elective offices, the school library and cafeteria, music, dramatics, and parties on the ground that they had broken the social code and would be a bad example for other students.

> The board of education evidently feared that their request for additional operating millage would be rejected by the voters. They instructed the superintendent of schools to send a letter to all parents, warning that loss of the millage election would mean elimination of athletics, music, and school trips.

> Two boys were involved in a fight with an adult, outside of school hours. While their case was waiting to be heard in justice court, and before any determination could be made of who was at fault, the boys were barred for the rest of the school year from participating in sports, class trips, or music productions.

It is evident that the nation is not unanimous in the belief that school activities are a basic part of the curriculum. Some people

---

[2] See, for example, *The Evaluative Criteria*, rev. ed., used as one part of the accreditation process in several accrediting associations (Washington, D.C.: National Study of Secondary School Evaluation, 1960), Section E.

believe that—(1) participation in activities is a reward for social conformity, and (2) of all that goes on in schools, student activities are the most easily dispensable.

At least one other interpretation might be placed on the occasional threats by school officials to deprive recalcitrant citizens of their student activities. It is possible that boards of education are aware that loss of the athletics or music program would be a more serious blow to parents than loss of some part of the classroom instructional offerings. There is some evidence that students and parents sense the values of the activities program more clearly than do school administrators and teachers. At any rate, these activities have stubbornly persisted in the face of considerable opposition from school people.

## What are activities?

Activities are variously referred to as "extracurricular," "extraclass," or "nonclass" experiences, all titles which seem to place them outside the realm of the instructional program. The terms "cocurricular" or "allied," also used in many schools, seem to imply a separate-but-equal status. "Student activities," the term we have used in this book, is perhaps too broad to be definitive, but at least has the merit of not implying separation from the curriculum.

Definition of the term becomes increasingly difficult as more and more activities enter the classroom and become credit courses offered in the regular schedule of classes. This "curricularization" process has brought into the classroom the school band, orchestra, and chorus; speech, forensics, and dramatics; journalism; and group guidance organizations such as the homeroom. Thus any definition which is based on extraclass or noncredit status would exclude many important school activities.

One might assume that the activities program could be defined in terms of its purposes. One such statement of goals for the activities program may serve to illustrate the difficulty of such separation:

> We are interested in having experiences provided for pupils through which they may develop their own abilities and powers more effectively, may learn to accept responsibility and to work cooperatively with their fellows, may contribute generously to the

common good, and may evaluate with increasing discernment the worth of their own contributions.[3]

As the authors of this statement point out, these goals are not confined to the extraclass part of the school curriculum. They are equally valid as statements of the purposes of the entire school program. As the concept of curriculum has broadened, its goals tend also to broaden and identify with those of the activities program.

Although definition is difficult, we can be fairly specific about what programs are referred to in this chapter:

> the social program
> school clubs
> assemblies
> student publications
> music
> speech and dramatics
> athletics
> school camping
> student participation in school government

*The social program.* Every major statement of the goals of secondary education during the twentieth century has stressed the importance of human relationships.[4] The developmental tasks concept developed by Havighurst emphasized, among other tasks, the need for adolescent youth to:

> achieve new and more mature relations with age-mates of both sexes
> achieve a masculine or feminine social role
> achieve emotional independence of parents and other adults
> prepare for marriage and family life
> desire and achieve socially responsible behavior [5]

This need to relate to other people is imperative in an increasingly interdependent world, where a premium is placed on the skills

[3] Edgar G. Johnston and Roland C. Faunce, *Student Activities in Secondary Schools*, p. 8. Copyright 1952, The Ronald Press Company. Used by permission.

[4] The reader may wish to review the purposes of secondary education quoted in Chapter 2, as stated by the Educational Policies Commission and the National Association of Secondary School Principals.

[5] Robert J. Havighurst, *Developmental Tasks and Education* (New York: David McKay Co., Inc., 1952), p. 2.

and attitudes of cooperation. There is a growing conviction that schools must do their part to help youth learn to understand people of other races, religions, and cultures, to accept them and relate to them effectively.

Many of the adolescent's basic interests and problems are in the realm of social relationships. He is in a period of rapid physical change which has its emotional echoes. He is trying to find out "who he is," a process which requires discovery of himself from his friends' perceptions. It is of great importance to him that he forms friendships and interacts with the others in the gang. One of his main fears is of being thought different. The schools have an important role to play in helping youth learn how to relate to others.

Some classrooms are so conducted as to promote friendly interaction. In others, the only relationships that develop are those between a teacher and an individual student. In such schools the social program outside the classroom becomes especially important.

Social contacts occur informally in the halls and at lockers before school, between periods, and after school. There is much opportunity in the cafeteria for conversations with friends. There are clubs and committees, sports events and concerts, play rehearsals and locker room banter. Whether the school promotes it or not, socialization goes on informally throughout the activities program. In some schools these social contacts are frowned upon and attempts are made to keep them at a minimum. In other schools these opportunities are deliberately created and systematically planned. Instead of a no-talking policy in the cafeteria, time and physical arrangements are adjusted to encourage conversation. Instead of keeping students moving in the halls, lounge space is provided in new, widened corridors which students can use at certain times. The library is used for quiet conversation in many schools. A game or activity room or a lounge is equipped for noon-hour and after-school social gatherings. Some older buildings have been converted or re-equipped to encourage socialization.

In addition to these informal opportunities, schools have planned regular social functions such as the following:

>     teas, parties
>     evening dances, after-school dances
>     game parties
>     picnics, hikes

class trips
movie nights
bowling nights
orientation week
noon-hour dances
pep rallies
banquets

In a school where the staff is interested in developing wholesome human relationships, both informal and planned social activities occur every day. A calendar of planned activities should be developed by student groups and coordinated by the student council to insure (1) that facilities will be available, (2) that plans for the affair are carefully made, (3) that all students can participate, and (4) that appropriate staff participation is provided. Parents, too, can contribute to and enjoy evening social affairs; they should be involved as much as possible.

How can the social program be evaluated? As we reflect on the developmental needs of youth, the facilities that are available, and the importance of human relationships, we might look at a particular school program and ask ourselves some questions:

1. Is it really the students' own program, planned and carried on by them with friendly staff guidance?

2. Do the building and the schedule of the school facilitate instead of restricting social interaction?

3. Does the program provide a wide variety of fun-experiences so that something in it will appeal to every student?

4. Is there particular effort made to reach the timid, lonely individual?

5. Is there a systematic plan for orienting new students?

6. Do teachers participate enthusiastically but without trying to run the program?

7. Is an effort made to evaluate the effectiveness of the program, or to relate it to the social structure of the classrooms?

Teachers who remain aloof from the social activities, or who doubt the educational value of school parties and noon-hour programs are missing a real opportunity to get acquainted with their students. Some of the most significant insights about students are acquired in the spontaneous, informal atmosphere of a party. It is no accident that coaches know their boys well, after a season of daily locker-room repartee. The English teacher who accompanies her class to a local theater to see a production of *Hamlet* can learn much more that evening than Shakespeare's lines. If we wish to help young people we must know them, and the social program can be an invaluable aid to us in this process of knowing. In addition to the value of getting better acquainted, there is also a lot of fun awaiting teachers who socialize with their students. This is one way to stay young in heart. It is a bonus the teaching profession offers, as compared to some other occupations.

*School clubs.* A well-organized club program enriches a secondary school in many important ways. A club offers regular opportunities to play and work with one's friends. Some clubs are proving grounds for hobbies that may develop into vocations. Others are a means of pursuing interests that will enrich one's whole life during leisure hours. Still other clubs provide a channel for service to one's school and community, or to less fortunate human beings anywhere in the world. A club of almost any kind offers students a means of developing their abilities—in such diverse ways as discussing, chairing meetings, reporting, constructing, dramatizing, recording, demonstrating, and, of course, cooperating with one's peers on mutually acceptable projects. All these are goals of good classroom teaching, it is true. In a good club they take place naturally, without teacher-pressure or "motivation," and in a climate free from marks, homework assignments, and promotion or failure.

There is, as John Dewey remarked in *Interest and Effort in Education,* no necessary conflict between interesting activity and good, hard work. In the classroom, teachers sometimes fail to arouse a keen interest in what is going on. They too readily conclude that their students are just not interested in anything. This is not the case, as thousands of club sponsors will testify. The curiosity and drive to learn are still there, but they must be tapped by the right means. Many a boy or girl has been observed doing some task voluntarily and eagerly as a club member which had been performed only under pressure as a student in a classroom. The significant difference may lie in the freedom to choose one's project and the resulting conviction that the club is "owned" by the students. They often refer to "my club"—seldom to "my class." One way to ruin a club is to supply a sponsor who makes all the decisions and assigns all the tasks.

The number and kinds of different clubs defy description. As early as 1931, Fretwell reported a total of 1,372 different clubs listed in one hundred high school handbooks.[6] In 1947 Gruhn and Douglass reported a survey of 498 junior high school clubs classified into the following categories:

> all-school
> physical education
> civic-social-moral
> agriculture
> art
> science and mathematics
> domestic arts
> manual arts
> commercial
> music
> miscellaneous [7]

Miller, Moyer, and Patrick have suggested classifying school clubs as (1) social and recreational, (2) service, (3) academic-area-related, and (4) special interests or hobbies.[8] Under this latter category the names of possible clubs are as numerous and varied as the interests of teen-agers. One list of hobby clubs in some secondary schools is reported by Kilzer, Stephenson, and Nordberg:

> Anagram Club
> Archery Club
> Art-Metal Club
> Athletic Club
> Automobile Club
> Aviation and Airplane Club
> Badminton Club
> Ballroom Dancing Club
> Basket-Weaving Club
> Book-lovers Club
> Bowling Club

---

[6] Fretwell, *Extra-Curricular Activities,* p. 253.

[7] William T. Gruhn and Harl R. Douglass, *The Modern Junior High School,* 2nd ed., pp. 355–359. Copyright 1956, The Ronald Press Company. Used by permission.

[8] Franklin A. Miller, James H. Moyer, and Robert B. Patrick, *Planning Student Activities* (Englewood Cliffs, N.J.: Prentice-Hall, Inc., © 1956), pp. 323–233.

Braille-Transcribing Club
Camera Club
Camp-Cookery Club
Candy Club
Cartoonist Club
Carving Club
Checker Club
Chess Club
Classical Club
Collectors Club
Craft Club
Designers Club
Draftsmen's Club
Folk-Dancing Club
Game (non-athletic) Club
Handicraft Club
Harmonica Club
Hi-Y Club
Hooked Rug Club
Household Arts Club
Indian-Basketry Club
Knitting Club
Magazine and Periodical Club
Marionette Club
Morse Radio-Code Club
Music-Appreciation Club
Novelty Club
Ping-Pong Club
Printing Club
Short-Story Club
Snapshot Club
Swimming Club
Who's-Who Club
Word-Puzzle Club [9]

A good club program will be flexible so that it can be readily adapted to the interests of students. This is especially important in junior high schools, because of the rapidly changing interests of early adolescents. The purposes and program of the club should be

[9] Louis R. Kilzer, Harold H. Stephenson, and H. Orville Nordberg, *Allied Activities in the Secondary School* (New York: Harper & Row, Publishers, 1956), p. 80.

expressed in a charter, which should be acted on by the student council. Sponsors should be selected on the basis of their interests. Competence or expertness in the club's chosen field of exploration is less important in a sponsor than interest, and the readiness to work enthusiastically with students. The following questions have been suggested as appropriate for evaluating the qualities of a good club sponsor:

1. Does he really like to associate with boys and girls?
2. Does he enlist the confidence of boys and girls?
3. Is he keenly interested in the world about him?
4. Has he contagious enthusiasm?
5. Does he seek to become expert in some of the fields of activity in which the club is engaged?
6. Is he able to give constructive suggestions for activities of the club?
7. Is he able to guide without dictation?
8. Has he the ability to plan systematically?
9. Is he willing to give time and thought to making the club work a success?
10. Is he democratic in spirit?
11. Has he a sense of humor?
12. Is he able to find his chief satisfaction in pupil growth and not in appreciation of his efforts? [10]

These twelve questions would provide a reasonably good basis for evaluating teachers, apart from their application to sponsors of clubs. This may be another way of saying that club sponsorship simply represents teaching at its best. In the good school club are found many of the requirements of an effective learning situation: high interest, freedom to choose, challenge to plan, learning by doing, absence of academic failure (or of marks, for that matter), and, above all, responsibility of each member for his own progress. The qualities which enable a sponsor to capitalize these important assets are precisely the qualities of a good teacher.

On the other hand, many a club has been limited in its success, or has in fact failed, because the sponsor tried to make it too much like a formal classroom. If the school's list of available clubs looks like its schedule of academic classes, some students will be skeptical

---

[10] Johnston and Faunce, *Student Activities*, pp. 133–135.

of the clubs' contributions to their own special interests. If a club's program is really controlled by the sponsor, it will begin to suffer the same atrophy as that which unfortunately characterizes many an academic class. If the members seldom get a chance to participate in discussion or planning, they will soon lose interest. If marks in class-work are used as the basis of eligibility for joining a club, the very students who most need to belong will be excluded. If financial costs are levied on the members this same effect will be produced.

In the club program it is not difficult to provide some area of success for every student. Teachers should do their utmost to preserve this significant advantage of clubs, in the hope that their own success as sponsors may help them learn how to function more effectively in the classroom.

*Assemblies.* Unlike many other school activities, the assembly program was an accepted feature of the early high school, as well as of its predecessor, the academy. The daily "chapel" or morning exercise usually featured a prayer, reading from the Bible, and a moralistic lecture or sermon. In the present century the religious motif has generally disappeared from the school assembly,[11] which has become a weekly or fortnightly forum for large-group presentations. Both instruction and entertainment are sought in assembly programs. The use of commercial entertainers is now giving way to student presentations, and the current trend is to give students a part in program planning also.

Various purposes have been assigned to school assemblies by secondary school principals. One summary of these purposes is given by Miller, Moyer, and Patrick:

1. To unify the school
2. To interpret the work of the school
3. To strengthen existing interests and to broaden horizons
4. To develop desirable attitudes and appreciations
5. To assist in the selection of a vocation
6. To develop a better understanding of critical issues and problems of our contemporary culture
7. To furnish opportunities to appear before an audience
8. To learn more about the community and how it functions

11 Prayer and Bible readings continue as program features in some public school assemblies, and in many private and parochial schools.

9. To recognize superior achievement
10. To encourage the development of good audience behavior
11. To furnish wholesome entertainment as well as to educate
12. To provide an opportunity to present certain administrative problems and to seek solutions of them [12]

These purposes suggest that the assembly, properly planned and geared to the interests of students, is a valuable feature of the activities program. It is the only opportunity for the entire student body and faculty to come together in one large group. Such large gatherings are a common experience in adult life. It is important for youth to gain some experience in planning and participating in large audience situations.

In spite of the many benefits to be derived from a good series of school assemblies, some secondary schools have scheduled them rarely or not at all. Some schools simply do not have an adequate auditorium and must repeat a program two or three times to audiences by shifts. More frequently the problem has been the fear on the part of teachers and administrators that students will not behave properly in assemblies. This challenge is, of course, one of the more cogent reasons for having assemblies. Good audience behavior is learned by practice. Through careful evaluation of behavior in assemblies it is possible to develop some criteria and improve the audience habits of students.

Inattention or discourtesy more often develop when the program is not of interest to most students. The planning of programs must take careful account of interests. Adult audiences often behave badly when they are bored, and it may be expected that students will also. A student-faculty committee should be set up to plan the programs, eliciting talent from classes and clubs, music groups, and community resources. The committee should have available the summary of students' evaluations of previous assemblies. Occasional discussions in homerooms or classes will provide clues for improving assembly programs. Some programs that have proved popular in many schools are:

> inauguration ceremonies for student officers
> town-hall discussions of school or teen-age problems

---

[12] Miller, Moyer, and Patrick, *Planning Student Activities*, pp. 499–504. Reprinted by permission.

concerts: band, orchestra, choir, and smaller ensembles
student variety shows
talent contests
song assemblies
previews of school plays
one-act plays
demonstrations: science experiments, pistol shooting
nomination of student officers
faculty variety shows
awards assemblies
pep rallies
foreign visitors to community
pageants, tableaus
exchange assemblies, other schools

Teachers have been known to dread "assembly day" in schools where audience behavior has become a perennial, unsolved problem. They are not much better off in strictly regimented assemblies where seats are assigned and teachers must spend the whole period watching their homeroom groups for minor infractions. Neither of these conditions need obtain if (1) students share responsibility for planning, carrying out, and evaluating assemblies, and (2) the programs are varied and interesting to the audience. In such schools, teachers can generally relax and enjoy the program with the students. Such an outcome does not happen without effort. It calls for careful planning and continuous appraisal. The benefits of a good assembly plan are so desirable that their achievement is worth the effort.

*Student publications.* Most secondary schools have newspapers. Some have yearbooks and handbooks for student orientation. A few publish magazines as outlets for literary and artistic talents.

The most popular of these is easily the school newspaper. Some schools publish the paper weekly, others fortnightly or monthly. Its purpose, like that of any newspaper, is to inform and entertain its readers. Some further purposes characterize a good school paper:

1. To unify the school; to improve school morale or school spirit; to develop pride and feelings of identification as students of a particular school.

2. To provide an outlet for various school activities; to interpret club, class, athletic, music, and speech activities to the students and faculty.

3. To strengthen and clarify school traditions.

4. To develop in students the faculty of critical reading; to develop canons of good taste.

5. To publicize school events.

6. To provide an experience in journalism for those students who are interested in it as a hobby or as a possible career.

Not all school papers achieve these purposes. Some are really the product of a teacher, rather than of students. Others are chiefly characterized by gossip columns and corny humor. Many papers carry news of school events long past, because of the infrequency of publication.

Perhaps the most common failure is concerned with the goal of making the paper a real organ of the school. If a journalism class or a small, carefully selected staff of good English students publishes the paper, without any real bridges to the entire school, it may be a fine journalistic product but not the voice of the students. The task of organizing so as to secure contributions from all homerooms, classes, and clubs is not an easy one. It is necessary to work for this kind of an organization, however, if the paper is to become really a *school* paper. News stories, editorials, and features can be derived from the entire school if reporters are appointed in each room and the staff maintains constant contact with them. Teachers can help this process in many significant ways if they, in turn, look upon the school paper as *their* project instead of an assignment for the journalism teacher.

The magazine has unfortunately lost ground in recent years in secondary schools. If a school has a regular monthly magazine, the school paper need not serve the dual function of reporting news and also being a medium for publishing creative writing and art. This purpose of providing an outlet for literary and other creative activities is more appropriate for the (longer) school magazine. It is possible to produce an attractive mimeographed magazine when funds do not make possible a printed one. Like the newspaper, the magazine should be an all-school project. No doubt an editorial and production staff will usually be recruited from interested students in English or core classes, but an organization is needed to reach out for contributions from the entire school. If each class publishes a small magazine containing the work of students in that class, the best of these products may appear in the school magazine. Art products such as line drawings and cartoons, as well as musical compositions, can be published in a magazine.

Yearbooks or "annuals" are most often published in senior high schools, usually by a staff selected from the senior class. Some junior high schools have copied this practice and publish a ninth grade annual, but it seems a dubious practice. It is an expensive kind of publication, usually supported by goodwill advertising. It emphasizes the terminal rather than the transitional motif which characterizes modern junior high schools. Even in the senior high school, the journalistic values of the work on the yearbook are confined to a small staff. Often the sponsor gets more experience than the students in making important decisions about design or format. However, students value the yearbook as a graduation tradition. It is difficult to discontinue the yearbook, once it is launched. Unlike the newspaper and magazine, which may be actually projects of advanced classes in journalism or English, the yearbook is usually an extracurricular assignment for both students and sponsor. It is an onerous task which usually does not produce training and other values commensurate with the effort involved.

The school handbook is a tool of the orientation program. New students are helped during their first weeks in a school by a good handbook. It has so much value that many schools subsidize its cost and supply it free to students. Students should help produce the handbook, if it is really to be a student handbook instead of an administrative or faculty instrument. It should not consist entirely of rules and regulations, threats or restrictions—and it will not be confined to these negative aspects if students produce it.

The handbook may contain something of the history and traditions of the school, its unique characteristics or purposes, the requirements and offerings, and the clubs and other school activities. It may well present some good reasons for participating in school activities. There may have to be a few school regulations included in the handbook. Other items may be:

school songs, yells
calendar of events
floor plan of school
roster of faculty
names and short biographies of student officers
photographs and greetings from the principal and student officers

policies regarding awards
assembly schedule
"what to do or where to go" (when tardy or absent, etc.)
functions and schedules of counselors

The handbook is often published by the student council, or by a staff selected by the council from the English classes. The cost should be kept low so that it can be revised each year.

Sponsors of journalism projects are often busy people. There are deadlines for teachers as well as for students. Yet it can be a rewarding activity to work on with students. The staff of a school publication has a real job to do, responsibility to the entire school, and a wide variety of roles for individuals to perform. At its best, a publication staff exemplifies some of the basic goals of all classes and activities.

*Music.* Music is one of the school activities which has moved into the classroom, at least in part. Most secondary schools schedule the band, orchestra, and choir on a regular daily basis and for credit. Some schools also schedule the glee clubs as classes, as well as some smaller ensembles, but these are more often extraclass activities which rehearse after school or during an activity period.

A well-rounded music program provides opportunities for all in both vocal and instrumental music, as well as special groups for those with talent and high interest. Music is a universal human need. Interest and pleasure in song is not confined to the gifted musician. An effective program will provide opportunities for all students to take part in group-singing, and to try their talents in a beginning band. This is especially important in the junior high school, which is obligated to provide many kinds of exploratory experiences. In general music classes, in glee clubs, and in the junior band any interested student should be able to participate for enjoyment. In schools where the music program is respected, there will also be song assemblies and group singing in classes and clubs.

In addition to these opportunities for all students, there should also be organized music groups for the more talented students. These might include advanced band and orchestra, *a cappella* choir, quartets, sextets, or double quartets, and small instrumental ensembles such as dance bands and woodwind, brass, or string ensembles. Solo work should be provided as a part of all these programs for the talented. A well-balanced music program will provide challenge and enjoyment for all, through a wide variety of activities.

This goal of music for all has sometimes been lost sight of by ambitious directors who have their eyes only on the product. As they seek to meet the mounting competition and produce a semiprofessional choir or concert band, the whole music curriculum may develop into a program for the gifted. Students who enter a large high school after years of experience in organized instrumental or vocal groups are capable of musical achievement of a very high order. It is not surprising that many music directors concentrate on these gifted few, who combine high interest with unusual talent, and spend all their time and energy in producing organizations that approach the professional level of excellence.

Yet this exclusive concentration on gifted students overlooks some of the basic goals of a good music program. There must be at least an equal amount of effort and direction devoted to the objective of music for all if a school is to have a really good program.

Sponsors of music activities should look carefully at their total program and ask themselves some questions:

1. Is the program basically the property of teachers, or of students?

2. Is there in the total program an adequate challenge for those who are gifted in music?

3. Is there at least an equal effort made to provide opportunities for all students to sing, to play, and to learn to appreciate good music?

4. Are we emphasizing enjoyable participation by all, as opposed to professional performance by the few?

5. Is there some definite impact by the music program on all students, through assemblies, classes, and clubs?

6. Does the program strengthen social ties instead of creating a music clique in the school?

7. Are we providing numerous opportunities for student leadership and participation in planning?

8. Have we provided a chance for students of limited economic means to participate in music?

9. Is there a place in our program for individual and small-group activities, as well as large-group rehearsals and performance?

10. Do other teachers know about and accept our goals as valid, instead of fearing our competition for students, facilities, and funds?

The music teacher who is really a member of the faculty team, and who is interested in helping all students to enjoy music, can have a most satisfying career.

*Speech and dramatics.* Speech and dramatics activities, like music, have a dual responsibility. First and foremost there should be an adequate program of speech for all students, whatever their talents. Both in classes, and in clubs, all students should have opportunities to sharpen discussion and reporting skills, to improve informal communication skills, to interview, to chair meetings, to interpret verse or prose, and to take part in dramatic productions. Those who have high interest and unusual talent should also have opportunities to engage in more specialized activities:

> interpretive reading
> class plays
> debating
> panel discussions
> extempore speaking
> radio and television productions
> choral reading

One other kind of speech activity is included in any complete program. A student who has a speech difficulty needs a corrective program. A clinical and counseling staff should be available to give skilled help to those students who have speech problems.

As in the case of music programs, teachers do not always remain faithful to the goal of speech activities for all students. As speech has moved into the classroom, the general speech program has tended to become the responsibility of English or core teachers. If such teachers have training in speech education, they may do very well indeed. If they either lack training or time for including speech experiences in general education, the students who have more need than talent may not get much help in speech. In such schools, unfortunately, the extraclass activities such as debating or dramatics tend to become programs for the gifted. In short, those who need the help least receive an inordinate amount of it. Those who need it most are often overlooked.

This situation can be corrected in any of several ways. In one school, all core teachers worked together for a year, studying the techniques of speech teaching under the direction of one of their number who had recently majored in speech. As they learned techniques they immediately tried them out with students. Since they had all the students in their classes, the general speech program soon achieved a high level of excellence. In other schools the "goals of effective speech" have been developed cooperatively by all teachers, and each teacher has assumed the responsibility of working toward these goals in his own classes. In some schools a required speech program replaces English on certain days.

There should be some extraclass activities provided for gifted students in speech. Perhaps at the eleventh and twelfth grade levels there is also a place for specialized courses for advanced students in radio speech, dramatics, etc. If the whole faculty is "speech-conscious," however, many other experiences will also be provided for less talented students—in clubs, in class organizations, in the student council, and in the school-community relations area. Teachers must be alert to such opportunities, help create them, capitalize them, and generally help students perfect their speech skills for communication purposes in real projects and group situations. The school assembly, discussed earlier in this chapter, offers many opportunities for speech experience to large audiences. More lifelike, however, is the small-group situation available in any class or club. The fact that communication is a universal cultural and vocational need must not be overlooked.

*Athletics.* The most familiar of all student activities is athletics. However small the school, efforts are made to field teams in at least one or two sports. Many a small community has based its very identity on the basketball teams at the high school. No other activity evokes such feverish community interest or commands such prestige among students.

Long before music and speech became programs for the gifted, interscholastic sports had achieved that dubious honor. Only a small percentage of those who are interested can remain on the squad. Those who need physical growth and coordination most are the first to be eliminated. Boys' activities are emphasized over those for girls. There is a drive to win at any cost. The athletics program basks in the sun of public interest, at the expense of almost all other activities and classes. Thus it tends to be somehow separated from the rest of the school program.

There is merit in a well-organized sports program for the talented. There is also a very real need for an athletics program for all students. The junior high schools seem to have come somewhat closer to achieving a program for all. Senior high schools which emphasize only interscholastic sports, and which carry minimum squads in all sports, are not reflecting sound values. The physical education program should reach all students and should have a much richer, more diversified program than team sports. It should have a respected status as a department in its own right, not a farm system for training prospective school athletes. There should also be a schoolwide intramural program, open to all boys and girls, with a varied game program that would interest everyone in some activity. The intramural program can, under proper direction, achieve as much status in the school as the interscholastic sports. It can include activities with high carry-over to adult recreational interests, such as softball, swimming, golf, and bowling. It can include large-group games such as volleyball and games for two such as tennis. It can reach out for those with nonathletic preferences by offering chess and bridge. It can be operated in smaller space than a gymnasium for such features as table tennis and shuffleboard.

Intramural programs can offer something for all students. This is a very important advantage, which should induce secondary schools everywhere to develop comprehensive intramural programs. Most junior high schools carry on such a program. Why is it so seldom achieved in senior high schools?

For one thing, no one appears to be giving vigorous leadership to organization of the intramural program in many high schools. The men and women who might be expected to exhibit interest in such activities are often absorbed in interscholastic coaching. The varsity teams not only use all the time of the available faculty, but monopolize the gymnasium, pool, and play fields after school. The schedule, as well as the financial backing, favors interscholastic athletics over the less glamorous intramural program.

The following criteria were offered for evaluating the intramural program by a recent volume on the junior high school. Most of them are equally applicable to the senior high school program.

1. The program should provide opportunities for all students to participate, not just to watch.

2. The object should mainly be fun for all, not success for a few.

3. A variety of sports should be offered as a means of interesting all students in some type of activity.

4. The program should be carefully administered to make allowance for health and safety.

5. The program should promote good social and emotional adjustment.

6. The program should be free to all students.

7. All students should be eligible to participate.

8. The program should be scheduled on school time.

9. The program should offer opportunities for student leadership in planning, administering, and evaluating the activities.

10. Adults should show interest, should help in every way, and should build the status of the program but avoid domination or control of policies.[13]

Perhaps the most urgent need of the intramural program is indicated in the last of these quoted criteria, that of status and importance in the eyes of students and parents. If we seem to be omitting any discussion of the interscholastic program, it is because we believe it has less need of status. Building up a good intramural program need not be done at the expense of the interscholastic program. Both can flourish in a secondary school if they are developed and administered with the dual goal of varied opportunities for all youth and selected programs for the talented. In any case, there appears to be a sound case for restricting the interscholastic program to the senior high school.[14]

*School camping.* The practice of taking elementary and secondary school youth to camp for one week during the school year has developed rapidly in recent years. Most of the goals of the activities program are capable of achievement in the well-conducted school

[13] Roland C. Faunce and Morrel J. Clute, *Teaching and Learning in the Junior High School* (Belmont, Calif.: Wadsworth Publishing Co., Inc., 1961), headings, pp. 148–149.

[14] In spite of convincing medical evidence (see the report *School Athletics,* cited at the close of this chapter) against interschool competition at the junior high school level, there has been a recent trend toward extending interscholastic sports downward. In 1958, over 85 per cent of the separately organized junior high schools had some program of interscholastic athletics.

camp. The camp setting facilitates learning. No matter how ingenious teachers are, or how fine the building is, the school does not seem as real or as natural as the camp. In urban centers, youth have had increasing difficulty finding responsibilities that they can assume and through which they can learn. In camp everyone has a real job, one that needs doing for comfort and survival. Such tasks as dishwashing, food preparation, and housekeeping need not be adult-assigned or "motivated" in the camp setting. Planning with others is a daily procedure. Social skills and democracy are learned by their constant practice, around the clock. Learning by doing is natural in camp. All kinds of stimuli for learning about nature and about man are all about one.

A common plan is to send two or three sections to camp for a week accompanied by their homeroom or core teachers, two or three other interested teachers, and some parents who have volunteered. In some states a considerable number of state camps are available and winterized. Elsewhere private or church camps are leased. A few school systems own camps. If no kitchen or maintenance staffs are provided at the camp, the school may supply all personnel needed from its own staff.

Preplanning is the rule in school camping. Students are involved, well in advance of the actual camping experience, in planning the week's activities, making rules or policies, setting up responsibilities, developing menus and schedules. Both cabin groups and program groups offer leadership opportunities at camp. A counselor is usually assigned to each cabin group of eight or ten boys or girls. Program groups may be larger and composed of both sexes. Program groups facilitate the alternating of activities planned by students and teachers for each day.

Besides taking care of the housekeeping, groups of students hike, study and photograph wild life, write poems and stories, see films, listen to lectures, and read in the camp library. In addition to these experiences, which are somewhat similar to those carried on in school, they plan and carry out many service projects. School campers have built roads, bridges, fire lanes, pathways, retaining walls, docks, and overnight shelters. They have planted trees and flowers, cleaned away forest debris, and in general improved the resources around the camp. Social and recreational activities are natural and frequent at camp. Swimming, hiking, campfire song-fests, cook-outs, skiing, snowshoeing, skating, talent shows, square dancing, and story hours offer rich opportunities for planning and for fun. Evaluation of the week at camp has often revealed significant growth in the important process of socialization.

The following steps seem important in developing a school camping program:

1. Staff planning in which the administrators and teachers discuss the philosophy and purpose of camping in education
2. Community planning
3. Student planning
4. Board of education approval
5. Resource-use planning (securing camp and personnel, both permanent and temporary)
6. Planning camp activities
7. Pre-camp planning sessions for camp staff
8. Camper-teacher program planning [15]

Costs of the week at camp should be kept minimal if not assumed by the board of education. Means should be developed to take care of all students financially, without embarrassment to those unable to pay their entire cost.

More than any other school activity, the school camp offers an opportunity to learn democracy through practicing it. Such learning is possible in any school, with or without school camping. At camp it is achieved more readily, in a climate of reality. Whatever problems must be solved in order to extend the camping experience to more students can be overcome by systematic planning.

*Student participation in school government.* The school student council is in one sense the capstone and symbol of the whole activities program. It is not only a means of learning democracy by participating in government. It is also the one organization thus far devised for involving all students in a school in developing and reviewing policies. But this is only true insofar as the council succeeds in becoming representative of the whole school. The goal is for every student and teacher to become a participating citizen with a personal stake in planning, executing, and evaluating significant projects.

[15] *Community School Camping* (Lansing, Mich.: State Department of Public Instruction, 1951), pp. 27–28.

Unless the council is really a representative body, this goal is not achieved even for its own members.

What prevents a typical student council from being a representative group? What is the reason for the rather common apathy on the part of most students, and the deterioration of the council into a private club or clique? Any of several conditions may be the cause:

1. No machinery may exist for communicating with those who elected the councilmen. If the council is elected by grade-level classes or at large, there may be no opportunity for them to discuss with their own constitutents the vital business of the school. If councilmen are elected by homerooms, time for such discussions can be provided.

2. Administrators or sponsors may have demonstrated by repeated vetoes or warnings that the council cannot make any very important decisions. If there is a definite lack of faith in the ability and common sense of youth, the council will soon lose interest in the whole affair.

3. Teachers may be apathetic or even hostile to the council's operation. If teachers consider discussions of school policies or projects a waste of time, they are unlikely to cooperate with the council's efforts to communicate with their own constituents.

4. The council may view their own members as a privileged part of the power structure, who are not obliged to consult with ordinary students. If they are unable to listen they will fail to build an all-school participation plan.

5. A large segment of the student body may be ineligible to serve because of their marks.

All these problems can be overcome if adults have faith in the democratic process. Time can be found for communicating to the whole school, and the skills can be learned. The first ingredient needed is faith and interest on the part of administrators and teachers.

Ideally, the council should be the voice of all the people. The youngest, poorest, least articulate, and least influential student in the entire high school should firmly believe, with all his fellows, that he may present an idea which will affect the whole school through its transmission to the floor of the student council.[16]

[16] Johnston and Faunce, *Student Activities,* p. 152.

Provision must be made in classes or homerooms for regular weekly discussions with a council member present. The whole student body and faculty must have time to share in developing and reviewing policies. In the administration of decisions, too, students and teachers not on the council can serve on boards or commissions for special projects. An active council needs many such committees for planning school assemblies, improving the school grounds, chartering clubs, developing the budget, planning noon-hour activities, developing the school handbook, improving the social program, conducting drives, and dozens of other service projects which a lively student organization will initiate. Other continuing services will call for volunteers. Examples of these are fire drills, locker inspections, cheerleading, hosting special occasions, film-projecting, library service, ushers, and office aides. There can and should be an almost endless variety of services which can be shared with the entire student body and faculty. Young people want to serve and share in planning. The most suitable areas for such services are those which arise from and faithfully reflect the students and their interests. Teachers will discover that students tend to live up to their expectations for them.

## Administering activities—some recommendations

A few recommendations regarding the administration of the program seem indicated. The *cost* of activities to students should be kept low or largely eliminated by board of education subsidy. An activity ticket plan may enable a school to spread the cost. The *schedule* should be largely included in the school day, through use of an activities period and the noon hour. Some few activities may have to be carried on after school, but each of these should be paralleled by a similar or identical activity during the school day. There should be no academic *eligibility restrictions* for any activity beyond the minimum required by the state for interschool competitions. Awards should be minimized by spreading them more generally throughout the whole program. It should be possible to gain awards by participating in any of a wide variety of activities. Efforts should be made to avoid *overparticipation* or *domination* of a whole program by a few students. Perhaps a point system may be useful in spreading participation. Under this plan each activity earns a specified number of points and a maximum is established for any particular semester.

## Evaluation of activities

Both students and sponsors should engage in evaluation of the entire activities program. A good program is likely to be one where all participants are striving to make it a better one. They will be asking themselves such questions as the following, with regard to all student activities:

1. Is the stated purpose of each activity a legitimate one in a public school which serves all youth?

2. Is there opportunity somewhere in the program for every student to participate successfully?

3. Does the program build stronger social relationships and cooperative attitudes?

4. Is it in gear with the classroom-centered curriculum?

5. Does it offer opportunities for youth to plan, to assume leadership, to accept and carry out real responsibilities?

6. Does the program reflect the real interests of students?

7. Is it supported with enthusiasm by teachers, administrators, and parents?

If the answers to such questions continue to be in the affirmative, it is likely that students and teachers are carrying on a rich and vital program which will supplement classroom efforts to build better citizens.

*In conclusion.* Teachers should consider the activities program a legitimate part of their assignment. The values of sponsoring such activities have been pointed out in various ways in this chapter. It is also true that the activities program cannot thrive without the enthusiastic participation of the teachers. The particular group or activity which they assume should be based on their interests. But whether it represents their first love or favorite hobby, it will become a satisfying experience if a teacher learns to relax and enjoy the activity instead of trying to direct it. He will discover in the activity a freedom from subject-matter expectations, flexibility to adapt to students' interests, and a fine opportunity to learn what his students are really like when the pressure of the classroom is removed.

In the next chapter, we turn to the more general problem of evaluating students' growth in all aspects of their school programs.

## FOR FURTHER READING

American Association of School Administrators and Educational Policies Commission, *School Athletics*. Washington, D.C.: The National Education Association, 1954. A strong policy statement on athletics. Opposes interschool contests below grade nine.

Educational Policies Commission, *Learning the Ways of Democracy*. Washington, D.C.: The National Education Association, 1940. Dramatic description of citizenship-education activities in American secondary schools.

Faunce, Roland C., *Secondary School Administration*. New York: Harper & Row, Publishers, 1955. Chapter 9 surveys the whole field of student activities. Chapter 10 is devoted to "Student Participation in School Government."

————, and Morrel J. Clute, *Teaching and Learning in the Junior High School*. Belmont, Calif.: Wadsworth Publishing Co., Inc., 1961. Chapter 6 contains recommendations for a program uniquely adapted to junior high school youth.

Frederick, Robert, *The Third Curriculum*. New York: Appleton-Century-Crofts, Inc., 1959. History and modern practices of school activities. Comprehensive and interesting.

Fretwell, Elbert K., *Extra-Curricular Activities in Secondary Schools*. Boston: Houghton Mifflin Co., 1931. A pioneer text on student activities that is still a useful and stimulating analysis of the basic goals of such programs.

Hand, Harold C., *How to Conduct the Participation in Extra-Class Activities Study*. Illinois State Department of Public Instruction, 1949. A useful handbook for surveying and evaluating an activities program.

————, *Principal Findings of the 1947–48 Basic Studies of the Illinois Secondary School Curriculum Program*. Illinois State Department of Public Instruction, 1949. A report of the extraclass participation studies in Illinois is included in this summary pamphlet.

Johnston, Edgar G., and Roland C. Faunce, *Student Activities in Secondary Schools*. New York: Ronald Press Co., 1952. Analysis and examples of all aspects of student activities. Contains a chapter on school camping.

Kilzer, Louis R., Harold H. Stephenson, and H. Orville Nordberg, *Allied Activities in the Secondary School*. New York: Harper & Row, Publishers, 1956. Contains a good chapter on school clubs, and one on the social program of the schools.

Kirkendall, Lester A., and Franklin R. Zeron, *Student Councils in Action.* New York: Chartwell House, Inc., 1952. Many illustrations of junior and senior high school councils at work.

McKean, Robert C., *Principles and Methods of Secondary Education.* Columbus, Ohio: Charles E. Merrill Books, Inc., 1962. Chapter 10 provides a brief overview of the activities program. Special treatment of pros and cons of athletic program.

McKown, Harry C., *Extra-Curricular Activities.* New York: Macmillan Co., 1952. A widely used volume on all aspects of student activities, written by one who has made a career of their study.

Meier, Arnold, *et al., Let's Look at the Student Council.* Detroit: Wayne State University Press, 1949. A report of the Detroit Citizenship Education Study. Brief, graphic outline of ways to build better student councils.

Miller, Franklin A., James H. Moyer, and Robert B. Patrick, *Planning Student Activities.* Englewood Cliffs, N.J.: Prentice-Hall, Inc., 1956. A good comprehensive volume on all secondary-school student activities, based on a substantial survey of high schools and junior high schools throughout the United States.

Strang, Ruth, *Group Activities in College and Secondary School.* New York: Harper & Row, Publishers, 1946. In the latter portion of this volume the author includes much analysis of ways of working with students in the activity program.

Trump, J. Lloyd, "Extra-Class Activities and the Needs of Youth," in *Adapting the Secondary School Program to the Needs of Youth,* Fifty-second Yearbook, National Society for the Study of Education. Chicago: University of Chicago Press, 1953.

# 13

# Evaluating and reporting student progress

Evaluation is as much a part of our lives as anything we do. Whenever we change our plans or act consciously and deliberately in a manner in which we did not expect to act, we do so because we have engaged in the process of evaluation. We have examined our intended plan of action, have decided against it in the light of circumstances or matters we had previously failed to consider, and have decided to make changes.

> Mrs. Brown was expecting guests for dinner on Saturday evening. She had found a new recipe for sweet and sour pork which interested her. She had not tried it before but was an accomplished cook so was confident that the result would be very satisfactory. On Thursday Mrs. Brown had a telephone conversation with Mrs. Davis who was to be among the Saturday evening guests. In the course of the conversation Mrs. Davis mentioned that she and her husband had had some "wretched Chinese food" at the Anderson's two weeks ago and that Mr. Davis had vowed he would eat no more home-cooked Chinese food if he could help it. Mrs. Brown decided to serve a ham loaf.

It seems likely that Mrs. Brown had considered the consequences of serving sweet and sour pork anyway. She had confidence in her

323

culinary ability. Mr. Davis might be convinced that home-cooked Chinese food could be good if prepared by an expert. His regard for Mrs. Brown might be enhanced. On the other hand, Mr. Davis might be so prejudiced against home-cooked Chinese food that he could not enjoy it even at its best. He might even make some derogatory remarks which would be embarrassing for all concerned. Mrs. Brown had done some evaluating and decided to adjust her plans accordingly.

Bill and Harold were walking to their third hour classes when they passed Sue and Bob at Sue's locker.

"Hi Bob," said Bill. "Did you know I'm taking Sue to the J-Hop?"

Sue looked puzzled but Bill and Harold walked on so she kept talking with Bob before both scurried for their classes.

"You didn't say anything to me about having asked Sue to the Hop," said Harold.

"Oh, I hadn't asked her before," replied Bill, "but she knows I'm taking her now."

"You sure take a lot for granted!" Harold admonished as the boys took their seats in chemistry class.

Bill proceeded to make his plans for the dance including securing the use of his uncle's convertible, a sizable advance on his allowance, and a new suit. Finally, after some urging by his mother, he called Sue about the color of her dress so he could order the corsage.

"But Bill," Sue protested, "what ever made you think I was going to the Hop with you? You never even asked me!"

Bill's explanation that he had intended to follow up on his statement that day at the locker but had decided it wasn't necessary failed to impress Sue. Anyway Jim had asked her to go with him and she had accepted.

Nearly a month before the Prom, Bill called Sally. "I'd like to take you to the Prom if you'd go with me," he said. "Unless you promised to go with someone else," he added.

Apparently Bill had done some evaluating. He seems to have concluded that his approach to the problem of making a date for the J-Hop left something to be desired, hence he changed his tactics.

## When do people evaluate?

We are constantly evaluating our behavior and modifying it in relation to our estimate of the degree of success we have achieved previously under somewhat similar circumstances—or how successfully things are going for us now. We profit by our failures and our successes. When we fail we are inclined to look for the causes; when we succeed we tend to try in similar circumstances in the future to follow the pattern of behavior which led to success before. We evaluate through all stages of the activity, not only at the end. Usually, we are not even conscious of the fact that we are evaluating, the process has become such a common experience.

*Evaluation as a personal endeavor.* People exhibit various degrees of proficiency in the evaluation and consequent modification of their behavior. Some are very skillful. We say they are well adjusted. We call those maladjusted who are least skillful at the process of evaluation and consequent modification of their behavior on the basis of experience and reflection.

Evaluation, then, is the process of appraising our actions, including our thinking. Its purpose is to improve our behavior (overt action and thinking) both now—as the behavior is proceeding—and in the future. Since all behavior is goal oriented, we evaluate our behavior in order that we may achieve a greater degree of success in reaching our goals. By the same token evaluation is an integral part of the learning process, inseparable from it—except artificially for purposes of analysis and examination as we are now doing.

*Evaluation as a group endeavor.* Evaluation is not always a personal matter involving only the individual's appraisal of his own behavior. Often the process is carried out by a group that has objectives which it desires to reach as soon as possible. In order to accomplish this, the planning must be precise and correct, and the action must be according to plan. But sometimes unforeseen circumstances develop. Obstacles appear. Some members may shirk their duties. Events may occur in improper sequence. Some acts which appeared promising in the projection are revealed to be useless. In order to achieve its goals the group must evaluate as it lays its plans and as it proceeds to carry them out, making changes along the way. If it is a continuing group which will tackle other problems, or other aspects of the same problem, it must also do some evaluating at the end of the project, or when the current phase of the project has been completed.

Tom, Linda, Mary, and Joe were the members of a student council committee to prepare a report on the council's annual project of beautifying the school grounds. At the first meeting of the committee, Linda was chosen chairman. The committee "free-wheeled" for awhile, then settled on a proposal which involved a courtyard area completely surrounded and overlooked by the library, the arts and crafts room, the principal's office, and hallway. There were some tulip and daffodil beds along the border near the building on three sides. Along the hallway the border consisted of a privet hedge. The center area was grass.

The council committee first made notes from which a statement could be prepared which would present reasons for selecting this particular portion of the school grounds for the council project. They listed the fact that the hedge was seldom properly trimmed, and it seemed out of place anyway to have a hedge on only one side of the court. The hedge had now grown so high that the entire surface of the court was hidden from the view of anyone passing the hall windows, unless they walked very close to the windows. The grass had encroached on the flower beds so that the beds were barely distinguishable from the lawn area. No one on the committee could ever remember the grass having been cut. It was noted that the custodians seemed very lax about caring for the courtyard and should be reprimanded by the principal.

The committee planned to preface its report with a statement of their reasons, then recommend that the council secure volunteers from the student body to clean out the flower beds, dig up and replant the bulbs at the proper time, and plant new bulbs which the council would purchase. The committee would ask the head custodian if the hedge could be trimmed down to about two feet in height and the lawn cut regularly. They also decided to ask the principal if the school would plant a hedge on the other side of the courtyard to match the one already there.

Consultation with the head custodian revealed that the school did not own a hand mower and it was impossible to bring the large power mower through the arts and crafts room, which provided the only access to the courtyard. The custodian said he had brought an old mower he had at home but that it had been broken and had been taken to the dump because it wasn't worth repairing. The only way to keep the grass cut would be to have the school purchase a new hand mower or get someone to donate one. The custodian agreed to trim the hedge and keep it trimmed and plant the new one if the principal would authorize it. He thought the committee would be unsuccessful in getting students to clean out the flower borders and keep them clean, however. The committee members were not pleased with this attitude but said nothing. The principal said he could purchase the hedge plants but didn't see how he could justify the purchase of a lawn mower for such a small area of grass. He, too, thought it might be possible to get someone to donate one which they no longer used.

At what was supposed to be the final meeting of the committee, called for the purpose of preparing the report to the council, Mary stated that she didn't think the custodian was likely to take care of the grass even if they did get someone to donate a lawnmower to the school. She wished some other solution could be found. The committee then discussed planting various kinds of flowers over the whole area but decided this would be too expensive and wouldn't look good anyway. Tom suggested using paving blocks in various colors to replace the grass, with groups of shrubs in each corner. This seemed like a good idea to all of the committee members but now the principal would have to be consulted again, since some considerable expense would be involved even if the students and custodians did the work. Since the principal was not available at that time, and the committee was expected to report the next day, they decided to take a chance on the principal's approval of the expenditure for shrubs and paving blocks. Linda insisted on including a recommendation in the report that the head custodian be reprimanded by the principal for failure to take adequate care of the courtyard.

The council took several actions. They complimented the committee on the thoroughness of their study and the completeness of their report. The committee charge was changed from a planning function to an action (implementing) function. The recommendation regarding the reprimand of the head custodian was deleted from the council minutes. The council authorized a sum which could be expended for bulbs but thought that the planting and clean-up should be done by council members instead of volunteers from the student body "so the students could see some tangible results of the council's work." One council member whose father operated a landscaping business said he thought his father could suggest a cheaper solution to the problem presented by the grass-covered center area. The council added that member to the committee and directed the committee to secure the advice of the new member's father.

Obviously, both the committee and the council were engaged in the process of evaluation from time to time as this project unfolded. The committee weighed proposals for beautification of various portions of the school grounds before deciding on the courtyard. They considered, perhaps somewhat unconsciously, the effects of their selection on the council if they did not present their reasons for choosing this particular area. The committee had to revise its plans when confronted with the problem of getting the grass cut. The council evaluated the committee's report, accepted most of it in principle, and decided it was sufficiently satisfactory with some modifications to implement. They must have evaluated the likelihood also that these particular committee members would be likely to carry the project through to completion so the council assigned this task to them. The council evaluated the effect of the committee's recommendation that the head custodian be reprimanded by the principal, particularly in view of the fact that the council minutes were distributed widely among the student body. The council also appears to have evaluated the recommendation regarding the use of paving blocks and shrubs and decided this question deserved further study and expert advice. They were also conscious of the image of the council in the eyes of the student body. They weighed (evaluated) the anticipated benefits which might accrue from calling for volunteers to clean the flower beds as opposed to making it a council project.

## Some misconceptions regarding evaluation

Even though evaluation is closely associated with most aspects of living, its function in relation to learning and the school is frequently misunderstood. Many teachers regard evaluation as a means of acquiring some basis for assigning grades. They prepare the tests, grade them, and average the grades according to an arbitrary but complicated formula, in order to be able to give each student a grade for the period in question. Many school administrators also see evaluation as limited to the process of securing grades in order that parents may be informed regarding the school progress of their children. Although one of the outcomes of the evaluative process may be the assignment of a grade which may be reflected in a report to the students' parents, the grade is simply a by-product. Evaluation serves much broader purposes.

Teachers frequently attempt to use evaluative devices as a means of motivating students to greater effort. They warn their classes that they will be quizzed on the assignment. The implication is that the students had better study hard in order to achieve the highest possible score on the test since this score will affect the mark they receive for the course. Such behavior on the part of the teacher suggests to students that evaluation is a device which teachers use to make them work harder. Since most parents have been subjected to this procedure, at least sometime during their own schooling, they tend to view such practice as entirely proper. When the test results in a mark, as it usually does, the parents think of evaluation as a means of determining whether their children are studying hard enough. Although some students probably redouble their efforts under such circumstances, the practice at best leads to "cramming" with temporary rather than more permanent learning as a result. At worst it leads to cheating and other forms of dishonesty. Evaluation is a process for measuring successes and failures in the attempt to improve prospects of goal attainment. It cannot be used properly as a substitute for a learning goal.

Some teachers view evaluation as a device that facilitates the comparative rating of students, a sort of screen which strains out the nonachievers, leaving the achievers. Many parents and students follow along with this conception of evaluation as a process that enables college admissions officers to decide whom to admit. Some parents also use the resulting grades to compare one child with another, either within or outside of the family. All such comparisons, of course, fly in the face of all that is known regarding individual differences. We can measure the height of James and John and report truthfully that John is three inches taller than James. We are in error, however, revealing disrespect for individual dignity, when we say that John is better than James because John is taller—or that James is better because he is shorter. Unfortunately, college admissions officers sometimes base their decisions concerning admission to college exclusively on marks, rank in class, and grade-point average. Many of them, however, would prefer to make their selections on more comprehensive information. They use grades and the by-products of grades only because this is the only kind of information the secondary school makes available.

Occasionally, one finds teachers who regard evaluation as a method of acquiring a high rating in relation to other teachers, as a result of the superior performance of the students in their classes on standardized achievement tests. Teachers with this point of view are usually found working in a school where the administrator tries to use test scores to compare the efficiency of the various teachers. Being assigned to the classes which have the largest percentage of students from the "right side of the tracks" is a real asset to the teacher in such a situation. Also of considerable value is having students who have had the best teachers in previous years. The use of achievement test scores to measure teacher efficiency could be justified only if (1) goals were known and understood by all parties concerned, including the degree of emphasis which should be accorded to each goal, (2) the tests used were known to be valid and reliable,[1] and (3) student achievement were conceived as individual growth, limited to the period of time the student was a member of the teacher's class, and adjusted for all factors of individual difference, e.g., the influences of other school and nonschool environmental factors, the physical, emotional, social, and intellectual development of the student, etc. The present degree of precision in goal definition, test making, and appraisal of individual differences falls far short of the level required for effective evaluation of teaching efficiency on the basis of students' scores on achievement tests.

Much like the use of achievement test scores for teacher evaluation is the practice of judging the relative quality of a school system by the percentage of students who scored above the established norm for the test, the number of students admitted to college, and the number of students who won scholarships of one kind or another. This is not to say that all schools are equal in efficiency. Schools vary in effectiveness over an extremely wide range from very poor to excellent. But there is much variation in such matters as goal emphasis, characteristics of student bodies, community mores and traditions, and level of financial support, so that any attempt to place schools in a "better than," "poorer than" classification must be arbitrary.

Many students view evaluation as a dreaded exercise which peri-

---

[1] A test is said to be *valid* if it measures what it purports to measure. It is *reliable* to the extent that it produces consistent results.

odically leaves their fate hanging in the balance. Students who view
the evaluative process in this light are not likely also to see it as an
essential part of all human endeavor—a means of increasing the
probability of goal achievement, hence, a skill in which one should
constantly strive to become more proficient. When teachers limit
their concept to the traditional variety of testing, students are not
likely to seek ways to use evaluation as a wholesome route toward
more effective living.

## Evaluation in the school

Both students and teachers often view evaluation as something
the teacher does, perhaps because schools offer too few opportunities
for students to appraise their own progress or to share in assessment
of their own growth. In Chapter 8 we gave a number of illustrations
of student self-evaluation in reference to group membership and the
productivity of small groups in the classroom. Some teachers have
helped students to translate such self-evaluations into school marks.
Individual and group goals have been reproduced on a self-marking
check-list, with a place for a rating by both student and teacher.
When the ratings tend to agree, the mark may be considered to have
been arrived at in this manner. When there seems to be some disagreement between student's and teacher's ratings, a conference is
usually called for and data should be supplied by both parties in
support of their ratings.

Whether or not such self-evaluations are translated into school
marks, they contribute significantly to the education of the student.
It is probable that self-evaluation is much more important and
significant an activity than is teacher-appraisal. Only through self-
evaluation can a student gain control of the crucial business of setting standards for himself, and only self-established standards have
any meaning in education. Teachers should work systematically on
methods of helping students assess their own progress.

*The teacher's role in evaluation.* The teacher has a dual role in
evaluation. He must serve as an observer, guide, adviser, and counselor to his students as they seek to evaluate the products of their
learning, including the improvement of their ability to evaluate
effectively. The teacher is also the designated agent of the society to
determine the extent to which the goals society has set for the schools

are being achieved. A part of this responsibility involves individual self-evaluation, since the teacher is charged directly with the achievement of certain goals. It also involves participation in group self-evaluation, since the teacher is a member of a team which shares the total charge to the school. These two facets of the teacher's role in evaluation are not discrete. As the teacher helps students in self-evaluation, evaluates his own teaching activities, and works as a member of the faculty team in evaluating the success of the program, he constantly assumes both aspects of his responsibility for evaluation.

*The purposes served by evaluation.* The foremost purpose of evaluation is to improve the problem-solving process by keeping each aspect of it—identification and description of the problem or problems, planning for the solution or partial solution of the problem or problems, and implementation of the plans decided on—under constant surveillance.

A second purpose is to determine levels of goal achievement so that next steps may be identified. Such knowledge is essential to both the student and the teacher. The student cannot select appropriate projects and study materials unless he can make a fairly accurate estimate of the various kinds of skills required to complete the alternative choices in relation to the skills he possesses. The teacher needs this same information in order to help the student assess his potential and select his tools. The eleventh grade student who reads at the seventh grade level cannot learn much while trying to use eleventh grade books. The student who has little or no knowledge of English grammar will not be very successful in a foreign language course in which the methods and materials used depend heavily on comparison and contrast with English grammar. The student who has difficulty writing a few sentences is unlikely to find the assignment of a 2,000-word composition one which he can complete over a weekend. On the other hand, students of high ability are frequently bored by the uniform class assignment. These individuals should be encouraged to discover more challenging experiences. The information concerning each student collected by the teacher, using evaluative procedures, enables the teacher to adjust his expectations (and, therefore, assignments) to the capacities of each student. From time to time special problems, unique to individual students and groups of students, will be revealed. If the teacher shares appropriate information with the students, they will be able to make more intelligent choices too.

Evaluative procedures are also an aid to the discovery of aptitudes and interests. Teacher-counselors and other guidance workers need this information in order to help students in career selection. Moreover, such knowledge aids students and teachers in the identification of promising fields for further study and training.

*Making the evaluative process more precise.* Since the purpose of evaluation is to render goal achievement more likely, the evaluative process must begin with goal definition. Progress toward a goal is impossible unless the goal is known. In Chapter 2 we treated in some detail the goals set by the society for secondary schools. We have defined learning as changed behavior. We illustrated one attempt to define purposes in behavioral terms. We suggested this as a point of departure for teachers, working individually and in groups, who wanted to take full advantage of the evaluative process in improving their own teaching as well as the total influence of the school. The important question, of course, in all such endeavor is "How may the student who is making progress toward this goal be expected to act?"

One group, in attempting to establish behavioral guidelines for the evaluation of the goal of learning to appreciate literature, decided that such appreciation could be manifested in seven general types of behavior as follows:

1. Satisfaction in the thing appreciated.
2. Desire for more of the thing appreciated.
3. Desire to know more about the thing appreciated.
4. Desire to express one's self creatively.
5. Identification of one's self with the thing appreciated.
6. Desire to clarify one's own thinking with regard to the life problems raised by the thing appreciated.
7. Desire to evaluate the thing appreciated.[2]

Each of the seven general types of behavior was described in considerable detail. We present here the detailed description of the ways

[2] "Ways in Which the Appreciation of Literature May Manifest Itself in Behavior," Evaluation Staff of the Progressive Education Association (mimeographed), pp. 1–10.

in which the "desire to express one's self creatively" might be revealed in behavior.

> Appreciation manifests itself in an active desire on the part of the individual to go beyond the thing appreciated: to give creative expression in ideas and feelings of his own which the thing appreciated has chiefly engendered. The person who really appreciates a given piece of literature is desirous of doing for himself, either in the same or in a different medium, something of what the author has done in the medium of literature.

### Subjective

1. He feels that he can achieve for himself, through his own creative activities, a pleasure comparable to the pleasure which the creative activities of the author have given him.

2. He plans in his imagination the particular creative product which he would like to achieve.

3. He tries to imagine what would have happened if the piece had been extended beyond the compass which the author gave to it, or if certain other situations had been introduced, or if the order of events had been changed.

4. He wants to discuss the piece with others because of the opportunity which such discussion affords for the expression of his own ideas and feelings about the life problems with which the piece deals.

5. He re-constructs, in his own reading of the piece, something of the creative feelings which the author himself must have experienced in writing it.

6. He is interested in writing *about* the piece.

7. He feels the urge to rewrite for himself certain scenes which do not seem to him entirely acceptable, or to add new scenes which he feels desirable to the sequence of the narrative.

8. He attempts in his imagination to picture the theme of the piece represented in some other art medium.

9. He attempts to picture accurately in his imagination the persons, places, situations, actions, etc., depicted by the author.

### Objective

1. He discusses with his friends particular pieces of writing, or other creative products, which he himself would like to achieve as a result of the inspiration received from the thing appreciated.

2. He discusses with his friends certain of his own ideas and feelings about life which have been engendered by the thing appreciated.

3. He produces, or at least undertakes to produce, a creative product more or less after the manner of the thing appreciated.

4. He writes to the author, to the publisher, or to his friends expressing his own ideas or feelings concerning certain phases of life dealt with by the thing appreciated.

5. He writes [expressing] critical appreciation of the piece.

6. He elects to discuss the piece, or the work of its author, before a literary or social group to which he belongs.

7. He writes a sequel to the piece, he rewrites certain scenes which he does not find entirely acceptable, or he adds scenes which he considers desirable to the sequence of the narrative.

8. He transfers the structural elements of the plot to another artistic medium—drama, opera, scenario, etc.

9. He illustrates the piece in some one of the graphic, spatial, musical, or dramatic arts.

10. He transfers the mood or feeling-tone of the piece to some artistic creation of his own.[3]

Obviously, each student would not be expected to exhibit all of the behaviors described in this illustration. It does seem likely, however, that each student would exhibit some of the behaviors in the complete list if he were, in fact, progressing in the direction of the achievement of the goal "to appreciate literature." As we have noted previously, the teacher has to adjust his expectations to the individual's capacity in the area in question. The fact that the list of behaviors is divided into *subjective* and *objective* manifestations suggests clearly that the list was intended for use by students for self-evaluation as well as by teachers.

The dovetailing of student self-evaluation and teacher evaluation of the students should characterize all such activity. The student is concerned with the answer to the questions "How well did I do?" "How close did I come to achieving my goal?" "What can I do next time to come closer to complete satisfaction of my goal?" The teacher is concerned with helping the student to evaluate, but also with the success of the experience itself. If the progress seems slight the teacher should seek other, more promising learning experiences.

3 *Ibid.*, pp. 5–6.

*Specific aids in the process of evaluation.* The reduction of learning goals to behavioral terms is a general device used to aid in evaluation. Let us now turn to a discussion of more specific procedures from which the teacher may select, according to the particular kind of behavior he proposes to measure or appraise.

1. *Observation* is the only method of evaluating many kinds of behavior. This is true of several of the items in the illustration relative to the appreciation of literature ("the desire for more of the thing appreciated," "the desire to express one's self creatively") and the various behaviors involving discussion. Most of the behavior that must be expressed in a group setting or in relation to one or more other individuals is not subject to appraisal by means other than observation. This is also true of some of such study skills as use and allocation of time, concentration on the work at hand, and efficient arrangement of the study environment.

Observation may be performed by either students or the teacher or by both. It may be either planned in advance or incidental. The observer's success is directly related to the extent to which he is objective in his observations. Often the observer reports to the group or individual immediately following the activity. In this case notes for future reference are unnecessary as far as the observer is concerned. If the observation is designed to provide data which may contribute to a more comprehensive evaluation, some record of the observed phenomena will usually have to be made. Note-taking during the observation will frequently detract from the activity being observed unless the observer cannot readily be seen by the persons being observed. This implies, of course, that the record must be prepared as soon as possible following the observation.

2. *Anecdotal records* are closely related to observation since they are prepared as a result of observed behavior. They are descriptions of incidents or events that are believed to have bearing on some aspect of the learning process. Although usually prepared in relation to individual students, anecdotal records may be used with equal success to describe group behavior. As an evaluative device, they throw light on degree of goal achievement, possible obstacles to satisfactory progress, and readiness for various learning experiences.

One teacher recorded the following incidents in relation to one aspect of the behavior of one student:

November 9: Jim's project group elected him chairman today. After class Bill and Mary asked me how they could get another chairman. They complained that Jim clowned and "talked all the time." Observed some of this myself. Caught Jim after his last class and asked him if he liked being chairman. He said he did. Asked him if he had read the mimeographed sheet on duties of chairman. He said he had but he didn't remember much of it. Asked him to reread it and see me again Monday.

November 12: Jim came in at noon. Said he read sheet. Asked if he got any ideas about the chairman's job as a result. We talked about other things for a while. Before leaving Jim said he didn't think his actions on Friday were "like it said on the sheet." He said he thought his group was "mad at him" and maybe he should be changed to another group. I suggested he might want to apologize to the group.

January 14: Jim volunteered to act as chairman of the panel discussion on Group A's final report. The group seemed reluctant to accept him but there were no other volunteers.

January 15: Jim came in after school and went over his plans for the Group A report. Plans seemed good. I mentioned that it was important to clear plans with the group.

The teacher who prepared the above record was concerned about Jim's development in leadership roles. She viewed Jim as a very bright boy, shy, somewhat lacking in the social graces, and with little encouragement at home. She believed Jim had a great deal of potential which had thus far been unrealized. It disturbed her when Jim "muffed" his opportunity to chair a discussion group. She seems to have experienced some success, at least temporarily, in her efforts to help him.

Obviously, the teacher must discriminate carefully among the many possibilities in the writing of anecdotal records, the preparation of which is very time-consuming. It is important to develop the ability to write a meaningful description of the incident in question using as few words as possible. It is also necessary to decide on the purpose which the anecdotal record will serve before preparing it. If it is to be used only by the teacher who writes it, within a limited period of time, the record may be prepared less carefully than when several persons may have to understand it. Some teachers find single-sentence records sufficient to call to their minds the details of the incidents they wish to remember.

Anecdotal records have many uses. They are helpful in counseling students, in planning learning experiences for individuals and groups, and, of course, in evaluation. They are an excellent example of the manner in which evaluative activities intertwine with all other aspects of living. Anecdotal records are especially helpful in teacher-parent conferences. They are also useful in case conferences and as illustrative data in faculty curriculum planning. Many teachers use anecdotal records to assist them in arriving at grades. Although the anecdotal record is primarily a device prepared by a teacher for his own use, it sometimes becomes a part of the student's cumulative file. In such cases much caution must be exercised to make certain that the observation is as objective as possible and carefully written in sufficient detail so that the meaning is clear. Probably such records should be based on a series of incidents over an extended period of observation rather than occasional single events.

3. *The periodic log* is one of the most useful of the evaluative devices. It is equally valuable for student self-evaluation and teacher evaluation of student progress. Like the other good evaluative devices, it contributes as much or more to the on-going learning process as it does to the strictly evaluative function. It enables the teacher to keep in touch with each student on a periodic basis.

The log consists of a few short questions or statements that are answered by the individual or group. Answers are usually in writing for the sake of clarity and recording, but the log is sometimes answered orally. Under the latter circumstance it may become a part of a student-teacher conference. Sometimes the log becomes the basis for a report by a small group to the class, or for a discussion by the larger group.

Teachers usually experiment with slightly different phrasing until they settle on some particular questions or statements that produce the results they desire. The following form is typical:

1. Our group (I) accomplished the following things this week:
2. We (I) have encountered some obstacles:
3. We (I) plan to try to overcome these obstacles in the following ways:
4. We (I) need the following kinds of help:

The above format is illustrative of the type of log that is used for periodic evaluation of a continuing activity. The questions or statements which make up a log to be used to assist in the evaluation of a completed activity will be similar to the following:

1. Our (My) accomplishments were as follows:
2. Things we (I) liked about this project:
3. Things we (I) disliked about this project:
4. If we (I) were to repeat this project, I would change certain things:

4. *Informal pencil-and-paper instruments* are those evaluating devices that call for essay responses to questions, various kinds of check-lists and rating scales, and so-called objective-type tests. These are used by teachers to secure various kinds of information. The informal instruments are of two general kinds: (1) those designed to measure factual knowledge or the ability to perform some task and (2) those designed to secure information relative to attitudes, interests, beliefs, associations, relationships, etc.

Accumulation of factual knowledge and development of concepts are only two of the several purposes of education. If teachers limit their evaluation to these two purposes, they will direct the major emphasis in their teaching and in the students' minds toward these purposes and away from other equally important purposes.

The first step in any evaluative process is to decide what is to be measured. This must be known before the best type of instrument to do the job can be selected. If the teacher desires to measure only the students' ability to recall information, and if the goal of the test is also to cover as much knowledge as possible in the time available, the teacher will probably decide to use a so-called objective-type test. If, on the other hand, the purpose of the test is to measure students' ability to select from their knowledge that which is pertinent to a certain topic or problem and respond in their own words, the essay-type test is indicated.

The teacher who sets out to construct a test must also decide how the results will be used. If the major purpose of the test is to diagnose weaknesses so that remedial steps may be taken, the test will be different from one designed to rank students on the basis of their relative success in learning facts, remembering facts, and/or applying facts learned. The diagnostic test must have items covering each weakness to be identified. It will also be necessary to have a range of difficulty in each set of items in order that different levels of weakness may be identified. Furthermore, the number of items must be sufficient to sample the various ways in which the weaknesses may be revealed as well as to eliminate the possibility of "lucky" answers.

The teacher must also consider the amount of time available— for students who will take the test, and for the teacher to prepare the test and score it. Generally speaking, essay tests require less of the teacher's time to prepare than do objective tests, but much more time to score. In an objective test, the students can cover a substantial amount of content or knowledge in a short time. Even a student who knows a great deal about a question or topic can cover only a limited amount in a short time when responding to an essay test.

The following summary cites advantages and disadvantages of both types of tests.

|  | ESSAY | OBJECTIVE |
|---|---|---|
| Abilities Measured | Requires the student to express himself in his own words, using information from his own background and knowledge. | Requires the student to select correct answers from given options, or to supply an answer limited to one word or phrase. |
|  | Can tap high levels of reasoning such as required in inference, organization of ideas, comparison and contrast. | Can also tap high levels of reasoning such as required in inference, organization of ideas, comparison and contrast. |
|  | Does *not* measure purely factual information efficiently. | Measures knowledge of facts efficiently. |
| Scope | Covers only a limited field of knowledge in any one test. Essay questions take so long to answer that relatively few can be answered in a given period of time. Also the student who is especially fluent can often avoid discussing points of which he is unsure. | Covers a broad field of knowledge in one test. Since objective questions may be answered quickly, one test may contain many questions. A broad coverage helps provide reliable measurement. |

| | | |
|---|---|---|
| Incentive to Pupils | Encourages pupils to learn how to organize their own ideas and express them effectively. | Encourages pupils to build up a broad background of knowledge and abilities. |
| Ease of Preparation | Requires writing only a few questions for a test. Tasks must be clearly defined, general enough to offer some leeway, specific enough to set limits. | Requires writing many questions for a test. Wording must avoid ambiguities and give-aways. Distractors should embody most likely misconceptions. |
| Scoring | Usually very time-consuming to score. | Can be scored quickly. |
| | Permits teachers to comment directly on the reasoning processes of individual pupils. However, an answer may be scored differently by different teachers or by the same teacher at different times. | Answer generally scored only right or wrong, but scoring is very accurate and consistent.[4] |

Having decided what type of test to use, what it is to measure, how the results will be used, and how much time is available, the next step is to prepare the items. The questions or statements should be presented as simply as possible unless, of course, one is attempting to measure reading ability or some particular aspect of it such as vocabulary. The probable interpretation of the item and the indicated answer should be specific; the item should not be subject to various interpretations. Many teachers go over the test item by item with their students after scoring, and cull out the items which seem to have been interpreted in ways that differ from the teacher's intention. The number of items should be sufficient to cover adequately the facts or skills to be measured.

The identification and recording of proper answers is a normal part of the preparation of an objective test. The proper response is known as soon as each item is completed, frequently even before the item is prepared in its final form. The essay does not force the

4 "Making the Classroom Test, A Guide for Teachers," 2nd ed. (Princeton, N.J.: Educational Testing Service, 1961), p. 16.

teacher to identify the proper response. A better scoring job can be done, however, if the teacher outlines the "ideal" answer before completing the essay test. This precaution not only greatly aids the scoring task by providing the teacher with a frame of reference for scoring but also tests the item itself before it is presented to the students. Many times the statement of the item will be refined after the teacher has attempted an "ideal" answer. Sometimes the item will be abandoned entirely and a better one found. The items in an essay test may be either questions or statements.

Items in an objective test are of four general kinds, true-false, completion, multiple-choice, and matching.[5] The preparation of items has been extensively discussed in the professional literature.[6] Only brief illustrations will be given here.

The true-false item is simple to construct and easy to score. An obvious disadvantage is the automatic fifty per cent chance of accidental proper response. Examples follow:

> T  F  1. Franklin D. Roosevelt was born into a wealthy family.
> _____ 1. Soon after Franklin D. Roosevelt became president, a stock market crash ushered in a great economic depression.

In the first instance the student was instructed to underline or circle the *T* or *F*. In the second the response would involve placing a *T* or *F* (or + or *o*) on the line preceding the item.

The completion item may be either a question or statement. Usually it is intended to elicit a specific word or phrase as a response, although occasionally some latitude in the answer is permitted. The student is expected to write the correct answer in the space provided. Examples follow:

> 1. The procedure used by scientists to discover new knowledge is called the _____. (*scientific method*)
> 2. What are the three states of matter? _____ (*gas, liquid, solid*)
> 3. The energy of _____ is known as kinetic energy. (*motion*)

---

[5] Other names are sometimes used to refer to these four kinds of test items.
[6] See especially Robert M. W. Travers, *How to Make Achievement Tests* (New York: Odyssey Press, 1949).

The proper responses for the examples above are shown in parentheses. Because of the more precise nature of the response required, the completion item tends to reward memorization. Its application is, therefore, quite limited except where precise knowledge is required.

The multiple-choice item has more flexibility than either the true-false or completion types. Since the student is required to select from among two or more possible answers, the dependence on memorization is not so great. There is also more opportunity for reasoning by the student, since he may be required to distinguish between good, fair, and poor or wrong answers. Examples follow:

1. The immediate circumstance which brought the United States into World War I was

_____a. President Wilson's pledge to assist the Allies by all means short of war.

_____b. the desire on the part of American businessmen for war profits.

_____c. the German government's submarine campaign against American merchant vessels.

_____d. the imperialistic goals of the German militarists.

(correct response is c)

1. Place an x on the line preceding each of the following words or phrases which correctly describe Miss Lyons in *Zone of Quiet* by Ring Lardner.

_____ Well-educated, highly literate

__(x)__ Tactless

__(x)__ Talkative

_____ Conscientious about the doctor's orders

_____ Honest

__(x)__ Lacking in integrity

_____ Reluctant to talk about herself

_____ More concerned about the welfare of her patients than herself

__(x)__ Egotistical

__(x)__ Inconsistent

The illustrations above are but two of the many possible forms which the multiple-choice item may take. In the first example the students were instructed to place an x on the line preceding the phrase which best (most factually) completed the statement. Both *a* and *b* would be deemed incorrect by the student who knew something of the facts. Alternative *d* could be considered a more general cause of United States entry into the war but is not an "immediate circumstance." The preference of answer *c* over answer *d* requires more careful reading of the item, more extensive knowledge of the events preceding entry into the war, and more discrimination on the part of the students.

The second illustration requires the student to recall the events of the story and to assign certain traits to one of the characters on the basis of those events. In this particular case the events consisted of a series of monologues by Miss Lyons.

The matching item is much like the multiple-choice item. It is usually set up in two columns. The student is directed to pair the items that are most closely related across columns. An example follows:

| A | | B |
|---|---|---|
| a. Verb phrase | (d) | To the store. |
| b. Dependent clause | (b) | Since the tire was already flat. |
| c. Simple sentence | (f) | If the Bay of Pigs invasion had been successful, our attitude toward Cuba would have been quite different. |
| d. Prepositional phrase | (a) | Had been running. |
| e. Compound sentence | (c) | The black dog with white spots seemed to insist on barking far, far into the night. |
| f. Complex sentence | (e) | Mary came but Jim remained at home. |

In this case the students were directed to pair the items in column A with those in column B by placing the letter which identified the column A item on the line preceding the proper column B item. The correct responses are shown in parentheses.

Before we leave the discussion of informal (teacher-made) pencil-and-paper instruments designed to measure knowledge or skill, we must remind ourselves of two things. In the first place both essay and objective tests depend heavily on reading ability. The student who is deficient in reading ability but has nevertheless learned some or all of the matters to be tested by listening, viewing films or TV, or some other way will not reveal this knowledge on tests that require him to read. Some other means must be found to test his knowledge, e.g., teacher-student conference, observation, completion of a project that involves little or no reading, or the like. Since students who are deficient in reading skill are usually also handicapped in the skills of written communication, the essay test is at least as invalid for them as the objective test.

Secondly, we must remember that the only thing that is *objective* about the objective test is the way in which it is scored. The exact response to each item has been identified and the test is scored on this basis. Once the proper response has been identified, the scorer's judgment is no longer a factor. No matter how carefully the teacher outlines the "ideal" response to an essay item, sufficient latitude for variation in the students' responses will always remain, so that the scorer's judgment must be exercised. Furthermore, the selection of what is to be measured, why it is to be measured, and the wording and organization of items, as well as any decision as to what is acceptable in terms of percentage of correct responses, is fully as subjective in the objective test as it is in the essay test.

5. *Attitudes, beliefs, interests, and associations* may be measured, at least crudely, by informal, teacher-constructed pencil-and-paper instruments using the same techniques as those described above. Such knowledge is useful to the teacher in his role as a counselor. It also helps him to plan learning experiences for and with his students. The development of attitudes, interests, beliefs, and relationships are either explicit or implicit in all of the composite statements of educational purposes and goals which we examined in Chapter 2. Some cautions must be observed, however, when this type of evaluation is attempted.

Traditions exert a strong influence on teachers to view any evaluative instrument as a test or examination that requires responses which are either right or wrong. The line that divides right from wrong is much less distinct in the area of attitudes, interests, and beliefs than in the area of knowledge and skill. In certain areas there are no right or wrong positions. Choice of occupation, friends and mates, leisure-time pursuits, and a multitude of other matters are left to the discretion of the individual. Some areas such as religion (and sex in some communities) are not considered within the purview of the publicly supported school. Any encroachment into such matters may result in parental and community protest.

These cautions should not deter the teacher, however, from showing a legitimate concern for the development of suitable interests, attitudes, and beliefs in his students, and from using appropriate means to evaluate their achievements. The teacher who understands the role of the school in society and the cultural values of the society can discriminate between the areas in which the school is expected to function and those which are reserved to other institutions such as the church and the family. A belief in the worth and dignity of each individual, for example, is one of the most revered democratic ideals. The school has an obligation to help students develop and strengthen this value. The supernatural and the avenue to eternity, however, are not among the matters on which the teacher may bring influence to bear on the student.

Sometimes the process of collecting information about students' attitudes, interests, and beliefs yields results that suggest serious emotional problems that require expert opinion for appraisal. It is essential that the teacher secure advice under such circumstances, both on whether the condition is serious and also on the person to whom a referral may be made. Teachers are not trained to do psychotherapy and should not attempt it. The school psychologist, school social worker, director of guidance, or principal should be consulted about such conditions. The early discovery of potential problem situations is one of the benefits of teachers' activities in evaluating beliefs, attitudes, and interests.

6. *Miscellaneous additional evaluative devices* that are related to some of those we have discussed include (a) conferences with students about various aspects of their work, (b) preparation by students of reports, both oral and written, on materials read, movies, telecasts, and dramatic productions seen, and discussions observed or participated in, and (c) situational activities such as sociodrama. Like most other methods of evaluating, these contribute as much to the on-going process of learning as they do to evaluation.

Student-teacher conferences may be used to collect information needed to evaluate any learning activity. Ordinarily, the conference is used to supplement data collected by other means. The conference is especially useful in encouraging student self-evaluation. Even the most mature adult sometimes has difficulty achieving sufficient objectivity to make a good self-appraisal. The teacher can help the student to return to a question such as "How could I have done a better job of this?" when the answer is a little embarrassing, and the natural tendency is to avoid a careful analysis. The conference also has the advantage of producing a greater volume of information in a given period of time than can be secured through writing. Some teachers use an outline of matters which they wish to cover during the conference. The outline is presented to the students prior to the conference so that they may do some advance thinking and organize their thoughts. There may be times, however, when impromptu answers are desired.

Student reports may be oral or written, structured or unstructured. From them the teacher will get evaluative clues of many kinds, including strengths and weaknesses, needs, likes and dislikes, attitudes, interests, beliefs, knowledges, and skills. Some arrangement should be made for orderly retention of some of the students' written reports in order that long-range progress may be appraised. Some teachers make it a practice to file reports which are thought to be significant because they reveal a particular strength or weakness or a special problem which should be watched.

Although sociodrama is usually thought of as a learning experience, it can contribute valuable evaluative information also. The student who succeeds in casting himself in the role of someone quite different from himself reveals much about his attitudes and beliefs, and frequently something, at least, about his knowledge or lack of it.

7. *Standardized, published tests* have a place in most schools. All of our discussion thus far of devices which aid the evaluative process dealt with instruments that are planned and constructed by the teacher. We have used the term "informal" to indicate that the teacher-made instrument is intended to be used with a relatively small number of students. It is likely to be designed with a specific group of students in mind, perhaps a single class, who have engaged in a series of learning experiences which were probably, in some ways at least, different from the experiences of any other group. It has not been subjected to careful statistical analysis *in toto* or item by item. It is not available in published form for purchase by other teachers, nor has much thought been given to the exact manner in which the instrument is to be administered.

The formal or standardized test is the exact opposite of the teacher-made device in the ways noted above. It is like the informal objective test, however, in that it uses the short-answer kind of items. Standardized tests are probably overused in American secondary schools, but they do have their place in the evaluative process. They are useful in identifying particular skills or areas of knowledge that must be strengthened if a student is to achieve his goals. Standardized reading tests, for example, measure both rate of reading and comprehension. A student who scores high in comprehension (of the part of the test he covers) and low in rate needs a kind of help that is different from that required by the student whose rate is high but who produces a low comprehension score. Some tests also measure other specific aspects of the reading process, such as word recognition. Some distinguish between different kinds of content, such as scientific, literary, and social science material, and yield separate scores on each.

It is usually desirable to have some general idea of a student's scholastic aptitude. In our society at this time, for example, a career goal which involves becoming a physician is unrealistic for a student whose scholastic aptitude is average or lower. Such a student will encounter serious obstacles in the process of attempting to achieve his career goal. It is not unusual, however, for such a student by virtue of considerable effort to receive high grades in school. Information about the student's scholastic aptitude is essential to helping the student and his parents set their aspirations at a realistic level.

Standardized test results are not always used in a manner that takes advantage of their potential contributions to student and teacher welfare but eliminates their negative effects. Sometimes tests are selected without regard to the particular goals of the school or the particular students to be tested. It is very difficult to separate aptitude from achievement. Both depend heavily on environmental influences which are not subject to control by the school. Generally speaking, students from homes in the higher socio-economic brackets score higher on standardized tests than students from homes lower on the socio-economic scale. Unless a test is geared to important goals of the school and its particular students, the scores produced by the test are worthless at best. At worst, they may destroy or misdirect proper aspirations.

Sometimes teachers have little or no voice in the selection of tests. They may then give little more than casual consideration to the results. Occasionally, it appears that tests are given in order to produce scores which may be filed! The expense and time required for a standardized testing program can hardly be justified unless maximum use is made of the results.

Sometimes too much emphasis is placed on a comparison of the scores of students of a given school or school district with national or state norms. As indicated above, environmental influences outside the school play too large a part in aptitude and achievement to make it possible to attribute superior performance on standardized tests entirely to the excellence of the school program. Moreover, the student mobility rate is so high in many schools that the school can hardly take full credit (or blame) for the scores its students as a group make on standardized tests. When test scores are used in this way, the tendency to adapt the school program so that students will score as high as possible is difficult to resist. To the extent that teachers are able to "teach for the test," the local community transfers some of its rightful control over the curriculum to test makers.

Some tests are administered and scored locally; others are controlled by agencies external to the school. The total number of both kinds of tests has sharply increased in recent years, with the added incentive of scholarships from industries and colleges. A recent publication [7] of the National Association of Secondary School Principals warns of such proliferation of external tests, and points out that one such test was administered in a recent year to 800,000 students in high schools, and involved nearly 400,000 student days in this one evaluation of academic achievement.

In summary, standardized tests are but one of the many devices which teachers find helpful in evaluating progress in learning, and in improving the educational process. Like most other devices, they can, when wrongly used, detract from, rather than aid, the work of the school.

## Reporting student progress

The job of the school is to help its students progress toward achievement of the goals society has set for the school and the purposes the students set for themselves. Evaluation is both continuous and periodic. Students evaluate themselves and each other. They are also evaluated by the teacher. Teachers usually report the results

---

[7] *Testing, Testing, Testing* (Washington, D.C.: National Association of Secondary School Principals, 1962).

of their evaluations to the students in a variety of ways: by written and oral comments on papers and projects prepared by the students or concerning activities in which the students engage, and by grades or other symbols.

All schools have some means of reporting student progress to parents. The goal, of course, is to use the method which best communicates to the parents the information they should have and which they desire regarding their children's educational achievement, again in terms of the goals as indicated above. Earlier in this chapter we discussed some of the common misconceptions regarding evaluation. One reason that these misconceptions exist is that school people have fostered them. They will continue to exist as long as practices, particularly in communicating the results of evaluative activities, continue to foster the misconceptions. Teachers should evaluate reporting practices with this in mind.

The most common method of reporting student progress involves the use of the symbol mark, most frequently the traditional A, B, C, D, F. Sometimes two symbols are used, one to indicate academic achievement, the other to denote citizenship (which often means conformity to the teacher's standards of behavior). In other instances in which two symbols are used, one signifies achievement in relation to the other students in the class while the other relates to achievement in relation to the student's ability. The latter is often labeled "effort." When two symbols are used they are likely to be different; for example, A, B, C, D, F may be used for achievement and 1, 2, 3, 4, 5 for citizenship or effort.

The use of symbols has many shortcomings, some of which may be alleviated somewhat by the use of additional means of reporting such as letters, check-lists, or teacher-parent conferences. Probably the major weakness in symbol marking is the utter impossibility of packing all of the necessary information into one or two symbols. The symbols simply do not say enough.

Any mark must be highly subjective. Even the most conscientious teacher cannot avoid making many arbitrary decisions in marking. When the entire results of the evaluative process over a given period of time must be compressed into one or two symbols, many teachers compromise by including only academic accomplishments in the mark that is placed on the report cards and in the students' permanent records. When this is done the mark reflects only part of the schools' and students' goals. Moreover, the students' previous achievement or reputation, his personality, the standing of his parents in the community, the good record made by an older sibling, his prowess in athletics, his usual mode of dress, and many other extraneous matters tend to creep into the mark.

School marks tend to become ends in themselves. Good teachers seek constantly to develop in their students a real appetite for learning, which must stem from the pursuit in the classroom of real interests and problems. Such efforts are sometimes unsuccessful because students tend to absorb mark-consciousness from their culture. The mark is the goal, they feel, and their own interests and concerns are irrelevant in the classroom. In effect, they are constantly saying to the teacher: "show us a simple, clear-cut way to pass the course, to get a better mark, for that is our definition of success." The development of intrinsic motivation for learning involves awakening to the fact that marks are not the main goals of education.

In addition to these weaknesses, marks vary widely from one teacher to another and from one school to another. For most teachers they vary from one year to the next. Furthermore, the symbol mark does not clearly suggest to either the parent or the student what the student can do to improve, or what he did that was deemed by the teacher to be successful or unsuccessful.

We have found a great deal of fault with symbol marks. Unfortunately, teachers will usually find that the school policy and tradition require them to issue marks periodically. We would like to be able to tell teachers how to perform this task so that the weaknesses we have cited would be converted into strengths. But there is no way to do something right which cannot be done. Meaningful reporting is impossible if limited to a few symbols.

A more intelligent approach to reporting is the parent conference. Parents are asked to confer with the teacher once or twice each semester, either during school hours with the students dismissed for this purpose, or after school in some cases. At least twenty or thirty minutes are needed for each conference. Both parents should be present for the most effective use of this device, which has had widespread success in both elementary and junior high schools. Some senior high schools have also experimented successfully with the use of the conference plan as a supplement to the report card.

Teachers can gain many new insights about their students from well-conducted parent conferences. Conferences are also the best means yet discovered of reporting to parents the progress of their children. Plans for improving the achievement and adjustment of students can be developed by teacher and parents cooperatively, with the aid of more complete data available as a result of the interview. Teachers often report that the conference plan has great value in forcing them to study their students carefully, since it is unwise to enter into the conference without data. Parents, too, have discovered that the conference plan provides them with better understanding of the progress of their children. Cunningham has reported the following values that parents have seen in the conference plan:

1. It helped the parent to become clear in his own mind as to what he wanted his child to gain from his school experiences.

2. The parent was given an opportunity to explain any pertinent facts about the child that would enable the teacher to work with him effectively as an individual and as a group member.

3. Any maladjustment of the child at school was pointed out. If there was a difficulty at home, the parent and teacher were often able to find tentative means of solution for this mutual problem.

4. The parent was assured of the fact that he was welcome at school at all times.[8]

The parent conference plan requires some careful planning for its success. The teachers and administrators must be in favor of its use. Time must be provided in order to avoid exploitation of either teachers or parents. Teachers must collect and organize information about their students in advance of the conference. Parents must understand and accept the purposes of the conference if they are expected to cooperate with it. Perhaps most important of all, teachers must have some skills in conducting a good interview.

Fortunately, all of these requirements can be met with systematic planning and in-service education. Conferences with parents can be provided if time is allowed and if personnel involved are ready to assume their responsibilities. This means spending money, but a good plan of reporting to parents is well worth the investment. The special problems in the secondary school of deciding which teacher is to contact the parents, when teachers have five or six classes daily, can be solved if there is a decentralized guidance plan in operation

---

[8] Ruth Cunningham et al., *Understanding Group Behavior of Boys and Girls* (New York: Bureau of Publications, Teachers College, Columbia University, 1951), p. 331.

such as described in Chapter 7. Either homeroom or core teachers can become responsible for carrying on the actual conference; they receive information systematically from all teachers who have the student involved.

Letters to parents are another alternative or a supplement to the symbol marking system. Such letters describing the progress of individual students are sent to parents in some secondary schools once each semester. The letters should be friendly and informal, but they should contain useful information, too. Teachers should have some help in learning the techniques of writing such letters: learning how to keep them to the point, to avoid stereotypes and clichés, and to report a student's progress without the necessity of invidious comparison with others. This process will take time, and stenographic help should be provided. The letters need not all go out at one time, as we send out the report cards, but can be composed and sent at intervals with the aid of dictation equipment available in turn to each teacher. An example of such a letter follows:

Dear Mr. and Mrs. Pollock:

Jim has made some important progress since my last letter. He no longer disturbs the class, or his own small group, with wisecracks and personal remarks. He has been working well with his work group and assumed some responsibilities on his own for their forthcoming report. (You may know about that, since I understand he enlisted the cooperation of his father in arranging for the group to visit the Great Lakes Steel plant last Thursday.) One indication of the attitude of the class toward Jim is his recent election as class chairman for the next six weeks. We regard this as a rather important assignment in our class, and I have congratulated Jim on the outcome of the election.

Jim has read and reported on two books since I wrote, but I know he has read others. His writing remains rather uninspired, though he is checking his spelling more carefully. It is just that he sticks with reporting the obvious and trite, and that he has some difficulty letting his imagination carry him into the wonderful land of poetry and fantasy. Still, he is now coming to me to ask my advice on how to say certain things in his written work, and I hope to persuade him to try some more imaginative kinds of writing next time.

Jim scored well in his midyear achievement tests. I would like to go over these scores with you at our next parent conference. I am also eager to ask you for some advice about how to help Jim use sound criteria for his choice of friends, not because he is in any trouble at this point, but because he has told me he wants to talk about this matter of new friendships sometime.

Thank you for your letter of last month. It was very helpful. I am looking forward to our conference. I think it is in February, but you will be hearing from the office about the schedule.

Most sincerely,

Lucy Houghton

Less time consuming than the letter, but also less descriptive, is the checklist. This device consists of a list of traits, skills, or competencies representing some or all of the purposes of the school (or of a particular grade, subject, or course) with provision for the teacher's estimate of the pupil's achievement. Some checklists are several pages in length.

*In conclusion.* Reporting student progress is a basic professional problem which will require diligence if teachers are ever to find a solution. Furthermore, no adequate method of reporting will be found which will be equally appropriate for every community. Communities, like students and teachers, are characterized by individual differences.

If the symbol grade has to be retained—and it cannot be abandoned until a better way is found and accepted—it can be greatly improved by supplementing with check-lists, letters, or conferences, separately or in combination. The conference is the best supplement, the letter next in effectiveness, and the check-list a poor third. Obviously, any of the supplements take time—as do most things which are worth doing. A careful examination of how teachers use their time presently may reveal that they are doing some things which could well be sacrificed to a better job of reporting the results of the evaluative process. Any method of reporting student progress cannot be better than the methods of evaluation.

Since parents are the major consumers of the reporting practices, any change will have to have their consent. Surveys of parent preference usually result in a large majority favoring the *status quo,* especially if the present method has been in use for several years. People tend to feel comfortable with the familiar. Besides, most parents are not aware of the shortcomings of present methods of reporting.

They tend to have much more faith in symbols, for example, than teachers do. "Educating" the parents to accept a change is not likely to be as successful as involving them with teachers in making the change. Any way it is done, it will be a long term project in most communities. It will not happen, however, until teachers start it.

At this point in our discussion we may well turn to a consideration of the role of the teacher in school-community relations.

## FOR FURTHER READING

Alexander, William M., "Reporting to Parents—Why? What? How?" *NEA Journal,* 48:9 (December 1959), 15–18. Consideration of the basic problems that confront the teacher who wants to report student progress adequately.

Durost, Walter N., and George A. Prescott, *Essentials of Measurement for Teachers.* New York: Harcourt, Brace and World, Inc., 1962. Chapters 2 and 3 contain relatively nontechnical discussions of standardized tests of achievement and capacity. Chapter 9 is "How to Tell Parents about Test Results."

Heffernan, Helen, "Evaluation—More than Testing," *NEA Journal,* 47:4 (April 1958), 227–229. Emphasis on the comprehensive nature of evaluative activity. Author cautions against too much dependence on testing. See also in the same issue "Tests and What They Test" by J. Wayne Wrightstone and "ABCs of Test Construction" by Julian C. Stanley.

Jersild, Arthur T., *In Search of Self.* New York: Bureau of Publications, Teachers College, Columbia University, 1952. Self-evaluation is discussed in Chapters 19–21.

Lindvall, C. M., *Testing and Evaluation: An Introduction.* New York: Harcourt, Brace and World, Inc., 1961. Chapters 4, 5, 6, and 8 contain helpful suggestions for the teacher concerning the construction of tests.

"Making the Classroom Test, A Guide for Teachers." 2nd ed. Princeton, N.J.: Educational Testing Service, 1961. Illustrations of various kinds of teacher-constructed tests of subject matter at different grade levels and in different subject areas.

National Society for the Study of Education, *The Measurement of Understanding,* Forty-fifth Yearbook. Chicago: University of Chicago Press, 1946. As implied by the title, the emphasis in this excellent volume is on measurement of the ability to apply knowledge.

"Reporting Student Progress—Grades Seven through Twelve." Columbus,

Ohio: The Ohio State University, 1953. Contains examples of teachers' anecdotal reports to parents covering various grade levels and subjects with a few examples of records of parent-teacher conferences.

*Short-Cut Statistics for Teacher-Made Tests.* Princeton, N.J.: Educational Testing Service, 1960. A simplified explanation of many of the concepts used in measurement practices. Points out some of the fallacies of too heavy dependence on the scores produced by teacher-made tests. Suggestions for improvement of these instruments.

Simpson, Ray H., *Improving Teaching-Learning Processes.* New York: David McKay Co., Inc., 1953. Chapters 7 and 8 deal with the development of evaluative abilities including self-evaluation.

Strang, Ruth, *How to Report Pupil Progress.* Chicago: Science Research Associates, Inc., 1955. A good presentation of methods of improving reporting to parents, including parent conferences.

Thorndike, R. L., and Elizabeth Hagen, *Measurement and Evaluation in Psychology and Education,* rev. ed. New York: John Wiley & Sons, Inc., 1961. A comprehensive discussion of kinds and uses of tests written for the teacher as a maker and user of tests and as an interpreter of test results.

Traxler, Arthur E., "Standardized Tests," *NEA Journal,* 48:8 (November 1959), 18–20. Discussion of the uses of standardized tests and their limitations. Also in this issue are seven additional articles on various aspects of evaluation.

Wood, Dorothy Adkins, *Test Construction.* Columbus, Ohio: Charles E. Merrill Books, Inc., 1960. The scope of this book is limited to an attempt to aid teachers in the understanding and interpretation of standardized achievement and ability tests and in the construction of teacher-made "objective" tests.

Wrightstone, J. Wayne, Joseph Justman, and Irving Robbins, *Evaluation in Modern Education.* New York: American Book Co., 1956. Part II contains separate chapters on short-answer, essay, and oral examinations; observation and anecdotal records; questionnaires, inventories, and interviews; checklists and rating scales; personal reports and projective techniques; sociometric methods; case studies; and cumulative records. In Part III, the authors treat techniques of evaluation in specific subjects and skills. Similar content is covered in several other books. See, for example, Swartz, Tiedeman, and Wallace, *Evaluating Student Progress in the Secondary School* (New York: David McKay Co., Inc., 1957), R. M. Thomas, *Judging Student Progress* (McKay, 1960), and Gerberich, Greene, and Jorgensen, *Measurement and Evaluation in the Modern School* (McKay, 1962).

Wrightstone, J. Wayne, "Teacher-Made Tests and Techniques," *Educational Leadership*, 19:3 (December 1961), 170–172, 199–200. A brief description of the more common techniques of evaluation. The fact that tests for measurement of subject-matter learning are but a small part of the total process of evaluation is emphasized.

Yauch, Wilbur A., "School Marks and Their Reporting," *NEA Journal*, 50:5 (May 1961), 50, 58. A summary of the research on this topic during the past fifty years.

# 14
# The teacher and school-community relations

"Come on, Sally. You'll have to leave those papers until tomorrow if you're going to have time to get Fred's dinner and get back to PTA by 7:30. You're coming, aren't you?"

Jean Borden had stopped by the teachers' lounge to get her thermos bottle on her way out of the building. Sally Regan, who taught tenth grade English in the room next to Jean's, was apparently "correcting" some of her students' themes.

This was Jean's first year at Roosevelt High but she was not a beginning teacher, having taught four years in a small high school on the other side of the state. Sally Regan was about Jean's age but had taught two years longer than Jean. Although Roosevelt High had no formalized "buddy system" for the orientation of new teachers, Sally had taken Jean under her wing and the two had become fast friends.

"You know how I feel about PTA," retorted Sally. "Schools are to educate kids, not provide a cheap social club for parents. I spent five years at the University learning to be a teacher and I'm in my seventh year here. I don't need any parents to tell me how to teach their children."

Jean saw no reason to push the argument further with her friend. They had been over the same ground before, apparently without success from Jean's point of view. Sally had seemed to weaken last week and Jean thought she had been on the verge of agreeing to come to the PTA meeting with her. No definite arrangement had been made however, so Jean concluded that Sally had changed her mind—or perhaps Jean had not really understood what Sally had said. Anyway, it didn't matter too much.

Bill Borden had been able to leave the office on time and Jean's advance dinner preparations had paid off, so that there was time to talk during a leisurely dinner.

"I wish Sally weren't so anti-parents," Jean began. "I have been telling her about the way the faculty and community worked together in Junction City but she keeps saying that PTA is for the birds and the parents ought to let the teachers run the school," she continued. "I did think she was weakening a little and might at least go to the PTA meeting tonight but apparently I was wish-thinking. I suppose I should have offered to drive her. That might have made it harder for her to refuse."

"With her attitude the PTA is better off without her," said Bill. "She'd probably act like a sourpuss all evening. A lot of people already think teachers are snobs and aloof and it wouldn't help to have them meet up with Sally when she's on one of her 'parents keep out' binges. She and Fred are probably giving the PTA a going over right now."

And so they were! It was Sally talking: "Jean Borden has been at me off and on for two or three weeks about coming to PTA meeting. I don't know why she gets such a big kick out of that outfit. She's an awfully good teacher in other ways but she seems to think you ought to ask the parents every time you make a move in school. She says they had all kinds of enthusiasm with parents all over the building at Junction City High. The way she tells it I sometimes wonder how the students could tell the teachers from the parents."

Fred Regan was listening to his wife but he saw no reason to comment. He had his troubles at the store and was inclined to let Sally take care of her own career problems. He accepted her judgment on such matters as the value of the PTA and the responsibility of the citizens to the school.

"I guess Jean is harmless though," Sally continued. "Only a few of the Roosevelt teachers attend the PTA meetings and most of them go out of a sense of duty or because Mr. Jacobs (the principal) wants them to. As far as I can tell the parents expect the teachers to run the school and not bother them. Parents ought to come to school when their children misbehave and they're sent for. Their job is to pay their taxes so we can run a good school. Otherwise we don't need them around."

Whether or not parents and other lay citizens should be involved in matters pertaining to the school (except its financial support) is questionable to many teachers. Some, like Sally Regan, believe teachers could do a better job if parents came dutifully to concerts, plays, and athletic contests, urged their children to study hard, behave, and "do what the teacher says," provided proper study materials and conditions at home, and voted "yes" on all bond and millage issues presented by the board of education. Some laymen also share this view. Like Jean Borden, many teachers have experienced the benefits of close school-parent cooperation. They find it hard to visualize a school in which parents are not involved in many ways.

## The increase of citizen interest in the schools

Americans have always been interested in their schools. A variety of events and circumstances have combined to stimulate a sharp increase in this interest in recent years.

*Interest is increasing because of concern for youth.* Parents have always been concerned about the welfare of their children. Improved understanding of child development, communicated to parents through teachers, physicians, child study clubs, and the mass media, have recently produced a more intelligent concern that can be translated into action. Moreover, a larger percentage of the parents of teen-aged children are interested in secondary schools today than previously because of the schools' increased holding power. A higher percentage of young people remain in school longer these days.

Parents want their children to succeed in school. They prefer that the children work hard enough to keep out of mischief but not so hard that their health is impaired. Many would like their sons and daughters to have time also to engage in some social and recreational activity. A sizable proportion are at least as concerned about social success as academic achievement. Some value sports and music activities above all others and tend to support these activities with great enthusiasm. Some get much satisfaction from the fact that their children enjoy a higher level of success than other children. Parents are interested in the school because they are interested in all matters that involve their children. This does not mean that they are all interested in the same things, that their values are properly ordered so that they place "first things first," nor that the education of their children is necessarily a matter of central concern in their lives. It is up to the school, that is to say the professional staff, to nurture and guide parents' normal interest in the welfare of their children into those channels which will enhance the education of the children and hence the success of the school program.

*Because of concern for democracy.* We noted in Chapter 1 that the school in a democratic society is an instrument of public policy and therefore a responsibility of all citizens. Although by no means all adults are motivated by considerations of good citizenship, many do understand the unique dependence of a free society on education of a high order. Even though they may not have children in school, many citizens are strong school supporters and are willing to contribute cheerfully their time and talent as well as their tax dollars when provided with an opportunity.

*Because of improved communication.* The average citizen knows more about schools today than he did a few years ago. Methods of communication have improved; there are more newspapers, books, magazines, radios, and television sets in the homes. These media carry more content apropos of schools and education than ever before. Furthermore, the general level of literacy is higher. People know more about practically everything these days, including schools.

*As a reaction to criticism.* Some citizens who had little or no interest in schools prior to the deluge of critical commentary in the public media of communication during the past few years have now become anxious about education. Some are merely curious. They wonder if the schools are as bad as they are said to be. Others tend to accept the alleged shortcomings as established fact and express their dissatisfaction by talking and voting against millage and bond issues, critical comments of various kinds to their acquaintances, and generally negative attitudes. Many, on the other hand, are indignant about some of the criticisms but do not know how to combat the effects of these criticisms. They may believe the conditions identified as undesirable by the critics do not exist in their own community. Schools have a triple obligation in this regard. They should take advantage of the new interest stimulated by the debate; they should also take steps to combat the influence of unjustified criticism; to the extent that the criticisms are justified, the schools should take immediate steps to do everything possible to correct their inadequacies.

*Because of rising costs.* The increasing number of dollars expended for education, especially the portion which is raised locally, has motivated an increased interest in schools on the part of many citizens. People often fail to realize that in order to maintain the same level of service, the tax rates must go up as the dollar depreciates and other costs including salaries rise. Even more obscure to the average taxpayer are the facts of expanding enrollment because of the rise in the birth rate which began in the early forties, and the gradual improvement in the holding power of the secondary schools. The neglect of school plants during the years of the Great Depression and World War II have not been called to the attention of the general public except in isolated instances in certain communities. When we add the need for relocation of school facilities as a consequence of in-migration we have a formidable array of forces which have required extensive investment in school buildings and equipment during recent years. Citizens cannot fail to take account of the effects of these forces on their tax bills, but an understanding of the forces or their results is hardly a by-product of paying the taxes.

We have noted an increased concern with schools and the processes of education on the part of citizens. We have suggested that this heightened interest has resulted primarily from greater knowledge of child development, more extensive coverage of matters pertaining to education and schools in the mass communication media, including a vast upsurge in the incidence of alleged deficiencies in the schools, and higher dollar costs for buildings, equipment, and operation of schools, reflected in higher tax rates. The identification of phenomena which have stimulated a greater focus of citizen attention on the schools, however, does not complete the picture of how school patrons may be expected to feel about the schools. We still need to give attention to another dimension of the way citizens view their schools.

*Differences in citizens' attitudes.* We have given much thought in this volume to individual differences among students. We know, of course, that the principle of individual differences is equally valid when applied to adults. Here, we are concerned only with differences in attitude toward schools and education. Attitudes are slow in forming. They are not the product of reading one or two magazine articles, or the receipt of a larger than usual tax bill. Attitudes are influenced by one's values and how they are ordered, i.e., which things are most important and which are least important to us. To a large extent values depend on experiences and observations.

Many citizens have very friendly feelings toward the schools. They have a high regard for learning and the value of education. They are willing to delay or curtail the satisfaction of other desires and needs in order to support better education. They believe the schools are doing a good job. Many give willingly not only their tax money but also their time—as school board members, PTA officers, members of citizens' advisory committees, millage and bond campaign workers, and the like. Frequently, citizens who have positive attitudes toward the schools remember their own school experiences as being pleasant and rewarding. Many times their children are or have been successful and happy in school. In a few instances their feelings of good will are fostered by friendly relations with school personnel with whom they tend to identify.

Many school public relations programs are oriented primarily toward parents and other citizens whose attitudes are favorable or potentially favorable toward the schools. The extent to which such a policy is justified is not the province of this book. One thing is certain, however: wherever good school programs exist, there will also be found a sizable number of citizens whose attitude toward the school is generally favorable. In a democracy a school cannot consistently maintain an educational program of high quality without considerable support on the part of its patrons.

Some citizens are apathetic toward the public schools. Perhaps they have no children or their children are grown. They may derive their living or a substantial part of it from rental property. They may be wealthy and send their children to private schools because the mores of their social class require that their children attend private schools. A few parents are not concerned about this aspect of their children's lives. Some are busy with other matters; other concerns overshadow any latent interest they may have in the quality of education their children are receiving. Characteristically, one seldom sees evidence of great concern for school matters on the part of those at either extreme of the socio-economic scale, i.e., the very rich and the very poor. Sometimes, particularly among the lowest economic levels, there are those who feel inferior to teachers and are afraid of them. They may vote negatively at the polls on school welfare issues but take no other overt action against the schools.

A few citizens are disgruntled. Their own school experiences may have been unfruitful and unhappy. They may have left school before graduating. In some instances their children do not do well in school or perhaps have already dropped out. Some have been "stirred up" further by the attacks on the schools which we discussed in Chapter 1. Some may favor private or parochial education and resent having to support a system of public education in addition to their own independent schools. Whatever the reason or reasons, some citizens exhibit negative attitudes toward the schools. Furthermore, some of them will engage in acts designed to weaken the schools' position in the community. Their number will, of course, vary from one community to another. Their effectiveness will depend in large measure on the relative size of the group who are, or can be persuaded to be, favorable toward the schools.

Although the total school-community relations program must take cognizance of the entire range of citizens' attitudes, including those who are disgruntled and apathetic, the classroom teachers' contacts are primarily with parents who are, to some degree at least, potentially favorable. It is essential that teachers take advantage of their opportunities to foster good will toward the school, since all parties concerned—teachers, parents, and students—have much to gain from friendly school-community relationships.

*Benefits of close school-community relationships.* By establishing and maintaining close relationships with the parents of students in his classes, the teacher can substantially improve his knowledge about and understanding of his students. He will know the aspirations each parent has for his child and can form some useful judgments as to whether the aspirations seem realistic. The teacher is in a better position to counsel the student if he knows what the parent expects and hopes for. The teacher will have a better idea of the cultural and economic level of the home as he becomes better acquainted with the parents. He will also become aware of the general pattern of relationships in the home, especially among siblings, but also between parents and children. Such insights will greatly improve the teacher's ability to understand the student's behavior as well as to establish his own expectations concerning the student's achievement.

Good relationships with parents will pay off in other ways which affect the teacher's work with students less directly. Parents who find the teachers friendly and interested in the welfare of their children, whose counsel is sought in matters affecting their children, and who are sometimes invited to contribute their time and talents to make the school program more effective are likely to find their school tax bills reasonable. People tend to identify with and support those activities in which they feel personally involved. Close contacts with parents help the teacher to understand the community better, to know better the availability of community resources, and to arrive at a more realistic appraisal of the needs of his students. In a free society it is the citizens who decide what is to be taught in the school by the teachers, and, to some extent, at least, how well it is taught. Those who devote their lives to education have much at stake in how much value citizens place on good schools, the purposes they see for the schools, and the regard they have for those who work in the schools.

It is the student who benefits most from good parent-school relationships. Often parents have aspirations for their children that are unrealistic in terms of the students' interests and abilities. The teacher who is close to his students and knows them well can often help parents to adjust their expectations more in line with reality. This may require a change in expectation to greater, lesser, or different accomplishments.

Sometimes students are willing to reveal to teachers problems and concerns that they cannot bring themselves to discuss with their parents. The skillful teacher can frequently act in a liaison capacity between the parent and the student, or at a minimum, reveal to parents matters about which they had no inkling. It is understood, of course, that the teacher does not violate confidences. Many times, however, students will welcome the teacher's offer to convey to his parents "a message" which the student wants the parent to have but can't deliver himself.

Although adolescents demand a degree of independence from adult control, they do want adults to be interested in them. If teachers and parents find common grounds upon which this interest is shared, the student benefits. Stated negatively, the student is bound to be confused when teachers attempt to guide his interests and activities in one direction while his parents are counseling him in a different direction. A much more wholesome and productive condition exists when parents understand what the school is attempting to accomplish in relation to their son or daughter, and the teachers understand the parents' aspirations and values.

A condition of mutual good will and understanding benefits parents as well as teachers and students. We have already commented on the contribution teachers can make to parent understanding of their child's interests, abilities, and special problems. The secondary teacher has specific training in the field of adolescent growth, development, and behavior, as well as much experience in working with adolescents and youth. Many parents are aware of this fact and are ready to profit from the teacher's insights. They feel better about the quality of their success as parents when they are helped to understand both the normal problems of adolescents and youth and the unique problems of their particular children.

Many parents have little or no identification with community enterprise apart from their jobs and an occasional trip to the ballot box. They may not even work in the community in which they reside. Involvement with the schools, even if limited to infrequent consultations with the teacher, brings them a step closer to feeling that at least one community enterprise values their opinions and assistance. The parent who works with his child's teacher in order to secure an optimum education for his child may be expected to take pride in this achievement. He may have changed his expectations for his child's accomplishments quite drastically over a period of years but this he can accept if he has had a part in engineering the change.

## School-community relations—a shared responsibility

Only recently have school people begun to give more than sporadic attention to the establishment and maintenance of friendly relations with the general public. This concern manifests itself in such activities as wide dispersal of information about school personnel, problems, programs, and events; intensive bond and millage campaigns; and direct involvement of citizens in planning and advisory groups pertaining to a great variety of school matters. Most large systems and many of the smaller ones designate one or more persons on a full- or part-time basis to give leadership to the school public relations program. Although budget allocations by schools to this enterprise are small in comparison with the vast sums (exclusive of product sales advertising) spent by business and industry to woo the public to the support of their cause, schools are no longer overlooking the necessity for keeping in closer touch with the public.

More and more teachers, administrators, and school board members are realizing that a carefully planned, year-around public relations program results in better education for community members.

*The teacher's role is crucial.* Even though schools have become considerably more active in public relations enterprises in recent years, it is still not unusual to find teachers who would allocate all responsibility for such endeavor to the administrators and other school personnel having this specific responsibility. Such teachers take the position that their job is to teach, that anything else which is requested of them reduces their teaching efficiency and, hence, the quality of their product. Even if this argument were sound, it would still be impossible to leave the entire public relations job to the administrators and specialists. A school public relations program that limits itself to news releases to the community newspapers, special pamphlets and bulletins, and occasional speeches at PTA meetings and service clubs—things which the administrators and specialists conceivably could accomplish—falls short of an adequate effort. Administrators and specialists are too few. To be good, a school public relations program must be diversified. This makes the involvement of teachers mandatory. Beyond this, teachers are "in the driver's seat" as far as contacts with the parents are concerned. Teachers and parents have a focus of mutual interest—the student. This interest is a natural starting point for mutual trust and respect. No administrator or specialist in school public relations can ever have the easy access to the parents which the teacher enjoys. Furthermore, since parental attitudes of favor or disfavor are closely tied to the way they assess the quality of the school experience their children receive, the influence of administrators and specialists is limited, since teachers exercise primary control over what takes place in the classrooms. It is the teachers who have the greatest opportunity to determine whether or not school attendance will be a rewarding experience for the students.

## The teacher's responsibility as an individual

Some aspects of school-community relations cannot be carried out successfully except as a cooperative enterprise involving teachers, administrators, and other school personnel. There are other aspects, however, that are dependent on the individual teacher.

We have already referred to the relation between the parent's assessment of the school and the satisfaction his child gets from the school experience. Teachers who take account of individual differences by having different expectations for each student and, hence, adjusting assignments accordingly, who encourage their students to use a variety of instructional materials according to their interests and abilities, and who evaluate students on the progress they make rather than on their achievement in relation to a fixed, arbitrary standard have taken a giant step toward satisfied students and parents. The educational product will be greater too. Such a teacher will probably also treat students with respect and justice and make himself available to assist and counsel students outside of class time.

Many students are somewhat less than enthusiastic about their school experiences because they do not see much relation between what goes on in the school and their own goals and purposes. This student dissatisfaction is readily caught by the parent who desires success for his child and tends to wonder why the school cannot motivate the student to greater effort. After all, from the parents' point of view, this is the school's business and the school personnel ought to know how to perform their jobs! The parent tends to view the school as he does the garage. If his car needs repairing he takes it to the garage. If the mechanic doesn't repair the car to his satisfaction, he goes back and complains or goes to another garage. He assumes the function of the garage is to repair his car and the mechanic had better be able to do it. If the student believes he is learning worthwhile things in school, the parent is inclined to take the student's word for it. Students are more likely to see the value of their classroom experiences if they have a part in determining goals and planning means of progressing toward achievement of their goals. At the very least, the teacher can make sure that students know what they have been attempting to accomplish and why. Although the purposes of the lesson and their relationship to the assignment may be perfectly clear to the teacher, it does not follow that the students will automatically have the same knowledge, especially with a degree of clarity which will enable them to explain it to their parents. The student is certainly the most readily available public relations agent the school has. He is probably also the best one.

The conversation which follows is based on a report by the mother who took part. The conversation took place at the dinner table in the Joslyn home. Jim Raines and Bill Joslyn were in the same chemistry class. Jim had come to the Joslyn home immediately after school in order to study with Bill for a chemistry examination. Mrs. Joslyn had invited Jim to remain for dinner. Mr. Joslyn was attending a dinner business meeting. Bill had been promised that he could drive Jim home directly after dinner so that each boy could complete his homework for other classes. Mary, Bill's sister, was a grade below the boys. We enter the dining room as Mary is speaking.

*Mary:* Oh, Mom, I forgot to tell you. I stopped by at Clover's on my way home today and looked at that shirt, you know, the green and tan one with the mandarin collar. I could make it in homemaking class when we plan our next project if we could find the material. Think we could find some if we went downtown?

*Mrs. Joslyn:* I'm sure 'we could find something you'd like, all right. It might not be exactly the same as the print at Clover's. There's always plenty of variety in cottons. It is cotton, isn't it?

*Mary:* Yes, it's a drip-dry cotton. You remember, that abstract print in the green and white blocks. I asked Miss Deaver if we were going to plan again and she said we would plan all year. That's one of the things you learn in homemaking, she said. Last year Sue Lackey made two whole dresses and lots of other things. Some of the girls got to knit a sweater, too, as an outside project, but Sue thinks their mothers helped them.

*Bill:* Girls really have it soft! Imagine being able to decide on projects. Why don't they have homemaking classes for boys? (He laughs and so do Jim and Mary.)

*Mrs. Joslyn:* Maybe that's not as funny as you think. At least, Mary seems to know what's going on in the class all the time. That's more than I can say for you and that history class you're in. You couldn't even tell your father what period of history you were studying when he asked you the other day.

*Bill:* Oh, I remembered after I thought about it awhile. It's just that history is so boring! All you do is read several pages in that dry old book and then go to class and have Mr. Roberts ask questions all hour. Who can remember all the stuff in the footnotes? History is just a dry subject, that's all!

*Jim:* I bet you wouldn't say that if you had Mrs. Whipple for American history. We don't just read the book and answer questions. We never do that at all. Right at the first of the semester we talked about what history was for. Then we decided on a master plan. We said that all year we would take turns reporting on the biographies of the great men and women of history. We asked

Mrs. Smith to talk to us every two weeks about art objects of the period we were studying. She had us making some drawings of colonial life last week. A couple of the girls' drawings were a lot like the ones we projected on the wall from a book on colonial art. They're pretty good artists, those girls!

*Bill:* That sure isn't anything like our history class! Don't you have any tests or anything?

*Mary:* Do you plan projects like we do in homemaking?

*Jim:* It's sort of like projects. We put our ideas and the things we learn together. Like every Friday we have what Mrs. Whipple calls our evaluation session. We ask all kinds of questions about how we could have done it better. It's real interesting. Mrs. Whipple says we ought to be able to apply what we learn so we're always asking "What's this got to do with life today?" I was awful surprised at first to find out that almost everything in history had something to do with the things that happen today.

*Bill:* I don't see how history can help anybody.

*Jim:* I disagree with you. I didn't like it in tenth grade but I really had my eyes opened. Take, for example, when we had Mr. Jives in. He showed us how all of our American music—romantic songs, jazz, rock and roll, the whole business—can be traced right back in history. Did you see that program on TV last year? What was his name—Joplin, I think? It was like that. History is kind of like a brick wall. You can't lay the top bricks until you get the bottom ones in. Last week we just stopped everything because France kept Britain out of the Common Market. Mrs. Whipple said maybe it wasn't American history—what France and England were doing now—but she couldn't answer questions and make us understand what happened unless we put some time into it too. So we voted to table our project for a week to look into the Common Market. That's not the real name you know. It's the EEC, the European Economic Community. We divided into groups so we could study more parts. Some kids read up on French history in the world history books we had last year. We were talking about it after Hi Y meeting yesterday. We all agreed we understood the history of France a lot better now than we did last year. Maybe that's because we really wanted to find out why France wanted to keep England out. Of course, that wasn't in the history book. We had to get some stuff from magazines and the newspaper. Then we had to talk about it before we answered our questions.

Two boys read a book on modern France and her problems. I

was with a committee on the Common Market and how it got started. History can really help you to understand what's going on in the world.

Although this conversation is fragmented, one need not listen further to it to draw conclusions about which parents are going to think the history course is contributing most to their son's education.

*Use of newsletters.* Although student good will is the most important avenue to the community, it is not the only one available to the teacher. Many teachers do not depend entirely on the students to keep parents informed regarding what the class is doing. With the help of the class, these teachers prepare newsletters, or sometimes just simple letters, which tell of class goals, projects, events, and activities. Frequently, these are written from the viewpoint of the students after a discussion of what was done, why it was done, and how successful it was.

One student wrote the following letter to his parents.

Dear Mom and Dad:

Our English class has just finished our first unit on "writing for clarity." We will have another unit on this topic before the end of the year. We have two units on this because it's so important. These days you have to be able to have people understand exactly what you mean.

All of the kids in our class are writing to their parents because we want you to know what we did. Before we did this unit we read some short stories and decided whether the characters were real, I mean like somebody you know. Once the teacher just read half of the story to us and then we wrote the ending of it. After we had ours written he read the rest of the story. It was very funny how it came out. Some of the kids wrote better endings than the real one. That was what we did in our unit on short stories.

We also read two essays on politics and public health. We studied grammar about two weeks. We have a spelling lesson every Friday.

I didn't see my report card yet but Mr. Boyle says my grade will be C+. I think that is all right, but Mr. Boyle says I could do better if I would study my spelling harder and go over my themes before I hand them in. I think I can raise my mark for next period because our last swimming meet is next week and then I will have more time to study.

Well, I guess that's all I can tell you about English class now.

Your loving son,

Bill

In another version of the same idea, the letter may be a composite of ideas from the entire class. Another variation of this procedure involves the use of the district or building newsletter as the vehicle for communicating with the parents of students in the teacher's class or classes. The teacher or the students, or both, then prepare items for inclusion in the publication. Individually written letters based on group discussion appeal to junior high students; the more formal newsletter also prepared as a class project suits senior high students better.

A foreign language class prepared the following item for inclusion in the "Parents' Newsletter."

### French 1 (Mrs. Fournier)

At the beginning of the year the students in French 1 and the teacher decided on some purposes we would like to have for this year. In addition to learning enough about the grammar and idiom so we can read a little, we would also like to accomplish the following things:

1. Learn to speak well enough to "get by" on a trip to France.
2. Learn more about the French people: how they live, how they feel about world problems, in what ways they are like us.
3. Read some French magazines.
4. See one French movie, if possible.
5. Cook and eat some French food.

Since we are about half way through the course naturally we have not achieved all of our objectives. We have made a lot of progress, however. We have concentrated more on speaking than on reading but each of us can read a little French, too. We can speak quite well. Sometimes we can conduct our entire lesson for the whole class period using only a few words of English. All the rest is in French. Mrs. Fournier says most of us could travel in France already and order food, make purchases, and find our way around.

We have examined several French language magazines and

newspapers and read and reported on some of them. We have had four or five class periods during which we talked about life in France and the French people. Next semester we will have a unit on "The France of the Future." Mrs. Beverly La Duke, a house-wife who lives at 293 Riverside, has talked to the class twice about her trip to France last summer.

We are planning our French meal for April or May. If the weather is nice so we can eat outside, we will have a "French picnic" at Mrs. Fournier's. We shall probably have to call on parents for some help with transportation.

If a French movie that is OK comes to the Bijou, we shall make plans to attend. Mr. Boston, the manager, has two French films scheduled during the coming weeks but Mrs. Fournier has not seen either one. She is writing some friends who teach French in other schools to ask about these movies.

We like French 1 very much and are looking forward to the rest of the year.

The benefits of a newsletter are not limited to improved parent-school relations. There are other obvious results in the improvement of communication skills—a basic goal at all levels of education—and improved understanding of the why and how of classroom activity by the students themselves.

*Parents' nights.* Some schools schedule periodic open house pro-grams or parents' night programs which involve all teachers. The format of such programs varies. Sometimes the open house simply provides an opportunity for the parent to talk briefly with the teacher. The building is open and each teacher is in his room or other designated location. Sometimes teachers explain to the group of parents assembled the broad purposes of the course and some of the means used to achieve the goals. Frequently, parents follow the students' schedule of classes, moving from classroom to classroom for ten- or fifteen-minute periods. The open house can be as good or as bad as the teachers and administrators make it. It provides a con-tact with the parents. If it is carefully and imaginatively planned and has the support of the faculty, it should help to improve the parents' regard for the school. It must not follow the same pattern year after year, nor may it be expected to satisfy the full need for a school-community relations program. Above all, the open house must not be permitted to substitute for individual parent-teacher conferences. Talking with the teacher for five or ten minutes with a group of other parents within earshot may make parents and teachers feel more kindly toward each other but it hardly satisfies the need for an opportunity to discuss the student's progress in the course in question.

Some teachers use the open house idea on an individual room basis, i.e., they schedule such an event for only their own class or classes. They then have an hour or two to explain and describe the work they and the students have been doing and to answer parents' questions and hear their reactions. A display of students' work is usually a prominent feature of the open house whether building-wide or individual, as is the serving of light refreshments before or following the more formal activities.

*Room parents' club.* The individual open house can be regularized by the establishment of a room parents' club. Although highly effective in the elementary school, little has been done with this idea at the secondary school level. Such a club must include both parents, not just mothers as is so frequently the case at the elementary level. The activities and concerns of the group may be broadened beyond the teacher's class into social and/or cultural pursuits. Whether or not the room parents' club concerns itself with matters other than those directly associated with the activities of the classroom and school will vary from one community to another and from one group of parents to another. After the group has met a few times, the question of interest in other activities of a social or cultural nature is appropriate. Picnics, discussions, speakers, and cooperative projects in community improvement are possibilities. Whenever possible the students should be involved in such endeavors.

*Use of community resources.* One of the criteria of a good school program is the extent to which community resources have been identified and used. The contributions of people are the most valuable of the many community resources. The cooperation of lay citizens in the process of educating the young not only benefits the process directly through the contribution the citizens make but also builds good will toward the schools. People tend to support those things of which they feel a part.

Paul Bowman suggests examples of ways citizens can enrich the school program.

Most communities these days have residents or visitors from foreign countries who can contribute immeasurably to the child's (and the teacher's) understanding of language, geography, and history. Most communities will have residents in many different occupations, any one of which has contributions to make to the school program.[1]

One high school which keeps a register of the use of non-staff members in instructional activities compiled the following list during a three-month period:

| Kind of Resource | Topic or Subject |
|---|---|
| A former member of the state legislature | Political parties: purposes, contributions to the society, organization |
| The membership secretary of the local chamber of commerce | The objectives of the chamber, locally and nationally; common problems of businessmen |
| The president of a local labor union | The viewpoint of organized labor on selected state and national issues |
| The city clerk | The structure of our city government; some alternative plans; how the people are represented |
| A newspaper reporter | How newspapers serve the public |
| An employee of an advertising firm | The ethics of advertising |
| A housewife (war bride) | My impressions of London as a teen-age visitor |
| A chemist (employed by a nearby firm) | How to become a chemist and like it |
| A priest (born and partially educated in France) | Idiom and slang used among the peasants of northern France |

[1] Paul Hoover Bowman, "Developing Potentiality: Creed or Pipe Dream?" in *New Insights and the Curriculum,* Association for Supervision and Curriculum Development (Washington, D.C.: The Association Yearbook, 1963), p. 49.

| The local manager of a chain drug store | Qualities our firm wants in an employee |
| A community college chemistry teacher | What's new this year in chemistry? |
| The vice-president of the local affiliate of a national sorority for women in business | New challenges for the woman who wants a career in the business world |

It is obvious that the teachers in this high school were alert to the possibilities of involving citizens directly in the program of instruction.

*Home visits.* Some parents find it impossible to come to the school for a great variety of reasons. Sometimes the reasons are or seem to be phony. Regardless of the reason, if a teacher wants to enlist their help in understanding their children his only recourse is to go to them. In schools where the departmentalized organization has been modified by block or core-type scheduling, a program of home visitation is feasible. A good homeroom organization can also facilitate visits by the homeroom teachers.

In a completely departmentalized secondary school where most teachers have a hundred and fifty or more different students enrolled in their classes, a yearly visit to each student's home is well beyond the realm of reasonable expectation. Moreover, the school frequently provides an atmosphere more conducive to quiet conversation than many homes. If ample provision is made by the school (or the teacher) for scheduled parent interviews at the school as described in Chapter 13, the need for home visits should be sufficiently reduced so that teachers will be able to make such contacts when necessary without burdening themselves unduly. Unfortunately, the families who can profit most from close school-parent cooperation are often the ones who are least likely to initiate such contacts. Unless the teacher "breaks the ice," the relationship is not established. In many cases, however, once the first contact is made and the parent finds the teacher nonthreatening and sincerely interested in the student's welfare, the parent is more willing to come to the school for future conferences.

*Other opportunities for teacher-citizen contacts.* Thus far we have been discussing formalized means available to the teacher to enlist the cooperation of parents and other citizens in the education of the community's young people. There are also many incidental opportunities for teacher-citizen contacts. Citizens attend school-sponsored events such as plays, concerts, and games. If teachers are in the halls and foyers before and after such events and during intermissions, many students will introduce their parents. The teacher who resides in the community has an advantage. Teachers who reside outside the school community can make it a practice to do much of their shopping in the community. Students will introduce parents in this situation also. Merchants who are conscious of the taxes they pay for school support are quick to notice the teachers who patronize them. When they want information about the schools they turn to their school-connected patrons. Other opportunities for contacts are found in the churches, clubs, and other community organizations.

Merchants are not the only citizens who address their inquiries about the schools to the teachers.

> When you have a question about the schools, whom do you ask for an answer?
>
> The answer in a survey of one Michigan community was "a teacher."
>
> It did not matter if the question was about the high school and the teacher named taught in kindergarten. The same answer was given if the question concerned a budget which the teacher never saw or heard explained.
>
> The teacher is a natural communicator of the schools to the community. Even if the teacher is a poorly informed communicator, he still holds this role. In most instances, the community is more aware of the teacher's role as unofficial representative of the schools than is the teacher.
>
> The problems of school-community relationships can be reduced and objectives more speedily reached if the teachers can see their unavoidable roles as important and influential representatives of their school system and of education in general.[2]

Teachers and other school personnel have an obligation to help citizens understand the schools. In order to do this they must be in-

2 Ernest G. Lake, "The School Staff—Each Member an Ambassador," *The Bulletin of the National Association of Secondary School Principals*, 44:257 (September 1960), 39.

formed about school matters. Each teacher has a minimal obligation as a professional employee of one of the community's most important institutions to be informed regarding the action taken at each meeting of the board of education, the general policies and procedures existent in the district and in his particular school, the broad facts of school finance in his state and in the district where he works, the general pattern of the curriculum and extracurriculum in the district as well as in his building, and the methods used to keep citizens informed about school matters. This is a big order if each teacher has to undertake to secure this knowledge on his own. Fortunately, such individual effort is seldom necessary. The state and national teachers' organizations make a valiant effort to provide their members with pertinent information pertaining to education on the state and national scene. Many of the local affiliates do the same at the district level. Many school systems have regular or periodic fact sheets, newsletters, or other means to keep teachers informed. If such means are not available it is appropriate for teachers to request the information they require in order to carry out this aspect of their public relations obligation. Citizens who are busy with other matters cannot be expected to know as much as they should about the behavior and development of young people and the role of the school in society, unless they have help. The teachers are the only experts in these matters sufficiently numerous in each community to carry out this task with success.

## The responsibility of teachers as a group

We have noted that some school public relations efforts require the cooperation of all school personnel or at least a sizable group. The Parent-Teacher Association is such an activity. Although such an enterprise may on occasion come into being as a result of the initial enthusiasm of one person, the support of many others is necessary before the project can be launched and continue to prosper.

*The Parent-Teacher Association.* Secondary schools as a general rule have not taken full advantage of the opportunities for school-parent contacts afforded by the PTA. Whether or not some kind of organization involving parents and teachers (and perhaps students) will succeed in relation to a given secondary school depends on a number of factors. It must have leadership, perhaps initially from school personnel, but eventually from both school patrons and teachers. It will have to fulfill needs for both groups. The programs will have to be interesting to both teachers and parents (and students too, if they are included). Programs will have to confront significant issues; an organization that limits its concern to raising money for school activities may provide an outlet for a few people and hence continue to sustain itself but it will never approach the limits of its potential of service to the school and community. There are better ways to get money to operate school-sponsored activities than through parent-teacher sponsorship of carnivals, fun nights, dinners, and the like.

Some high schools are decentralized administratively so that an administrator, one or more counselors, and several teachers are responsible for a specific group of students, frequently a complete grade. When such an administrative-instructional unit occupies and has all or most of its activities confined to a specific wing or section of the building, the arrangement is known as the house plan. Whether or not the house plan or some less inclusive form of administrative decentralization is used, the formation of the teacher-parent organization on a grade-level basis deserves careful consideration. Tying the teacher-parent organization to a grade-level base as opposed to a schoolwide base has a number of advantages. The relatively smaller number of parents and teachers involved make it possible for people to get acquainted more readily. If teachers are already working together as grade-level groups on curriculum development, the teacher-parent group is a natural extension of such cooperative effort. Also, the formation of a grade-level association can proceed without involving the entire school, especially at the beginning, and can thus be confined to a particular group of parents and teachers who seem ready for it. In some communities where a strong organization of parents and teachers has existed in the junior high building, the grade-level organization has been initiated at grade ten, then moved along year by year through the senior high grades.

*The need for actual involvement.* Perhaps the best way to stimulate interest in an endeavor is to involve people in it. In a study conducted by Richard Carter

. . . a community which was in deep trouble was examined in comparison with three other communities which had long records of successful bond issues and happy community relations. The troubled community could not get its bond issues accepted, and the superintendent was in real difficulty. When a large sample of the voters was interviewed, there were surprisingly few differences in their attitudes from those of the healthy communities. For example, education was valued just as highly, and, in general, the voters knew as much about current educational issues and methods. But there was one glaring difference. A much smaller percentage of the voters in the troubled community participated in any way in the schools—visited them, talked with school officials or teachers, went to meetings about school matters, and discussed school problems.[3]

All contacts between school personnel and citizens include an element of involvement. The casual contact exemplified by the annual open house, the school newsletter, or the occasional written communication does not represent involvement in sufficient depth to inspire a feeling of "pride of ownership." Advisory and planning committees of various kinds offer almost limitless means of involving parents and other lay citizens in school matters. The value of such groups, properly organized and assisted by professional personnel, has been demonstrated repeatedly in hundreds of school communities. The most frequent use of such groups has been in connection with bond and millage campaigns, but many other instances can be found. The following are illustrative of the many kinds of concerns with which citizens' advisory committees have dealt successfully:

> long-range building and site planning
> millage and/or bond proposal
> millage and/or bond campaign
> attendance area boundaries
> job placement of graduates and nongraduates
> auto mechanics curriculum
> vocational preparation curriculum
> school-sponsored dances

[3] Reported by Wilbur Schramm, "Mass Media and Educational Policy," in *Social Forces Influencing American Education*, Sixtieth Yearbook, National Society for the Study of Education (Chicago: University of Chicago Press, 1961), pp. 227–228.

*Meeting the needs of all citizens.* We have noted that the schools' normal and most productive avenue of communication to the community is through the students. Generally, only the parents can be reached via the students. In every community there are many adult citizens who do not have children in the public school. Some are childless, some have children who are above or below school age, and some send their children to private and parochial schools. While some of the school effort designed to promote and maintain good school-community relations does reach these citizens, they cannot be expected to respond with the same degree of enthusiasm as those who have children who are profiting from the school program.

One of the benefits of the true community school, in addition to its contribution to general community welfare, is the good will it generates by serving the needs of all citizens, rather than limiting itself to serving only those between the ages of five and seventeen. Probably the best example of community service beyond the basic educational program for young people is the adult education program. Many citizens who have no occasion for contact with any other school endeavor become staunch school supporters as a result of their experience in adult education classes. The same could be said for adult recreation activities. One could certainly make a strong case for support of recreation activities for adults and even for children by some governmental or volunteer agency other than the school. There are many communities, however, especially in sparsely settled areas where no recreation program for either adults or children will exist if the school does not sponsor it. Having a school-sponsored recreation program seems preferable to having none at all.

Many community schools also recognize their role as one of the major foci of culture in the community. They sponsor, either alone or in cooperation with other community institutions or organizations, such events as concerts, travelogs, dramatic performances, and forums of one kind or another. Frequently, the school contribution consists primarily of the volunteered time and talent of its personnel and the use of the school buildings. All of these community services help to build community good will toward the school and to assure the highest reasonable level of local financial support.

*Teaching the school in the school.* Probably one of the most effective means of securing long-term citizen interest in the schools is

the inclusion in the secondary school curriculum of systematic attention to the major issues concerning education. Strangely, this is
something teachers have done only infrequently and sporadically.
The intent of such an endeavor would be to acquaint students with
the necessity for universal, tax-supported education in a free society,
the major ways in which such education must differ from the type
one would expect to find in a more authoritarian culture, and the
fundamental issues concerning education that remain unresolved
at present, such as the separation of church and state in educational
matters and the extension of federal aid to education. Negative attitudes regarding taxes are deeply rooted in our culture. The tax col-
lector has been almost equivalent to a "public enemy" since ancient
times. Few citizens realize that the public services they purchase
through taxation are the greatest bargain they enjoy. Admittedly,
there are limits to the success the schools might achieve in changing
such deep-seated attitudes. But education is a powerful force! The
quality of education in a free society depends to a large degree on
the willingness of citizens to sacrifice other desires in order to support their schools. The tendency has been to treat school finance and
other issues related to the quality of the educational program as matters that concern adult citizens only. Teachers have tended to forget
that their high school students are fully capable of giving intelligent
attention to a matter that is intensely interesting to them—the quality of the education they are receiving. It seems reasonable to expect
that an opportunity to consider issues at a time when one has a vital
personal interest in them may have an impact that will continue to
influence one's attitudes and behavior for many years to come.

Although such a program of "teaching the school within the
school" contemplates the acquisition by the students of lasting attitudes favorable to the continuation and extension of high quality
education available to all, it would automatically reap much direct
and immediate benefit from the resulting communication from students to their parents.

*In conclusion.* In this chapter we have examined the attitudes of
citizens toward their schools, the benefits of close school-community
cooperation, and the ways in which teachers can establish, maintain,
and improve good relationships between the school and its various
publics. The older "leave-us-alone" policies of the school no longer
suffice. If school programs are to be changed in such ways that they

will better meet the needs of individual learners, maximum understanding of the people who own the schools is essential. This understanding can come about only through the involvement of more and more citizens in planning, implementing, and appraising the school's program. But citizen participation will not occur unless teachers work skillfully toward such a goal.

In the next chapter we shall consider trends in curriculum planning in secondary schools.

## FOR FURTHER READING

American Association of School Administrators, *Educational Administration in a Changing Community,* Thirty-seventh Yearbook. Washington, D.C.: The National Education Association, 1959. Chapters 2–6 provide a good overview of the contemporary American community in relation to the major challenges involved in the establishment of optimum school-community relations.

————, *Public Relations for America's Schools,* Twenty-eighth Yearbook. Washington, D.C.: The National Education Association, 1950. Chapters 1 and 2 include background information on the several aspects of school-community relations.

Carter, Richard E., "Voters and Their Schools," *Phi Delta Kappan,* 42:6 (March 1961), 244–249. A summary of the findings of a government-sponsored research study.

Cuony, Edward R., "Helping Parents Understand Adolescence," *The Bulletin of the National Association of Secondary School Principals,* 45:265 (May 1961), 27–31. The outline that formed the basis for a multiple-session parent study group is presented.

Fine, Thomas W., "Parent Conferences in the Junior High School," *The Bulletin of the National Association of Secondary School Principals,* 44:259 (November 1960), 104–105. A description of the use of the parent conference method of reporting in one school.

Grant, Eva H., *Parents and Teachers as Partners.* Chicago: Science Research Associates, Inc., 1952. This booklet contains suggestions for improving parent-teacher interaction. Part II is based on a national survey conducted by the National Congress of Parents and Teachers.

Hymes, James L., Jr., *Effective Home-School Relations.* Englewood Cliffs, N.J.: Prentice-Hall, Inc., 1953. An insightful book written in semiconversational language. See especially Chapter 4, "Teachers' Attitudes and Aptitudes."

Jones, J. J., and Irving W. Stout, *School Public Relations: Issues and Cases.* New York: G. P. Putnam's Sons, 1960. Several current issues in school public relations are illustrated by case studies.

Kindred, Leslie W., *School Public Relations.* Englewood Cliffs, N.J.: Prentice-Hall, Inc., 1957. Background information is presented in Chapters 1 and 2. Suggestions for teacher-student relationships in regard to interpretation of the school to the community are found in Chapter 7. Various kinds of parent-teacher associations are discussed in Chapter 10.

Lake, Ernest G., "The School Staff—Each Member an Ambassador," *The Bulletin of the National Association of Secondary School Principals,* 44:257 (September 1960), 39–43. The responsibility of teachers for school-community relations from the viewpoint of the superintendent.

Langdon, Grace, and Irving W. Stout, *Teacher-Parent Interviews.* Englewood Cliffs, N.J.: Prentice-Hall, Inc., 1954. A comprehensive treatise on this topic. See especially section 9 D, "Types of suggestions a teacher can give" to parents of teen-agers, and section 11 C, which includes accounts of interviews with parents of high school students.

Menge, J. Wilmer, and Roland C. Faunce, *Working Together for Better Schools.* New York: American Book Co., 1953. The rationale for extensive involvement of citizens in the development of improved community schools with many illustrations of actual practices.

Moehlman, Arthur B., and James A. van Zwole, *School Public Relations.* New York: Appleton-Century-Crofts, Inc., 1957. Readers desiring sociological background information on the place of the school in the society in relation to the problems of school-community relations will find Chapters 1–3 helpful.

National School Public Relations Association, *Pebbles.* Washington, D.C.: The National Educational Association, 1960. One of a series of booklets prepared especially for teachers, featuring practical suggestions of ways teachers can help to improve the citizen's image of the school. See also *Person to Person* (1956) and *It Starts in the Classroom* (1951).

Steele, Henry Benton, and Harold R. Bottrell, "How Much Community Participation?" *Phi Delta Kappan,* 39:5 (February 1958), 229–233. A description of a study, including the techniques and the results. Sufficient information is provided to enable any faculty to replicate the results in its own school.

Stout, Irving W., and Grace Langdon, *Parent-Teacher Relationships.* Washington, D.C.: The National Education Association, 1958. Research findings are interpreted and woven into this commentary, which concerns itself primarily with attitudes and feelings as elements in teacher and parent relationships. No. 16 in the series "What Research Says to the Teacher."

# 15 Recent trends and issues in secondary education

In our consideration of teaching and learning in the secondary school, we have thus far explored several related problems. Chapters 1 through 4 were devoted to such basic matters as the history and current status of secondary schools; the purposes of secondary education as our culture has defined them; the nature of the learner himself; and the principles of effective learning. In Chapters 5, 6, and 7 an analysis was made of the various, related roles that a teacher must play. Chapters 8 through 13 consisted of a look at the teacher in action within a secondary school: teaching classes, exploring resources, sponsoring student activities, and evaluating the progress of his students. In Chapter 14 we examined the teacher as a key figure in school-community relationships.

One factor which affects the daily operation of the teacher has not yet been discussed: the way in which the curriculum is organized. At this point we shall look briefly at some alternative curriculum organizations, and examine current trends in respect to both curriculum and methods. Finally, we propose in this chapter to present some of the issues regarding curriculum that secondary school people must confront during the years that lie immediately ahead.

No attempt will be made to present all the curriculum trends that have been observed in secondary schools, or to analyze the rationale on which such trends have been based.[1] Instead we shall highlight some of the most significant trends and perhaps sharpen the issues that confront teachers and students of secondary education.

Many books and pamphlets, as well as articles in professional journals are available to the reader who has a special interest in the trends unique to a particular subject. Some of these references will be included in a later section of this chapter, as we consider the current trend toward subject specialization.

## The high school before 1930

We have noted that the early high school was very like its predecessors—the grammar school and the academy—in its curriculum. It was mainly a college preparatory institution. As enrollments in secondary schools increased during the twentieth century, educators were confronted by more and more high school students who had neither aptitude for, interest in, nor use for the traditional college preparatory curriculum. The Committee of Ten of the National Education Association began its report as early as 1892 with a clear statement that the high school was not and should not be a college preparatory institution for all students. Subsequent recommendations in this early report did not, however, depart very much from the narrow curricular concepts prevalent at that time. In 1918 the Commission on the Reorganization of Secondary Education published a statement titled *Cardinal Principles of Secondary Education*. This widely discussed report recommended that the secondary school curriculum should be "comprehensively reorganized" to meet its constantly changing responsibilities, including "the needs of the society to be served, the character of the individuals to be educated, and the knowledge of educational theory and practice available."[2]

Some changes in the curriculum occurred during the 1920's in an

1 Among the many excellent books which provide such analysis in some depth, see especially Harold B. Alberty and Elsie J. Alberty, *Reorganizing the High School Curriculum*, 3rd ed. (New York: Macmillan Co., 1962); J. Paul Leonard, *Developing the Secondary School Curriculum*, rev. ed. (New York: Holt, Rinehart and Winston, Inc., 1953); and Edward A. Krug, *The Secondary School Curriculum* (New York: Harper & Row, Publishers, 1960).

2 Commission on the Reorganization of Secondary Education, *Cardinal Principles of Secondary Education*, Bulletin No. 35 (Washington, D.C.: Bureau of Education, 1918), p. 7.

effort to respond to the changing responsibility of the high school. Such "vocational" subjects as agriculture, homemaking, industrial arts, and commercial subjects were added. More art and music classes were developed. Physical education became strongly emphasized. Citizenship, civics, and economics were added in most high schools. By about 1930, the typical high school had made such adaptations as these to the changing needs of the still growing student population. By this time the new trend toward the junior high school had become established, at least in urban schools. In 1930 there were already 1,842 separate junior high schools and 3,287 six-year schools that included junior high school grades.[3] The new junior high school (launched about 1910) was destined to have a significant influence on the general education curriculum of the secondary school.

## The decade of studies

Yet there was growing evidence during the early 1930's that the high schools needed to make some more basic adjustments in their programs. Although enrollments increased almost 50 per cent between 1930 and 1940, the drop-out rate remained high. About half our youth were rejecting the high school after a brief trial. Since jobs were scarce during the depression years, millions of young people found no constructive role to play in the society. Many of them simply roamed the country, unemployed and homeless. As a result of growing national concern for this problem, the National Youth Administration and the Civilian Conservation Corps were established as federal programs. This entry of the national government into the realm of secondary education was evidence that high schools across the country had failed generally to gear their curricula to the needs and interests of youth.

The 1930's have been referred to as the era of secondary school studies. Never before had there been so many national, regional, and state studies of the curriculum of the secondary school. At least three forces were at work in motivating these numerous studies. One of these forces—the growing conviction that high school programs were ineffective—has already been mentioned. Another significant influ-

3 U.S. Office of Education, "Statistics of Public Secondary Day Schools, 1951–52," *Biennial Survey of Education in the United States, 1950–52* (Washington, D.C.: Government Printing Office, 1954), p. 23.

ence was the questing, experimental climate of the national culture during this period. The re-examination of the secondary school was only one facet of the tendency to look critically at social and political institutions during the 1930's, and to try any remedy at least once.

The interest in the secondary school curriculum also stemmed, in part, from certain developments in the elementary schools. These included experiments with the project method, with problem solving as a means of integrating various subjects, and with the activity movement, which focused on use of activities as a means of learning fundamental knowledges and skills. Some schools had developed the "experience curriculum," which added certain criteria for evaluating the validity of such activities:

> Under this concept, activities are regarded as educative when they (1) stem from real purposes in the learner, (2) are geared to his present problems and interests, (3) derive their sequence from the learner's normal growth and development, and (4) are interpreted, analyzed, or intellectualized as an aid to the possible redirection of the learner's purposes.[4]

This concept led many elementary teachers to base learning activities on units that cut across many subject fields and correlated these subjects around a single problem.

Not all elementary teachers were using any of these experiments by 1930. There had, however, been enough interest in various types of curricular change in the elementary schools to accent the cleavage between the elementary and secondary levels. Both teaching methods and curriculum organization [5] tended to reflect this difference in philosophy, and constituted a source of pressure on the secondary schools to re-examine their own curricula.

*The Eight-Year Study.* In some ways the most important of all the secondary curriculum studies was launched in 1932 by the Commission on the Relation of School and College of the Progressive Edu-

---

[4] Roland C. Faunce and Nelson L. Bossing, *Developing the Core Curriculum,* rev. ed. (Englewood Cliffs, N.J.: Prentice-Hall, Inc., © 1958), p. 37. Reprinted by permission.

[5] As curriculum is increasingly regarded as the sum total of the student's school experiences, this implied distinction between curriculum and method becomes meaningless.

cation Association. The thirty member schools, freed by agreement from the usual pattern of subjects for college entrance, were enabled to study and try out various ways of organizing courses and to experiment with new teaching methods. The five volumes that summed up the outcomes of these experiments deserve the attention of everyone interested in secondary education.[6] One of these books, *Did They Succeed in College?* is a report of a careful evaluation of the college success of the graduates of these thirty schools, when compared with graduates whose transcripts showed the traditional preparatory pattern. A special further study was made of the graduates coming to college from the six schools that had the largest amount of experimentation. These graduates were significantly superior to their matched control partners from conventional schools in college achievement, in citizenship, leadership qualities, ability to think, and intellectual curiosity. The study revealed that no single pattern of high school subjects can be considered indispensable for the preparation of students for college. It thus invalidated the separate curriculum (still almost universal) called the "college preparatory curriculum." Further, this investigation revealed that "the more experimental the [high] school, the greater degree of success in college." [7]

Thus one of the significant findings of the Eight-Year Study was that freedom for each high school faculty to plan the curriculum for their own school will not penalize the college-bound students, since there is no single curriculum pattern that best prepares students for college. In spite of this finding, the separate college preparatory curriculum has continued generally in most high schools. A study of 1,351 secondary schools made by the Educational Records Bureau in 1950 revealed that "most of the high schools have a fixed pattern of requirements for college preparation. In fact, the percentage of

[6] Wilford M. Aikin, *The Story of the Eight-Year Study* (New York: Harper & Row, Publishers, 1942); H. H. Giles, S. P. McCutchen, and A. N. Zechiel, *Exploring the Curriculum* (New York: Harper & Row, Publishers, 1942); E. R. Smith *et al.*, *Appraising and Recording Student Progress* (New York: Harper & Row, Publishers, 1942); Progressive Education Association, *Thirty Schools Tell Their Story* (New York: The Progressive Education Association, 1942); Dean Chamberlin *et al.*, *Did They Succeed in College?* (New York: Harper & Row, Publishers, 1942).

[7] Chamberlin *et al.*, *Did They Succeed in College?* p. 209.

secondary schools reporting a fixed curriculum for college preparatory pupils was greater than the percentage of colleges reporting a
similar requirement." [8] This study seemed to indicate that freedom
from specific subject requirements for the college-bound is really not
wanted by most teachers and administrators in the secondary schools.
More recent studies appear to support the conclusion that high
schools are not moving very far or very fast in the direction of abol-
ishing the traditional curriculum for the college preparatory student.
There is much greater interest in revising methods of teaching
within the traditional curriculum pattern, as we shall note later in
this chapter.

*Other national and regional studies.* Brief reference should be
made to certain other secondary school studies made, or at least
launched, during the 1930's. In 1933 the Cooperative Study of Secondary School Standards began an investigation of the high school
accreditation process. A major result was the instrument called
*Evaluative Criteria,*[9] which has been a basic tool for initial accreditation of high schools since 1940. It is a collection of materials for
self-study by school staffs, preparatory to a visit by an accreditation
team. A recent revision of the criteria for evaluation of junior high
schools is gaining some acceptance.

In 1935 the New York State Board of Regents began an inquiry
into the character and cost of secondary schools in that state. Their
reports [10] were excellent early examples of follow-up of former high
school students.

The American Youth Commission also launched in 1935 a study
of the problems and needs of adolescents.[11] The Southern Association Commission on Curriculum Studies and Research began their
work in 1935, as did the Educational Policies Commission of the

---

[8] Arthur E. Traxler and Agatha Townsend, eds., *Improving Transition from
School to College,* A Study of Admissions by the Committee on School and
College Relations of the Educational Records Bureau (New York: Harper & Row,
Publishers, 1953), p. 46.

[9] *Evaluative Criteria,* rev. ed. (Washington, D.C.: National Study of Secondary
School Evaluation, 1960).

[10] Prominent among these reports was Francis T. Spaulding, *High School and
Life* (New York: McGraw-Hill Book Co., Inc., 1938).

[11] See Howard M. Bell, *Youth Tell Their Story* (Washington, D.C.: The American Council on Education, 1938).

National Education Association. One of their reports has been briefly quoted in Chapter 1.[12]

*State studies.* The 1930's also witnessed a number of state studies of secondary education. Among these were a five-year study of ten California high schools (1935); the Ohio Plan for Curriculum Reorganization in Secondary Schools (1938); the Florida Program for the Improvement of Schools (1938); and the Michigan Study of the Secondary School Curriculum (1938).

An example of a state study somewhat patterned after the Eight-Year Study was the Michigan Study launched in 1938, after a year of planning and surveys. This study enrolled fifty-five high schools for the twelve-year period 1938–50. The schools were protected in respect to the admission of their graduates to Michigan colleges, in much the same manner as in the Eight-Year Study. A number of curriculum innovations were developed in these schools. In 1946 their agreement with the colleges was revised and extended to all secondary schools whose staff and administration would agree to (1) conduct regular studies of their curriculum, (2) make follow-up studies of graduates and drop-outs, (3) improve their guidance records, and (4) intensify guidance in vocational and college selection. This "Michigan Secondary School-College Agreement" was endorsed by nearly all Michigan colleges and universities, and eventually enrolled nearly three hundred member high schools. In 1962 their organization was formalized as "The Michigan Association of Schools and Colleges." [13]

A somewhat similar curriculum program has been carried on in Illinois. Their "local consensus" studies have been jointly staffed by the State Superintendent of Public Instruction and the University of Illinois. Their numerous reports have included studies of "hidden tuition costs," participation in extraclass activities, guidance

---

12 See pp. 12–13. See also their report (in 1944) *Education for All American Youth* and (in 1952) *Education for All American Youth: A Further Look* (Washington, D.C.: The National Education Association).

13 For a report of the initial Michigan Study, see J. C. Parker, J. W. Menge, and T. D. Rice, *The First Five Years* (Lansing, Mich.: State Department of Public Instruction, 1942). See also T. D. Rice and R. C. Faunce, *The Michigan Secondary Study* (Lansing: State Department of Public Instruction, 1945); and Leon S. Waskin, "The Michigan Secondary School-College Agreement," *Bulletin of the National Association of Secondary School Principals* (January 1949), 49–64.

services, holding power, and human relations programs, among others.[14]

*The Life Adjustment Program.* In 1945 the United States Office of Education launched a national program aimed at improving guidance and instruction for that neglected group of students whose needs were not being served by either the college preparatory or the vocational curriculum. This group, originally estimated by leaders of the Life Adjustment Program at 60 per cent of the enrollment, were described as floundering in an unsuitable curriculum or dropping out of school when they reached the legal age of school-leaving. The emphasis of this program was subsequently changed to apply to all students, and had as its goal the adaptation of all instruction to the real needs, problems, and interests of students.[15] During the late 1950's it came under virulent attack from critics who described it as a campaign for mediocre, anti-intellectual education. Under the term "Life Adjustment," at least, efforts to improve the curriculum became unpopular. Many of the basic goals of the program survive under other banners.[16]

## Alternative curriculum patterns

We have been discussing some of the numerous studies that have been made of the total secondary school curriculum since about 1930. We have made little reference as yet to the outcomes of these studies within the schools themselves. Given some freedom and some leadership from state and national resources, what alternative patterns of curriculum organization have emerged?

It is no doubt obvious that the separate subject curriculum is still prevalent, at least in the senior high schools. Indeed, it has been so firmly established for so many years that all the studies since 1930 have seemed to make little impact. It is even difficult for many sec-

---

[14] A number of the early Illinois studies are reported in Harold C. Hand, *Principal Findings of the Illinois Secondary School Curriculum Program,* Bulletin No. 2 (Springfield, Ill.: State Superintendent of Public Instruction, 1949).

[15] The Life Adjustment Program was discussed from another point of view in Chapter 1.

[16] For an account of this program at its peak, see J. Dan Hull, "Progress in Life Adjustment Education," *Educational Leadership,* 7:6 (March 1950), p. 361.

ondary teachers to imagine any other way to organize the curriculum than by separate subjects. Nevertheless, alternative patterns have been successfully tried.

Critics of the separate subject approach have for at least thirty years been pointing out disadvantages that inhere when schools are divided into distinct subject segments and sharply departmentalized. These criticisms may be summed up as follows:

1. The separate subject approach has no built-in relationships between one subject and another. The pupil is expected to achieve the difficult task of relating each of his separate learnings to some broad theme or problem with which he is confronted in life outside the classroom.

2. The periods are too short and the school days too segmented to permit time for extended activities that vitalize learning. For example, fields trips and community studies do not fit the single-period lock step.

3. The number of students who confront a teacher during a typical five-period teaching day is too great to permit development of teacher-pupil relationships. This renders the guidance program ineffective.

4. The separate subject commitment of teachers tends to create in each class an aura of specialization that places more importance on the subject itself than upon the learner or the learning process.

5. As a result of increasing specialization, the separate subjects tend to be regarded as material to be conveyed to the learner by textbooks and by lecture. The learner gets little experience in assuming responsibilities or in making choices.

Those who regard the separate subject curriculum as suffering from these and other related handicaps have looked for alternative patterns. It has been their goal, in general, to reorganize the curriculum in ways that will embody or facilitate certain basic goals:

1. *Experience must be integrated.* In general education—that segment of the program that is required of all—the various subject disciplines should be related to certain broad problems or topics that cut across subjects and departments.

2. *Subject matter is a means.* Instead of serving as an end in itself, the subject should point toward a broader purpose or goal.

3. *Education is problem solving.* All learning should contribute to the solution of some problem faced by the learner.

4. *Learning demands resources beyond the printed word.* When learning is defined as problem solving, the search for resources will extend beyond the classroom into the community and the world outside the school.

5. *One must know the learner in order to help him learn.* This is the guidance motif in relation to teaching methods. It demands the assignment of fewer students to each teacher and for longer time periods.

A number of curriculum trends stem from these five goals. The integrated curriculum, the personal-social problems approach, the community school movement, and the guidance-in-the-curriculum advocates all build their various approaches on one or another of these five premises. It is significant that all these movements have prospered first in the self-contained elementary school. As their proponents viewed the secondary school, with its typical separation into subjects, they have attempted to find relationships between subjects. Some of the approaches resulting from this search for relationships will be described in the section that follows.

## Efforts to build relationships

*Correlation.* One simple device to build relationships between two or more subjects is planned correlation. Example: an English teacher and an American history teacher plan to have literature classes read such works as those of Bret Harte, Joaquin Miller, or Dorothy Canfield Fisher at the time they are studying the westward movement in history. This planning can be carried much further and involve several teachers, or even all teachers at a given grade level.

*Broad fields courses.* Some efforts to restore unity in the curriculum have been in the direction of broadening the subjects within each department. For example, social studies embraces the once-separate history and geography. "American Problems" courses combine the fields of government, economics, and sociology. English embraces spelling, penmanship, grammar, composition, and literature. Botany and zoology have merged into biology. General science has replaced separate classes in natural and physical science. General mathematics was originally planned as a broad fields course also.

*Fused courses.* A more radical extension of the broad fields approach is the fused course, usually with at least two periods daily, achieved by merging two related courses into one. A rather common illustration is a fused course in "American culture," which combines the goals but eliminates the separate text materials in American history and American literature. More common in recent years is the humanities course, which has fused such separate subjects as art, music, history, and literature.

*Unified studies.* The line of distinction is perhaps less clear and not universally accepted between fused courses, unified studies, and the core curriculum. Some curriculum theorists define "unified studies" as a further step in the continuum of integration. This type of organization is sometimes described as a combination of two subject-fields into one course, with the retention of the basic objectives of both subjects but with planned correlation of the two fields throughout most of the course. It is thus a more systematic way of building in the correlation goal. It is sometimes distinguished, however, from either fused or core courses because the purposes and basic materials of each (formerly) separate subject are retained in a unified studies course. (In spite of this distinction, the terms "unified studies" and "core" are often used interchangeably.)

*The core curriculum.* Unlike the fused or unified studies course, the core curriculum in theory departs sharply from any commitments to present or cover any particular subject. It derives its subject matter from any appropriate source and uses it to pursue learning experiences that are considered fundamental for all learners. Thus it is organized around the common problems of the learners, which in turn derive from the common needs of a democratic society. The core is problem centered and usually enjoys a block of two or more periods daily. Core teachers are committed to the unit approach by the nature of their assignment. They are supposed to organize their work around the problems of living, cutting across any and all subject lines.

In practice it has proved easy to create core classes by combining required courses in English and social studies, or (less commonly) in mathematics and science. If these courses remain merely combinations of two subjects, they might more accurately be described as unified studies than as core. A core teacher is committed to the practice of planning with his students the goals, procedures, and content to be used in the class. In Chapter 11 the device known as the resource unit was discussed. Such progress as the resource unit has thus far made has been generally due to the interest of core teachers in planning for the use of materials from several subjects in the pursuit of broad problems or teaching units in a core class.

The characteristics of the core curriculum have been summed up as follows in a recent volume on the junior high school:

> 1. The core program provides a larger block of time, which is obtained by combining or replacing two or more subjects. The longer block of time provides opportunity for teachers and pupils to engage in a wide variety of significant activities.
>
> 2. The core program uses problems that boys and girls recognize as important to themselves and society as the organizing center for learning experiences. Identification and selection of these significant problems provide opportunities for growth in cooperative planning, decision-making, critical thinking, and evaluation.
>
> 3. The core program emphasizes the problem-solving method and therefore draws upon the subject matter of many disciplines in the study and investigation of problems. Democratic processes of cooperative group work, individual and group planning, sharing of responsibilities, and leadership characterize the method. The core program recognizes the importance to youth of acquiring skill in democratic living by living it in the classroom. This goal is sharply reflected in the methods of evaluation.
>
> 4. In the core program, guidance is considered an integral part of the classroom function. The reduced number of different students with whom a core teacher works enables the teacher to know each student well. Such understanding fosters better adjustment to individual differences.[17]

Thus the core curriculum may be properly distinguished from either the fused or unified studies course by its freedom from any subject commitments, and its practice of deriving its content and procedure from the planning of teachers with students. In practice, however, the word "core" has been frequently used to refer to any block-time course in general education. Alberty's well-known "six

[17] Roland C. Faunce and Morrel J. Clute, *Teaching and Learning in the Junior High School* (Belmont, Calif.: Wadsworth Publishing Co., Inc., 1961), p. 90.

types of core" might even be regarded as a summary of all recognized curriculum patterns.

1. The core consists of a number of logically organized subjects or fields of knowledge, each of which is taught independently. [The separate subject curriculum]

. . .

2. The core consists of a number of logically organized subjects or fields of knowledge, some or all of which are correlated. [The correlated curriculum]

. . .

3. The core consists of broad problems, units of work, or unifying themes which are chosen because they afford the means of teaching effectively the basic content of certain subjects or fields of knowledge. These subjects retain their identity, but the content is selected and taught with special reference to the unit, theme, or problem. [Grade-level planning]

. . .

4. The core consists of a number of subjects or fields of knowledge which are unified or fused. [Fused or unified studies courses]

. . .

5. The core consists of broad, pre-planned problem areas, from which are selected learning experiences in terms of the psychobiological and societal needs, problems, and interests of students. [Core with commitment to pre-selected themes]

. . .

6. The core consists of broad units of work, or activities, planned by the teacher and the students in terms of needs as perceived by the group. No basic curriculum structure is set up. [Core without commitment to pre-selected themes] [18]

It appears that only Types 5 and 6 in Alberty's list are descriptive of the core curriculum as we have defined it here. Such a classification, however, is useful in clarifying the fact that not all block-time

---

[18] Abstracted from Harold Alberty, "Designing Programs to Meet the Common Needs of Youth," in *Adapting the Secondary School Program to the Needs of Youth*, Fifty-second Yearbook, National Society for the Study of Education (Chicago: University of Chicago Press, 1953), pp. 119–120. Type 3 of this classification has been omitted from the list in the Albertys' revised book, *Reorganizing the High School Curriculum*, pp. 204–225.

classes are core. Types 1–4 should be regarded as separate subject approaches, modified only by the block of time which, in effect, reduces the number of different individuals confronted by the teacher daily.

The distinction between Types 5 and 6 in the Alberty list is a useful one. In Type 5 the teacher has a commitment to certain themes or broad problems, preselected by the staff and furnishing a basic structure for the curriculum at each grade level. Student-teacher planning may be used to evolve units, but within the scope of the grade-level theme. In Type 6, on the other hand, there is freedom from any such commitment to a theme at each grade level. Thus the structure of the curriculum is not preplanned, but emerges from the student-teacher planning in each classroom. In either case, the teaching units may be drawn from larger resource units already developed.

During the 1930's and 40's core programs developed in both junior and senior high schools across the country. With some notable exceptions, senior high schools have tended to move away from either the unified studies or core approach and have returned to the traditional pattern of separate subjects. During this same period, the use of some kind of block-time approach has sharply increased in the junior high schools. Over half of the separate junior high schools employ block time, with most of the programs in grades seven and eight. The block most commonly replaces or combines the separate English and social studies programs. A decided majority of these block-time classes still retain the separate identity of the original subjects, or at best provide for occasional correlation of the subjects combined.[19]

## The separate subject curriculum

As indicated in the preceding section, critics have found serious defects in the separate subject approach. Since it still remains the pattern in nearly all senior high schools, and in a majority of the junior high schools, there must be some advantages claimed for it by its advocates.

[19] Grace Wright, *Block-Time Classes and the Core Program in the Junior High School*, U.S. Department of Health, Education and Welfare, Bulletin No. 6 (Washington, D.C.: U.S. Government Printing Office, 1958).

1. It is in harmony with tradition. Teachers are familiar with programming and teacher-assignment to the separate subjects, and it demands less thought than any departure from the conventional curriculum.

2. It seems a logical prelude to the kind of curriculum that characterizes almost all colleges.

3. It lends itself to separate packaging of course materials, especially textbooks and testing materials.

In recent years a number of other influences have been at work to reinforce the separate subject curriculum. Alberty has called attention to certain of these influences, in a recent lecture series:

1. The influential Conant Reports [20] include recommendations that make the development of a problems-of-living core program . . . impossible. Even in the junior high school, where he concedes that a block-time program may be valuable as a transition, English and social studies would be taught separately.

2. The tendency . . . to push the academic subjects of the high school down into the elementary . . . grades leads to further compartmentalization of subject-matter.

3. All of the national studies under way . . . are predicated on the assumption that the curriculum is to be made up of separate and discrete subjects. . . .

4. Teacher education institutions . . . have returned to compartmentalized "methods" courses.

5. The growing popularity of educational television, which now provides complete courses presented by "master-teacher" specialists and is beamed to several states, encourages a subject-centered approach. The same may be said of the use of teaching machines and programmed learning. . . .[21]

Alberty's third point regarding current national studies deserves further comment. Among the various committees presently studying the secondary school curriculum, the commitment to separate subjects is almost universal. There are national committees working on

[20] James B. Conant, *The American High School Today* (New York: McGraw-Hill Book Co., Inc., 1959), and *Education in the Junior High School Years* (Princeton, N.J.: Education Testing Service, 1960).

[21] Harold B. Alberty, *Public Education in the Sixties: Trends and Issues*, Bode Memorial Lectures, The College of Education, Ohio State University, Columbus, 1962.

science and mathematics, and separately on chemistry, economics, English, history, and social studies, but few if any on broad, interdisciplinary problems.[22] Ample funds and leadership are being provided by foundations and by the federal government for many of these studies, all of which reinforce the traditional separation of subjects.[23] Another powerful influence is the College Entrance Examination Board, whose recommendations regarding course organization and content cannot be taken lightly by high school principals.

The testing movement has also been instrumental in reinforcing separation of subjects by large-scale standardized testing, linked in some instances to granting of college scholarships. In 1962 there were no less than twenty national testing programs being administered, one of which was given that year to 800,000 high school students. As pointed out in a recent bulletin of the National Association of Secondary School Principals in cooperation with other organizations, such tests influence the curriculum rather powerfully. "Students—even gifted students—will score well on a national test only if their program of studies is similar to the program of studies envisioned by the test maker." [24]

The various forces that have been cited as reinforcing the separation of subjects have been referred to above as "traditional," but only in the sense that the curriculum pattern which they generally accept is traditional. As for content and methods within the separate subjects, their position is often far from the traditional one. This point will be elaborated later in this chapter as we illustrate some of the current trends in certain subjects. One line of thought that has permeated many of the current studies relates to various proposals for changes in teaching methods within certain subjects. Cer-

[22] For a resume of current national studies, see Dorothy M. Fraser, *Current Curriculum Studies in Academic Subjects* (Washington, D.C.: The National Education Association, 1962). This is a publication of the NEA Project on Instruction.

[23] These direct and indirect investments by the federal government furnish some evidence of a movement toward a national curriculum. The National Education Defense Act has buttressed certain of the separate subjects by pouring huge funds into improvements in science, mathematics, and foreign languages.

[24] *Testing, Testing, Testing* (Washington, D.C.: National Association of Secondary School Principals, 1962), p. 13.

tain phrases and concepts recur in the writings of Bruner,[25] for example, who rejects the time-honored practices of memorization and drill. He believes instead that children can learn the structure of a subject discipline through discovery of its basic principles and organization, much as a scientist or historian arrives at generalizations within his respective discipline. He holds that "any subject can be taught to any child in some honest form," beginning with the "inactive" (knowing by doing) and proceeding to the "ikonic" (using visual images) and ultimately to the symbolic (either words or mathematical symbols). He emphasizes the use of "intuitive thinking," which has been discussed under the term "reflective thinking" in Chapter 4.

In short, the advocates of studying "the structure of the disciplines" reject traditional methodology but reinforce traditional curriculum patterns, at least with reference to the time-honored separation of subjects. An interesting proposal embodying both the structure and the problems approaches has been advanced by Alice Miel. She proposes that the grade-level curriculum from grade four through grade twelve be planned in three cycles:

1. grade 4: The arts
   grade 5: The natural and physical sciences
   grade 6: Social sciences

2. grade 7: Communication
   grade 8: Social sciences
   grade 9: Natural and physical sciences

3. grade 10: Communication and aesthetics
   grade 11: Social sciences
   grade 12: Religion, philosophy, and ecology.[26]

25 Jerome S. Bruner, *The Process of Education* (Cambridge, Mass.: Harvard University Press, 1961). See also the articles by Philip H. Phenix and Arthur W. Foshay in *Curriculum Crossroads*, A. Harry Passow, ed. (New York: Bureau of Publications, Teachers College, Columbia University, 1962).

26 Abstracted from Alice Miel, "Knowledge and the Curriculum," in *New Insights and the Curriculum*, Association for Supervision and Curriculum Development (Washington, D.C.: The Association Yearbook, 1963), Chapter 4. Miel groups the specific subject disciplines under these classifications given for each grade level.

Miel sums up the "structural" point of view in the following words:

> The attention to the separate disciplines being urged today is of a different character from that practiced in relation to school subjects of yesterday. Today's proposals reject a curriculum based on outmoded, insignificant, isolated bits of subject matter as vigorously as did the "progressives" in the 'twenties and 'thirties. The proposals reflect confidence in understanding of fundamental principles and ideas in learning how to learn as the main road to "transfer of training."
>
> Surely it is desirable to build a curriculum that includes both approaches, problem-centered and discipline-centered. Both ways of viewing the world are needed by the individual and the society. Given our experience with problem-centered studies that integrate information from various fields of knowledge and given our newly developing insights with respect to the most transferable elements of the separate disciplines, it now seems possible to develop such a curriculum.[27]

Aside from the question of whether the separation of subjects is a valid approach to curriculum development, current proposals also raise the issue of national vs. local control of curriculum planning. As subject specialization increases and extends even downward into the elementary school, it is difficult to believe that there can be much freedom or challenge for local school faculties to share in curriculum development.

## Some current trends in selected subject-fields

It may be useful to take a brief look at developments in some of the subject-fields currently under study. In general, the new directions may be summed up in the following principles referred to in the previous section of this chapter.

1. Some subject disciplines are becoming increasingly specialized.

2. Study of the subjects is to be carried on in repeated spirals or cycles of increasing intensity and depth.

3. Difficult concepts are introduced earlier than previously, since

[27] *Ibid.*, pp. 94–95.

it has been proved that younger children can learn abstract concepts.

4. The structure or basic principles of a discipline are to be emphasized more than knowledge of isolated facts.

5. Discovery of new truth or ways to think are more to be sought than repetition or rote learning.

*Science.* Earth science courses are being widely introduced in high schools throughout the country, following experiments in Pennsylvania and New York. This area of science is concerned with the scientific phenomena of the earth and of space, and draws on the subjects of geology, geophysics, oceanography, meteorology, astronomy, and space science.

The Biological Sciences Curriculum Study [28] brings ideas and concepts in biology up to date, emphasizes "investigative" laboratory work, and stresses the process of inquiry over presentation of statements of conclusions. Three alternative versions, complete with text materials, introduce biology respectively through (1) the molecular or biochemical approach, (2) the "inquiry into life" approach, or (3) the ecological and behavioral approach. All three are built around the same nine themes. An advanced biology course and one for slow learners are currently being added to the materials.

Two curriculum programs in chemistry are receiving attention: the Chemical Bond Approach Project [29] and the Chemical Education Materials Study.[30] The first of these builds the beginning chemistry course around the concept of the chemical bond, with emphasis on atomic and molecular structure of substances. Problem solving is strongly emphasized in both textbook and laboratory materials. Conceptual schemes, represented by mental models in such fields as structure, kinetic theory, and energy, are used in this process.

The "discovery" principle is accented in the Chemical Education Materials Study. This course is aimed at furthering interest and understanding of the function of chemistry in human activities. The textbook is entitled *Chemistry: An Experimental Science.* In keeping with this theme there is a strong emphasis on laboratory work, for

[28] Organized in 1958 by the Education Committee of the American Institute of Biological Sciences. Headquartered at University of Colorado, Boulder, Colo.

[29] Chemical Bond Approach Project, Earlham College, Richmond, Ind.

[30] Information available at Chemical Education Materials Study, University of California, Lawrence Hall of Science, Wing B, Gayley Road, Berkeley 4, Calif.

which it is recommended that three single periods and two double periods be provided each week.

A new course in physics has been developed by the Physical Science Study Committee,[31] complete with textbook, laboratory manual, teacher's guide, films, monographs, and tests. It aims to present the interrelationships of various concepts in physics, treat the science as a product of experiment and investigation, and reveal the cultural impact of physics. It is intensive rather than extensive and designed for "most" high school students instead of physics majors. The four basic divisions of the course are (1) the universe, (2) optics and waves, (3) mechanics, and (4) electricity and modern physics.

Recommendations for K-12 science curricula have emerged from the National Science Teachers Association [32] and from the Science Manpower Project [33] of Teachers College, Columbia University. The curriculum proposals for elementary, junior high school, and senior high school students are generally aimed at understanding the natural, physical world, gaining respect for scientific method, and learning about the body. Content from several sciences is integrated in the courses up through the junior high school.

*Mathematics.* General recommendations are made by the Commission on Mathematics of the College Entrance Examination Board and by the Secondary School Curriculum Committee of the National Council of Teachers of Mathematics. In addition, two complete course proposals deserve attention. The first of these, by the University of Illinois Committee on School Mathematics,[34] comprises a new four-year sequence in "college preparatory" mathematics, beginning with "the arithmetic of the real numbers" in grade nine and concluding with polynomial functions in grade twelve. The textbook contains a number of "discovery" exercises to encourage students to

31 Physical Science Study Committee, Educational Services, Inc., 164 Main Street, Watertown, Mass.

32 See *It's Time for Better Elementary School Science* (1958) and *Planning for Excellence in High School Science* (1961) (Washington, D.C.: The National Education Association).

33 See *Science Manpower Project* (New York: Bureau of Publications, Teachers College, Columbia University).

34 University of Illinois Committee on School Mathematics, Max Beberman, 1208 W. Springfield, Urbana, Ill.

formulate, test, and refine their understanding of a principle. Sequence of the four-year program is regarded as important.

The second project, the School Mathematics Study Group,[35] has developed new text materials for the "college capable" students, grades seven through twelve, and is releasing materials for other students in grades four through eight. These materials emphasize a new set of modern mathematics concepts and vocabulary, along with a deeper approach to traditional mathematics. Such matters as number systems, probability, and deductive reasoning are emphasized in grades seven and eight. The ninth grade course is called a first course in algebra but deals with the properties of the real number system, quadratic equations in one variable, and linear equations in two variables. Grade ten carries the student beyond plane geometry to solid geometry and analytic plane geometry. Grade eleven introduces trigonometry and advanced algebra, coordinate geometry, and vectors. The twelfth grade course goes on to elementary functions preparatory to calculus, and an introduction to matrix algebra. Again the emphasis throughout is on discovery of principles by the student and understanding of concepts as opposed to manipulation of numbers and symbols.

Two other proposals for mathematics have emerged from the National Association of Secondary School Principals [36] and the University of Maryland Mathematics Project.[37] These two proposals, unlike those already discussed, are aimed at all students instead of the higher ability group. In the Maryland Project, the curriculum proposals are confined to the junior high school. Both plans include emphasis on problem solving and, in the Maryland Project, the use of mathematical language and the discovery principle.

*English.* The College Entrance Examination Board has established a commission on English, which is at work preparing new text materials. Such other groups as the National Association of Secondary School Principals and the National Council of Teachers of English

35 See E. G. Begle, School Mathematics Study Group, School of Education, Stanford University, Stanford, California.

36 See "The Place of Science and Mathematics in the Comprehensive Secondary School Program," *Bulletin of the National Association of Secondary School Principals,* 42:239 (September 1958), 5–12.

37 University of Maryland Mathematics Project, John R. Mayor, College of Education, Skinner Building, T114, University of Maryland, College Park, Md.

have drafted reports that include recommendations regarding emphasis and sequence. As yet, no such detailed course materials have been produced for the English curriculum as are in wide use in science and mathematics.

Nevertheless, certain trends are evident in publications, if not in classroom practice. One of these is an urge to develop more clear-cut sequence or articulation in the K-12 language arts program. The literature program is to be aimed at development of values, skill in reflective thinking, and appreciation rather than memorization or classification. The grouping of stories and poems around a theme is therefore replacing chronological selection of authors. Emphasis in creative writing is on self-understanding and personal values. Individualized reading procedures are being facilitated by classroom libraries.[38] Every English teacher is urged to regard himself as a teacher of reading, and to gain competence in developmental and remedial reading techniques.

The structural linguistics movement has had some impact on how English teachers look at language. This represents, in brief, a move away from rote memorization of rules and grammar-for-grammar's-sake toward understanding of the structure of language. The study of elementary semantics and of uses of mass media in propaganda are also urged by leaders in this field. How many of these changes have yet occurred in the thousands of widely disparate English classrooms is not known.[39]

*Foreign languages.* Under the leadership of the Modern Language Association, aided by Titles III and VI of the National Defense Education Act, rather widespread changes have already occurred in the curriculum and methods of teaching modern foreign languages:

1. The number of students enrolled has increased markedly.

2. Foreign language instruction has been rather generally introduced in elementary schools.

3. The oral-aural method has become accepted as the way to begin instruction. This means emphasis on speaking and hearing as opposed to reading and writing, which come later.

[38] This development was described in Chapter 9.

[39] In preparing this entire section on trends in specific subject fields, the authors have received much help from the summary by Dorothy M. Fraser, *Current Curriculum Studies in Academic Subjects.*

4. The sequence of study in the same language has extended to four or more years.

5. The language laboratories with individualized use of tapes have been generally added to secondary schools.[40]

6. Emphasis is placed on cultural comparison and understanding of other peoples.

The Modern Language Association published a policy statement in 1956 which may serve as a summary of the aims of today's foreign language program. They urged that (1) the student should gain real mastery of at least one foreign language, (2) he should gain new understanding of the structure of language, and (3) he should learn to understand other cultures.[41]

Some questions may be asked regarding the foreign language curriculum. How early should such instruction begin? Is it sufficient justification that a child can learn a foreign language in, for example, the fourth grade, or should we also ask whether this is the most profitable way for him to spend time in school? For how many years should he study the same language? How can continuity of instruction be provided in the same language? Who should study languages—those with high ability, or all? Can teachers be found? These and similar questions must be answered if teachers are to move beyond the "tinkering" stage in the foreign language curriculum.

*Social studies.* Like the English curriculum, the social studies have been characterized by more recommendations than by actual changes to be seen in classrooms. The National Council for the Social Studies published in 1957 *A Guide to Content in the Social Studies,* which introduced the theme device as a framework for K-14 curricula.[42] The National Association of Secondary School Principals published a position paper on the social studies in 1961,[43] which recommended

---

[40] This development was described in Chapter 9.

[41] Further information may be obtained from the Modern Language Association of America, Donald D. Walsh, MLA Foreign Language Program Research Center, 70 Fifth Ave., New York 11, N.Y.

[42] National Council for the Social Studies, *A Guide to Content in the Social Studies,* Report of the Committee on Concepts and Values (Washington, D.C.: The National Education Association, 1957).

[43] "Social Studies in the Comprehensive Secondary School," *Bulletin of the National Association of Secondary School Principals,* 45:266 (September 1961), 1–17.

six years of required social studies (grades seven through twelve) with careful provision for continuity. They also urged strong attention to study of controversial issues, use of teaching aids such as films and ETV, participation in community affairs by students, practice in critical thinking and investigative methods, and provision for independent study. No radical changes in sequence of courses were proposed, but the report urged the need of a national model for such a sequence.

Other groups have been at work preparing supplementary materials to illuminate particular areas of the social studies: the teaching of world affairs, understanding of economic problems, conservation of natural resources, intercultural understanding, propaganda analysis, and communism compared with capitalism.

As in the case of mathematics, science, and foreign languages, if current pressures and curriculum proposals in the social studies were widely implemented, the secondary school would have to lengthen the school day and diminish the elective offerings.

*In conclusion.* Trends in many other subject fields might be cited. Perhaps the subject-fields described may serve as examples of certain general trends:

> toward greater specialization
> toward emphasis on reflective thinking
> toward understanding the structure of a subject
> toward more required subjects
> toward fewer electives outside the five "academic" fields
> toward understanding today's world scene
> toward building of personal values
> toward intensive study of selected subject areas
> toward training of the mind as opposed to the development of the total individual
> toward national standards, accompanied by federal aid
> toward separation of the subjects within broad fields
> toward extending separate subject approaches into the elementary school
> toward curriculum development by subject-experts at the national level

When we consider certain currently popular adjuncts to teaching method, in relation to the above-mentioned trends, we must ask ourselves in what direction we want to move in secondary schools. For example, educational television appears to be reinforcing the lecture method. Team teaching is also accenting the presentation skills of the so-called master-teacher. If we continue present trends toward increased specialization, will we reach the point where large-group instruction is inevitable because of pressures of time and lack of skilled teachers? Do we really want a national curriculum in place of local responsibility for curriculum development? Can we do anything about total development of our students in highly departmentalized, separate subject curricula? Can we help them attack the broad social and political problems of our time through the separate subject approach? Will increasing specialization drive more and more students to drop out of school? As this problem becomes more serious, are we to abandon our goal of universal secondary education and maintain only schools for the talented?

Every thoughtful teacher must answer for himself such questions as these if he is to become a professional resource for teaching and learning. In our final chapter we turn to the vital problem of how to improve as a teacher.

## FOR FURTHER READING

Alberty, Harold B., and Elsie J. Alberty, *Reorganizing the High School Curriculum*, 3rd ed. New York: Macmillan Co., 1962. This edition is an improved version of an already excellent book on curriculum development. Chapters 5 through 8 contain a scholarly analysis of factors influencing curriculum planning.

Alexander, William M., and Paul M. Halverson, *Effective Teaching in Secondary Schools*. New York: Holt, Rinehart and Winston, Inc., 1956. Chapter 14, "Planning the Organization of Instruction," is largely concerned with the process of curriculum planning but presents also some of the alternative products of such planning.

Association for Supervision and Curriculum Development, *New Insights and the Curriculum*. Washington, D.C.: The Association Yearbook, 1963. Various chapters include discussions of potentiality, knowledge, self-management, and creativity. See especially Miel's chapter on "Knowledge and the Curriculum."

Bruner, Jerome S., *The Process of Education*. Cambridge, Mass.: Harvard University Press, 1961. Presents the case for understanding the structure of the subject disciplines. Argues for the "discovery" concept and the "spiral curriculum."

Conant, James B., *The American High School Today*. New York: McGraw-Hill Book Co., Inc., 1959. An influential report whose recommendations support, among other things, ability grouping, more homework, and "tougher" subjects for the academically talented students.

———, *Education in the Junior High School Years*. Princeton, N.J.: Educational Testing Service, 1960.

Douglass, Harl R., ed., *The High School Curriculum*, 3rd ed. New York: Ronald Press Co., 1964. Includes several chapters on curriculum trends in the various subject fields.

Faunce, Roland C., and Nelson L. Bossing, *Developing the Core Curriculum*, rev. ed. Englewood Cliffs, N.J.: Prentice-Hall, Inc., 1958. Defines and illustrates the core curriculum and distinguishes it from its antecedents.

Faunce, Roland C., and Morrel J. Clute, *Teaching and Learning in the Junior High School*. Belmont, Calif.: Wadsworth Publishing Co., Inc., 1961. Chapters 4 and 5 include proposals for the curriculum structure of the junior high school, both general education and exploratory experiences.

Foshay, Arthur W., "A Modest Proposal for the Improvement of Education," *Educational Leadership*, 18:8 (May 1961), 506–516. Presents the case for including study of the structure of subject disciplines among the fundamental sources of curriculum development.

Fraser, Dorothy M., *Current Curriculum Studies in Academic Subjects*. Washington, D.C.: The National Education Association, 1962. A useful resume of the history and outcomes, up to 1962, of the various studies launched by national groups of the separate subject fields.

Krug, Edward A., *The Secondary School Curriculum*. New York: Harper & Row, Publishers, 1960. An excellent basic book on the curriculum. Separate chapters depict current trends in the subject fields.

Leonard, J. Paul, *Developing the Secondary School Curriculum*, rev. ed. New York: Holt, Rinehart and Winston, Inc., 1953. Parts III and IV of this comprehensive book on curriculum discuss the "determinants" of the curriculum and conflicting theories of education.

National Education Association, *Schools for the Sixties, Report of the NEA Project on Instruction*. New York: McGraw-Hill Book Co., Inc., 1963. This first report of the Project on Instruction opens with a chapter titled "The Right Questions," dealing with the process of decision-making. Subsequent chapters contain a series of specific recommendations, grouped under "Deciding What to Teach" and "Planning and Organizing for Instruction."

Romine, Stephen A., *Building the High School Curriculum*. New York: Ronald Press Co., 1954. Part II, "Curriculum Foundations," provides an introduction to the sociological bases of curriculum building, and foundations furnished by the learner and the nature of the learning process.

Stratemeyer, Florence B., *et al., Developing a Curriculum for Modern Living*, 2nd ed. New York: Bureau of Publications, Teachers College, Columbia University, 1957. The first six chapters furnish a base for curriculum planning. They are grouped under "Part I: Foundations of Curriculum Planning" and "Part II: A Curriculum for Learners in Our Times."

Taba, Hilda, *Curriculum Development: Theory and Practice*. New York: Harcourt, Brace and World, Inc., 1962. The second section on the process of curriculum planning is excellent.

Wiles, Kimball, *The Changing Curriculum of the American High School*. Englewood Cliffs, N.J.: Prentice-Hall, Inc., 1963. See especially the final chapter, "The High School of the Future."

# 16

# Improving as a teacher

We have discussed the many challenges that face the teacher, challenges sufficiently complex to demand the utmost use of his intelligence and energy. We have traced the significant movements in curriculum development. We have identified important issues and trends that teachers must confront during the next few years. We have described teaching and learning as we think it ought to be, not as it actually exists in most secondary schools of this nation.

## Teaching as a profession

The teacher is the key to educational advance. Education as a total process improves when teachers improve. We have assumed that the rewards to be earned from teaching are sufficient to deserve the commitment and dedication required of teachers. We must now give our attention to a closer examination of this assumption, after which we shall consider ways in which teachers can develop ever higher levels of competency as their careers unfold.

One often hears the word "profession" used loosely as a synonym for occupation. The word has a more precise meaning. In order to determine whether or not a given occupation may properly be called a profession, certain tests are applied. Common among these are the following:

412

1. A relatively long period of preparation is required before the practitioner is eligible to assume his duties as a member of the occupational group, i.e., before he is admitted to practice. The required preparation includes the pursuit of learning at an institution of higher education, usually a college, university, or specialized institution.

2. Some form of state licensing is required before admission to practice. This licensing may be based on the completion of a more or less prescribed course of study and/or a comprehensive examination. Under certain circumstances the license may be revoked.

3. Some control over the manner in which persons enter the occupational group is exercised by the occupational group. This control is exercised in various ways, e.g., through legally guaranteed seats on a licensing board, through advisory influence on the preparatory course of study, and through participation in the preparation program.

4. The occupational group has a voluntary system of ethics that is observed at least to a reasonable degree by the group members.

Teaching meets these four criteria rather well. Some occupations such as law, dentistry, and medicine may meet these standards more positively, while others would be ranked lower than teaching, yet still be considered as professions.

Leighbody has suggested a somewhat different measuring device. He lists the following "characteristics associated with true professional status":

> The professional worker does not require close supervision or direction.
> The professional worker does not regard himself as an employee.
> The professional worker does not work by the hour.
> The professional worker does not expect to be paid by the hour.
> The professional worker takes full responsibility for the results of his efforts and actions.
> The professional worker continually seeks self-improvement.
> The professional worker contributes to the skill and knowledge of the profession.
> The professional worker respects the confidence of others.
> The professional worker is loyal to his fellow workers.
> The professional worker avoids rumors and hearsay.
> The professional worker adjusts his grievances through proper channels.

The professional worker meets his professional obligations.
The professional worker is sensitive to the problems of his fellow workers.
The professional worker does not advance himself at the expense of others.
The professional worker is proud of his profession.
The professional worker's chief desire is to render service.[1]

Although more idealistic and detailed than the four qualities most commonly proposed as criteria for determining whether or not an occupation may properly be considered a profession, Leighbody's list is useful, especially in connection with individual evaluation.

## Prestige and status of teachers

As the occupation of teaching has become increasingly professional, i.e., as the preparation period has become longer and longer, the licensing provisions more stringent, and the code of ethics more generally known and observed, teachers have evidenced increasing concern regarding the prestige and status accorded to the profession by the general public.

*The teacher stereotype.* Relative prestige depends on many factors. One important factor is the tendency of the culture to "type" people according to occupation. This "typing" appears in novels, motion pictures, stage productions, comic strips, and television plays. We see the industrialist as strong-willed, aggressive, confident, hard-working, prosperous, and vigorous. We see the nurse as devoted to her patients, kind, sympathetic, stolid in the face of pressure, submissive to the demands of the physician, and neatly groomed both on and off duty. The teacher stereotype is not so complimentary. The male teacher is often cast as effeminate, nonassertive, physically unattractive, perhaps even forbidding, awkward, shabby, "fuddy-duddy," and humorless. The female teacher often appears as middle-aged, unmarried, stern, homely, prudish, old-fashioned, conservative, lonely, opinionated, and Victorian in manners and morals.

An examination of several investigations into the status of the

---

[1] G. B. Leighbody, "What Makes a Profession Professional?" *Phi Delta Kappan,* 34 (April 1953), 295.

teacher-image as portrayed in various media was made by Belok and Dowling,[2] who described their findings as follows:

> Erskine investigated the characterization of teachers in forty-six Broadway plays presented between 1920 and 1950. Teachers were characterized as maladjusted in 68 per cent of the cases, as having economic troubles in 37 per cent, as experiencing sexual tension in 33 per cent, and as being poorly clothed in 19 per cent. Erskine states that teachers for the most part were treated seriously but with what amounts to pity, and concluded that the characterization of teachers as neurotic does damage to the status of the profession.[3] (Unfortunately, Erskine does not tell us what per cent of the representatives of other professions are similarly characterized by the dramatists.) Foff examined the teacher stereotype in American novels. He selected sixty-two novels published since 1900, twenty-two of them since 1945. He found that novelists insist that the male teacher is solitary, effeminate, and impractical. The same attitude prevails toward women. They were characterized as either young and unmarried or as old maids, sexless creatures devoid or depleted of femininity. Foff concludes that the stereotype of the school teacher harms the profession.[4] He maintains that an effect is to attract this type to the profession and produce more of the type within it.
>
> Deegan, studying the stereotype of the single woman in novels, found that teachers were often depicted as very unfeminine women. In several cases they are shown as wielding a destructive influence in the community.[5] Gurko, writing about the treatment of teachers in both fiction and motion pictures, makes the point that the teacher fares no better in films than he does in fiction and that the characterizations are almost always very unfavorable.[6]

2 Michael Belok and Fred Dowling, "The Teacher Image and the Teacher Shortage," *Phi Delta Kappan*, 42:6 (March 1961), 255.

3 Andrew H. Erskine, "An Analysis and Evaluation of the Characterization of American Teachers in Broadway Productions, 1920–1950" (Doctoral dissertation, New York University, 1951).

4 Arthur Foff, "Teacher Stereotypes in the American Novel" (Doctoral dissertation, Stanford University, 1953).

5 Dorothy Yost Deegan, *The Stereotype of the Single Woman in American Novels* (New York: Columbia University Press), 1951.

6 Leo Gurko, *Heroes, Highbrows, and the Popular Mind* (New York: Bobbs-Merrill Co., Inc.), 1953.

*Origins of the stereotype; its relation to prestige and status.* How did this unfavorable picture of the teacher develop? Why is the teacher often displayed as a person with objectionable character-istics? What effect has the classical teacher stereotype on the relative status accorded to teachers by the public? Is the stereotype, on the average, a true picture of the teacher in our society? What can teachers do to improve their image in the eyes of the public?

Some of the answers to the first two questions are probably lost in history. It seems probable that most teachers never did fit the classical stereotype. It may well be, however, that a greater number of teachers came closer to the stereotype in the past than do today. Some aspects of the stereotype were certainly borrowed from "Old World" literature and became distorted in the process of being transplanted from one culture to another. Once established, a stereo-type tends to feed upon and perpetuate itself.

There was a period in our own history when teachers were sub-jected to stringent restrictions on their behavior. Boards of educa-tion made it quite clear, sometimes as part of the legal contract, that female teachers were not to marry. As recently as the years of the Great Depression many school districts refused to employ married teachers and dismissed those who did marry as soon as the fact was known, or at least at the end of the contract year. Even when no contract provisions were involved, it was fairly common, years ago, to notify the female teacher that dress, behavior, and general de-corum had to follow certain prescribed patterns. The teacher was expected to be a kind of moral paragon. Such restrictions could not help but have an effect on the teachers' behavior with a resulting image on the part of nonteachers as to what teachers were like.

It may be, too, that the stereotype of the teacher has been influ-enced by the child's teacher image carried into adulthood. Time might be expected to distort somewhat these childhood memories. The traditional role of the teacher, however, including the great emphasis on drill, rote learning, and physical punishment as a device to motivate learning could not be expected to inspire fond memo-ries of school days.

The assignment of a relatively low status to teachers is not a product of Western culture, but seems limited to the United States. Teachers in Western Europe, although financially poor, are accorded a relatively high degree of prestige. This contrast seems strange in view of the almost unbounded and perhaps naïve faith in education the American people have traditionally exhibited. The educational enterprise is held in highest esteem; those who implement the enterprise are placed much lower on the scale of values.

Social phenomena are usually the result of many factors. On the American frontier the skills needed for survival depended on physical stamina, strength, and agility. Such essential traits as character, integrity, and the ability to outwit the hunted were not the concern of the early school. The ability to read and cipher—the concerns of the pioneer schools—were far down the list of important values. The teacher's contribution to the society was not sufficiently associated with matters of life and death to be assigned a high priority.

Even as the society became more sophisticated and affluent, with more leisure available for its young, and schools and teachers more numerous, the prevalent theories of learning focused the activities of the teacher on routine and drill. Teaching was seen by many as a mundane occupation. Even today the general public has no inkling of the spirit of adventure the creative teacher injects into his work.

Probably the major reason why teachers as a group are not normally ranked among the community members who enjoy the highest status is the tremendous value the society places on material things. People value education, but they also value the possession of automobiles, ranch houses, dishwashers, and an endless variety of mechanical gadgets. The simple fact is that people value education because they have found it to be a vehicle of social mobility, a method of movement from a lower to a higher socio-economic class. Teachers usually do not belong to the exclusive clubs, nor associate extensively with those who do, because they cannot afford it. For better or worse, status is accorded those who have the highest incomes.

Before teachers become too disturbed by this set of circumstances, however, they should ask themselves whether they want the kind of prestige that high income alone brings. Many would prefer to settle for the satisfaction of knowing they are doing a good job, of being involved in an endeavor that continually challenges the imagination and that ties them to the future by virtue of their influence on the young. The vast majority of citizens have to earn their prestige. Those who achieve it do so because the community values their services. The good teacher or carpenter or postman or dentist has more status, other things being equal, than the one whose performance is poor or mediocre. There are also ways unrelated to one's job in which contributions may be made to community welfare. Interested and enthusiastic participation in community service groups, churches, political parties, and other organizations will lead to opportunities for leadership of various kinds, hence greater service. In the long run, status based on what one does is more rewarding than the kind based on what one owns.

*The decline of the stereotype.* The time may be near at hand when teachers need not be concerned about their public image and the prestige accorded their profession. No one could deny that some teachers exhibit some of the negative characteristics cited earlier in this chapter. Perhaps a few could be found who exhibit all or most of these qualities. But so could "butchers, bakers, and candlestick makers" as well as members of any other occupational group.

Most modern teachers do not fit the classical stereotype—or any other stereotype, for that matter. Casual observation of a large group of teachers—at an educational convention, for example, or at a districtwide faculty meeting in a large city—reveals that most teachers, male and female, are attractively dressed and well groomed. Many are married. Most have above average cultural and social interests, and are alert and well informed on a great variety of subjects. It would seem that some of the authors of fiction and drama are not realistic in their portrayal of teachers.

*The improving status of teachers.* There is other evidence, perhaps more persuasive, that the status of the teaching profession is improving in the public mind. One excellent criterion for measuring the relative prestige of the various vocations is the occupational choices young people say they would make if their selection could be completely free of parental pressure, economic problems, and college admission difficulties. What little evidence is available from this source seems to indicate an improvement during the past few years in the status accorded to teaching as a vocation.

Gallup Poll results reveal definite improvement in the way adults view the teaching profession if "theoretical advice" to young people may be considered valid.

In a nationwide survey—identical to the 1953 report—a representative sample of adults received a card listing various major professions and were asked: "Suppose a young man asked your opinion about choosing a profession. Assuming that he was qualified to enter any of them, which one would you recommend to him?"

The three "best" professions to enter today are medicine, engineering, and teaching, according to those interviewed. The following table shows the differences in the public's rating of occupations between 1962 and 1953: [7]

Which profession would you recommend?

|  | Today | 1953 |
|---|---|---|
| 1. Doctor | 23% | 29% |
| 2. Engineer-builder | 18 | 20 |
| 3. Professor-teacher | 12 | 5 |
| 4. Clergyman | 8 | 7 |
| 5. Government career | 7 | 3 |
| 6. Lawyer | 6 | 6 |
| 7. Business executive | 5 | 7 |
| 8. Dentist | 4 | 6 |
| 9. Banker | 2 | 2 |
| Other | 4 | 7 |
| None, don't know | 11 | 8 |

The lowest age group in the sample ranked teaching higher than the group as a whole as shown in the following table: [8]

Which profession would you recommend?
(Views of 21–29 age group)

| 1. Doctor | 26% |
|---|---|
| 2. Professor-teacher | 18 |
| 3. Engineer-builder | 17 |
| 4. Lawyer | 17 |
| 5. Government | 8 |
| 6. Dentist | 5 |
| 7. Clergy | 4 |
| 8. Business executive | 3 |
| 9. Banker | 2 |
| Other | 4 |
| None, don't know | 6 |

[7] "Gallup Poll Ranks Teaching High," *Michigan Association of Secondary School Principals Bulletin,* 4:6 (March 1963).
[8] *Ibid.*

O'Dowd and Beardslee investigated the views of about 1,200 undergraduate liberal arts college students in seven institutions. They report the results of their study, in part, as follows:

> It is possible to derive from the responses of students a portrait of the male school teacher which summarizes the patterns of responses for all major groupings of students. The school teacher image is quite different from the images of other occupations. Liberal arts college students share an image of the teacher dominated by the limitations on his social and economic standing in the community. The teacher is rated not well-to-do, lacking in opportunity for advancement, relatively low in social status and power in public affairs. Even his wife is only neutral on a scale from pretty to not-pretty. A second prominent feature of the school teacher is his lack of strength, activity, hardness, assertiveness, and confidence. According to students, the teacher does not play poker or become involved in activities that have a cast of vigorous masculinity. At the same time, he is realistic about life and adaptable in habits. He is fully in touch with real problems, but his role does not call for or permit the expression of strong, vigorous sentiments. Foremost among the many positive features associated with the teacher is his unselfish devotion to people. Students see the school teacher as a self-sacrificing public servant who performs a most valuable service and who is rewarded mainly by the sense of satisfaction that he derives from his work. This is reflected in the very high score he receives on "having a happy home." Associated with these traits is a good deal of sensitivity and wisdom. The teacher is rated as reasonably intelligent, but this is overshadowed by the great capacity of the teacher to draw on experience and to guide and direct others—essentially his behavior represents the highest order of good judgment. The teacher is also perceived as a person concerned with artistic and cultural matters. The teacher certainly belongs to the community of cultured people, but he is by no means a leader in this company. The teacher is rated somewhat high in emotionality and low in impulse control. He is seen as a moderately sociable person, but he would not be rated as gregarious. Rather, the teacher is the pleasant and friendly neighbor who chats over the back fence but rarely invites you in for a highball. The style of the teacher is seen as relatively individualistic and at the same time quite conservative. The teacher goes his own way, but he rarely chooses to be flamboyant or excessive in his personal tastes.

According to college students, then, the teacher is an unselfish, wise, sensitive, thoughtful, intelligent person whose material and social success is very limited. The male teacher is both soft and impulsive; in these respects his masculinity is suspect in spite of the rather close attention to real and concrete problems that is required of him. Apparently, these are seen as problems to be faced by women, not men. The teacher is an independent, friendly person who devotes time and energy to his family and perhaps a limited circle of conservative friends. He reads, he attends to art and music, and he must derive most of his pleasure from the rewards intrinsic in his work.[9]

There are negative aspects to this picture but one gets the impression that these students had considerable respect for teachers as a group and tended to view them quite positively. Some additional insight into the attitudes of these college students may be gleaned from their responses to the "career choice" question.

> . . . male students were instructed to "Rate each of the following occupational positions according to how much you would like to enter them if you were free to make the choice without regard for training, ability, or time and expense required for specialized study. . . ." Responses to this question produced a cluster of four highly attractive occupations leading the list, namely: college professor, lawyer, doctor, business executive. The next distinctive grouping was composed of scientist, ranked five, and the school teacher at a considerable distance. Clearly, there are many features of the life of the school teacher that attract college men.[10]

*The teacher's attitude.* It would be misleading to leave the impression that the modern teacher has become the prototype of an ideal citizen or that no room remains for improvement. A study conducted by the National Education Association Defense Commission revealed that nearly one-fifth of the nation's teachers were not active members of a church or any other common community group and another 25 per cent were active in only one group. We could also add that teachers tend to restrict their social contacts to other teachers.[11]

[9] Donald D. O'Dowd and David C. Beardslee, "The Student Image of the School Teacher," *Phi Delta Kappan,* 42:6 (March 1961), 251.

[10] *Ibid.,* 253.

[11] "Profile of the Metropolitan Teacher," *NEA Research Bulletin,* 30:3 (October 1962), 67–74.

Furthermore, many teachers tend to think of themselves as second-class citizens, underpaid, and unappreciated by the citizenry. One writer has put it thus:

> Education is the worst "poor-mouthing" profession in America. We approach legislatures and the general public with hand outstretched for charity, dragging our tales of woe behind us. . . .
> These are the standards which have guided us: pity and poverty. The common teacher stereotype is not of a strong minded, highly intelligent person; it is of a public servant in the same category as "good old Joe," who swept the floors of City Hall for forty years. At best, teachers are considered slightly down-at-the-heel intellectuals somewhat looney about education.
> We are ourselves at least partially responsible for this attitude. It has been our inclination to commit the sin of self-pity. We have considered that our best chance of getting necessary financial support was to beg, to make the public sorry for us. But we have sold our birthright—the birthright of every American teacher—to hold his head erect, knowing that his is the Master Profession, the creator of the professions.[12]

Some teachers do not seek means of improving their competency and become steadily poorer while they continue to teach, protected by tenure laws, the shortage of teachers, and a profession which has not yet come to grips fully with the challenge of policing its own ranks.

## Developing professional competency

Let us summarize some of the major points we have made thus far and draw out some further implications.

1. Teaching is a profession. The teacher is a professional worker. A modern professional worker in a free society is obligated to continue to grow in his professional competency. This responsibility is to the building and district faculty of which he is a part, to his professional colleagues everywhere, and to himself.

2. The teacher has been the victim of stereotyping in fiction and drama over a period of many years. This image has had a derogatory

---

[12] Sim Wilde, "The 'Poor-Mouth' Profession—or the Master Profession," *Phi Delta Kappan,* 40:7 (April 1959), inside back cover.

effect on both the public's teacher image and the image the teacher has had of himself.

3. But things are looking up! Most modern teachers do not fit the classical stereotype. Moreover, high school students, adults in general, and college students rank teaching fairly high among desirable occupations.

4. Teachers can change the public image and increase their relative status in the public eye by making a greater contribution to nonschool community endeavor and setting high standards of performance for themselves—standards which can be reached only when the great bulk of teachers continually make themselves better teachers.

5. Teaching is a complicated endeavor requiring extensive knowledge, insights, skills, and abilities. Optimum professional competency cannot be achieved in the four-year preparatory program, most of which is devoted to a general liberal arts education and the development of academic majors and minors.[13] This fact is recognized by the certification codes in many states, which require formal study beyond the bachelor's degree for certification as a career teacher. Teacher salary schedules frequently reflect this belief also.

6. The increase of knowledge characteristic of our time has made continuing professional study more urgent than ever before. This situation is, of course, by no means unique to teaching. Persons in other professions are also finding it necessary to devote increasing amounts of energy and time to studying current developments.

7. Satisfaction with teaching increases as competency increases. The better teachers become, the more they realize that each new day presents new challenges, new opportunities for discovery and exploration, new ways of dealing with new problems. Knowing how to attack problems and solve them and putting one's skills to use for this purpose are most rewarding.

*Self-evaluation—the first step.* Early in this chapter we quoted Leighbody to the effect that the "professional worker does not require close supervision or direction." He has to be his own evaluator. We saw in Chapter 13 that evaluation must be based on goals or purposes.

---

[13] Typically in a four-year preparation program for secondary teachers, only one-sixth of the time is devoted to professional studies.

One way to get some tentative criteria which may be useful in evaluating level of competency is to examine ways in which students cast their "ideal" teacher. One teacher asked 2,042 students at the elementary, intermediate, and secondary levels to identify the "qualities, traits, and practices they would mention if they were to describe a perfect teacher." The results are described by Powell as follows:

> The ability to maintain good discipline was mentioned twice as often as any other quality. Students wanted the ideal teacher "strict but not too strict," "not to let the class get away with murder," "warn twice then really 'lay it on.'"
>
> Students asked that teachers "look neat and nice," "not be overdressed," "not let themselves get fat and sluggish," "not wear the same clothes every day," and "watch personal habits."
>
> Suggesting that "all work and no play makes Jack a dull boy," they advocated teachers with a "good sense of humor," those who "kid around a *little bit*" and "let the class have some fun."
>
> Many students expressed the desire for a helpful teacher. He should, they said, "be willing to work extra with poor students," "reason with students and tell them why something is right," "never be too busy for you," "be someone you can come to with difficult situations," and "be helpful outside of the class as well as in."
>
> Their ideal teacher would "be friendly in and out of class," "show understanding of students," "have a good disposition," and "be able to smile and be happy most of the time."
>
> In their opinion, an ideal teacher need not abolish homework as long as assignments are justifiable and the amount is reasonable. They recommend "a break on holidays and vacations," and "no busy work." Other respondents wanted teachers who "keep the amount of work consistent" and "really make you work."
>
> "Patience and an even temper" are held in high regard by the sample group, as is the ability to "handle unexpected situations with ease."
>
> The ideal teacher should "understand each and every one in the room," "be able to put himself in the child's place."
>
> Students also want a teacher who can "explain assignments," "express himself clearly and concisely," "make hard things look easy," and "use effective methods to get the point across."
>
> Fairness is another trait frequently mentioned. The ideal teacher "treats all students alike," and "doesn't let one or two students do everything."

Often mentioned was the teacher's voice. He should have "a modern vocabulary," "use a clear, normal voice," "talk to the students and not into space," "pronounce words correctly."

Superior knowledge of subject-matter was called for, but primarily on the secondary level.

Ideally, the teacher "knows what he is talking about," "has vastly superior knowledge," "teaches without leaning on a textbook," and "has knowledge but isn't smart about it." [14]

What many would call a more scholarly and sophisticated technique is described by Barr. In this case two groups totaling eighty-three experienced teachers, supervisors, and administrators examined the literature, then listed and categorized (after discussion) a descriptive vocabulary. The following is adapted from one of the lists of categories developed by the group:

> *Behaviors associated with:*
> Identifying pupil needs
> Setting and defining goals
> Creating favorable mind sets and motivation
> Choosing learning experiences
> Providing for individual differences
> Making activities meaningful
> Analysis and organization of learning experiences
> Direction of group activities
> Use of learning aids
> Teacher-pupil relations
> Evaluation of pupil growth and achievement [15]

The list could serve as a starting point for a teacher's self-assessment. Using the first category, "identifying pupil needs," as an example, he would ask himself such questions as the following: Am I familiar with the general needs of students of this age level? Do my students have some special needs that are different from those of the "average"? Do I establish proper priorities in dealing with the needs of my students? Do I have systematic ways of discovering the special needs of my students—techniques that work quite well? Do I usually involve my students in the process of identifying their own needs?

---

[14] C. F. A. Powell, "The Ideal Teacher," *NEA Journal,* 45:1 (January 1956), 31.
[15] A. S. Barr, "Characteristics of Successful Teachers," *Phi Delta Kappan,* 39:6 (March 1958), 282–284.

Such questions as the following would be appropriate to the category "providing for individual differences": Have I developed means of appraising differences in interests, abilities, skills, talents, background, and the like among my students? Do I have different levels of expectation for the various students in my classes according to my appraisal of their individual abilities to achieve? Do I convey this fact of difference in expectation to my students in a satisfactory manner? Do I vary lesson assignments according to my appraisal of reasonable individual levels of achievement? Do I regularly use with my students study materials of varying degrees of difficulty and with a variety of foci of interest appeal? Am I constantly on the lookout for additional study materials of various levels of difficulty and with various kinds of interest appeal?

A similar approach but using different criteria is based on the various teacher roles discussed in Chapter 5, viz., participant, expediter, resource, counselor, architect, and sight-lifter. Several questions, helpful in the process of personal assessment, were implied in the discussion of these roles. It seems likely that no one method or set of criteria will suit every teacher. Care should be taken to make certain that the assessment is done on a broad base in order to eliminate the possibility of judging one's self only in those areas in which one is superior. Some teachers, for example, do very well in making assignments clear, in maintaining a businesslike atmosphere in the classroom, and in finding enriching experiences for the academically gifted students in their classes but do nothing at all about varying the expectation level for students whose interests and aptitudes do not facilitate a high level of achievement, or providing a variety of learning experiences and study materials for these students. All teachers, if they are honest with themselves, will be able to identify relative strengths and weaknesses in their repertoire of professional skills.

*Opportunities for improvement.* Recognition of the aspects of one's competency that need strengthening is a major step toward professional improvement. Once the personal assessment has been accomplished, the problem becomes one of selecting the kinds of experiences that lead to improvement.

The assessment will probably reveal that strengthening is needed in one or more of the following general categories:

Skill in working with colleagues.

Knowledge about and skills in the use of methods and materials.

Knowledge about and application of knowledge concerning the learning process and other aspects of human behavior, including research results.

Knowledge about subject(s) taught including recent developments.

Opportunities for growth will be found in both individual and group activity. One of the most fruitful fields for continued professional improvement is the activities the teacher undertakes to do a better job with the students in his classes. These efforts will vary according to the teacher's personal assessment and also with reference to the kind of community in which the teacher works, and the particular students in the teacher's classes at any given time. The teacher's professional development activities will encompass any or all of the matters discussed in Chapters 3–13. All teachers would probably find the building of resource files and the collection of bulletin board display materials helpful. The professional literature is, of course, a vast source of information that is readily available. Most school districts and buildings have collections of professional books. Most teachers have professional books in their own libraries.

The various activities of the building and district faculties afford excellent opportunities for extending professional competencies, as do the programs of the professional associations. One of the most rewarding means of self-improvement is to become involved with others in curriculum evaluation and development projects. Many of the faculty groupings regularly found at the building and district level—whole faculty, department, grade level, committee, case conference—will usually be concerned with improving one or more aspects of the school program. When the group proceeds in an atmosphere of scientific problem solving, the procedure is sometimes called action research. Action research has been defined as the "process by which practitioners attempt to study their problems scientifically in order to guide, correct, and evaluate their decisions and actions. . . ." [16] It differs primarily from traditional research in the following ways: [17]

[16] Stephen M. Corey, *Action Research to Improve School Practices* (New York: Bureau of Publications, Teachers College, Columbia University, 1953), p. 6.

[17] Adapted from Corey, *Ibid.*

| Traditional Research | Action Research |
|---|---|
| Distinguishes between scientific inquiry and educational practice | Scientific inquiry and educational practice are interrelated and proceed simultaneously |
| Value is judged by the extent to which new knowledge is added to what is already known | Value is determined by the effect the findings have on the practices of those who do the research |
| Careful provision is made for application of the results to populations other than those involved in the research | The researchers are concerned about extending their findings to specific populations only—usually the students in a given community at present and in the near future |
| Those who perform the research are not likely to be the ones who will apply the results | The primary motivation of the researchers is to improve their own practices |

Hilda Taba saw "much need in curriculum development for practical action research, over and above general educational research." [18] Such activities as the study in practical situations of problems investigated by formal research methods and the application of principles derived from formal research to a variety of situations in an effort to establish the practicality of these principles were urged by her. She also expressed the belief that teachers are more likely to be conscious of research findings and more sophisticated in applying these findings to their own practices if they make more general use in their day-to-day activities of the methods used by researchers. Although action research is usually carried on by a group, it can be performed by individual teachers.

Formal study in college and university classes is used by most teachers as a device to assist in the process of professional growth. A course is most helpful and meaningful when selected carefully—in relation to one's self-assessment, the experiences of other teachers, the help of a college adviser. It is least helpful when selection is in-

---

18 Hilda Taba, "Problem Identification," in *Research for Curriculum Improvement,* Association for Supervision and Curriculum Development (Washington, D.C.: The Association Yearbook, 1957), p. 42.

fluenced by the location of the course offering and the time of day and day of the week it is scheduled. A course planned with particular reference to the problems of the school or district is likely to be superior to a course without this point of reference. Certification requirements and salary schedules that give salary increments for credit earned beyond the bachelor's degree have not always succeeded in accomplishing their goal, i.e., encouraging teachers to improve their professional skills, because courses were selected on bases other than their probable contribution to increased competency. Such credit requirements improve secondary education only when the teachers themselves make intelligent adaptations to the rules.

*In conclusion.* Someone has defined a good school as one in which everyone is busy trying to make it a better one. No matter how good a secondary school is, it can be improved if teachers will set out to know and accept the individual learner, and to work with him in the application of the skills of problem solving to his development as a person and as a citizen. As he grows and changes, the teachers can take genuine satisfaction from the help they gave him. This is the reward of working with dynamic, human material. It is not easy work. It is often perplexing, and frequently frustrating. But it offers rich rewards to those who accept the challenge to help individuals develop.

Teaching can be the most challenging and satisfying occupation our culture provides. Every teacher can be a pioneer in a real sense. There is so much to learn about teaching that one can go on learning throughout his entire career. In fact, he can hardly keep from doing so if he remains alert and interested. Few other callings can offer as much.

> Teaching is an invitation to youth, because those who live creatively do not grow old. They cannot, because each move is new. Old age comes from repetition, routine, and life devoid of exploration and adventure. Age is a symptom of already anticipated action; action which has occurred many times before, and out of which all juice has long been squeezed. The universe is in process of being created, and a teacher can be one of the architects. He cannot, however, if he values security and habit over adventure. If he becomes a creative teacher, he will have adventure abundantly.
>
> —Earl C. Kelley

## FOR FURTHER READING

Alexander, William M., and Paul M. Halverson, *Effective Teaching in Secondary Schools.* New York: Holt, Rinehart and Winston, Inc., 1956. Several means of improving one's professional competency are discussed in Chapter 16, "The Teacher's Role in the Improvement of Instruction."

Association for Supervision and Curriculum Development, *Research for Curriculum Improvement.* Washington, D.C.: The Association Yearbook, 1957. A critical aspect of action research, problem identification, is analyzed and illustrated in Chapter 3 by Hilda Taba.

Barr, A. S., "Characteristics of Successful Teachers," *Phi Delta Kappan,* 39:6 (March 1958), 282–284. Three different approaches to the listing of characteristics of successful teachers. The need for further definition is emphasized.

Belok, Michael, and Fred Dowling, "The Teacher Image and the Teacher Shortage," *Phi Delta Kappan,* 42:6 (March 1961), 255–256. A review of the research concerning the stereotype of the teacher in novels and plays. See also in the same issue "The Student Image of the School Teacher" by Donald D. O'Dowd and David C. Beardslee, in which the findings of a recent study involving the attitudes of college undergraduates are presented.

Corey, Stephen M., *Action Research to Improve School Practices.* New York: Bureau of Publications, Teachers College, Columbia University, 1953. The process of action research is described in detail. Characteristics which distinguish action research from formal research and common-sense problem solving are pointed out.

Denemark, George W., "Continuing Growth: Today's Imperative," *Educational Leadership,* 20:2 (November 1962), 85–89, 133, 135. The author lists and discusses six reasons why teachers must continue to improve professionally.

Flanders, Ned A., "Teacher Behavior and In-Service Programs," *Educational Leadership,* 21:1 (October 1963), 25–29. Two studies of the effectiveness of in-service teacher education programs are reported, followed by three assumptions concerning the improvement of professional competency by in-service teachers. Unanswered questions pointing toward further research are posed.

Gordon, Julia Weber, "Action Research," *NEA Journal,* 44:9 (December 1955), 546–548. A simulated description of the action-research activities of a school faculty during one school year. Although applied to the elementary school, the illustration is readily applicable to secondary schools.

Grambs, Jean D., William J. Iverson, and Franklin K. Patterson, *Modern Methods in Secondary Education,* rev. ed. New York: Holt, Rinehart and Winston, Inc., 1958. Chapters 22 and 23, "The Teacher in School and Community" and "Becoming a Teacher," are especially helpful to the prospective teacher.

Lieberman, Myron, *Education as a Profession.* Englewood Cliffs, N.J.: Prentice-Hall, Inc., 1956. A comprehensive appraisal of the teaching profession.

National Society for the Study of Education, *Mental Health in Modern Education,* Fifty-fourth Yearbook, Part II. Chicago: University of Chicago Press, 1955. See "The Mental Health of the Teacher" by Paul Witty for an excellent discourse on maintaining mental health. Especially helpful for beginning teachers.

Powell, C. F. A., "The Ideal Teacher," *NEA Journal,* 45:1 (January 1956), 31. Results of a student opinion poll carried out by a high school teacher.

Saylor, J. Galen, and William M. Alexander, *Curriculum Planning for Better Teaching and Learning.* New York: Holt, Rinehart and Winston, Inc., 1954. Opportunities for participation in curriculum development activities are discussed in Chapter 16.

Sharp, D. Louise, ed., *Why Teach?* New York: Holt, Rinehart and Winston, Inc., 1957. Statements about the rewards of teaching by 120 famous men and women in various walks of life.

Smith, Mary Neal, "Action Research," *NEA Journal,* 44:4 (April 1955), 229–230. A participant describes an action-research project carried out by a junior high school faculty.

Stiles, Lindley J., ed., *The Teacher's Role in American Society,* Fourteenth Yearbook of the John Dewey Society. New York: Harper & Row, Publishers, 1957. Many aspects of the teacher's role are examined by several authors. See especially Part IV, "The Profession and the Teacher."

# indexes

## NAME INDEX

433

Fine, Thomas W., 383
Flanders, Ned A., 95, 430
Foff, Arthur, 415
Ford Foundation, 254
Forkner, Hamden L., 164
Foshay, Arthur W., 401, 410
Foster, E. M., 244
Fraser, Dorothy M., 400, 406, 410
Frederick, Robert, 321
Freedman, Leonard, 28, 45
French, Will, 38, 41, 45
Fretwell, Elbert K., 295, 302, 321
Friedenberg, Edgar Z., 54, 64

Garry, Ralph, 71, 93
Gates, Arthur, 79
Getzels, J. W., 86
Giles, H. H., 389
Gilmore, James L., 169
Glaser, Robert, 75, 93, 225
Goedeke, M. Thomas, 156
Golden, Ruth, 209
Goodlad, John I., 59
Goodman, Paul, 65
Gordon, Ira J., 158, 169
Gordon, Julia Weber, 430
Grambs, Jean D., 139, 169, 233, 265, 294, 431
Grant, Eva H., 383
Gruhn, William T., 302
Guilford, J. P., 86
Gurko, Leo, 415

Hagen, Elizabeth, 356
Halverson, Paul M., 139, 143, 168, 192, 199, 200, 205, 233, 239, 264, 269, 293, 409, 430
Hand, Harold C., 9, 19, 276, 321, 392
Hanna, Paul R., 19, 263
Hardin, Garrett, 58, 59
Havighurst, Robert J., 36, 45, 53, 62, 65, 298
Heffernan, Helen, 355
Heller, Frieda M., 245
Hilgard, Ernest R., 71, 74, 92
Hill, C. M., 20
Hill, Thomas J., 201
Hock, Louise E., 201
Hollingshead, August B., 61
Hughes, Marie M., 99
Hull, J. Dan., 7, 392
Hullfish, H. Gordon, 86, 92
Hymes, James L., Jr., 139, 383

Inlow, Gail M., 255
Iverson, William J., 139, 169, 233, 265, 294, 431

Jackson, P. W., 86
James, William, 74

Jersild, Arthur T., 92, 355
Johnston, Edgar G., 139, 145, 147, 148, 150, 169, 176, 201, 216, 298, 304, 318, 321
Jones, Arthur J., 142
Jones, J. J., 384
Jones, Mary C., 52, 54
Justman, Joseph, 356

Karpas, Melvin, 139
Kearney, Nolan C., 51
Kelley, Earl C., 20, 35, 36, 61, 65, 87, 92, 201, 429
Kelley, Janet A., 169
Keough, Jack, 233
Kettlecamp, Gilbert C., 294
Kilpatrick, Franklin P., 78, 92
Kilzer, Louis R., 303, 321
Kindred, Leslie W., 384
Kingsley, Howard L., 71, 93
Kirkendall, Lester A., 322
Klausmeier, H. J., 265
Koerner, James D., 73
Krug, Edward A., 386, 410

Lake, Ernest G., 377, 384
Lallas, John E., 169
Lane, Howard, 57, 58, 65, 139
Langdon, Grace, 384
Larson, Knute, 139
Leighbody, G. B., 413, 414
Leonard, J. Paul, 45, 159, 294, 386, 410
Lichter, Solomon O., 19
Liddle, Gordon P., 20
Lieberman, Myron, 431
Lindvall, C. M., 355
Lounsbury, John H., 155
Low, Camilla M., 143
Lumsdaine, A. A., 75, 93, 225
Lurry, Lucile, 201

Manning, John, 138, 140
Marani, Jean Victoria, 243
Maslow, A. H., 93
Mayor, John R., 405
McCann, Lloyd E., 132
McCutchen, S. P., 389
McDaniel, Henry B., 146, 147, 169
McDonald, Frederick J., 93
McKean, Robert C., 45, 140, 169, 265, 294, 322
McKim, Margaret G., 164
McKown, H. C., 155, 322
Meier, Arnold, 322
Melby, Ernest O., 11, 12, 20
Menge, J. Wilmer, 88, 169, 384, 391
Metropolitan School Study Council, 234, 265
Michael, Lloyd S., 289

434

Travers, Robert M. W., 342
Traxler, Arthur E., 356, 390
Trow, W. C., 93
Trump, J. Lloyd, 227, 322
Tyler, Ralph W., 116
Van Zwole, James A., 384
Veatch, Jeanette, 107

Walsh, Donald D., 407
Ward, Arthur E., 210
Waskin, Leon S., 391
Waskin, Yvonne, 183, 201
Wattenberg, William W., 66, 93, 138, 140
Wendt, Paul R., 265
Wickman, E. K., 137, 140
Wigren, Harold E., 258
Wilde, Sim, 422

Wilds, Elmer H., 22
Wiles, Kimball, 116, 202, 234, 411
Wilhelms, Fred T., 212, 220, 234
Wilson, Sloan, 2
Withall, John, 95
Withers, William, 45
Witty, Paul, 431
Wood, Dorothy Adkins, 356
Wright, Grace, 398
Wrightstone, J. Wayne, 234, 355, 356, 357

Yauch, Wilbur A., 357

Zapf, Rosalind, 185, 202, 204
Zechiel, A. N., 389
Zeron, Franklin R., 322

# TOPIC INDEX

tion of literature, 333–335; of athletics, 314–315; through conferences, 346–347; of group efforts, 189–191; as a group endeavor, 325–328; by logs, 152, 190, 338–339; misconceptions regarding, 328–331; of music activities, 311; by observation, 336; as a personal endeavor, 323–325; of planning, 291–293; and purposes, 16, 42, 100, 333; of social program, 300; by standardized tests, 347–349; of student progress, 323–355; by students, 331; of teacher, 423–426; by teacher-made tests, 339–346

Field trips, 262–263
Foreign-language study, 25, 406–407
Fundamentals, 35, 36
Fused courses, 395

Group activity: based on study of group, 174–178; evaluating, 189–191; importance of group relations in, 89–90; in improving classroom, 179; individual roles in, 191; need for, 170–172, 197; organizing for, 187–188; reporting, 188–189; resources for, 188; in selecting goals, 181–183; in selecting problems, 183–187; stages of, 172–174; steps in, 196
Grouping, ability, 4, 228–232
Guidance: aided by studying the learner, 150–154; through core classes, 158–162; as counseling, 146–150; through curriculum, 163–167; as description of good teaching, 142–145; through homerooms, 154–155; modern concept of, 141–142; plan for, 154–158; by specialized counselor, 156–158; through teaching teams, 162–163

Handbook, school, 309–310
History of secondary education, 4
Homeroom, 154–155
Home visits, 376
Homework, 3, 73, 248–250

Illinois Secondary School Curriculum Program, 391–392
Individual differences, 2, 6, 46–50; and ability grouping, 228–232; in achievement, 57, 59; in cultural factors, 59–61; and discipline, 135–136; and elective courses, 221–222; implications for teaching, 62–64, 67; increase with improved schooling, 60; in interests, 55–56; in mental development, 56–57; and organismic psychological theory, 76; in physical characteristics,

51–53; and reading interests, 313; in social maturity, 53–55; in socio-economic background, 61; and student activities, 222; and teacher preplanning, 292; and unit method, 270
Individual learning activities: in art and music, 209–212; through elective program, 221–222; within groups, 202–208; through independent study, 224–227; in literature, 212–215; in science and mathematics, 217–221; in speech, 208–209; through student activities, 222; in writing, 215–217
In-migration, 27–28
International relationships, 24–25

Kalamazoo case, 6
Knowledge, expansion of, 29–31

Language laboratories, 259
Large-group instruction, 26, 288–291
Latin grammar schools, 5
Learning: basic principles of, 78–91; definition of, 78; as problem-solving, 84; and purposes, 42; theories of, 71–78
Lecture method, 98–99
Lesson plan, 272–275
Letters to parents, 353–354; by students, 371–373
Library: in classroom, 213, 242–244; departmental, 244; school, 244–245
Life adjustment, 7, 392
Literature: teaching of, 212–215; appreciation of, 333–335

Magazine, class, 210, 215–216
Marks, 350–351
Mathematics, 217–221, 404–405
Motion pictures, 251
Motivation, 91
Music activities, 209–212, 310–312

National Defense Education Act, 157, 406
Needs: and purposes, 21; of teachers, 63–64; of youth, 34–35
Newspaper, class, 215–216

Parents: attitudes toward schools, 358–364; differences in attitudes of, 362–364; letters to, 353–354, 371–373; open house for, 373–374; organizations for, 378–379; room clubs for, 374; use of as resources, 259–264, 374–376; ways of influencing, 364–366
Parent-teacher organizations, 378–379
Perception, 77, 87, 253
Physics, 404
Planning: extent of, 108–111; evalua-